# Negotiating Mughal Law



Based on a completely reconstructed archive of Persian, Hindi and Marathi documents, Nandini Chatterjee provides a unique micro-history of a family of landlords in Malwa, central India, who flourished in the region from at least the sixteenth until the twentieth century. By exploring their daily interactions with imperial elites as well as villagers and marauders, Chatterjee offers a new history of the Mughal Empire from below, far from the glittering courts of the emperors and nobles, but still dramatic and filled with colourful personalities. From this perspective, we see war, violence, betrayal, enterprise, romance and disappointment, but we also see a quest for law, justice, rights and righteousness. A rare story of Islamic law in a predominantly non-Muslim society, this is also an exploration of the peripheral regions of the Maratha empire and a neglected princely state under British colonial rule. This title is also available as Open Access on Cambridge Core.

NANDINI CHATTERJEE is Associate Professor of History at the University of Exeter. She has published widely on the British and Mughal empires, including her book *The Making of Indian Secularism: Empire, Law and Christianity, 1830–1950* (2011).

# Negotiating Mughal Law

## *A Family of Landlords across Three Indian Empires*

Nandini Chatterjee
*University of Exeter*

CAMBRIDGE
UNIVERSITY PRESS

**CAMBRIDGE**
**UNIVERSITY PRESS**

University Printing House, Cambridge CB2 8BS, United Kingdom

One Liberty Plaza, 20th Floor, New York, NY 10006, USA

477 Williamstown Road, Port Melbourne, VIC 3207, Australia

314-321, 3rd Floor, Plot 3, Splendor Forum, Jasola District Centre, New Delhi - 110025, India

103 Penang Road, #05-06/07, Visioncrest Commercial, Singapore 238467

Cambridge University Press is part of the University of Cambridge.

It furthers the University's mission by disseminating knowledge in the pursuit of education, learning and research at the highest international levels of excellence.

www.cambridge.org
Information on this title: www.cambridge.org/9781108736961
DOI: 10.1017/9781108623391



First published 2020
First paperback edition 2022

*A catalogue record for this publication is available from the British Library*

*Library of Congress Cataloging in Publication data*
Names: Chatterjee, Nandini, 1976– author.
Title: Negotiating Mughal law : a family of landlords across three Indian empires / Nandini Chatterjee, University of Exeter.
Description: Cambridge, United Kingdom ; New York, NY, USA : Cambridge University Press, 2020. | Includes bibliographical references and index.
Identifiers: LCCN 2019051903 (print) | LCCN 2019051904 (ebook) | ISBN 9781108486033 (hardback) | ISBN 9781108623391 (ebook)
Subjects: LCSH: Law – Mogul Empire – History. | Law – India – History – 19th century. | Law – India – History – 20th century. | Landlord and tenant – India – Malwa (Madhya Pradesh and Rajasthan, India) – History. | Law – India – Islamic influences.
Classification: LCC KNS130.5 .C47 2020 (print) | LCC KNS130.5 (ebook) | DDC 349.54/30903–dc23
LC record available at https://lccn.loc.gov/2019051903
LC ebook record available at https://lccn.loc.gov/2019051904

ISBN 978-1-108-48603-3 Hardback
ISBN 978-1-108-73696-1 Paperback

# Contents

# Figures and Tables

**Figures**



**Tables**

# Maps

# Acknowledgements


The happiest part of writing a book is recalling all the generosity that has made it possible. This book has lived and grown with me over seven years, and, in the process, I have received enormous kindness, from teachers, friends, colleagues and complete strangers.

The first person to thank is Professor Chander Shekhar, Professor of Persian at the University of Delhi and currently Director, Lal Bahadur Shastri Centre for Indian Culture, Tashkent. From that day in early 2012, when I walked into his class at Jawaharlal Nehru University, New Delhi, as an informal student, with only a beginner's knowledge of Persian, he has taught me so much that it is hard to delimit. With his encyclopaedic knowledge of Persian literature, his delight in cross-linguistic etymology and his forensic interest in untangling the 'curls of the beloved' – the confusing ligatures of the dreaded cursive Persian script, *shikasta* – he nurtured in me a wonder about the Indo-Persian world that I hope shows through in the pages of this book. Professor Chander Shekhar joined me as co-investigator in a small British Academy-funded project in 2014, grant number SG132595, during which time he helped me read the first set of documents – from the National Archives of India – training me on the job. I hope to assist him in publishing the results of that work as an annotated sourcebook of Indo-Persian legal documents as a small token of my gratitude.

I was able to secure the second set of documents – that from the Al-Sabah Collection of the Dar al-Athar al-Islamiyyah Museum, Kuwait – because of the support of my friend, the brilliant economic historian, Fahad Bishara. Fahad put me in touch with the amazing staff members of the museum, especially Ahmad Najadah, who helped me apply for a copy of the documents. I sincerely thank the Dar al-Athar al-Islamiyyah Museum for providing me with digital copies of all the relevant documents in the Al-Sabah collection, and for giving me permission to reproduce one document in this book, all without charging any fees.

The discoveries that allowed me to open the third and final store of documents for this book were made in Dhar, India, in December 2016. They were made possible through the astounding generosity of strangers, starting with the tradesmen in the old *rājwāḍā* of Dhar who led me to Mr Karan Singh

Pawar, ex-M.L.A. for Dhar. Karan Singh and his wife, Nandita, let a complete stranger (together with husband and son) into their homes, listened to my bizarre queries, and miraculously connected me to Amit Choudhary, direct descendant of the protagonists of this book. Since that day, Amit has been a collaborator, friend and, at times, counsellor, as the research crawled on and my analysis developed. He and I have thought, argued and investigated together, and a great deal of the research, especially in Chapter 6, is as much his as mine. I thank him, and his gracious mother, the late *Thākurānī* Abha Choudhary, for allowing me unstinted access to the family archives. I regret that the book was not completed soon enough for me to present it to Abha ji. I also thank Meenal Shrivastava, whose own book *Amma's Daughters*, not only completed the story for me but also pushed me to think more carefully about family history.

Prachi Deshpande read through the first full draft of the manuscript and offered me the kind yet precise advice that I needed at that point to sharpen my arguments, correct my errors and, generally, not lose heart. She also shared her time and linguistic skills to read the Marathi documents for me and Hindi documents with me. Prachi's intelligence and compassion has kept this project, and me, afloat over difficult times. I hope to learn to write like her one day.

A five-year Starting Grant from the European Research Commission, grant number 714569, which I have held since 2017, gave me the time and resources necessary to analyse my documentary collections and write this book; I am eternally grateful.

This grant has funded my Forms of Law in the Early Modern Persianate World project, which has given me the luxury of considering legal documents as historical artefacts in their own right. It also allowed me access to the scholarship and abilities of two outstanding early career scholars, Dominic Vendell and Elizabeth Thelen. Dominic has helped me read several Marathi documents written in the Modi script; his linguistic skills and intellectual generosity never cease to amaze me.

I thank the two anonymous reviewers of this book, whose encouragement and meticulous corrections and suggestions have made it a much better piece of scholarship. I particularly thank them for pushing me to reflect systematically on the methodological component of the book and for catching the various errors and faux pas I had made.

Lucy Rhymer and Emily Sharp at Cambridge University Press deftly guided this book through the process of publication; many thanks to them for their constant good humour.

Erik Goosman produced two beautiful maps at short notice, and Arnia van Vuuren produced a professional index; I am very grateful to them for their expertise and support.

Finally, my husband, Vikas, and our son, Armaan, have accompanied me on this quest over years, including on road trips across central India. Vikas valiantly helped me manage my spreadsheets and produced charts at the drop of a hat, booked cars, spoke to shopkeepers in a village called Ahu and held my hand when I wanted to give up. Armaan was the best research assistant a mum can ask for, besides, of course, the best son. A big hug to you both.

As India seems to be flattening itself out in straitjacketed religious, linguistic and political identities, this book is a record of what the cosmpolitan Indo-Persian world that used to be like. Of course, all errors are my own, but I hope the joy is yours too.

# Note on Transliteration and Dates

This book, and the materials it is based on, uses many words that are shared across Arabic, Persian and Hindi. When transliterating those words in the Latin script, I have relied on the Library of Congress Romanization tables for Persian and Hindi. The LOC system offers accurate one-to-one correspondence in orthography and also the best intuitive fit with the phonetic patterns of the Persianate world, which would help the reader who does not read the Arabic script. The only deviation from this system is the transliteration of the diphthong represented by 'au', for which I find the LOC-recommended 'aw' producing visually unfamiliar results for common names and words. I have indicated vowel lengths but I have not always transliterated the word terminal silent h or the *ta marbuta*. I have followed Indian pronunciation in transliterating the vowel before the word final –h, so *nāma*, not *nāmah* or *nāme*. For a small number of Arabic-origin words, such as *ḥadīth*, I have used the LOC Romanization system for Arabic. I have retained the transliteration choices made by other authors in book titles, not added diacritic marks for person names and have utilised standard Indian-English orthography for the names of well-known figures, such as Aurangzeb Alamgir.

The documents used in this book use a variety of calendars, most commonly, the Hijri Qamri, but also the Islamic months in combination with regnal year (Julus). The conversion of Julus dates represents serious challenges, especially since the materials cluster in the reign of the emperor who was crowned twice. An explanation of the conversion formula used is presented in the Appendix. There are also Vikram Saṃvat and Faslī calendars in use, which, being solar years, are converted simply by subtracting/adding years, and there is also the Turkish twelve-year cycle, which, thankfully, is only present in combination with other calendars.

# Abbreviations

| | |
|---|---|
| BRD | *Baḍā Rāolā*, Dhar |
| DAI | Dar al-Athar al-Islamiyyah, Kuwait |
| *IESHR* | *Indian Economic and Social History Review* |
| NAI | National Archives of India |

# Introduction: Law in Many Forms

In the late 1620s, Prince Khurram was serving his punishment posting as governor of Deccan, while his sons were held hostage at the imperial court by his own father, Emperor Jahangir. Prince Khurram, who would eventually assume the imperial Mughal throne as Shah Jahan in 1628, was being punished for armed rebellion, which had also seen him attempting to build a military and political base in the *sūba* (province) of Malwa, until he was chased across the country by the imperial army and eventually defeated.[1] While embroiled in imperial high politics, Prince Khurram found the time to issue a *nishān* (a princely order) confirming the appointment of a man called Mohan Das to the post of *qānūngō* (local official maintaining tax records) of the *pargana* (district) Dhar.

The document revealed that the grantee Mohan Das had been going through upheavals of his own. Although once the *qānūngō* of Dhar, he had, for reasons unstated in the document, been transferred to Asirgarh, a significant hill fort marking the boundary between Hindustan and Dakhin. Asirgarh happened to be an important base of activity for Khurram in his period of rebellion; perhaps Mohan Das managed to catch the prince's eye at that place.[2] In any case, the document recited that since Mohan Das had proved his loyalty, he was glorified (*sarfarāz*) by being granted the office of *qānūngō* of the district in accordance with ancient custom (*ba-dastūr-i sābiq*). A certain village (*mauza'*, in the terminology of revenue administration) was granted as *'inām*,[3] as emolument or by way of reward for the unstated special services, or both. Several decades down the line, a descendant of Mohan Das, having lost this vital document, had a copy made, and endorsed by the local *qāẕī* (Islamic judge), Muhammad Mustafa, who notarised the document with his seal bearing the date 1103 AH

[1] John F. Richards, *The Mughal Empire* (Cambridge: Cambridge University Press, 1993), pp. 114–15.

[2] Ibid., p. 115.

[3] This Arabic-origin word literally means reward. In Mughal and post-Mughal usage, it is generally translated as a grant of 'tax-free' or 'rent-free' or 'revenue-free' lands. See H. H. Wilson, *A Glossary of Revenue and Judicial Terms*, ed. Ganguli and Basu (Calcutta: Eastern Law House, 1940), pp. 338–40. This entitlement, which, at its most general, included the right to take a share of the peasant's produce, and could be combined with a range of conditions, is typical of the kind of nested and relational rights that this book is concerned with.

(1690 CE), and inscribed on it: *muṭābiq ba-aṣal ast*, 'It is in line with the original'.[4]

In the National Archives of India, there are eighty-four (principally) Persian-language documents, spanning just over a hundred years, and pertaining to four generations of a single family of village-level landholders, who doubled as petty state officials based in the central Indian Mughal province of Malwa. There are also forty-three complementary documents, pertaining to the same family and clearly derived from the same family's dispersed collection, in the museum Dar al-Athar al-Islamiyyah, Kuwait. Finally, there are around sixty-one documents, and other materials, still in the possession of descendants of the family, housed in their ancestral homestead in the city of Dhar, in the central Indian state of Madhya Pradesh. The majority of these documents are from the Mughal period – that is, the seventeenth and early eighteenth centuries – with a slim but narrow tail running through the era of Maratha imperialism and then into British indirect rule. These documents are all, broadly speaking, legal documents – whether they be official orders creating property rights, copies of such title-deeds notarised by court officials, contractual documents involving rent, debt, repayment and guarantee or judgements following disputes over property and inheritance. As in the document just summarised, each one of these documents offers a glimpse of the interweaving of imperial politics, military manoeuvres, taxation, co-option of local powerholders into the state structure and the contours of agrarian economy – all of which have been themes of classic works on Mughal history.[5]

While being informed by that scholarship, this book will approach such material in a different way, aiming to discover how petty rural grandees and minor stakeholders, such as members of Mohan Das's family, attempted to negotiate the local power dynamics as well as the structures of governance in order to further their individual and family interests. In tracing the nature and methods of those efforts, we will take note of the protagonists' in-between status, being both of the state and subject to it. Thus, this book is inspired by Farhat Hasan's characterisation of the Mughal state as both shaping local societies and being shaped and sustained by them.[6] Indeed, the protagonists

[4] Persian manuscript 2703/31 (dated by cataloguer in 'Jahangir's period', which refers to the date of the original document, rather than this copy), National Archives of India (NAI), New Delhi.

[5] For a survey of the literature, see 'Introduction' in Muzaffar Alam and Sanjay Subrahmanyam, *The Mughal State, 1526–1750* (Oxford: Oxford University Press, 1998); some classics are Irfan Habib, *The Agrarian System of Mughal India 1556–1707* (3rd edition, New Delhi: Oxford University Press, 2014); Jos Gommans, *Mughal Warfare: Indian Frontiers and Highroads to Empire, 1500–1700* (London: Routledge, 2002).

[6] Farhat Hasan, *State and Locality in Mughal India: Power Relations in Western India, c. 1572–1730* (Cambridge: Cambridge University Press, 2006). This itself related to an older debate about the extent of centralisation and bureaucratisation of the Mughal state, especially in relation to

of this story are very similar, if somewhat less grand and cosmopolitan, than the Mughal officials, businessmen and their families studied by Hasan in connection with the great Indian Ocean port cities of Surat and Cambay. Quite like the port officials, the limited eminence of men (and women) of Mohan Das's family was based on their local connections and landed power, but they could not thereby afford to rest on their laurels: the continuity and growth in their fortunes required them to access the state for offices, rewards and recognition, but also to inhabit it, thus turning the state apparatus into family property.

Unlike Hasan, however, the purpose of this book is less to evaluate the nature of the Mughal state (or the polities that succeeded it), and more to uncover the motivations, ideas and approaches of such little people who manned it, but who have remained woefully ignored in Mughal historiography, which is still predominantly concerned with either macro-historical structures and processes – the state, the economy, the military market – or grand individuals such as members of the royal family, great nobles, administrators and venerable saints. In particular, it is an effort to trace the ideas and activities of some not very eminent people through archives created in – broadly speaking – legal settings. While it may appear as such, I do not see this book as an effort to recover and represent an isolated fragment of history poised against normalising meta-structures.[7] It is a micro-history, and as such, it is premised on the assumption that looked at up close, we always discover variations from what appear to be the overarching patterns, but we also discover conformity. The crucial point, however, is that we get close enough to the workings to be able to explain both deviation and conformity, and as such, use the part to explain the whole by illustrating their mutual relationship.[8]

Unlike the majority of micro-histories, however, this is not a study of a highly evocative single episode in time. The availability of a substantial and continuous series of documents, covering nearly four hundred years, pertaining to a single landed and locally powerful family who rode out three

corporate groups – of caste, kin and so on. M. Athar Ali, 'The Mughal Polity: A Critique of "Revisionist" Approaches', in his *Mughal India: Studies in Polity, Ideas, Society and Culture* (New Delhi: Oxford University Press, 2006), pp. 82–93.

7 The classic formulation in Partha Chatterjee, *The Nation and its Fragments: Colonial and Postcolonial Histories* (Princeton: Princeton University Press, 1993), p. 13.

8 Giovanni Levi, 'On Microhistory', in Peter Burke (ed.) *New Perspectives on Historical Writing* (Cambridge: Polity, 1991), pp. 93–113. Within the broad parameters, the best known examples of micro-historical writing demonstrate distinct analytical aims; Natalie Zemon Davis, *The Return of Martin Guerre* (Cambridge, MA: Harvard University Press, 1983); Carlo Ginzburg, *The Cheese and the Worms: the Cosmos of a Sixteenth-Century Miller* (translated by John and Anne Tedeschi) (London: Routledge, 1980 [1981]); Richard Darnton, *The Great Cat Massacre: and Other Episodes in French Cultural History* (London: Allen Lane, 1994). Very few micro-histories have been produced for South Asian history – biographies being a distinct genre: one of those few is Partha Chatterjee, *A Princely Impostor? the Strange and Universal History of the Kumar of Bhawal* (Princeton: Princeton University Press, 2002).

regimes, presents us with opportunities for discerning patterns and connections as well as transformations. We have the opportunity to trace the networks of kinship, association, affection and disaffection, to study strategies of personal and collective advancement, to uncover structures of authority and notions of rights and righteousness, and see how all this evolved as the Mughal empire gave way to other regimes in the region.[9]

This is a book about entitlements, and the efforts of some people in Mughal India and afterwards, for asserting and securing them. As such, this is a book about law, which is not conflatable with institutions or rules/norms.[10] This book's conception of law does indeed encompass all the above, but also sees 'law' as a specialised language used by common people, with the help of low-brow specialists, to record, assert and dispute claims, to articulate popular expectations of the state, of peers and of betters, and (most usefully for a micro-historical study), to make striking statements of self-description. I also see law as an arena of contests, in which power is sublimated through normatively stated disputes, sometimes with the norms themselves in conflict. As this book argues, law is not just a code for power and an instrument for its application; it is also a site for the legitimation of power, so, therefore, also for challenging it.[11]

## Empires, Islam and Islamicate Law

By writing the history of a part of the Mughal empire through law and legal records, and commenting on the Maratha and British empires in the same book, I am inspired both by the growing literature on the legal geographies of entangled early modern Eurasian and Atlantic empires,[12] and the only very partially connected literature on Islamic cultures of legal documentation, in the Middle East and North Africa, Iran and Central Asia.[13] Like many others

[9] For an effort in this direction in connection with law in the British empire, see Nandini Chatterjee, 'Muslim or Christian? Family Quarrels and Religious Diagnosis in a Colonial Court', *American Historical Review*, 117: 4 (2012), 1101–22.

[10] Which was Subrahmanyam and Alams's concern in their introduction to *The Mughal State*, p. 6.

[11] E. P. Thompson, *Whigs and Hunters: the Origin of the Black Act* (London: Allen Lane, 1975), pp. 258–69.

[12] Lauren Benton, *A Search for Sovereignty: Law and Geography in European Empires, 1400–1900* (Cambridge: Cambridge University Press, 2009); Eliga Gould, 'Entangled Histories, Entangled Worlds: the English-Speaking Atlantic as a Spanish Periphery', *American Historical Review*, 112: 3 (2007), 764–86.

[13] Maiike van Berkel, Leon Buskens and Pertra M. Sijpesteijn (eds.), *Legal Documents as Sources for the History of Muslim Societies* (Leiden: Brill, 2017); Paolo Sartori, *Visions of Justice: aiʿa and Cultural Change in Russian Central Asia* (Leiden: Brill, 2017); Paolo Sartori, 'Colonial Legislation Meets Sharīʿa: Muslims' Land Rights in Russian Turkestan', *Central Asian Survey*, 29: 1 (2010), 43–60; Christoph Werner, 'Formal Aspects of Qajar Deeds of Sale', in Kondo Nobuaki (ed.) *Persian Documents: Social History of Iran and Turan in the Fifteenth to Nineteenth Centuries* (London: Curzon, 2003), pp. 13–50.

working on the history of empires, I have been struck by the bold imaginary provided by Lauren Benton – the idea of 'lumpy landscapes' of law as it spread unevenly along oceans, waterways and other difficult terrain, sometimes on the invitation of indigenous populations, sometimes despite their resistance. However, I am also cautioned by Paolo Sartori's insistence on the need to pay attention to the particularities of legal pluralism in empires, rather than rushing to generalise about uneven terrains and jurisdictional jockeying.[14] Now, Mughal India was an empire too, and since Benton's own passing reflections on the nature of legal layering therein are tantalising rather than explanatory, we are left with the necessity of conceiving how law in the Mughal empire may have been arranged and negotiated, so that we have more than a pleasantly hazy idea of what law in precolonial India may have looked like.[15]

The banal but oft-ignored fact that the Mughals and their predecessors ruled over the only persistently and predominantly non-Muslim population in the Islamic world should give us pause, and encourage us to reflect upon the variant forms and dispensations of Islamic law in the early modern world. And in this connection, I believe it is worth retrieving Marshall Hodgson's under-utilised concept of 'Islamicate law', because it allows us to conceptually grapple with several overlapping processes of cultural, institutional and political imbrication. This included the syncretic self-legitimation efforts of Mughal dynasts; the ubiquitous presence of the classical Islamic judge (*qāẓī*) in and alongside multiple loci of dispute resolution; the work of scribes who recorded, or coded happenings in Indian villages and cities in broadly Islamic legal language; and the many villagers, townsmen, soldiers and officials, Muslim and not, who showed themselves to be not only aware of these forms of law and procedure, but also articulate in the relevant jargon and adept at negotiating the necessary processes. In coining the term Islamicate to refer to the broader cultural and social complexes associated with Islam and not limited to Muslims, Hodgson himself specifically contemplated 'Islamicate law' as a more capacious and effective way of thinking about law in the world of Islam, including *sharīʿa* but extending beyond it;[16] it is time now to take up that suggestion.[17]

In this connection, it is important to acknowledge Shahab Ahmed's rejection of the term 'Islamicate' for its tendency to reify its obverse: an artificially reduced notion of Islam-as-religion, falsely separated from all its cultural instantiations, including the Persianate 'Balkan-to-Bengal' complex that

[14] Paolo Sartori, 'Constructing Colonial Legality in Russian Central Asia: On Guardianship', *Comparative Studies in Society and History*; 56: 2 (2014), 419–47.

[15] Lauren Benton, *Law and Colonial Cultures: Legal Regimes in World History, 1400–1900* (Cambridge: Cambridge University Press, 2002), at p. 80.

[16] Marshall Hodgson, *The Venture of Islam: Conscience and History in a World Civilization*, Vol. I (Chicago: University of Chicago Press 1974), pp. 57–60, at 57.

[17] Shahab Ahmed, *What Is Islam?: the Importance of Being Islamic* (Princeton: Princeton University Press, 2016), especially pp. 113–29; 157–75.

produced the classics of Sufi religious poetry, replete with anti-doctrinaire motifs of wine drinking and pederasty. Ahmed's argument, for a capacious vision of Islam, encompassing all its historical forms, is powerful and attractive as a hermeneutic for studying Islam. But as a conceptual matrix designed specifically in opposition to law, by which Ahmed meant a doctrinaire version of *sharīʿa*, it does not provide the necessary tools for understanding the precise relational matrix – of authorities, institutions, laws and languages – within which the legal documents of this book were produced. And more specifically, it does not offer sufficient tools for understanding the mental and social worlds of the Hindu landlords who form the principal protagonists of this book.

A large volume of exciting new research has now suitably put to rest the notion of Islamic law being a system of rigid rules, derived from unquestionable sources, with no internal capacity for evolution with the times. It has been argued forcefully, and convincingly, that in fact *sharīʿa*, or more accurately, *fiqh*, was an elaborate body of jurisprudence, systematically developed by legal scholars, *fuqahā'*, through a doctrinally systematic but also situationally responsive procedure. The core of this procedure involved the issuing of responses (*fatwá*, pl. *Fatāwá*) by qualified scholars (*muftīs*) to queries (*iftā'*) related to concrete legal problems. In framing their responses, *muftīs* drew on a hierarchically organised body of textual material – from collections of previous responses, to texts summarising the principles therein, back to recorded Prophetic tradition (*hadīth*) and ultimately the Quran. And while *muftīs* were not bound by precedent, they were constrained by a range of rules in their choice of authority – among other things the need to remain within 'schools' (*mazhabs*) that worked with the opinions of certain eminent scholars and not others.[18]

No *fatwā* was binding on the judge (*qāẓī*), who could decide to rely on one *fatwā* among several, or ignore them all, but in practice *fatāwá* definitely guided adjudication, and fed back, through compilations and summarisation, into the legal tradition.[19] And while clearly one's experience of the system could vary hugely between contexts, scholars have shown that in early modern Islamic empires, such as that of the Ottomans, it could offer substantive possibilities of justice to women as well as non-Muslim minorities.[20] This

[18] Christopher Melchert, *The Formation of the Sunni Schools of Law, 9th–10th Centuries C.E.* (Leiden: Brill, 1997)

[19] Wael Hallaq, *Shariʿa: Theory, Practice, Transformations* (Cambridge: Cambridge University Press, 2009); Wael Hallaq, 'Was the Gate of Ijtihad Closed?', *International Journal of Middle East Studies*, 16: 1 (1984): 3–41; Wael Hallaq, 'From *Fatwās* to *Furūʿ*: Growth and Change in Islamic Substantive Law', *Islamic Law and Society*, 1: 1 (1994): 17–56; David Powers, *Law, Society and Culture in Maghrib, 1300–1500* (Cambridge: Cambridge University Press, 2002); Muhammad Khalid Masud, Brinkley Messick and David S. Powers (eds.) *Islamic Legal Interpretation: Muftis and Their Fatwas* (Cambridge, MA: Harvard University Press, 1996).

[20] Judith Tucker, *In the House of the Law: Gender and Islamic Law in Ottoman Syria and Palestine* (Berkeley: University of California Press, 1998); Najwa Al-Qattan, 'Dhimmis in

was because of the clear, if not equal, rights accorded to such groups in Islamic law, which were often substantively superior to those afforded by community norms; also in part because of the possibility of systematic juristic discretion built into the system as a whole.[21]

Despite general agreement on the bare bones of this picture, approaches vary widely even among scholars studying the Muslim-majority parts of the world. It is my opinion that this variation arises from the nature of source material used. Those asserting the systematic proximity of academic jurisprudence and adjudicative practice have naturally focussed on material produced by those jurists themselves. They have used the prolific genre of *fatāwā* collections and higher-level *ʿuṣūl al-fiqh* (principles of jurisprudence) texts, arguing that these simultaneously offer evidence for the progress of legal thought as well as practice, since such *fatāwā* were not only in conversation with other, and higher, jurisprudential texts, but also written as if in response to specific disputes, including descriptions of court procedures that featured *qāẓīs*.[22] Within such an analytical and evidentiary mode, scholars are then able to demonstrate both the principled and systematic nature of Islamic law, and the centrality of jurists, but also their flexibility in choosing from a range of acceptable authorities and their situational intelligence in interpreting them.

On the other hand, those historians who have worked from different categories of material, such as registers of the imperially sponsored courts preserved in various Ottoman archives, have revealed a more blurred image of Islamic law with multiple co-situated, competing or even unclear legal jurisdictions, with the king (and his representative) playing as important a role as jurists. The Ottomans, for example, appear to have institutionalised the *muftī-qāẓī* arrangement, but very much under the thumb of the emperor, their jurisdictions defined, and increasingly restricted by imperial authority, whether through the accepting of petitions,[23] or through outright legislation. Petitions to emperors and governors also abounded in the Safavid empire in Iran, and many people in the Ottoman empire[24] as well as the Central Asian kingdoms[25] preferred (or were pushed towards) arbitration by local notables over, or

the Muslim Court: Legal Autonomy and Religious Discrimination', *International Journal of Middle Eastern Studies*, 31: 3 (August, 1999), 429–44.

21 J. Makdisi, 'Legal Logic and Equity in Islamic Law', *The American Journal of Comparative Law* 33: 1 (1985), 63–92

22 David Powers, *The Development of Islamic Law and Society in the Maghrib: Qadis, Muftis and Family Law* (Burlington: Ashgate, 2011); Tucker, *In the House of the Law.*

23 James Baldwin, 'Petitioning the Sultan in Ottoman Egypt', *Bulletin of the School of Oriental and African Studies*, 75: 3 (2012), 499–524.

24 Leslie Peirce, *Morality Tales: Law and Gender in the Ottoman Court of Aintab* (Berkeley: University of California Press, 2003).

25 Paolo Sartori, 'The Evolution of Third-Party Mediation in Sharīʿa Courts in 19th-and early 20th-century Central Asia', *Journal of the Economic and Social History of the Orient*, 54: 3 (2011), 311–52.

alongside adjudication by the *qāẕī*. There is debate as to whether and how such processes of arbitration were aligned with the formal *muftī-qāẕī* structure; those wishing to align them have pointed to the doctrinal preference for peaceful resolution (*sulḥ*) in Islamic law,[26] the availability of documentary rubrics for recording such resolutions, and (in some cases) the official interrelations between the king, judge and arbitrator. Thus when the historical record reveals the working of law in Islamicate societies as tantalisingly Islamic in language, terminology and ethos, but not quite in line with the procedures outlined in the jurisprudential texts, scholars have attempted to see deviations as mere additions,[27] or point to generic pious statements within the intellectual tradition, or to discover hidden principles at work which aligned classical political theory (if not quite jurisprudence) with the observed practice.[28]

This urge to prove the intellectual and procedural systematicness of Islamic law is of course a prolonged reaction to Weber's sweeping characterisation of Islamic law as an exemplar of *kadijustiz* – personalised arbitration rather than impersonal and formally rational jurisprudence and adjudication.[29] However, given that we now have sufficient scholarship available to attest to the sophistication of Islamic jurisprudence, it may be productive to think about 'the multilayered nature of Islamic law 'sources',[30] and indeed of the legal traditions in practice, whether in the Middle East or elsewhere that there have been Islamic empires, such as South Asia.

Not doing so leaves the history of law in the Mughal empire in a strikingly underdeveloped state, and denies the study of Islamic law data from a very important and large Muslim and Islamicate context. Current geopolitical dynamics have obscured the fact that the early modern Islamic world had very different centres from the ones we know now. It was dominated by three great Turko-Persianate empires – the Mughals, the Safavids and the Ottomans. If we wish to know how Islamic law really worked in the day of its glory, it is to these empires and their workings that we should turn.

[26] Boğaç A. Ergene, 'Why Did Ümmü Gülsüm Go to Court? Ottoman Legal Practice between History and Anthropology', *Islamic Law and Society*, 17: 2 (2010), 210–44; Aida Othman, '"And Amicable Settlement Is Best": Sulh and Dispute Resolution in Islamic Law', *Arab Law Quarterly*, 21 (2007), 64–90.

[27] Haim Gerber, *State, Society and Law in Islam: Ottoman Law in Comparative Perspective* (Albany: State University of New York Press, 1994).

[28] Irene Schneider, *The Petitioning System in Iran: State, Society and Power Relations in the Late 19th Century* (Wiesbaden: Harrassowitz, 2006).

[29] David S. Powers, '*Kadijustiz* or *Qāḍī*-Justice? A Paternity Dispute from Fourteenth-Century Morocco', *Islamic Law and Society*, 1: 3 (1994), 332–66; Gerber, *State, Society and Law*, esp. chapter 1; James Baldwin, *Islamic Law and Empire in Ottoman Cairo* (Edinburgh: Edinburgh University Press, 2017), p. 15.

[30] Chibli Mallat, 'From Islamic to Middle Eastern Law: a Restatement of the Field (Part II)', *The American Journal of Comparative Law*, 52: 1 (2004), 209–86. Mallat also offers a magisterial survey of the themes and sources used for the study of what he calls 'Middle Eastern law'.

On the other hand, as far as the discrete historiography of the Mughal empire is concerned, despite some excellent efforts,[31] a persistent Indo-centrism has allowed it to continue not only at a disconnect from that of the other Persianised empires, but also with little systematic attention to Islamic law. Despite continuing and frequently politicised interest in the 'religious policy' of the Mughal emperors, research on the location of Islam under this Persianised Turko-Indian dynasty has remained limited to the periodic influence of certain sectarian Sufi *silsilas*[32] and the uneven relationship of the *'ulāma* with individual Mughal emperors. Traditionally, historians of Mughal India have tended to say little about matters such as dispute resolution and adjudication (the stuff of a huge volume of Ottoman historiography). This is not because of the absence of comparable judicial and legal structures. Based on the ubiquitous Persian manuals and chronicles, historians of Mughal India have duly noted the existence of the office of the *qāẕī*, but taken it to be a minor and relatively uninteresting part of the imperial administrative structure, and associated with other sectarian offices, such as that of the *sadr* who managed grants to the Muslim religious scholars, and the *muḥtasib*, a kind of public censor who was meant to control drinking, gambling and the selling of sex.[33] Since Mughal policy was taken to have moved away from confessional Islam, and given that most people in Mughal-ruled India were not Muslims, these offices are taken to be of minor significance, except in times of sectarian oppression. Alternatively, some scholars have attempted to explain the prolific documents bearing the *qāẕī*'s seal by placing these randomly within an archaic notion of 'Islamic law', generally derived from eclectically selected classical *fiqh* texts from very different periods and places. Such scholars also noted, without comment, the judicial activity of the emperors and other officials. Anachronistic efforts to align the Mughal system with that of the hybrid 'Anglo-Muhammadan' law produced during colonial rule led to misapplication of English legal terms, such as precedent, which is alien to Islamic law; and a widespread but poorly evidenced belief, that apart from 'criminal' matters, most non-Muslims in the Mughal empire would have been left to resolve their own disputes or take

31 For example, Lila Balabanlilar, *Imperial Identity in the Mughal Empire: Memory and Dynastic Politics in Early Modern South and Central Asia* (London: I.B. Tauris, 2011); Stephen Dale, 'The Legacy of the Timurids', *Journal of the Royal Asiatic Society*, 3: 8 (1998), 43–58; Stephen Dale, *The Garden of the Eight Paradises: Bābur and the Culture of Empire in Central Asia, Afghanistan and India (1483–1530)* (Leiden, Boston: Brill, 2004).

32 Yohanan Friedmann, *Shaykh Ahmad Sirhindi: an Outline of His Thought and a Study of His Image in the Eyes of Posterity* (New Delhi: Oxford University Press, 2000); Yohanan Friedmann, 'The Naqshbandis and Awrangzeb', in Marc Gaborieu, Alexandre Popopvic and Thierry Zarcone (eds.) *Naqshbandis: Cheminements et Situations Actuelle d'un Ordre Mystique Musulman* (Istanbul, Paris: IFEA, 1990), pp. 209–20

33 Jadunath Sarkar, *Mughal Administration* (Patna, 1920), pp. 35–41.

them to Brahmin councils.[34] This final belief has proved the most durable, and, being embraced by scholars of Islamic law with little knowledge of Mughal administrative and documentary sources, it has acquired the status of truth merely by repetition, rather than research.[35]

While there are still occasional works produced on law in the Mughal empire,[36] the study of Islamic law in India has proceeded at a strange disconnect from Mughal history. The most fruitful work on the precolonial period has been about the proliferation of the non-juristic elaborations of a broader sense of the 'right path', or about the many other sources of norms that appear to have displaced *sharīʿa*-as-law almost entirely in the Indian subcontinent.[37] Predominantly, however, Islamic law in India tends to be studied from a post-diluvian point of view: its resurgence and reformulation following the damaging and destructive effects of the imposition of British colonial rule.[38] And while scholars recognise the novelty of the proliferating projects of pedagogy and pastoral care from the late nineteenth century, aimed at training a body of religious scholars capable of guiding an inward-looking community of pious Muslim individuals, they rarely explore whether Islamic law ever had a wider jurisdiction.[39] Also, notwithstanding the very long history of Islamic *imperial* law, scholars tend to study Islamic law *and* empires. This suggests that, despite denunciations of older Orientalist works, scholars implicitly hold the outlines

[34] Muhammad Bashir Ahmad, *The Administration of Justice in Medieval India* (Aligarh: Aligarh Muslim University, 1941), which also included a table of cases in a modern adversarial format, pp. 17–22; S. M. Ikram, *Muslim Civilization in India* (ed. Ainslee T. Embree) (New York: Columbia University Press, 1964), pp. 221–2.

[35] For examples, see Mouez Khalfaoui, 'Mughal Empire and Law', in *The [Oxford] Encyclopedia of Islam and Law. Oxford Islamic Studies Online*, www.oxfordislamicstudies.com/article/opr/t349/e0066, last accessed 04-Aug-2016; Scott Alan Kugle, 'Framed, Blamed and Renamed: the Recasting of Islamic Jurisprudence in Colonial South Asia', *Modern Asian Studies* 35: 2 (2001), 257–313, at 263; Ayesha Jalal, *Self and Sovereignty: Individual and Community in South Asian Islam since 1850* (London: Routledge, 2001), 139–52.

[36] S. P. Sangar, *The Nature of the Law in Mughal India and the Administration of Criminal Justice* (New Delhi: Sangar, 1998); M. P. Bhatia, *The Ulama, Islamic Ethics and Courts under the Mughals* (New Delhi: Manak, 2006). Bhatia is among the very few scholars after Muzaffar Alam to have made substantial use of Persian legal documents in Indian archives; he offers some very useful insights, including that of the mediating role of the *sadr* between the emperor and the *ʿulāma*.

[37] Muzaffar Alam, *Languages of Political Islam: India 1200–1800* (London: Hurst, 2004); Katherine Ewing, *Sharīʿat and Ambiguity in South Asian Islam* (Berkeley: University of California Press, 1988).

[38] Hallaq, *Shariʿa*, pp. 371–88; Kugle, 'Framed'; Rudolph Peters, *Crime and Punishment in Islamic law: Theory and Practice from the Sixteenth to the Twenty-First Century* (Cambridge: Cambridge University Press, 2005), pp. 103–41, esp. 109–19 on India.

[39] Barbara Metcalf, *Islamic Revival in British India, Deoband, 1860–1900* (Princeton: Princeton University Press, 1982); Muhammad Qasim Zaman, *The Ulama in Contemporary Islam: Custodians of change* (Princeton, 2002); Justin Jones, '"Signs of Churning": Muslim Personal Law and Public Contestation in Twenty-First Century India', *Modern Asian Studies*, 44: 1 (2010), 175–200.

of Islamic law to have been settled through the stabilisation of the Quranic text, the collection of traditions, and the production of juristic commentaries within the first three centuries of Islam.[40] Both these assumptions lead to the anachronistic view that Islamic law had always been community law. In a preliminary essay using a small selection of materials comparable to that which are used in this book, I suggested that such a community-centric conception of Islamic law is anachronistic for the Mughal period;[41] this book takes up that idea more fully.

It does so, for two interconnected reasons. The first is my previous work in the field of law and colonialism, particularly with relation to religious identity and its co-formation with laws that worked through the ascription of confessional status.[42] As I learnt about the endless potholes in the legal landscape of the British Empire, and about ubiquitous colonial protagonists hopping over and around them, I was tempted, first, to discover what they thought while they hopped,[43] and then led to wondering how exactly people may have negotiated structurally comparable problems in the Mughal empire. In choosing to follow that question beyond the assumption of a colonial rupture, and attempting to find out what exactly it was that had changed,[44] I discovered that while there is widespread awareness among scholars of Islamic law that the Indian continent, especially under the Mughals, offers a crucial case worth comparing to the frequently studied Ottoman empire, research into Islamic law in Mughal India is plagued by the incapacity or unwillingness of scholars of Islamic law to use Persian and Indic-language source material, and by the very simplistic ideas of Islamic law entertained by historians of Mughal India, who disregard most findings of the former group. It is only by combining the insights from the former and the skills of the latter that we can prevent the reification of particular

[40] Even scholarship based on traditional jurisprudential sources, but sensitive to the historical role of the state, offers a different narrative. Guy Barak, *The Second Formation of Islamic Law: the Hanafi School in the Early Modern Ottoman Empire* (Cambridge: Cambridge University Press, 2015).

[41] Nandini Chatterjee, 'Reflections on Religious Difference and Permissive Inclusion in Mughal Law', *Journal of Law and Religion*, 29: 3 (2014), 393–415.

[42] The reference here is to the 'personal laws', which, in the Indian case, are distinct sets of laws, purportedly, but very tangentially based on religious codes, and applicable according to the legally recognised religious identity of the party. These laws, of which there are four separate sets, regulate family life, inheritance and the management of religious institutions. See J. D. M. Derrett, *Religion, Law and the State in India* (first published 1968; New Delhi: Oxford University Press, 1999).

[43] Nandini Chatterjee, 'Muslim or Christian?'; Nandini Chatterjee, 'Hindu City and Just Empire: Banaras and India in Ali Ibrahim Khan's Legal Imagination', *Journal of Colonialism and Colonial History*, 15: 1 (2014), online only.

[44] A recent effort in that direction, from a maritime perspective, is Lakshmi Subramanian, *The Sovereign and the Pirate: Ordering Maritime Subjects in India's Western Littoral* (New Delhi: Oxford University Press, 2016).

Mughal-era jurisprudential texts, such as the late-seventeenth-century *Al-Fatāwā Al-ʿAlamgīriya* (*Fatāwā-yi ʿAlamgīrī* in Persian), and enable proper analysis of their contents, especially what appears to be clear evidence of the Mughal jurists' deep interest in the implications of confessional diversity.[45]

I am inspired to attempt to make that connection, especially by scholarship on other Islamic empires that conceive of an institutionally complex field united by the legal consciousness of users who saw it as one terrain.[46] Although differently conceived, insights derived from the broad field of Jewish studies[47] and Mediterranean history[48] are also illuminating, since attention to multi-confessional legal subjects under Islamic rule is of core interest to scholars working on these areas. If Jewish women and men from Morocco to Afghanistan learnt to get their transactions recorded in forms acceptable to Islamic tribunals, and if the Mameluk and Ottoman empires as well as smaller Central Asian kingdoms[49] created procedures for accommodating non-Muslims, then it is surely worth investigating what happened in Mughal India. This book tells the stories captured in the documents related to the central Indian go-getter Mohan Das and his family, and tells them as a story of Islamic law.

## The Language of Law: Persian and Persianate

That is a story whose scattered pages are written in specific languages. Unlike Islamic jurisprudential literature, which, prior to the nineteenth century, was always written in Arabic, documents recording the rights, obligations and transactions of Mughal subjects – grandees to commoners – were written in Persian, sometimes in combination with other, more local Indian languages.

45 Mouez Khalfaoui 'Together but Separate: How Muslim Scholars Conceived of Religious Plurality in South Asia in the Seventeenth Century', *Bulletin of the School of Oriental and African Studies*, 74 (2011), 87–96; as indicated above, I do not agree with Khalfaoui's speculative conclusions about the existence of separate legal systems for Sunnis, Shiʿas and Hindus.

46 These three works have been most useful for me in conceptualising my own analytical framework: Baldwin, *Islamic Law and Empire*; Sartori, *Visions of Justice*; Fahad Ahmad Bishara, *A Sea of Debt: Law and Economic Life in the Western Indian Ocean, 1780–1950* (Cambridge: Cambridge University Press, 2017).

47 This includes the paleographic studies of the famous Cairo Genizah documents: Geoffrey Khan (ed. and translated), *Arabic Legal and Administrative Documents in the Cambridge Genizah Collections* (Cambridge: Cambridge University Press, 1993), and also more recent analyses of litigants traversing multiple jurisdictions, Jessica Marglin, 'Cooperation and Competition among Jewish and Islamic Courts: Double Notarization in Nineteenth-Century Morocco', in Moshe Bar-Asher and Steven Fraade (eds.) *Studies in the History and Culture of North African Jewry*, Vol. III (New Haven and Jerusalem: Yale Program in Judaic Studies and the Hebrew University Center for Jewish Languages and Literatures), pp. 111–29.

48 Francisco Appellaniz, 'Judging the Franks: Proof, Justice and Diversity in Late Medieval Alexandria and Damascus', *Comparative Studies in Society and History*, 58: 2 (2016), 350–78.

49 Claude Markovits, *The Global World of Indian Merchants, 1750–1947: Traders of Sind from Bukhara to Panāma* (Cambridge University Press, 2000), pp. 57–109.

That writing was highly conventional, and its conventions were derived not only from Arabic-language jurisprudential texts but also the chancellery traditions of Persianate empires, including pre-Islamic ones of the Near East, Iran and Central Asia and post-Islamic ones of South Asia. Since such legal documentation, and the processes documented therein, was the principal mode through which most Mughal subjects encountered law, the material pushes us to think of 'law' as more than jurisprudence, but as a mode of communication which shared and reoriented the juridical lexicon. Placing adepts and laity on the same sheet of paper, it encourages us to explore Islamic law as vernacularised in the Mughal empire, or conversely law as a specific trajectory of cosmopolitanism in the Indo-Persianate and Indo-Islamic world, as important as those other lines of interaction with Iran and Persianised Central Asia, in which interest has been growing since the 1990s.[50] Studies following the migratory patterns, circular and otherwise, of various skilled and enterprising groups, such as poets,[51] painters, administrators, jurists,[52] medical doctors[53] and traders,[54] between India, Iran and Central Asia underline that cosmopolitanism was borne by many who were not destined to be kings or anything particularly grand. This book shows that you did not have to travel very far from home in order to be cosmopolitan; the world came to you with your Persian-language title deeds.

Of course, the cosmopolitan entails its obverse: the vernacular. South Asia, with its persistent multiplicity of languages, affords us ample opportunity for reflecting upon this relationship, and law is an unfairly neglected location for doing so. As far as languages are concerned, the relationship between the potentially infinite scope of a cosmopolitan language and the necessarily limited and localised scope of a vernacular implies not just multiplicity but also hierarchy, even if that hierarchy is actuated in different ways. Sheldon Pollock has shown how during the first millennium after Christ, the two great cosmopolitan languages of Eurasia – Latin and Sanskrit – bore very different relationships with the vernacular languages they encountered. This difference appears to have been mainly about prescription and compulsion, or the lack thereof, in the South Asian case. Sanskrit's non-coercive and permissive

[50] Balabanlilar, *Imperial Identity in the Mughal Empire*; Dale, 'The Legacy of the Timurids'; Dale, *The Garden of the Eight Paradises*; Richard C. Foltz, *Mughal India and Central Asia* (Karachi, Oxford: Oxford University Press, 1998).

[51] Mana Kia, *Early Modern Persianate Identity between Iran & India* (Unpublished Ph.D. Thesis, Harvard University, 2011).

[52] James Pickett, *The Persianate Sphere during the Age of Empires: Islamic Scholars and Networks of Exchange in Central Asia, 1747–1917* (Unpublished Ph.D. dissertation, Princeton University, 2015).

[53] Seema Alavi, *Islam and Healing: Loss and Recovery of an Indo-Muslim Medical Tradition, 1600–1900* (Basingstoke: Palgrave, 2008).

[54] Scott Levi, *The Indian Diaspora in Central Asia and Its Trade, 1550–1900* (Leiden: Brill, 2002).

attitudes towards many scripts and other languages seems to have given way, in the 'vernacular millennium' that followed, to non-combative, localised vernaculars in South Asia, while European vernaculars turned into tools of the nation-state.[55]

Pollock suggested a somewhat unilinear movement from the Sanskrit cosmopolitanism to vernacularism to the flattening cosmopolitanism of the present day (linguistically borne by English, no doubt). Scholars have used his concept of the cosmopolis to explore the functions of other trans-regional, prestige languages that clearly had a role to play in the Babel that is South Asia. Of these, the study of Arabic cosmopolitanism remains oriented towards the Indian Ocean circuit, including the south-western margins of India.[56] Persian, on the other hand, was *the* language of courtly culture and administration in Indo-Islamic India from the twelfth century onwards, placing India in an overland cultural-imperial circuit that reached up to the borders of China on the one hand and into Europe on the other. Richard Eaton, who has been drawing attention to this world-historical role of Persian from the 2010s, has proposed that Pollock's concept of the cosmopolis, specified as the 'Persian cosmopolis' is a better framework for understanding cultural-societal formations in South Asia (such as the profuse use of domes in the architecture of the sixteenth-century Hindu empire of Vijaynagar), than the distorting 'Islamicate' model.[57] One principal reason for the inapplicability of a religion-derived adjective, according to Eaton, is that the Persian cosmopolis transcended religion, just as the Sanskrit cosmopolis had done before.[58]

Three collective publications, including one featuring an essay by Eaton, have offered the term 'Persianate world' to offer a sense of this vast, supra-religious, multi-polity and multilingual sphere that loomed large in Eurasia in the second millennium, united by the prestige language of Persian.[59] Some

[55] Sheldon Pollock, 'Cosmopolitan and Vernacular in History', *Public Culture*, 12: 3 (2000), 591–62; also Sheldon Pollock, 'India in the Vernacular Millennium: Literary Culture and Polity 1000– 1500', *Daedalus* 127: 3 (1998): 41–74.

[56] Ronit Ricci, *Islam Translated: Literature, Conversion and the Arabic Cosmopolis of South and Southeast Asia* (Chicago and London: University of Chicago Press, 2011).

[57] Richard Eaton, 'The Persian Cosmopolis (900–1900) and the Sanskrit Cosmopolis (400–1400)', in Abbas Amanat and Assef Ashraf (eds.) *The Persianate World: Rethinking a Shared Sphere* (Leiden: Brill, 2018), pp. 63–83.

[58] Richard Eaton and Philip Wagoner, *Power, Memory, Architecture: Contested Sites on India's Deccan Plateau, 1300–1600* (Oxford: Oxford University Press, 2014), pp. 19–28. This idea, and the interaction between the Sanskrit- and Persian-oriented cultures is further substantiated in Richard M. Eaton, *India in the Persianate Age, 1000–1765* (London: Penguin Books, 2019).

[59] Brian Spooner and William L. Hanaway, *Literacy in the Persianate World: Writing and the Social Order* (University of Pennsylvania Press, 2012); Abbas Amanat and Assef Ashraf, *The Persianate World: Rethinking a Shared Sphere* (Leiden: Brill, 2019; Nile Green, *The Persianate World: the Frontiers of a Eurasian Lingua Franca* (Oakland: University of California Press, 2019).

scholars have drawn attention specifically to the phenomenon of writing (in Persian), without the associated skill of speaking it – proposing, therefore, the phenomenon of Persographia, rather than Persophonie.[60] Nile Green has moreover emphasised that in order to understand how this cultural complex functioned, it is necessary to identify the 'various relational profiles' of Persian with other languages in the various regions of this world zone, and identify what 'forms of social interaction or organisation' could be facilitated by Persian and which ones lay beyond its scope. This is a very attractive call with a vast scope of study in the Indo-Persian sphere, in which these relational profiles are many and the social layering of languages is specific to those regional profiles. Thus far, substantive research related to Persian in South Asia has remained largely limited to literary production; this book takes the search into the dusty world of legal documents.

Our documents are written in Persian, the administrative language of the Persianised Turkic and (occasionally) Afghan dynasties that established their empires in northern and central India from the eleventh century onwards, including that of the Mughals, but they are also written in other languages and scripts. We still know strikingly little about the procedural and practical relationship of Persian with the non-Arabic Indic scripts, as well as the South Asian vernaculars, especially those that may have been adopted for some administrative writing under the less-Persianised Afghans.[61] Barring epochal, shakily evidenced events such as Emperor Akbar's famous revenue minister, Todar Mal, prescribing the exclusive use of Persian in administrative documents,[62] we know very little of how Persian and the many languages of India (generically referred to by Persian writers as Hind-ī or Hindawī) were utilised; our knowledge about the use of Persian in the Mughal empire being most systematic in connection with the production and consumption of high-

60 Nile Green, 'Introduction' in Green ed. *The Persianate World*, pp. 1–71; Hanaway and Spooner, 'Introduction: Persian as Koine: Written Persian in World-Historical Perspective', in Hanaway and Spooner (eds.) *Literacy in the Persianate World*, pp. 1–68.

61 Momin Mohiuddin, *The Chancellery and Persian Epistolography under the Mughals, from Babur to Shah Jahan, 1526–1658* (Calcutta: Iran Society, 1971), p. 28; Muhammad Shafi, '*Ahd-i Sher Shah ke do farmānein*', *Lahore Oriental College Magazine* IX (1933), pp. 115–128. As it happens, this is poor evidence of Afghan documentary procedures and practice, because the two documents reported are not *farmāns* (imperial/royal orders) at all, but lower-level documents, which, as we shall see continued to be bilingual and bi-scribal even in Mughal times. This will be discussed in more detail in Chapter 4.

62 Habib, *Agrarian System*, p. 324, note 43; as Habib notes, the sources for this purported order are from much later and offer only anecdotal evidence; among them is the anonymous *Khulāṣat al-siyāq*, completed 1703. Nabi Hadi expressed clear doubts as to the accuracy of its version of events. Hadi, *Dictionary of Indo-Persian Literature* (New Delhi: Indira Gandhi National Centre for Arts, 1995), pp. 311–12. The *Akbar Nāma* itself only mentions a series of revenue and administration reforms introduced by Todar Mal in the 27th regnal year (1582–3), but nothing about language use. Abul Fazl, *Akbar Nama*, translated Henry Beveridge (3 vols., Calcutta: Asiatic Society, 1907–39), Vol. 3, pp. 560–6.

brow literature.[63] As our documents show, not all Mughal documents were in Persian,[64] but there was also a pattern to the way in which languages and scripts were combined in different types of documents, which this book will discuss in some detail.

We have learnt a lot about the education of budding Mughal scribes or *munshīs*,[65] who must hold the key to understanding exactly how Islamic legal terms – such as *iqrār* (legally binding declaration; confession) – came to be part of the everyday vocabulary of several South Asian languages, and the stuff of Bollywood musical declarations of romance. These archetypically non-Muslim scribes, ubiquitous and occasionally subject to the frustrated ire of Muslim jurists, learnt Persian through classical texts of poetry, moralistic prose and the *munshāts* (formularies) we are interested in; some also learnt accountancy and its cryptic numerals. A select few among them secured employment with the highest nobles, even the imperial court, while the rest slogged it out in districts and villages, where highbrow Persian literature may have had a limited audience,[66] but Persian legal writing certainly had its market.

And not just Persian; as this book will demonstrate, certain kinds of transactions attracted recording in at least two languages and scripts. In the majority of bilingual documents in our collection, this other language can be broadly designated Hindawi, but it is more accurate to call it Rangri, the scribal form of Malwi associated with Rajput courts, that is very similar to Rajasthani.[67] The script in the Rangri sections of the documents is an archaic form of Nagri, with some eccentric letters. Subsequent to the passing of the Mughal empire in Malwa, the family's archive continued to acquire documents in Persian, but now also began to collect royal (Maratha) orders in Marathi (written in the cursive Moḍi script) as well as Rangri/Hindi. Finally, with the advent of British indirect rule, the princely state of Dhar occasioned the production Urdu and English documents. There were thus many layers to translation – literal and cultural – of Islamic law, but we are only beginning to learn about the Mughal scribes' training in administrative Hindawi, and also about their makeover under Maratha and then British rule. And in this book, I can only attempt to

[63] Muzaffar Alam, 'The Pursuit of Persian: Language in Mughal Politics', *Modern Asian Studies*, 32: 2 (1998), 317–49.

[64] As Alam suggests was the case in Ibid., p. 328.

[65] Muzaffar Alam and Sanjay Subrahmanyam, 'The Making of a Munshi', *Comparative Studies of South Asia, Africa and the Middle East* (2004) 24: 2, 61–72; Kumkum Chatterjee, 'Scribal Elites in Sultanate and Mughal Bengal', *IESHR*, 47: 4 (2010), 445–72; Rajeev Kinra, 'Master and *Munshī*: A Brahman Secretary's Guide to Mughal Governance', *IESHR*, 47: 4 (2010), 527–61; Rosalind O'Hanlon, 'The Social Worth of Scribes: Brahmins, Kayasthas and the Social Order in Early Modern India', *IESHR*, 47: 4 (2010), 563–95;

[66] As Hayden Bellenoit argues in 'Between Qānūngōs and Clerks: the Cultural and Service Worlds of Hindustan's Pensmen, c. 1750–1850', *Modern Asian Studies*, 48: 4 (2014), 1–39 at p. 13.

[67] On Rangri, see George Abraham Grierson, *Linguistic Survey of India* (Calcutta: Office of the Superintendent of Government Printing, 1903–1928), Vol. 9, Part II (1908), pp. 52–9.

present a speculative pattern about the rules and conventions for using these Indic languages and scripts within the bilingual documents, which were clearly prolific, in which I do not always agree with previous scholarship.[68]

Texts prescribing the norms of language use and writing abounded in the Persian-reading sphere. These were the *munshāts* – formularies containing models of 'letters' in the broadest sense, including diplomatic missives between emperors, orders of various kinds, as well as exchanges between family members and relatives.[69] Available from the eleventh century in Iran, they were first produced in the fourteenth century in the Indian subcontinent. This Indo-Persian genre really took off in the seventeenth century, with proliferating formularies also adding a new section on legal deeds. Very few recognisable *munshāts* in any regional Indic languages have been discovered; a tradition of Sanskrit formularies, which is difficult to date,[70] appears to have largely (but not entirely) yielded place to the Persian. Isolated compositions continued to be produced in Sanskrit, the purpose of such productions remaining unclear.[71] The Marathi-speaking and writing area appears to have been distinctive in producing a genre of manuals called *mestak* which, while grammatically Marathi, drew very heavily on Persian vocabulary as well as forms. These do not, however, contain models for legal documents, and are more concerned with offering instructions on correct writing methods and writerly behaviour.[72] For the core Mughal regions, Persian manuals dominated the field;

[68] Najaf Haidar, 'Language, Caste and the Secretarial Class in Mughal India', unpublished paper, on author's academia.edu pages.

[69] Jürgen Paul, '*Inshā*' Collections as a Source of Iranian History', in Bert Fragner et al. (eds.) *Proceedings of the Second European Conference of Iranian Studies (Bamberg, 1991)* (Rome: IsMEO, 1995), pp. 535–40; Colin Mitchell, 'Safavid Imperial Tarassul and the Persian Insha Tradition', *Studia Iranica*, 27 (1997), 173–209; Emma J. Flatt, 'Practicing Friendship: Epistolary Constructions of Social Intimacy in the Bahmani Sultanate', *Studies in History*, 33: 1 (2017), 61–81; Nandini Chatterjee, '*Mahzar-namas* in the Mughal and British Empires: the Uses of an Indo-Islamic Legal Form', *Comparative Studies in Society and History*, 58: 2 (2016), 379–406.

[70] *Lekhapaddhati: Documents of State and Everyday Life from Ancient and Early Medieval Gujarat, 9th to 15th Centuries*, (ed.) Pushpa Prasad (New Delhi: Oxford University Press, 2007).

[71] Pankaj Jha has drawn attention to the Sanskrit-language formulary – *Lekhanavali* – composed by the fifteenth-century Maithili polymath Vidyapati, and speculated about its twin connections with the conventions of Sanskrit grant deeds, inscribed on copperplate and stone, as well as Persian *insha*. While the connections deserve further study, a formulary for writing royal deeds in Sanskrit could only be a literary venture in the fifteenth century. Pankaj Jha, 'Beyond the Local and the Universal: Exclusionary Strategies of Expansive Literary Cultures in Fifteenth Century Mithila', *IESHR*, 51: 1 (2014), 1–40. Jürgen Hanneder kindly drew my attention to the nineteenth-century composition by Sahib Ram, apparently aimed at the court of Ranbir Singh of Kashmir.

[72] Sumit Guha, 'Serving the Barbarian to Preserve the *Dharma*: the Ideology and Training of a Clerical Elite in Peninsular India, c. 1300–1800', *IESHR*, 47: 4 (2010), 497–525; Prachi Deshpande, 'The Writerly Self: Literacy, Discipline and Codes of Conduct in Early Modern Western India', *IESHR*, 53: 4 (2016), 449–71.

bilingual lexicons offering mnemonic techniques for effective memorisation of corresponding vocabulary appear to have sufficed; a working knowledge of Persian grammar and intimate knowledge of a limited number of Persian texts, including the formularies, providing the rest of the toolbox of the multilingual Mughal scribe.

Scholars working in southern Indian contexts and working backwards from the angst of British East India Company officers and Protestant missionaries, who raged endlessly against what they saw as the linguistically and morally distorted world of 'cutcherry Tamil', have offered perceptive suggestions for how such multilingualism might have worked in practice. In the early nineteenth century, Tamil-speaking scribes who used this polyglossic language, deeply imprinted with administrative Persian, worked with a combination of skills related to reading, writing, computing and memorising. Here too, there were no Tamil formularies as such.[73] There is clearly no necessity for linguistically distinct manuals presenting the same content when users have sufficient cross-lingual competence, which could just mean oral/aural familiarity with key terms without full facility in the source (i.e., Persian) language and script. Books in the high-status source language could provide models to be translated and transcribed *in situ* by adept specialists, but the same results could also be achieved through memorisation of models and stabilisation of a core technical vocabulary across languages.[74]

This book will make some preliminary forays into exploring the modus operandi of multilinguality, within the specific, but widespread realm of law and legal documentation. In the absence of reliable programmatic statements from contemporaries explaining the purpose and modalities of using multiple languages and scripts in legal documents, I will work from the documents themselves. It is clear even from our family's collection that certain documents invited multilinguality while others did not. Also, within the typology of material that this book works with, the multilingual types are themselves various in the way that they deploy the different languages and scripts in use. Relating language use to the form, content and purpose of the documents allows us to work back to the manner in which they may have been written and correlate specific kinds of social and institutional situations with particular kinds of language use.

In thus attempting to work out the normative, procedural and social relationship of co-situated languages, I will work with the axiom that language is never just a functional vehicle; what can be said (or written) is always determined by

[73] Bhavani Raman, *Document Raj: Writing and Scribes in Early Colonial India* (Chicago: University of Chicago Press, 2012), pp. 57–62, 106–34.

[74] Sumit Guha, 'Margi, Desi and Yavani: High Language and Ethnic Speech in Maharashtra', in H. Kotani (ed.) *Marga: Ways to Liberation, Empowerment and Social Change in Maharashtra* (Delhi: Manohar, 2008), pp. 129–46.

the medium through which it is said (or written). Understanding the relevant conventions, allusions and lexicons is necessary for reconstructing the conceptual landscape of our protagonists, for getting at what they thought they were doing. In this connection, it is always worth reminding ourselves that the lives and indeed written traces of our protagonists spilled far beyond the limited cache of distinctive Persian legal documents that form the core of this book. Memorabilia, photographs and a manuscript Hindi-language family history shared with me by the family members offer at least some glimpse into those other worlds that they simultaneously inhabited, and prompt us to remember a heterogeneous, even discordant, field of language use, with concepts varying dramatically from one end to another.

## The Everyday Mughal Empire

Of course, law is not simply a product of culture or intellectual traditions. Our protagonists and the material they have left behind also force us to rethink the category of law as extending beyond an autonomous body of rules and procedure, and resituate it along a conceptual and coercive spectrum extending from state policy on the one hand to formal academic jurisprudence on the other, littered with un-academic manuals and pragmatic users in between. This spectrum was naturally negotiated by the heroes of my story through the use of several tribunals, languages and, when needed, force. In addition, their own view of themselves was frequently quite different from the meanings and functions that the regime attached to the offices that they were so keen to retain and display. One part of that difference derived from the well-known gap between the regime's aims and its abilities, especially in terms of its relationship with the *zamīndārs*, that ubiquitous class of heterogeneous origins, whom the Mughals wished to see as minor servants but had to handle as militarised rural powerholders who saw themselves of kings of their (admittedly) small realms.[75]

It is not quite enough, however, to think of Mohan Das's family as part of an entrenched and sullen rural gentry, encased in the 'hard shelled structures'[76] of clan dominance in the countryside, their position secured for most of the time by the regime's unwillingness to spend excessive resources on extracting relatively small returns, their belligerence making them useful, but ultimately unconvinced allies of any overarching regime. There was no insulated rural society forever waiting to throw off Mughal rule and peel off Perso-Islamic political legitimation; if those quintessential

[75] Habib, *Agrarian System*, pp. 169–229; S. Nurul Hasan, 'Zamīndārs under the Mughals', reprinted in Alam and Subrahmanyam (eds.) *The Mughal State*, pp. 284–98.

[76] This is John F. Richards' term, in Richards, *The Mughal Empire*, p. 82.

rebellious *zamīndārs*, the Marathas, did eventually assert a *Svarājya* in the late seventeenth century, they were able to do so after rising and growing under Deccani and Mughal overlords.[77] It is debateable whether the explicitly and self-consciously Hindu Brahminical political norms articulated by the Maratha rural rebels-turned-kings indicated the submerged but persistent existence of an alternative political vision, or indeed, whether it was a kind of planned 'renaissance' where Brahmin scholars found the political opportunity to rediscover classical texts, and for the first time in several centuries, apply them in adjudication. Whatever the answer as far as the Maratha effort is concerned, we cannot assume attachment to, or even knowledge of, any alternative universalist political ideology in Dhar in the seventeenth century, where our story is set.

What I mean, therefore, by a disjuncture between the Mughals' view of the *zamīndārs* such as Mohan Das and the latter's view of themselves, is that there was a clear gap between the hyper-formal vocabulary of the Mughal manuals of governance, and the way in which such people really worked for the government. In Mughal theory, there was a ranked body of imperial nobles, known as *mansabdārs*, who held various specific offices (governor, treasurer, paymaster-general, etc.) at different points in their career. The ranks were expressed in multiples of ten, and were composed of two parts – the personal (*z̠āt*) rank and the number of horsemen (*sawār*) rank. Together, the rank determined the salary of the *mansabdār*, which, in turn, had to be collected from a certain area which was given in *jāgīr*. While in theory there was an independent body of revenue officials undertaking collection of taxes, in reality the *mansabdār-jāgīrdār* had to make his own arrangements to get the taxes collected. Among other measures, the *mansabdār-jāgīrdār* could choose to farm out the collection of taxes to a lessee – an *ijāradār* – or several of them, although this was officially frowned upon. As for the amount of taxes to be collected, some provinces were *ẕabtī* – they had been measured and assessed and there was a schedule of taxes, prepared by the famous revenue minister of the third emperor, Akbar, in 1592, but everybody knew that the *jama ʿdāmī* – the revenue demand – was generally unrealistic, and, in fact, separate accounts were maintained of the *ḥāl-i ḥāṣil* – current collections. And besides, several provinces were not surveyed at all, so tax-collection was a matter of yearly negotiation.[78]

[77] André Wink, *Land and Sovereignty in India: Agrarian Society and Politics under the Eighteenth Century Maratha Swarajya* (Cambridge: Cambridge University Press, 1988).

[78] This outline, which will be elaborated further in the subsequent chapters, is based on W. H. Moreland, 'Ranks (Mansab) in the Mughal Service', *Journal of the Royal Asiatic Society* (1936), pp. 641–5; I. Habib, 'The Mansab System, 1595–1637', *Proceedings of the Indian History Congress,* 29: 1 (1967), 221–42; Shireen Moosvi, 'Evolution of the Mansab System under Akbar', *Journal of the Royal Asiatic Society*, 2 (1981), 173–85; Athar Ali, *The Mughal Nobility under Aurangzeb* (Bombay: Aligarh Muslim University, 1966), pp. 38–68; Noman Ahmad Siddiqi, *Land Revenue Administration Under the Mughals (1700–1750)*

All of this extraction process sat on top of a generic group of rural power-holders whom Abul Fazl's great chronicle-gazetteer only called *zamīndārs*. Our Mohan Das and his family were *zamīndārs*, but this term was only a description of status (like *mansabdār*) rather than of specific duties and entitlements; some *zamīndārs* might be elevated to court and become *mansabdārs* themselves, others would remain limited to a few villages. The numerous administrative manuals (*dastūr al-ʿamal*) written from the seventeenth century onwards elaborated what these less-eminent *zamīndārs* might do for the government. When recognised as *chaudhrī*, they were deemed as holding an office, which entailed getting the taxes collected. In playing that role – of government-sponsored arm-twisters – they were supposed to complement the role played by another kind of village officer, the *qānūngō*, who was meant to keep records of such extractions. These offices – *chaudhrī* and *qānūngō* – were supposed to be distinct,[79] and both deemed part of the revenue officialdom, sitting below *amīns*, *ʿāmils, karōrīs*, and so on.

In reality, of course, a *zamīndār* like Mohan Das could be a *chaudhrī* who doubled as a *qānūngō*, and might even take to being an *ijāradār*. That would mean that a *jāgīr's* monetary worth would depend on a man, or group of men, who rolled record-keeping, revenue-extraction and tax-speculation into one, being able to be super-extractors because of their private armies. In fact, as with the protagonists of our story, they may have been able to acquire that bundled position because of specific military services provided to the *mansabdār-jāgīrdār*. In effect, in a certain district, such men might be the state.[80]

These pragmatic modes of functioning were not unknown to the regime, for they are revealed to us through our documents – which formally recorded the various transactions undertaken by our protagonists in their different capacities. Because we have a continuous record of such transactions by the same family and its members over several generations, we can see how these rural go-getters 'managed' the system. Micro-history, when applied to such an archive, provides us with a methodological alternative to ethnography, which was used by Akhil Gupta to access the 'everyday practices of local bureaucracies and discursive construction of the state in public culture'.[81] Pertinently

(Bombay: Asia Publishing House, 1970), pp. 41 ff. My argument follows that of Sumit Guha, 'Rethinking the Mughal Economy: Lateral Perspectives', *Journal of the Economic and Social History of the Orient*, 58 (2015), 532–75.

79 On the distinction between the two roles, see Habib, *Agrarian System*, pp. 331–8.

80 And by recognising this, we can be guided by insights derived from the concept of the 'everyday state', which has been explored in South Asian history exclusively with relation to the twentieth century. Taylor C. Sherman, William Gould and Sarah Ansari, *From Subjects to Citizens: Society and the Everyday State in India and Pakistan, 1947–70* (Cambridge: Cambridge University Press, 2014); William Gould, C. J. Fuller and Véronique Bénéï, *The Everyday State and Society in Modern India* (Delhi: Social Science Press, 2009).

81 Akhil Gupta, 'Blurred Boundaries: the Discourse of Corruption, the Culture of Politics and the Imagined State', *American Ehtnologist*, 22: 2 (1995), 375–402, at 376.

for us, Gupta's perceptive analysis was with reference to the activities of a range of officials in a village in postcolonial India. There really is no reason to believe that such assessment has to be limited to the proximate past in South Asian history. The record for the Mughal empire is prolific; what we need is method and imagination for reconstructing the archive and putting the story together.

As we shall see, despite being district *qānūngōs*, that is, petty officials concerned with tax assessments, Mohan Das and his descendants were also represented in the family's documents as *chaudhrīs*, that is, local *zamīndārs* co-opted by the Mughals for the purpose of collecting taxes. This overlap in roles pushes us to make two modifications in our understanding of Mughal governance at the village level, the first of which is the translation of practice into theory through documentation. Documents consistently maintained clear distinctions between offices, but they also recorded simultaneous office-holding. Rather than see this as a conflict between Mughal theory of state and its reality, I see it as the percolation of a vocabulary of governance – everybody knew what the offices meant, they just wanted more of them. The second point is sociological: since whole idea of co-opting local *zamīndārs* rested on the regime's need to use local land-based power, we are pushed to relinquishing any anachronistic expectations we may have of *qānūngōs* being mere meek pen-pushing clerks. In so holding multiple official positions and bearing what might appear in retrospect to be conflicting social status, this family was neither unique nor symptomatic of imperial decline.[82] The answer lies in finding out what exactly people of this kind did to get their jobs, salaries, grants, perks and most importantly, promotions, and indeed, how they saw themselves and justified their entitlements.

I propose that despite the undeniably turbulent quality of this level of the state, there was no clean cultural and political line dividing the regime from its rural social bases. This book cannot tell the story of what the Mughal regime looked from the other side, it will instead explore what it looked like on an 'everyday' basis,[83] especially when viewed from 'below', by those who were near the bottom of the pile and scrambling to get a bit higher.[84] As André

82 The largest *zamīndārī* of Bihar, that of the Darbhanga Rajas, owed its origin to a very similar set of conjoint appointments as *qānūngō* as well as *chaudhrī* of the pargana, under the reign of Emperor Akbar. Qeyan Uddin Ahmad, 'Origin and Growth of Darbhanga Raj (1574–1666), based on some Contemporary and Unpublished Documents', *Indian Historical Records Commission*, 36: 2 (1961), 89–98.

83 I am borrowing the concept of the 'everyday state' from the special issue of *Modern Asian Studies*, edited by Taylor C. Sherman, William Gould and Sarah Ansari on the theme 'From Subjects to Citizens: Society and the Everyday State in India and Pakistan, 1947–1970', *Modern Asian Studies*, 45 (1) (2011), 1–224; and from the broader project within which this publication was located.

84 This use of the 'history from below' is closer to E. P. Thompson's concept, which suggested the sharing of paternalist norms between patricians and plebeians in early modern England, which

Wink's powerful formulation continues to remind us, such turbulence, or *fitna*, was an essential part of the continuous process of state formation.[85] The languages and formulae of legal and administrative documentation that they used, the activities that these documents recorded and the self-representation that they enabled, all point to a deep social penetration of Persianate and Islamicate forms and the loyal Mughal soldier and courtier model – deeper than we may have expected.[86] The Bollywood obsession with badlands, replete with gun-toting *rāja sāhebs* with elaborate *harems* and private armies but also fluent in English and occupying various offices and franchises of the modern Indian state, perhaps offer us useful reminders of both the ubiquity of the state and its alter egos.

This then, is the story of part-time landlords, part-time clerks, occasional businessmen (or women) and amateur strongmen. They raised armies, fought others like themselves, dealt with nobles, robbers and the infrequent prince, were well-known to the local *qāẕīs* and sometimes judges themselves. They were mostly not Muslim, but their lives, loves and conflicts resist such simple categorisation, and instead invite us to rethink modern-day categories whose neatness is anachronistic and misleading, and which obscure the nature of Mughal India as a unique Islamic polity with predominantly non-Muslim subjects.

## Family, Lineage, State

In many ways, this book is about powerful households in South Asia, and is inspired by insights related to the history of the family from a wider world. It is impossible not to notice that the protagonists of this story were active agents in a matrix of emotional and material resources and that they drew sustenance from those accumulated resources, which included reputation, and worked hard to sustain and improve on them. But, as we shall see, they also competed among themselves to eliminate weaker and undeserving lines and individuals, and in doing so, they drew upon broader institutions of the state, seeking endorsement

the plebeians could still appeal to in the eighteenth century in defence of their customary rights. It is less reliant on the *Subaltern Studies* formulation, in which the underdogs/plebeians/subalterns were credited with a fully distinct normative world of their own. Compare: E. P. Thompson, 'The Moral Economy of the English Crowd in the Eighteenth Century', *Past and Present*, 50 (1971), pp. 76–136, with Ranajit Guha, *Elementary Aspects of Peasant Insurgency in Colonial India* (Delhi: Oxford University Press, 1983).

85 Wink, *Land and Sovereignty*, pp. 23–35, 38, and throughout the rest of the book.

86 On the cultural model presented by the Mughals, and its social penetration within the aristocracy and the service gentry, see J. F. Richards, 'Norms of Comportment among Mughal Imperial Officers', in Barbara Daly Metcalf (ed.) *Moral Conduct and Authority: the Place of Adab in South Asian Islam* (Berkeley: University of California Press, 1984), pp. 255–89; for its persistence, see David Lelyveld, *Aligarh's First Generation: Muslim Solidarity in British India* (Princeton: Princeton University Press, 1978), pp. 35–101.

by princes and nobles or adjudication by state-appointed judges. These fissures, purges and reformations of the family flash into view during disputes over property and distribution of entitlements, which will be discussed in detail in Chapter 5. But they also appear in the repeated recitation of the history of services rendered to the regime by specific individuals, leading to the acquisition of specific rights, and the reiteration of genealogies connecting present-day claimants to their illustrious ancestors. Thus the formation of this powerful lineage was not a self-contained process; it was formed within an active, and at least partly recoverable, network of relationships with specific nobles and particular officials, some over significant periods of time. These were the higher, or at least broader, powers, who were invited to weigh in during conflicts within the family, and who subsequently used that restructured family, and their clients within it, to extract services for their own households, or further upwards. Prior to the (never fully successful) efforts of the colonial state to separate the domain of the state from that of the family, the state used to be family business, from the imperial dynasty down to the rebel warlord's household. Given that the 'formation of families and the formation of states were ... implicated in each other',[87] by studying this family, we are also studying the formation and transformation of states in South Asia.

Thus, in terms of subject matter, this book is related to studies of persistent landed lineages – both those that became 'little kingdoms' at some stage of their evolution[88] and those that rose and fell in economic, social and/or religious eminence, among other things by partaking of royal largesse, without aspiring to shares in sovereignty.[89] As far as royal households were concerned, it has often been pointed out that the Mughal emperors personally distributed power in a 'patrimonial-bureaucratic' manner.[90] More recently, we have learnt how Mughal princes created similar eddies of power, wealth and loyalty around themselves as competing power bases.[91] But it was André Wink who took the concept down the social ladder by telling the story of powerful lineages in a constant state of rebellion or *fitna*, supporting the state, but threatening to

[87] Sumit Guha, 'The Family Feud as Political Resource in Eighteenth Century India', in Indrani Chatterjee (ed.) *Unfamiliar Relations: Family and History in South Asia* (New Brunswick: Rutgers University Press, 2004), pp. 73–94 at p. 78; the same idea also in Frank Perlin, 'The Precolonial Indian State as History and Epistemology: a Reconstruction of Societal Formation from the Western Deccan from the Fifteenth to the Nineteenth Century', in H. J. M. Claessen and P. Skalnik (eds.) *The Study of the State* (The Hague: Mouton, 1981), pp. 272–302.

[88] Nicholas Dirks, *The Hollow Crown: Ethnohistory of an Indian Kingdom* (Cambridge: Cambridge University Press, 1987).

[89] Laurence W. Preston, *The Devs of Cincvad: a Lineage and the State in Maharashtra* (Cambridge: Cambridge University Press, 1989).

[90] Stephen P. Blake, 'The Patrimonial-Bureaucratic Empire of the Mughals', *Journal of Asian Studies*, 39: 1 (1979), 77–94.

[91] Munis Faruqui, *The Princes of the Mughal Empire, 1504–1719* (Cambridge: Cambridge University Press, 2012).

replace it as well.[92] Following Wink, I do not try to judge whether it is the lineage or the state that is the primary historical and/or social phenomenon; I see the story of the lineage, actuated through households, as also the story of the state as it appeared in Mughal and post-Mughal Dhar.

If we accept that proposition, then it also becomes productive to place the story of this family in the social and political hierarchy that the documents constantly indicate. As historians of the family have taught us, household implies much more than the site of habitation by an ultimately nuclear (i.e., heterosexual, procreative) family; slaves, servants, retainers and relatives were all very much part of the spectrum of relations which extended upwards, towards the Mughal nobles and later Maratha warlord-princes. Studying the principal protagonists with relation to their kinsmen and women, social and political superiors, associates and subordinates, we thus have access to an unusually rich burst of social history, one which refuses to be contained either by an institutional matrix or a community-centred one. Mughal princes, Muslim scholars, Afghan servants, Rajput and Maratha warlords, elusive courtesans and travelling peddlers all form part of the fabric of a story for which hierarchy and mobility are two faces of the same coin.

Methodologically, however, there are difficulties with this approach. The cache of Persian documents that enabled this study is hyper-masculine; it ostensibly looks towards the outside world. Although family relationships are so crucial to the shaping of the lineage and its claims, women make only fleeting, albeit evocative appearances in these documents, in all cases (except one) in the context of distress or a breach. Those breaches – of norms, of boundaries of kinship, of mutual obligations between master and servant – sometimes allow us a glimpse of the *ghar* behind the *gharāna*.[93] These glimpses supplement the picture we glean from the documents overall – that of a feudal household, with its patriarch, conflict between male heirs at generational boundaries, widows and black sheep, all encircled by armed retainers supplementing the ambit of kinship, and constituting a resource cluster that could be usefully offered to an incumbent regime. However, this being a Hindu family, we are deprived of the one documentary form that may have told us something more about kinship strategies – the *nikāḥ-nāma*. We are also deprived of a persistent series of interpersonal letters that may have allowed us to reconstruct the ways in which relationships were formed and sustained. On the other hand, some of these limitations are compensated for by a Hindi-language family history, produced sometime in the eighteenth or nineteenth

[92] Wink, *Land and Sovereignty in India*.

[93] For a work similar in spirit to this book, and situated within the wider field of histories of the family, see A. R. Kulkarni, 'The Jedhe *Gharane* (the House of the Jedhes)' in Irina Glushkova and Rajendra Vora (eds.) *Home, Family and Kinship in Maharashtra* (Delhi: Oxford University Press, 1989), pp. 173–84.

centuries, which elaborates further on the preferred feudal and martial self-image of the lineage. I will discuss this text in Chapter 7, but my interpretation of the seventeenth- and eighteenth-century Persian documents is influenced by what I know the family wished to believe about themselves several generations down the line.

## The Sources: Archives and Fragments

The core of this story rests on three stores of 'private papers', which clearly derive from a single family's collection. It is worth pausing here a while, to reflect upon this category from the archivist's trade. Scholars of relatively recent periods of history very often wade through messy and frequently tedious collections of diary notes, personal and official letters, theatre tickets and newspaper clippings in order to access the private person by reconstructing their emotional and social dynamics. Such people naturally have to be wealthy enough and regard themselves highly enough in order to create and preserve such collections, and eventually, public repositories have to consider such material of wide enough significance to transform these narcissistic collections into the 'private papers' of historians. The category assumes a certain clarity of distinction between the public and the private, even when the persons authoring or featuring in the documents are the same. For example, it is noted of the British Library's vast collection of 'Private Papers' of British officials and civilians in India that, 'Though often including papers similar to or complementing the much more extensive India Office Records . . . the Private Papers are distinguished from the Records by their provenance from private sources'.[94] Archivists today are aware of the difficulty of classifying documents and artefacts on the basis of provenance, leading to advanced distinctions based on function – thus the President's diary, as well as the records of his or her political party are comprised in 'private papers', since, these are not records of the 'official' functioning of the state.[95]

Paradoxically, private papers also remain premised on a notion of public significance. It is true that interest in the lives and thoughts of the working classes and marginal groups, such as immigrants, or, in other cases, a need to demonstrate the popular bases of national identity, has, since the 1950s, led to a widening of the source base. This trend has been strengthened by the availability of voice-recording technology, which can capture the memories of people who had not otherwise created a paper trail of their lives. Despite these developments, however, 'Private Papers' identified by the name of

[94] The National Archives, 'Mss Eur: Private Papers' online guide.

[95] Richard Pearce-Moses, *A Glossary of Archival and Records Terminology* (Chicago: Society of American Archivists, 2005).

a person require that person to have been of some eminence; the writings or words of those lacking such eminence are consigned to less individuated archives – of oral history or otherwise.

Thus, in characterising the records that form the core of this book, we are confronted with two problems, both related to the meaning of archives. As far as the question of eminence and significance is concerned, one might think that our protagonists have provided us with a clear answer. They collated their own collection, and in doing so, commented not only on the significance of the events recorded in those documents for themselves, but on their own continued significance within that local chain of events. However, the collection of papers that Mohan Das and his descendants accumulated was eventually dispersed, through mechanisms that are now impossible to fully reconstruct. It is only by doggedly pursuing a hunch, being rewarded by fortuitous coincidences and the unbelievable generosity of complete strangers that I was able to reconnect three parts of that dispersed collection, over a period of six years. The substantive results of those efforts and their results are contained in this book; the methodological insights that I gained thereby are elaborated in the conclusion.

Through conversations with present-day descendants, it appears that the substantial library and documentary collections of the patriarch of the family were held at the Dhar homestead until very recently, that is, until two generations ago. Some time during the decades following India's independence, the family lost its long-established ability to read Persian, and consequently, the ability to appreciate materials written in that language. Thus, some time in the 1950s or 1960s, unknown family members chose to donate or sell some of their documents, which had by then become obscure historical artefacts, to their mind interesting only to museums, libraries and private collectors. One such set, comprising exclusively of what must have been seen as higher value documents – entirely Persian-language stamp-bearing original *parvānas* – made their way to Dar al-Athar al-Islamiyyah Museum (DAI), Kuwait. A more miscellaneous collection, still mostly in Persian but including a variety of documents, a signficiant number of them including Hindi (in Nagri) sections or marginal notes, came to be acquired by the National Archives of India (NAI), Delhi. The remainder, including most material in Marathi in the Moḍi script, remained in the household.

There is a striking parallel, therefore, between the narratives underlying the archiving aims of repositories, and the collections they acquire and curate. Created in 1983 as the public repository of the private art collection of Sheikh Nasser Sabah al Ahmed al Sabah, the DAI's aim is to curate and present artefacts from across the Islamic world, from Spain to China. Naturally, the portion of the Dhar family's collection that was selected to travel to Kuwait was what appeared most Islamic, that is, was entirely in the Perso-Arabic script, including the seals, all of which were those of Muslim nobles/officials. The National Archives of India, on the other hand, acquired a more diverse collection of material, including those which appeared less grand and with a great deal of Nagri-script writing on them. Such material aligned well, in fact, with other such private collections acquired by the National Archives in the 1950s and 60s.[96] The remainer at Dhar was a mix – a few impressive-looking documents, several copies of documents held either in Delhi or Kuwait, and all the Marathi-language material, including long lists in vertically opening books, or *bahīs*. It is as if language, perceived prestige value and geographical relevance overlapped to decide how the household collection would be actually dispersed and relocated. In turn, those archiving narratives shape the stories that can possibly be told using material from each of those collections.

The journey of this book has consisted of the reaggregation of that dispersed collection. I will tell that story fully in the concluding chapter, where I will also discuss the rationale for my efforts. Suffice to say here that my journey began in the NAI, New Delhi, when I realised that the apparently amorphous collection of the 'acquired' papers of the NAI (around 14,000 documents), actually consisted of the collections of a handful of families – among them certain Bania merchants of Cambay, some Muslim scholars of Sandila and a family of *zamindārs* from Dhar. I also realised that, in line with still-current archiving (and research) principles, the NAI had either destroyed the integrity of the collections, merging and rearranging them chronologically and/or catalogued them in that exhaustive but haphazard fashion. As such, researchers seeking to reconstruct a particular collection must wade through the entire catalogues of the private papers, locating names, places and events that identify a paper as part of a certain collection. It was while doing so that the name Purshottam Das began to leap out at me from the pages, until I realised that there were dozens of documents that mentioned just this one man.

As I collated these documents together, and also learnt to recognise Purshottam Das's relatives and associates, I also learnt to read the cursive Persian, written in the fearsome 'broken' or *shikasta* script *and* in Arabic-inflected, Indian-usage-dominated Persian legalese, in the face of which all my hard-earned knowledge of Persian grammar and reading skills failed me completely. But I was fortunate then to find the best and most generous teacher one could have – Chander Shekhar of Delhi University – whose patience and endless love for anything written in Persian extended (very unusually) from sublime poetry to witness attestations on the margins of legal documents. He encouraged me to break the rules – instead of telling me to postpone reading

[96] *Calendar of Acquired Documents*, continues as *Descriptive List of Acquired* Documents, 4 vols. (New Delhi: National Archives of India, 1982–95). I discovered later that the principal archivist and cataloguer, Zakir Hussain, had also produced a short description of the portion of the Dhar family's collection acquired by the National Archives of India. Zakir Hussain, 'A "Zamindar" Family of "Sarkar" Mandu "Suba" Malwa during the 17th Century (Archival Evidence)', *Proceedings of the Indian History Congress*, 53: 9 (1992), 311–20.

difficult materials until my Persian was better, he told me to learn to read by reading what I was really interested in. And so I was trained to become, in my Persian reading skills at least, somewhat like the scribes or *munshīs* who wrote these documents in the first place.

Three short and intensive bursts of collaborative study of the documents, together with Chander Shekhar, funded by the British Academy, allowed me to understand these documents better. My obsession with them also led me to follow a footnote in Irfan Habib's encyclopaedic work on the *Agrarian System*, which mentioned a set of documents pertaining to a family of *zamīndārs* from Dhar. Habib noted that these documents were held at the Dar al-Athar al-Islamiyyah Museum in Kuwait. Working on a hunch, I contacted the museum, and its staff, incredibly generously, sent me digital copies of all forty-three documents in their collection.[97] These turned out to be derived from Purshottam Das's family, again, many of them featuring the man himself, bearing familiar seals and handwriting, both in the main text and on the margins. Many of them were also demonstrably originals of documents whose copies I had found in the National Archives.

Together, the documents from the National Archives and DAI Kuwait brought the story up to the 1720s. What happened to the family thereafter remained obscure, and all I have suggested above in terms of archiving, dispersal and re-archiving remained no more than speculative. Deeming this sufficient to write a plausible micro-history of a *zamīndār's* family in Mughal Malwa, examining thereby the formation of households and dynasties, the use of state resources and the recording of entitlements through the use of multiple languages, I considered my book nearly complete. On a whim, then, I decided to make a trip to Dhar, to see if I could take any photographs of the locations in which I knew my protagonists had operated that would be illustrative of context. And I ended up meeting the descendants of the family and discovering yet another portion of the archive, which extended my story from that of the Mughals, via the Marathas, right up to the British empire and up to the present day.

Dhar is a crowded city with an interesting but run-down fort, which rather pales in comparison with the beautiful Afghan mosques, forts, palaces and tombs in nearby Mandu. Driving and walking through the city, however, I came across a run-down, but still gorgeous complex of buildings, some of

[97] Twenty-four of the documents in the Kuwait DAI collection were summarised by Syed Bashir Hasan in 'Administration of *Jagirs* in Malwa in the Mid-Seventeenth Century: the Dhar Documents', in Shahabuddin Iraqi (ed.) *Medieval India 2: Essays in Medieval Indian History and Culture* (Manohar: Centre for Advanced Study, AMU, 2008), pp. 217–30. I assume that the scholar used photocopies that had been sent from Kuwait to Aligarh for Irfan Habib's evaluation; the same set of copies were probably used by Munis Faruqui in his *Princes of the Mughal Empire*.

which had life-size statues that were clearly of Maratha warriors. After asking around, I finally understood that these were the *chhatrīs* – the Rajput-style tomb complex of the Maratha Puwar dynasty that had become established in the region in the 1720s. Further asking around led me to the *rājwāḍā*, the erstwhile headquarters of the Puwar state, now a run-down complex of buildings bustling with everyday trade and business. From here, a generous young tailor took me to meet a knowledgeable lady whose name I did not learn, who told me that I clearly needed to meet one of the two highly respected Puwar brothers – the elder a former member of the State Legislative Assembly.

And so I imposed myself on the generosity of Mr Karan Singh Puwar, direct descendant of Anand Rao Puwar, who, together with Holkar and Sindhia, had invaded and conquered Malwa from the Mughals in the 1720s. Mr Puwar listened to what could have appeared to be preposterous queries about a family of *zamīndārs* who may have been subordinate post-holders under the Puwar-ruled Dhar state. The term *zamīndār* was alien to the region, he said, but on hearing the names of the protagonists, he smiled and called a number. And so I spoke to Amit Choudhary, direct descendant of Mohan Das and Purshottam Das *chaudhrī* of Dhar. Amit, a businessman and self-described history buff, recognised the names of his ancestors and was convinced by the research rationale I presented, and made arrangements for me to visit his ancestral home in another part of Dhar, where his mother Abha Choudhary, a beautiful and graciously intelligent lady, welcomed me, and showed me several boxes of documents, mainly in Persian, some in Hindi and a few in Marathi, bearing familiar handwriting, names and seals. Now I had the most complete archive of documents related to a single family in Mughal India, barring the Mughal dynasty itself.

Once again applying my old methods of careful transcription, translation and cataloguing, I now had almost two hundred documents, and more gaps in the story filled, especially that gaping hole after the 1720s. I learnt that the family had survived not one, but two, even three changes of regime – first the Maratha Puwar state, then indirect British rule, then the postcolonial Indian nation. I learnt what had been speculation until that point; that the male members of the family had tended to be fluent in Persian until about three generations back, that is, around the independence of India, which is approximately the time the documents began to be dispersed from the household. Amit also offered me photographs that helped, for the first time, to put a face to a name, and catch a glimpse of the manner in which this landed family of *Thākurs* in a princely state presented themselves using modern visual technologies. And I was able to access material that historians of the early modern non-European worlds only dream of: materials of self-reflection and self-representation, that can complement and gloss the formulaic material presented by the Persian documents. The most exciting of these was a scroll of family history written in Malwi/Rangri.

Despite all this, we still have no way of knowing the full limits of the archive, and in any case, that may be a false line of enquiry, because an archive is formed precisely because people wish to record certain things and erase others. This leaves us with difficulties in attempting interpretations that the papers themselves appear to be calling for. In our current collection, for example, once one gets to know the protagonists and their mutual relationships well enough, a clear plan of documentation begins to emerge. Certain lines of the family, and certain individuals within those lines, preponderate. The earliest document in the (reconstituted) collection, a grant to a certain Jayanti Das in 1574, is an outlier. The vast majority of documents are from the seventeenth and early eighteenth century, and about half of them name one person – Purshottam Das, son of Mohan Das, nephew of Chandar Bhan. Purshottam Das appears to have had a long and active career, which began in the 1620s. After some years of working in association with his father, and then his uncle, he came into his own in the 1650s, and had a long-term but occasionally turbulent professional relationship with a man called Paras Ram (the second most frequently named person in the collection). When Purshottam Das died in 1684, the family line appeared to stabilise, after a few very serious squabbles, on two of his sons, called Hamir Chand and Narsingh Das. This unilinear genealogy – Jayanti Das to Mohan Das to Chandar Bhan to Purshottam Das to Hamir Chand – was however a narrative that was very deliberately created by members of this line. It was created through repeated, periodic narrations of the family's antecedents, membership and entitlements; these narratives were produced and recorded during legal disputes, when other members and claimants made fleeting appearances, but were resolutely erased. Genealogies played a vital role in establishing that lineage and its claims; one such genealogy was produced in the early twentieth century, when Pratap Chand, a descendant of the main line, wrote a petition to the Resident of the princely state of Dhar, asserting the claims of his family against the expansive ambitions of the Puwar dynasty that ruled the state.

As such, the creation of this archive can be seen as a process of strategic commemoration, strengthening calls to extend the concept of 'sites of memory' to law.[98] For law insists on remembering, on eliciting multiple memories about what happened in the past, before authorising one version of that remembered past as the basis of actions in the future. Through documentation, it also materialises those memories, giving stories about the past a place in the present.[99] But law is

[98] Pierre Nora, 'Between Memory and History: Les Lieux de Memoire', *Representations*, 26 (1989), 7–24.

[99] Austin Sarat and Thomas R. Kearns, *History, Memory and the Law* (Ann Arbor: University of Michigan Press, 2002), Introduction by editors, pp. 1–24.

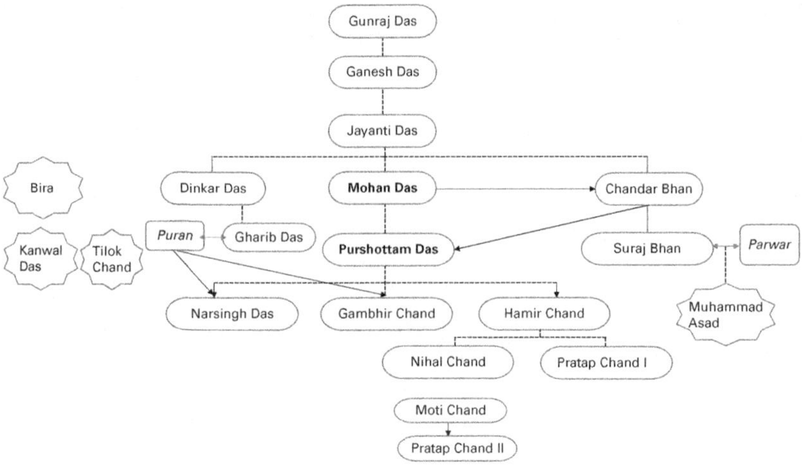


Figure I.1 Lines of descent, inheritance and rivalries

not an encrypting automaton: it is a field alive with purposive agents such as ours who told and recorded those stories; reinscribing but also reopening the narrative through repeated copying and notarising of rights-bearing documents; retelling antecedents that justified various futures. Ironically, law is our ally in reconstructing this family's conflict-ridden efforts, some of which were to remember, and others, to forget. The legally validated narrative that our documents produce is of course the dominant one; but since that narrative rests on disputes, we are afforded some glimpses of the other stories that may have been.[100]

Is this, however, a collection of private papers? To try to answer that question from an early modern context is of course to immediately stumble upon the anachronistic division of private and public, which assumes people's ability to distinguish their interior self from their public roles, and by extension, a workable distinction between the state and what is not the state. We also have the additional problem of knowing painfully little about Mughal archiving practices.

[100] Natalie Zemon-Davies, *Fiction in the Archives: Pardon Tales and Their Tellers in Sixteenth-Century France* (Stanford: Stanford University Press, 1987). Zemon-Davies' work is however more useful in analysing the narrative and documentary strategies used by particular individuals and particular times. In thinking about the boundary and structure of the archive as a whole, I have been inspired by Paolo Sartori's recent work on archives in Samarqand and Khiva, and encouraged by Irfan Habib's methodology in his 'A Documentary History of the Gosā'ins of the Chaitanya Sect at Vrindāvan', in Margaret H. Case (ed.) *Govindadeva: A Dialogue in Stone* (New Delhi: Indira Gandhi National Centre for the Arts, 1996), pp. 131–3. Confronted with a very large and also highly dispersed archive – that pertaining to the temples of Mathura, Vrindavan and Jaipur – Habib has chosen to organise his calendar of documents around key protagonists, rather than chronologically or by repository.

It is obvious, however, that the existence of such documents requires us to release ourselves from a vision of archival records that derives essentially from the Ottoman empire after the sixteenth century; clearly, what people wrote and stored, and where, varied very widely from one Islamic empire to another.[101] The history of Iran, as well as that of the Central Asian khanates of Khiva, Bukhara and Khokand, shows that the narrowly focussed quest for *qāẕīs*' registers or *sijillāt* of adjudicated cases, following the Ottoman model, may be a red herring, leading to false conclusions regarding the place of Islamic law in other empires, perhaps even about the Ottomans. It is quite likely that in most parts of the Islamic world, the authorities did not find it necessary to create and maintain registers, whether recording the adjudication of disputes or the activities of many other branches of government. Instead, it was found sufficient to maintain regional stores of documents, mainly related to military recruitment and pay, while the onus was on people to maintain records of their specific entitlements, or transactions with others. While necessarily speculative, this proposition would seem to explain the creation of the family archive that this book is based on.

## Orders as Legal Documents

The private–public divide, were we to keep pursuing it in characterising our documents, would become even more untenable as we looked through the contents of our collection closely. All forty-three of the documents now preserved in the DAI are a type of Mughal document called *parvāna.* Scholars and archivists studying documents produced during and under Mughal rule refer to the documentary types of the Mughal 'chancellery', with its hierarchy of documents, ranging from the *farmān*, which only the emperor could issue, through the *nishān*, which was in the gift of royal princes, to *parvānas*, which a range of high to middle-ranking nobles-cum-imperial-officials could issue. The picture of system and coherence they present becomes rather more blurred as we make our way down the hierarchy, or perhaps into a different documentary arena replete with generic orders called *ḥukums* and *dastaks*, but also interpersonal contracts of various kinds. Matters become even more unsure when we note that thus far we do not have single study of what can be called chancellery procedure – we do not know where exactly these offices were located, how many people worked in them, in what order the documents were written, super-scribed, checked, sealed and resealed, let alone how copies were produced and authenticated. All discussions of the Mughal chancellery assume an office at

[101] Tomoko Okawara, 'Reconsidering Ottoman Qadi Court Records: What Are They? Who Produced, Issued and Recorded Them?' in Vanessa Gueno and Stefan Knost (eds.) *Lire et écrire l'histoire ottoman* (Beirut: Orient-Institut Beirut, 2015), pp. 15–37.

the imperial centre,[102] with no reflection on the perpetual mobility of that centre, nor on the (also mobile) household offices from which high-ranking officials must have issued *parvānas* such as ours. As such, we have to work upwards from the documents, reading carefully what they say about the conditions of their own production, and relating them constantly with other documents, thus producing a story about the life of documents, as much as about the lives of people they reflect. This is the core of our jig-saw; but it will make sense as we invoke the broader textual field from whence these documents sprang – legal formularies, manuals of guidance for scribes and indeed, those always-disparaged but essential sources, the comments of outsiders who tried to do trade in India and struggled to make sense of this Persianate documentary world, while also acquiring their own share of 'firmans'.[103]

The word *farmān* was directly derived from the Persian verb *farmūdan*, to order. The *farmān* was a document that recorded an order of the emperor. In the Mughal empire, it was always written in Persian, on expensive paper (from Jahangir's reign) beginning with two indented lines, and topped with the royal seal and *ṭughra* (cipher, or stylised rendition of the emperor's name). They often had detailed inscriptions on the verso, with corresponding seals. As we move down the hierarchy, we have the *nishān*, the order of a royal prince, and the *parvāna*, that of a sub-royal, but high to middle-ranking official. The grammatical structure of *farmāns*, also of the lower-ranking *nishāns* and *parvānas*, was therefore always imperative – somebody was told to do something. As we shall see, orders and rights were not mutually exclusive matters; the order could consist of instructing somebody to take possession of certain entitlements.

Orders could be generic (Be good and loyal!) or specific (Go catch that thief!); they could create duties (Keep this village populated!) or entitlements (You may collect money from the peasants of this village, and do not need to pay taxes). Such duties and obligations were confirmed and modified by authorities other than the ones issuing them, and disputed in front of yet other authorities. We could say that some orders created rights, but that would be an inaccurate way of looking upon them; those orders that created specific entitlements were related to others that established the relationship that made the creation of such entitlements possible. Besides, orders led to other processes, which produced other kinds of documents – recording, for example, the resolution of a dispute by a *qāẕī*, the sale of an entitlement, or a debt secured on the resource that the order entitled the holder to. In trying to identify where

[102] Mohiuddin, *The Chancellery and Persian Epistolography under the Mughals*; also Mohammed Ziauddin Ahmed, *Mughal Archives: a Descriptive Catalogue of the Documents Pertaining to the Reign of Shah Jahan, 1628–1658* (Hyderabad: State Archives, 1977).

[103] See William Forster, *The Embassy of Sir Thomas Roe to the Court of the Great Mogul* (London, 1899), Vol. II, pp. 506–14.

'law' came from in Mughal India, it is this interlocking spectrum of orders and other documents that we look to in this book.

### Tax as Contract

Now, the other two subtypes of documents in this collection are not *farmāns, nishāns, parvānas* or indeed orders of any kind. Instead, in language as well as substance, they are transactional, including one-way transfers as well as immediate or deferred exchanges (i.e., contracts). I have conceived of these contracts as two, rather than a single subtype, based on their contents, and that is because agreements about tax payments, although recorded in a contractual form, involve a rather special party – the state.

Of course, the state and its precise location has been the holy grail of Mughal historiography. If taxation and military action are the two clearest loci of the relatively unambitious early modern state, then our substantial cache of documents, related to the contracts underlying tax-collection can offer an important corrective to the unilaterally extractive and coercive view of the state. Rural entrepreneurs such as Purshottam Das and his family, well equipped with private armies, engaged with the state through the noble who held a salary-account in the taxes of the region, offering to collect the taxes for him, for an implicit profit, of course. The fact that the same man who took on this 'franchise' was also the tax-collector and the tax recorder of the region, ensured his access to the coercive machinery of the state, which was essential for making the enterprise a success. These contracts are recorded in predominantly bilingual (Persian and Hindi or Rangri) documents that call themselves *qaul qarār pattā-yi-ijāra*, and are completed by documents of *qabẕ al-vaṣūl* or receipts secured when the contracted amount was paid into the *jāgīrdār's* treasury. However, there were always risks; a natural calamity such as a locust invasion might damage the harvest, competing landlords with their own private armies could attack the peasants, an unsympathetic imperial officer sent from the imperial court could demand extra cuts or different procedures. All such events required renegotiation of the deal, and produced a range of documents, but most importantly, *ʿarzdāshts* (petitions) which detailed the facts and sought to reopen the deal, with greater or lesser success.

### Legal Deeds as Instruments of Law

Finally, the men (and women) of Mohan Das's family dealt not just with their superiors, but also with their social equivalents and servants. These transactions were also recorded in a range of documents, which we may be tempted to call 'legal deeds', but this term, as all others derived from specific legal contexts, requires some modification. While English law defines a legal deed as an official written record of transfer of property, using the term in our early modern Islamicate legal context requires us to expand the definition to include all interpersonal transactions that create or fulfil entitlements or obligations. Consequently, this category includes documents recording not only sale and purchase, rent, mortgage, gift, debt and repayment, but also Muslim marriages and incidents to marriage and the manumission of slaves. These documents are self-identifying and marked by a distinct and formulaic vocabulary. Ironically, since these are transactions that were predominantly between members of the family and other non-Muslim protagonists, this is the document type that relates most closely to the documentary types described by Islamic jurists. They include *bāiʿ-nāmas* (sale deeds), *rahn-nāmas* (pawn or mortgage deed), *hiba-nāmas* (gift deed) and so on. These identifying terms (*bāiʿ, rahn, hiba*) relate to specific and highly developed areas of Islamic legal doctrine. They also contain stock phrases, some crucial ones in Arabic, which record the fulfilment of essential and widely known and practiced Islamic legal procedures. On the other hand, they bear phraseology and features that were distinctively Indian, and offer evidence of distinctive practices that are not discussed in any compendium of jurisprudence.

## The Structure and Contents of Household Archives

The specific types of legal deeds extant in different collections of 'family/private papers' indicate the social matrices within which such families or corporate entities operated. For example, the complex, and currently scattered, collections of documents pertaining to the temple complex of Mathura, Vrindavan and Jaipur, developed by *vaishṇava* priests from Bengal, nurtured by Mughal imperial grants from the sixteenth century onwards and eventually engulfed by Kacchwaha Rajput nobles are exceptionally well-stocked with *farmāns* and *parvānas*, and in the later period with Rajasthani *parvānaus* – orders creating, affirming and transferring rights in lands, but also of custodianship over the temples themselves.[104] Then there are several deeds of sale and gift, again related to land and its produce, as the temple functionaries and villagers made various deals among themselves. All this creating and recording of rights then threw up a substantive number of disputes, leading to declarations (*iqrārs* and

[104] On the early history of the complex, see Irfan Habib, 'From Arith to Rādhākund: the History of a Braj Village in Mughal Times', *Indian Historical Review*, 38: 2 (2011), 211–24. On the Kacchwaha Rajputs, who formed matrimonial ties with the Mughal dynasty from the mid-sixteenth century, and whose scions rose to the highest ranks within the Mughal nobility permitted to anyone outside the royal bloodline, see Jadunath Sarkar and Raghubir Sinh, *A History of Jaipur, 1503–1938* (Hyderabad: Orient Longman, 1968).

*maḥẕar-nāmas*) and records of judgements in the local *qāẕī*'s court.[105] A very similar spread of documents is seen in relation to smaller and less politicised sacred complexes – whether centred around an institution or certain persons. Orders predominate, including the highest status orders creating property rights, middle-ranking orders affirming and supplementing them, and lower-ranking orders dealing with the details of tax-collection and so on. As one works one's way through such collections, documents recording interpersonal transfers and disputes – related to the same property rights that the orders had created – inevitably begin to crop up, substantiating my arguments about the inseparability of orders from legal deeds.[106] Families of administrators with a flourishing side interest in commercial enterprise, on the other hand, created collections in which interpersonal transactions predominate. For example, the family collection of the Bhandaris from Batala, Punjab, was dominated by bonds and contracts of various kinds (*tamassuks*), gifts, loans, rental and mortgage agreements, quit-claims and records of disputes based on all of these.[107]

In the collection produced by Mohan Das and his descendants, there are no surviving original *farmāns* or *nishāns* (although there are a couple of purported copies); the highest level that the family reached directly was to imperial nobility. Hence the substantial collection of *parvānas*, all from the *jāgīrdārs* assigned the region. The orders that these nobles issued created both entitlements and obligations for the family, giving them access to the taxes of several villages, but more importantly, to offices in the same area – all concentrated in the district of Dhar, and spilling onto the neighbouring districts of Amjhera, Dewas, Nalcha and (the now-disappeared) Hindola.[108] It is in these very areas that the family undertook tax-collecting contracts and it is also here that they entered into endless interpersonal transactions – over money, property, offices and even lives.

105 Habib, 'A Documentary History'; for a detailed calendar, transcription and translation of documents issued exclusively by the chancery of the Kacchwaha nobles, including from the later period, when the idols of Govindadeva and Thakurani (Krishna and Radha) were taken to Jaipur and housed in a new complex there, see Monika Horstmann, *In Favour of Govinddevji: Historical Documents Relating to a Deity of Vrindavan and Eastern Rajasthan* (Manohar: Indira Gandhi National Centre for the Arts, 1999). These documents are bilingual (Persian–Rajasthani) and from 1712, in Rajasthani only.

106 B. N. Goswamy and J. S. Grewal. *The Mughals and the Jogis of Jakhbar: Some Madad-i Ma'ash and Other Documents* (Simla: Indian Institute of Advanced Study, 1967); Irfan Habib, 'Aspects of Agrarian Relations and Economy in a Region of Uttar Pradesh in the 16th century', *IESHR*, 4: 3 (1967), 205–32, in which he discusses the Bilgram and Shamsabad document collections of the Aligarh Muslim University Department of History Library.

107 J. S. Grewal, *In the By-Lanes of History: Some Persian Documents from a Punjab Town* (Simla: Institute of Advanced Study, 1975).

108 Hindola district, adjoining Amjhera existed as late as the 1920s. *Report on the Administration of the Dhar State, 1920–21 to 1925–26* (Dhar, n.d.).

## The Identity of Law

Where then, in this story, is Hindu law? When, the reader might ask, do we get to hear about how the *dharmaśāstras* regulated the lives and matters of Hindus such as these, in unadulterated precolonial times?[109] To answer that most directly and simply: there is no indication, anywhere in the collection, that the people whom we glimpse through these documents, had any awareness of an entity that we might call 'Hindu law', or that they expected or wished their transactions and disputes to be mediated by it. In fact, there is no explicit indication that the various parties – members of the family and their associates, the nobles involved, even the *qāẓī* who routinely turned up to notarise documents and mediate disputes, were working with the notion of an alternative body of non-Islamic law, related to any identifiable jurisprudential tradition. What we have in the orders, agreements, transactions and disputes are regular references to *sharīʿa*, as a body of norms without any reference to specific doctrines, but more often simply in adjectival form and in the sense of 'legal' or 'valid'; for example, when describing the validity of transactions or testimonies recorded. We have one explicit reference to *ʿurf*, or custom, again, without explanation as to what the custom amounted to, and several references to *dastūr* – rules, customs and/or entitlements based on these.

There is of course the possibility that the cache of documents that I have been able to retrieve represents only a portion of the household archive. It is possible that the family may have deferred to local single or multi-caste *jātī* councils, and even appealed to transregional Brahmin assemblies for the resolution of matters that related specifically to marriage, children, ritual status and so on.[110] I find it hard to believe, however, that records of such deliberations and decisions would be so systematically and completely lost from the family's collection, when in corresponding collections from the Marathi-writing zone, where such *jātī* and Brahmin councils were most effective, such documents have been most carefully preserved. Moreover, in one spectacular dispute from the late seventeenth century, where the legitimacy of a marriage of a member of the family and the legal status of his child was called into question, we see a panel of *qāzīs* making the decision, with no mention at all of any caste or religious council having been consulted. Rather than assuming the uniform

109 On *dharma* or righteousness as an area of expertise and exposition within the Sanskrit scholastic tradition, see P. V. Kane, *History of the Dharmaśāstra (Ancient and Mediaeval Religious and Civil Law in India)* (2nd ed., 5 vols., Poona: Bhandarkar Oriental Research Institute, 1968–77); on the more narrowly 'legal' implications of *dharma*, its continuities and transformations in colonial and post-colonial India, see J. D. M. Derrett, 'The Administration of Hindu Law by the British', *Comparative Studies in Society and History* 4: 1 (1961), 10–52.

110 Rosalind O'Hanlon, 'Speaking from Siva's temple: Banaras Scholar Households and the Brahman "Ecumene" of Mughal India', *South Asian History and Culture*, 2: 2 (2011), 253–77; Rosalind O'Hanlon, 'Letters Home: Banaras Pandits and the Maratha Regions in Early Modern India', *Modern Asian Studies*, 44: 2 (2010), 201–40.

presence and effectiveness of Hindu law as a shorthand for caste and religious councils and their preferred normative systems, it maybe more useful to learn of the specific historical and social conditions under which, for example, transregional assemblies of Marathi Brahmins acquired adjudicative power in the seventeenth century.

Moreover, in looking for Hindu law, we may be committing a conceptual error, thinking of 'law' as a body of abstract rules detached from the social relationships that it was intended to mediate. This is not to suggest a free-for-all, in which goons of various sizes settled matters by force, the rest being mopped up by some form of *kadijustiz*.[111] If nothing else, all categories of these documents are mutually self-referencing, thus whether considering an order, a contract or a dispute, documents refer to recorded rights; neither might nor tradition are cited as sufficient bases of entitlements. Also, they are highly regular – they clearly follow prescribed formulae: in the third sub-category of transactional documents, these formulae and conventions are those that would be recognisable throughout the Islamic world. Where does that leave us? If we conceive of our documents as the products of a system of Islamic law, modified by local custom, we are still thinking in terms of distinct jurisprudential traditions (Islamic law; customary law) and we are left with the rather unsatisfactory position of not knowing how people, including the judges, knew when to refer to the one and not the other. We also end up privileging about a third of the documents (the transactions recorded in Islamic legal forms) over the others, failing to incorporate the orders and contracts into the world of law, although they were clearly connected. Another explanatory possibility arises from the rather more insubstantial set of discussions regarding the Chingissid and Timurid legal heritage in Mughal India and its possible displacement by or coexistence with Islamic law. But while there were repeated references to the *yasa* of Chingis Khan, or the customary law of the Mongols, across the Islamic world, the scholarship does not suggest that this amounted to more than political ideology and practice of incorporation, exercised through court ritual, patronage of shrines and wartime behaviour.[112] It certainly does not appear to be a code of law, let alone a code of law detailed enough to deal with the petty entitlements of Indian village bosses. This leaves rather a lot more to be said about entitlements and obligations tied to Indian land, before we can make judgements about the genealogy and typology of those claims.

Here, I propose a tentative solution. I propose that 'law in Mughal India' consisted of rules derived from a number of sources – royal and sub-royal orders, administrative conventions and rules, Islamic jurisprudence and local

[111] For a discussion of Weber's concept of *Kadijustiz*, see earlier in this chapter.

[112] Balabanlilar, *Imperial Identity in the Mughal Empire*, pp. 10–11; Mathieu Tillier, 'Courts of law, historical', in *Encyclopaedia of Islam, THREE*.

custom – 'Islam' providing a general sense of order, together with royal grace.[113] *Dharmaśāstric* notions, for example, of exclusively male agnatic lines of inheritance may indeed have found their way in via local custom, or, if we follow the findings of Donald Davis with regards to a very comparable collection of material related to a temple town in Kerala, such local customs fed into Brahmanical jurisprudence.[114] Unlike Davis, however, I have not found a regional jurisprudential text – Brahminical or Islamic – that rationalises the observable legal practice as a coherent whole. For this work, it has been more productive to explore other bodies and sources of rules that clearly existed across the Mughal Empire, which multiple groups of specialists had systematic understanding of. By this I mean formularies that provided legal models and manuals of administration; while these do not present anything like jurisprudence, they offer a systematised view that may have informed the work of petty professionals, whose interests lay less in academic theory and more in getting the work done.

But I am not proposing to distinguish and separate specific elements and interpretively attach them to distinct legal traditions – this is Islamic law, that is administrative tradition, that again is custom. The documents that this book is based on suggest that my protagonists expected there to be systematic bodies of rules that could determine their entitlements; but this 'law' of theirs was that specific mixture that their social and geographical location exposed them to. There is no indication that they saw themselves as engaging with an eclectic system – Islamic law in parts and not in others – it appears that they saw it all as 'law'. If sectarian affiliation had any effect on determining the specific mix that a specific protagonist would recognise as law, it is not clear what that effect was, and it is certainly not in line with our present-day expectations. The predominantly Hindu protagonists in my story did not call for a specific 'law of Hindus' when disputing inheritance claims with their kin, for instance. The necessarily incomplete but nevertheless large archive I have been able to reconstruct reveals no pristine area of genealogical and affectionate relations immune to Islamic law where a recognisably 'Hindu' law and authority might prevail. Families were built and splintered around property and offices; royal orders, active contracting and recorded/reputed entitlements constituted a field in which records were produced using recognisable, but semantically open-ended, juridical forms and vocabulary.

[113] This is also the suggestion in Corinne Lefèvre, 'Beyond Diversity: Mughal Legal Ideology and Politics', in Gijs Kruitjtzer and Thomas Ertl (eds.) *Law Addressing Diversity: Premodern Europe and India in Comparison (13th-18th Centuries)* (Berlin: De Gruyter, 2017), pp. 116–41, specifically pp. 117–19.

[114] Donald Davis, 'Recovering the Indigenous Legal Traditions of India: Classical Hindu Law in Practice in Late Medieval Kerala', *Journal of Indian Philosophy*, 27 (1999), 159–213.

## The Story and the Structure

The core of the story of *Negotiating Mughal Law* is set in seventeenth- and eighteenth-century Malwa, straddling the reigns of last two 'great' Mughal emperors – Shah Jahan and Aurangzeb Alamgir. There is a slim long tail to that story, based on a thinner trail of records, that patchily but surely establishes the continued fortunes of the family through major political upheavals, as first the Marathas, and then the British took control of the region. Chapter 1 creates the setting. It discusses Malwa's political geography as it evolved from the late medieval period until the end of our story. It describes the dramatic and diverse landscape in its relationship with the local nodes of military and royal power, especially of those who referred to themselves broadly as Rajputs, and specifically, as *Rāthoḍs*. This includes those clans that congealed into states and those that remained more fragmentary, but all connected by a supra-regional notion of the land of Rajputs. On that real and imagined landscape is then imposed the arcs of military and commercial movements, evoking a zone that is defined both by entrenchment and mobility. This is offered as an essay on historical space, within which the protagonists of this story created an area of operations and entitlements for themselves, negotiating with successive and overlapping empires, wresting and recording their rights through all of them.

Chapter 2 introduces the protagonists and tells their story through the documents of order, issued by the occasional imperial prince, perhaps an emperor, but mostly, by high-ranking imperial nobles posted to the region. Together, these emanations of royal grace and authority, direct and delegated, explain the accretion of entitlements. They also allow us to retrace the process of structuration of a dominant line of the family – to the exclusion of other claimants who continue to haunt the edges of the story, producing creative tension and legal action. Emperors, princes and great nobles come and go in this chapter, giving orders and making grants, bringing the empire into the village and remaking it in the process. What remains constant is war, which both necessitates imperial intervention and provides opportunities for military entrepreneurs, such as members of this family, to work within unsubdued inner frontiers of the Mughal empire and lend themselves to the regime in order to ride to glory and wealth, at least on a local scale.

Chapter 3 discusses the business of tax-collection and uses tax contracts and associated documents in the collection in order to reveal how our family came to populate and dominate the extraction machinery of the state in their district and around. Showing how military prowess and sharp dealing were not mutually exclusive, we see how administrative offices, and a variety of transactions over associated perks, were yet another source of aggrandisement of this family of rural eminents. As such, this chapter speaks to the literature on the social history of Mughal and post-Mughal scribes and proposes correctives to the theoretical division between the worlds of the sword and the pen. It also widens the question of 'law', and explores further the range of vocabularies used to refer to it.

Chapter 4 uses documents in the collection that record interpersonal transactions, using it both to map the network of kin, creditors and employees that our protagonists lived in, and the specific procedures and documentary forms they used to record those transactions. The material used in this chapter allows it to address the literature on documentation and its procedures in Islamic law, explore the specificities of the Mughal Indian context and comment on their implications. In engaging with that literature, however, I will attempt to connect the documents in this collection to their precise modular source-texts. This will entail a discussion of Persian-language formularies called *munshāts*, which overlapped a little but also widely diverged from Arabic-language *shurūṭs* the latter usually appended to books of jurisprudence. From that textual matrix, the chapter will then proceed towards an exploration of the linguistic landscape in which these documents were located, opening up the 'Persianate' to reveal the multiple heteroglossic dispensations the term implied in Mughal India.

Chapter 5 looks at disputes and uses these recorded moments of friction to flesh out the interpersonal dynamics of the people in the story, and also investigate the notions of jurisdiction revealed by the disputants in taking their quarrels to specific tribunals at specific times. It then focusses on a major dispute in the family's history – in which a Muslim man tried to argue that he was part of this Hindu family, and was entitled to share in its possessions and privileges. After narrating what we can recover of the dispute and its long-drawn resolution, the chapter then reflects whether this dispute over inheritance – and also over belonging, entitlement, religion and family – may indeed have been the reason for the production of much of the documentation in the family's collection. Through a bald statement of rights, such documentation may have been specifically aimed at erasing a man and a woman who had a different story to tell.

Chapter 6 discusses the political turmoil that befell the region in the early eighteenth century, and the tortuous process of the region moving into Maratha country, and the consolidation of the Puwar dynasty. Using a highly evocative but strikingly less voluminous documentary cache, this chapter outlines negotiations undertaken by members of the family with these new rulers, and continues the story of that tense relationship into the nineteenth and twentieth centuries, when the Puwars were themselves compelled to submit to the supervision of an overweening British Empire. This chapter allows us to revisit, albeit passingly, some of the key ideas regarding the history of Persianate legal cultures, and to propose that this culture proved to be more resilient, and more pliable, than it may have previously been imagined to be.

Chapter 7 comments on the *Kāyasth* caste identity of the family, noting how, despite displaying various well-known characteristics of this archetypical Indo-Islamic service group, the family devised a specific self-identity to address its martial history. The chapter uses a family history narrative, possibly produced in the early nineteenth century, and reproduced several times in various languages and scripts (including as an annex to a petition to British authorities in the twentieth century). It uses that highly evocative narrative in conjunction with the material traces of self-conceptualisation left in other documents, such as identity markers and seals placed in the margins, to reveal a self-conceptualisation far more martial, and in communication with Rajput models of being, than the existing literature on Indo-Islamic scribes would suggest. That discussion then offers us the opportunity to map the relevant relational matrix of caste on the one hand, and to investigate the place of language in self-expression and self-identification on the other.

In the conclusion, we shall return to an evaluation of the micro-historical but also 'big-data' methods that may be used in conjunction in order to analyse documentary collections such as this one. It offers a demonstration of the kinds of enquiry that a reconstructed household archive and consequent serialised data can support. The aims, as in this book, are not to produce social history abstracted from individuals but rich narrative history that reaches much deeper down into the social fabric than may have been previously imagined. The book thus ends with a manifesto for reconstructing multiple archives and working towards narrative coherence within each. Only then can we make sense of the vast repositories of source material on early modern Indian history that is ubiquitous but meaningless without a story.

# 1 Malwa: Land of Many Empires

In the British Museum, there is a lovely statue of a female deity which is said to be from Dhar, the centre of our protagonists' zone of action, but from many centuries before they appeared. The museum's webpages note that this is a statue of Ambika, a deity shared by Hindus and Jains. The base of the statue bears a Sanskrit inscription which declares that the statue was commissioned and dedicated by a Vararūcī, who was intent on the Candranagarī and Vidyādharī branches of Jaina religion of Bhoja the king, and who had also dedicated a statue of Vagdevī and a triad of Jīnas (Jaina adepts). King Bhoja is a legendary king of the Rajput Parmar dynasty, who ruled from his capital in Mandu in the first half of the eleventh century; the date on the stela is 1091 Saṃvat, which corresponds to 1034 CE.[1]

There are other claims regarding the sectarian identity and historical provenance of this statue; claims which are of a piece with efforts to recreate a glorious Hindu past for India, anchored on to specific personalities and places. Bhoja Raja, and his legendary royal complex, Bhojaśālā, form a regional version of that story of the Hindu nation. According to this account of the story, the statue in the British Museum is not of the amphibious deity Ambika but of the Hindu goddess Sarasvatī, and that it was originally situated within the Bhojaśālā complex which was (predictably) later destroyed and built over by Muslim invaders.[2] The Mandu story and the historical wrongs it seeks to right are structurally identical with the more notorious efforts in Ayodhya, Mathura and Banaras: in each of these places, there is an intensified sacred geography, standing as symbol of a sectarian identity posing as national. That sacred geography is focussed on specific architectural complexes whose present and tangible reality simply do not match with the idealised past projected on to them. The ephemeral Bhojaśālā's historical existence is based on extrapolation from certain inscriptions, discovered inside a building which is also known as Kamal Maula's mosque (Figure 1.1). This building is currently under the surveillance

[1] www.britishmuseum.org/research/collection_online/collection_object_details.aspx?objectId=182355&partId=1&searchText=marble+jain&page=1.

[2] 'It's a Jain Statue, Clarifies the UK', *The Hindu*, 15 June 2003.

Figure 1.1 Latha Masjid/Bhojaśālā © Amit Choudhary

of the Archaeological Survey of India, which sells tickets saying 'Bhojashala/ Kamal Maula mosque'. Pious Muslim men offer prayers outside the building; Muslim women and men throng to the *dargāh* (tomb) of the thirteenth/fourteenth-century Chisti saint Kamal Maula, or Kamal al-Din Malawi[3] that stands next to it, and locals of all religions flock to the *ʿurs* (annual death anniversary celebrations) of Kamal Maula which enclose and enfold this disputed complex. In Mandu, as in all these other places, there are other people and inconvenient histories, which, with the convergence of a range of local and national aspirations in the early twentieth century, began to be seen as intrusions.[4]

[3] Muhammad Ghawsi Mandavi, *Gulzār-i Abrār*; I consulted the Urdu translation titled *Azkar-i Abrār*, translated Fazl Ahmad Jewari (Agra, 1908, reprint Lahore, 1975), p. 581.

[4] Archaeological Survey of India, 'Bhojashala and Kamal Maula's Mosque', www.asibhopal.nic.in /monument/dhar_dhar_bhojmosque.html#gallery; many of these inscriptions were discovered by K. K. Lele, the Superintendent of Education in the princely state of Dhar. K. K. Lele, *Parmar Inscriptions in Dhar State, 875–1310* (Dhar State Historical Records Series, 1944). Lele may also have been the source of the misreading of the inscription which led to the confusion of the statue of Ambika with that of Sarasvatī. Deborah Sutton has written about the conflicts between the Archaeological Survey of India and local devotional communities and priests in the process of conservation of Hindu temples in the early twentieth century. Deborah Sutton, 'Devotion, Antiquity and Colonial Custody of the Hindu Temple in British India', *Modern Asian Studies*, 47:1 (2013), 135–66. There remains to be told the story of Hindu nationalists who manned the

There are other ways of reading such material heritage, ways that permit us to view history as accretion, not epiphany.[5] At the same time, the competing aspirations that jostle to frame such heritage are themselves the stuff of history; stories themselves have histories. For example, a flattened notion of Hindu nationhood is not sufficient to understand riots over a proposed Bollywood film about a fourteenth-century queen; we need works such as Ramya Sreenivasan's to understand the evolution of the allegorical Sufi story of Queen Padmini and its entanglement with Rajput political aspirations in Mughal and post-Mughal times.[6] On that note, we have works by Prachi Deshpande,[7] Samira Sheikh,[8] Cynthia Talbot,[9] Chitralekha Zutshi[10] and Manan Ahmed,[11] which teach us how to tell stories about stories. All these scholars have explored creative as well as functional narratives about the past with which various South Asian martial groups – Rajputs, Marathas, Dogras, Mameluk Arabs – have repeatedly redefined themselves and their realms from the early modern era until the present day. In each of these cases, these royal stories have been subsequently discovered in the golden age of partnership between Orientalism and nationalism in order to establish the identity of a region.

This south-western corner of Malwa, our protagonists' hunting grounds, is not associated with a text quite as powerful as *Pṛthvīrāj Rāso* or *Chāchnāma*, but, as we have already seen,[12] Dhar has its own lost and found hero in Raja Bhoja of the Paramara dynasty. Rulers of the small princely state of Dhar have

lower to middle rungs of the archaeological bureaucracy in colonial and princely India, and the results of their efforts. Michael Willis, 'Dhār, Bhoja and Sarasvatī: from Indology to Political Mythology and Back', *Journal of the Royal Asiatic Society*, 3, 22, 1 (2012), 129–53.

5 Finbarr B. Flood, *Objects of Translation: Material Culture and Medieval 'Hindu-Muslim' Encounter* (Princeton: Princeton University Press, 2009); Finbarr B. Flood, 'Architecture of Malwa Sultanate', in Abha Narain Lambah and Alka Patel (eds.) *The Architecture of the Indian Sultanates* (Mumbai: Marg on behalf of IGNCA, 2006) pp. 81–91.

6 Ramya Sreenivasan, *The Many Lives of a Rajput Queen: Heroic Pasts in India, c. 1500–1900* (University of Washington Press, 2007).

7 Prachi Deshpande, *Creative Pasts: Historical Memory and Identity in Western India, 1700–1960* (New York: Columbia University Press, 2007).

8 Samira Sheikh, *Forging a Region: Sultans, Traders and Pilgrims in Gujarat, 1200–1500* (New Delhi: Oxford University Press, 2010).

9 Cynthia Talbot, *The Last Hindu Emperor: Prithviraj Chauhan and the Indian Past, 1200–2000* (New York: Cambridge University Press, 2016).

10 Chitralekha Zutshi, *Kashmir's Contested Pasts: Narratives, Sacred Geographies, and the Historical Imagination* (New Delhi: Oxford University Press, 2015).

11 Manan Ahmed Asif, *A Book of Conquest: The Chachnama and Muslim Origins in South Asia* (Cambridge, MA: Harvard University Press, 2017).

12 From that point of view, Samira Sheikh's study of formation of Gujarat through a continuous sedimentation of declarations, reports and reminiscences is most similar to mine in terms of its research base; as is Sumit Guha, 'Speaking Historically: The Changing Voices of Historical Narration in Western India, 1400–1900', *The American Historical Review*, 109: 4 (2004), 1084–103.

asserted descent from the Paramara dynasty since the nineteenth century, with the predictable combination of British Orientalism, Indian nationalist scholarship and political patronage. Like Gujarat, Marathwada, Sindh and Kashmir, Dhar and Malwa are located within an area of layered empires; it is just that, despite some significant and ongoing efforts, its story remains more interrupted.

The purpose of this chapter is not to tell the story of a region per se, nor to explore the successive formation of polities. The aim here is to conceptualise a zone – political, social and cultural – within which the protagonists of this book negotiated law. I am guided by the works mentioned, which both interrogate the concept of region and show us new ways of writing regional history. I am also inspired by those works that think of regions in terms of routes – not so much bounded territories, but significant circuits of circulation – of traders, merchandise, soldiers and war.[13] The protagonists of this story remained ensconced in the same region for at least four hundred years – more, according to family lore – and yet, that same family history was premised on the story of a journey. Settlement and movement are more complementary – as lifestyles but also as political styles – than we usually remember them to be.

In my case, I am interested in space because it is inherently related to law; and while the concept of jurisdiction – that combination of spatiality and authority, of geographical and abstract space – does leap to mind, here I would like to try and move beyond jurisdiction and all that Lauren Benton showed us it could do.[14] There are at least two reasons why I think that we need a better term than jurisdiction in order to conceptualise the negotiations with power and legitimacy – i.e., law – that the protagonists of this current story engaged in. The first reason is the wordiness of jurisdiction: derived as it is from the Latin pair *juris* and *dictio*, it renders a sense of law as words above all, captured best in texts and talking heads. The protagonists of my story expressed themselves in words, too, but their ability to speak derived from a range of activity and authority that I think needs a different word, one more closely linked to South Asian lexis and praxis. This is not an argument in support of the anti-intellectual conceptualisation of pragmatic 'jurispractice'.[15] As I have said elsewhere,[16] looking beyond formal institutions for law in South Asia (and maybe elsewhere, too) need not mean dismissing the possibility of abstract thought. It is here that the literature on regions offers interpretive models, for

[13] Tanuja Kothiyal, *Nomadic Narratives: A History of Mobility and Identity in the Great Indian Desert* (New Delhi: Cambridge University Press, 2016); Jos Gommans, *The Rise of the Indo-Afghan Empire, c. 1710–1780* (Leiden: Brill, 1995); Gommans, Mughal *Warfare: Indian Frontiers and Highroads to Empire, 1500–1700* (London: Routledge, 2002).

[14] Benton, *Law and Colonial Cultures;* Benton, *A Search for Sovereignty.*

[15] Lauren Benton, 'Introduction', *The American Historical Review*, 117: 4 (2012), 1092–100, at 1093.

[16] Chatterjee, 'Hindu City and Just Empire'.

the works I have cited on the history and identity of regions are about seeking out conceptual maps, through the clash and demise of empires.

I do not offer a 'background' essay, synthesised from recent scholarship and older works; I proceed, instead, to map the activities of my key protagonists against a palimpsest of shifting political formations, commercial and military circuits and physical environments. The method here is inductive – the description of the relevant 'region' proceeds from the material itself, from the distribution of persons, activities, locales and stories within that material. In that effort, the concept of *dāi'ra*, which includes the meaning of jurisdiction but circles far beyond it, appears to me to be a useful tool.

The word *dāi'ra*, which exists in Arabic, Persian as well as Hindi/Urdu, encompasses a range of meanings related to space and its encirclement. Derived from the Arabic root *d-vav-r*, it is part of one of those highly fecund word constellations which make Arabic such an evocative language; related words range from geometric to maritime and administrative. *Dāi'ra* itself, in all three languages, can be a circle, but its meaning also extends to other encircled spaces, such as a camp or monastery, and to spaces circumscribed in the abstract, that is, jurisdiction. In the thirteenth century, the historian Al-Juzjani, patronised by the Delhi Sultan Nasir al-Din, had placed Delhi at the centre of the *dā'ira* of Islam.[17] It is this semantic range – encompassing physical, social, architectural *and* legally defined space – that makes *dāi'ra* a useful conceptual tool for thinking of the zone of entrenchment and operations represented by Map 1.1.

Property owned by the family – in the form of houses, tax-free grants of agricultural or garden land, as well as various claims on shares of taxation – was clustered in south-western Malwa, just north of the Narmada river, nestling into the hills and forests that partially encircled it from the west and the south (see inset for details). This was the centre of their *dāi'ra*, but their long arms reached southwards, eastwards and northwards, with a scattering of property in the Mughal centre of Burhanpur, and with intelligence and political networks stretching towards pan-regional political centres: Agra in the Mughal period, Gwalior and Calcutta later. It was within the core area that the protagonists of this story owned and claimed property, fought most of their battles and lived out their lives. But the offshoots of their interests indicated that their *dāi'ra* was embedded in several other territories – ecological, political, commercial, military and administrative. The work of this chapter is to offer a palimpsest of those maps, as they are crucial for locating the characters of this story and for understanding what they did and said.

[17] Flood, *Objects of Translation*, p. 229.

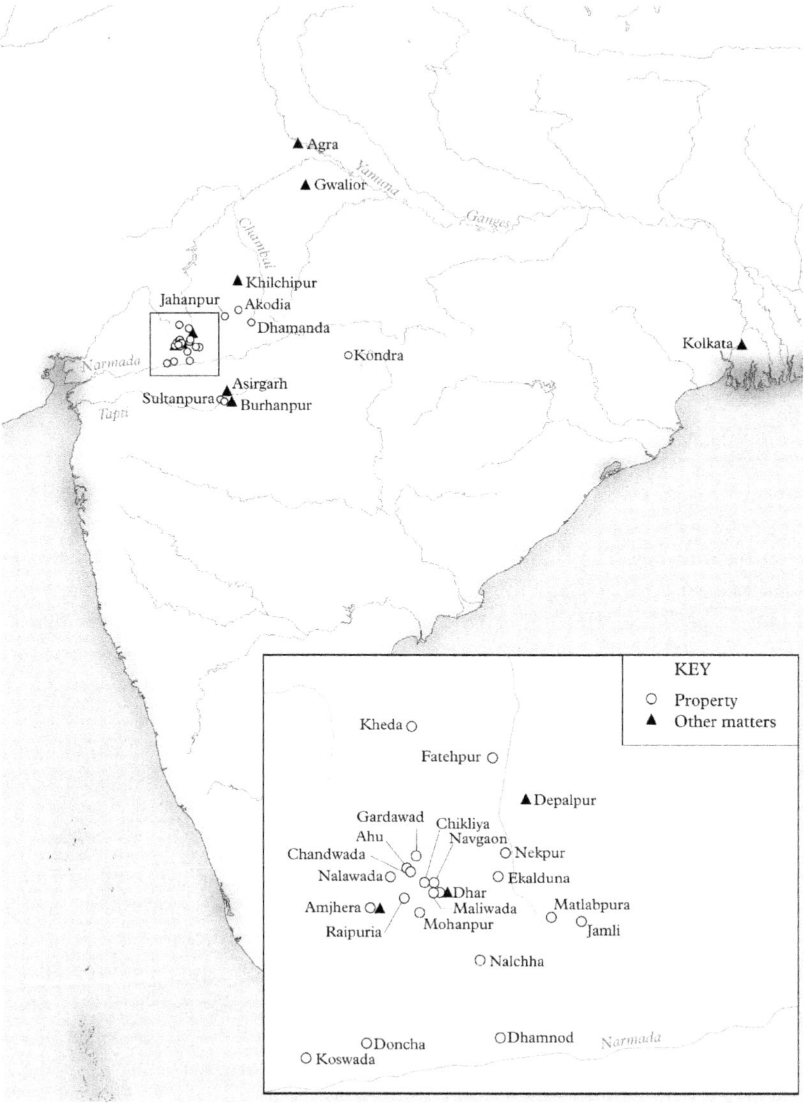


Map 1.1 The *dāi'ra* of the family

## Malwa: the Identity of a Region

The *dāi'ra* of Mohan Das and his family revolved around a dense cluster of villages in district Dhar, in the south-west corner of Malwa, nestling to the north of the Narmada river, the traditional dividing line between Hindustan and Dakhin. The range of their activities fanned out much further, however, with consequent entitlements scattered over a large part of Malwa. As twentieth-century colonial surveys noted, within the sprawling and politically fragmented zone of central India, Malwa formed a distinct region, geologically distinct for being a plateau as opposed to the hills to its west and the ravines to its east.[18] From at least Tughlaq times, that is, the fourteenth century, Malwa was considered the last frontier of 'Hindustan', beyond which began the geologically, linguistically, and politically distinct region of 'Dakshin'.

Geologically, there were both mountain and river boundaries that marked these limits – the foremost being the great river Narmada, which was difficult and dangerous to cross for several months of the year. The Vindhya and Satpura ranges ran parallel to the river, whereas the Aravallis stretched north-eastwards from the Narmada, creating a western boundary. To the north and north-east ran the Chambal, whose deep ravines remain a formidable natural barrier even today. Besides rivers and hills, there were also forests and animals: the hills to the north-west and the region beyond the Narmada river in the south were both densely forested. The region immediately south of the river Narmada was so well-known for its population of tigers, that the district took the Arabic name for tiger: 'Nimar'. Dhar, in particular, being at the south-western edge of Malwa, nestles in a corner created by forested hills in the west and the Narmada in the south. Geological and ecological challenges were not necessarily just barriers, however. They were also resources for those that inhabited them, among them ambitious soldiering groups who used the challenges of the landscape to entrench themselves, repulse rivals and prey on vulnerable traffic that passed through areas they had made their own.

Sometime around the twelfth century CE, heterogeneous nomadic and martial groups, including those that originated outside the subcontinent, began to cohere into royal dynasties with territorial claims, paired with genealogical assertions that traced their origins back to fictive progenitors capable of rendering a Kshatriya identity.[19] Some of these groups, spread from modern-day Rajasthan into central India and along the northern part of the Western Ghats, began to call themselves Rajputs (literally: sons of kings, or princes). Despite active efforts to secure and declare genealogical purity, 'Rajput' remained a relatively open social and occupational category well into the sixteenth century, perhaps even the nineteenth in central India, where this

[18] *Imperial Gazetteer of India* (new ed., Oxford: Clarendon Press, 1908), Vol. XVII, pp. 98–100.

[19] Among the various theories regarding the sources of such nomadic warrior groups, the Central Asian theory was popular in the early twentieth century, see Crooke's Introduction to James Tod, *Annals and Antiquities of Rajasthan* (ed.) William Crooke (first published 1829, 3 vols., London: Humphrey Milford, 1920), I, xxxi–xxxv.

story is located.[20] One such Rajput dynasty was that of the Paramaras of Malwa, established around the tenth century.

Contemporary records of this dynasty, which included the illustrious Bhoja (of the purported Bhojaśālā of Dhar), and Vikramjīt, to whom is attributed the Vikram Saṃvat era, are limited to fragmentary epigraphic evidence (such as the stela of the Ambika statue). Sources from a few centuries later (i.e., the fourteenth century) include Jaina Sanskrit *prabandha* literature aimed at documenting ideal 'Jaina' lives,[21] and legends reported fairly consistently by Persian-language histories[22] focussed on the victories of the Turkic and Afghan warriors, who were establishing a sultanate centred on Delhi at around the same time that the Rajputs were emerging into documented history.[23] Through the Mughal period[24] and by the eighteenth century, the story of Raja Bhoja, Vikramjīt and the Paramara dynasty became a standard part of local lore reported by gazetteers writing in Persian.[25]

[20] B. D. Chattopadhyaya, 'The Emergence of the Rajputs as Historical Process in Early Medieval Rajasthan', in Karine Schomer et al., *The Idea of Rajasthan: Explorations in Regional Identity* (Delhi: Manohar, American Institute of Indian Studies, 2001), II, pp. 161–191; B. D. Chattopadhyaya, 'Origin of the Rajputs: The Political, Economic and Social Processes in Early Medieval India', in *The Making of Early Medieval India* (2nd ed., Delhi: Oxford University Press, 2012), pp. 59–92; Dirk H. A. Kolff, *Naukar, Rajput, Sepoy: The Evolution of the Military Labour Market in Hindustan, 1450–1850* (Cambridge: Cambridge University Press, 1990), pp. 71–85; Dirk H. A. Kolff, 'The Rajput in Ancient and Medieval India: A Warrior-Ascetic', in N. K. Singhi and R. Joshi (eds.) *Folk, Faith and Feudalism* (Jaipur, New Delhi: Rawat Publications, 1995), pp. 257; Cynthia Talbot, 'Becoming Turk the Rajput Way: Conversion and Identity in an Indian Warrior Narrative', *Modern Asian Studies*, 43: 1 (2009), 211–43; Kothiyal, *Nomadic Narratives*, pp. 7–11; Sreenivasan, *Many Lives of a Rajput Queen*, pp. 66–7, and endnote 4, p. 111.

[21] Merutunga, *The Prabandhacintamani or the Wishing Stone of Narratives*, translated C. L. Tawney (Calcutta: Asiatic Society, 1899); Sreenivsan, *The Many Lives of a Rajput Queen*, p. 26.

[22] Most significantly, Ferishta, *History of the Rise of Mahomedan Power in India till the year A.D. 1612*, translated John Briggs (1st published 1829, reprint New Delhi: Oriental Books, 1981), Vol. IV, p. 101; and Abul Fazl, *Ain-i Akbari*, translated H. Blochmann and H. Jarrett, 4 vols. (Calcutta, 1873–94), Vol. II, pp. 215–17.

[23] On the five major dynasties that together made by the Delhi Sultanate, see Peter Jackson, *The Delhi Sultanate: A Political and Military History* (Cambridge: Cambridge University Press, 1999); Sunil Kumar, *The Emergence of the Delhi Sultanate, 1192–1286* (New Delhi: Permanent Black, 2007); on the localisation of the Sultanate through the entrenchment of Sufis and soldiers associated with them, see Simon Digby, 'Before Timur Came: Provincialization of the Delhi Sultanate through the Fourteenth Century', *Journal of the Economic and Social History of the Orient*, 47: 3 (2004), 298–356.

[24] Abul Fazl, *Ain-i Akbari*, Vol. II, pp. 215–17. Badauni, who had a specific connection, reported about the legendary Vikramjeet of the same dynasty, whose statue he said, was broken by Iltutmish, and who was also the hero of the thirty-two stories which he had translated to Persian under the orders of emperor Akbar – establishing the identity between Vikramjīt and Vikramaditya of *Siṃhāsana Battīsī*. Abdul Qadir Badauni, *Muntakhabu-t-Tawarikh*, translated George Ranking and W. H. Lowe (Calcutta: Asiatic Society, 1864), Vol. I, p.95.

[25] Rai Chatarman Saksena, *Chahar Gulshan*, (ed.) Chander Shekhar (Delhi: Dilli Kitab Ghar for National Mission for Manuscripts, 2011), pp. 107–8.

As far as administrative history is concerned, Malwa was won and lost by Delhi multiple times since the twelfth century. It was invaded by Sultan Iltutmish in 1233, leading to a plunder of Ujjain and its temples, including the Mahakal temple, which may then have contributed artefacts to the Qutb complex in Delhi.[26] Control was clearly fragile, for the region had to be reconquered by Alauddin Khalji in 1305 CE, resulting in a historical note by none less than the 'parrot of India' Amir Khusrau, the court poet, in his *Khazāin al-futuḥ* (treasuries of victories). Khusrau noted that on the southern border of Hindustan, Rai Mahalak Deo and his minister Goga possessed around 40,000 horsemen and innumerable foot soldiers. This minister and his king were defeated in an expedition led by Ain al-Mulk, the chamberlain, who then received the province of Malwa under his administration.[27] However, only a few years later, Sultan Balban appeared to need to subdue Malwa again.[28]

By the early fourteenth century, the geographical area of Malwa settled into the role of a sultanate province, retaining the old capital of Dhar. Composed in the same century, the Gujarati *Prabandha-Cintāmaṇi* referred to the 'kingdom of Malwa' several times throughout the text; this may have been a reflection of sultanate conquest and consolidation of the province as much as a pre-existing regional identity. In 1335, the Moroccan traveller Ibn Batuta went from Delhi to Malabar, passing through Chanderi, Dhar and Ujjain, before proceeding to Daulatabad. He reported that Dhar was the capital of Malwa and the largest district (*ʿamala*) of the province. He also reported that Dhar was in the *iqtaʿ* (similar to Mughal *jāgīr*)[29] of a certain Shaikh Ibrahim, who had come there from the Maldives. Ujjain, the next stop, was reported as a 'beautiful city', graced by a jurist who had come from as far as Granada.[30]

The control of Delhi over the region was fragile; as with Bengal and several other of the regions temporarily overwhelmed by armies from Delhi, Malwa developed into an offshoot autonomous sultanate, such localisation often actuated by the entrenchment of Sufis and soldiers associated with them.[31] Dilawar Khan, originally appointed governor by Delhi, made use of the disturbance caused Amir Timur's invasion in 1398 to declare his independence. Although he retained Dhar as his capital, Mandu began developing as a significant political, architectural and military centre, a process enhanced by his successor Hoshang Shah, who is credited with the building of some of the most spectacular buildings in Mandu, including the formidable Mandu

[26] Badauni, *Muntakhabu-t-Tawarikh*, Vol. I, p. 264.
[27] Henry Elliot and John Dawson, *History of India as Told by Its Own Historians*, 8 vols. (London, Trübner and Co., 1871), Vol. III, p. 76.
[28] Ferishta, *History of the Rise of Mahomedan Power*, Vol. IV, 101.
[29] I. H. Qureshi, *The Administration of the Delhi Sultanate* (4th ed. Karachi: Pakistan Historical Society, 1958)
[30] *The Rehla of Ibn Batuta*, translated Mahdi Husain (Baroda: Oriental Institute, 1976), pp. 167–8.
[31] Digby, 'Before Timur Came'.

fort.[32] Over the next one hundred years or so, Dilawar Khan's dynasty, and then that of his cousin and *wazīr*, Malik Mughis, created and ruled a kingdom whose ever-fluid boundaries were the function of constant alliance and warfare with the sultans of Gujarat, Khandesh and Jaunpur and the Ranas of Mewar, and of deals struck and revoked with the next rung in the political hierarchy: the Rajput *zamīndārs*, typically entrenched in significant forts. The detailed accounts of constant movement and warfare appear to indicate that contemporary political chroniclers saw the realm as an emanation of the roving king, rather than a settled territory. If we map Malwa in terms of Ferishta's sixteenth-century account, for example, we see a range of political power, centred on Mandu and Dhar, resting on the forts of Chanderi, Kalpi, Kherla, Keechiwara, Bhilsa (Vidisa), Sarangpur and Raisen, all manned by Rajput and other chieftains, and lunging out towards Baglana, Jaunpur, Chitor, Ajmer, Bundi and Champaran, in a penumbra of power.

At its peak in the fifteenth century, the Malwa Sultanate hosted and patronised several intertwined lines of cultural development, including the Jain religious tradition and literary composition in a language that is now considered old Hindi. The Jain tradition provided a powerful commercial and administrative strand in Islamic Malwa and its penumbra well into the seventeenth century, Muhnot Nainsi of Jodhpur being only the most outstanding example. Such eminence naturally also led to royal patronage as well as private sponsorship of literary and architectural creativity.[33]

Associated with the reign of Sultan Ghiyasuddin Khalji (r. 1469–1501) and his son Nasiruddin are outstanding examples of literary composition such as the *Candāyan* of Mulla Dā'ud, the oldest known Sufi *premākhyan* and model for Malik Muhammad Jayasi's *Padmāvat*. Written in Awadhi, a non-local old Hindi literary dialect, the *Candāyan* was a story of travelling in the quest of love, a common trope within the genre; the protagonists were Ahirs – pastoralists with martial aspirations comparable to the Rajputs. The *Ni'mat Nāma*, on the other hand, is a delightfully epicurean work; a highly illustrated book of recipes bearing testimony to the Sultan Ghiyasuddin's love of *samōsas* (and his rather wonderful moustache). Although written in Persian, the *Ni'mat Nāma* is peppered with Hindi words, and written in what is considered a distinctive Malwa *naskh* hand.[34] Alongside Hindi and Persian, Sanskrit too found a place

[32] Vishwanath Sharma, *Glimpses of Mandu* (Mandu, 1943).

[33] A richly illuminated *Kalpasutra* manuscript was commissioned at Mandu by the monk Kshemahansa Muni during Sultan Mahmud Shah's reign: see National Museum of India, Delhi, manuscript with Accession no. 48.29, www.nationalmuseumindia.gov.in/prodCollections.asp?pid=92&id=10&lk=dp10 (last accessed 10 May 2018); an inscription in a Jain temple near Barwani referred to the same sultan. Upendranath Day, *Medieval Malwa: A Political and Cultural History, 1401–1562* (Delhi, 1965), p. 199.

[34] Norah M. Tilley, *The Ni'mat Nāma Manuscript of the Sultans of Mandu: The Sultan's Book of Delights* (London: Routledge, 2005).

within the sultan's patronage – a Sanskrit *praśastī* (eulogy) was written and inscribed on the Suraj Kund tank for Sultan Ghiyasuddin.[35] Mandu remained the political, military, as well as cultural centre in the fifteenth and early sixteenth centuries; renamed as Shadiabad or 'City of Joy', it represented a regional pride fostered by Malwa sultans.

The Malwa Sultanate eventually crumbled, caught in a three-way imperialist struggle between their old allies/enemies, the Gujarat sultans, the eastern Afghans (Sher Shah Sur and his dynasty) and the incoming Mughals. Malwa was first incorporated into the Gujarat Sultanate and then the Afghan empire; but ironically, it is in that period of political annihilation that it acquired lasting cultural identity, typified by the romantic figure of Baz Bahadur. This Afghan soldier, originally called Bayazid, was the son of an official appointed by Sher Shah, and, typical of governors deputed to Malwa, declared himself independent in 1555. His rule was plagued by overwhelming imperial warfare that ultimately defeated him, but, in the meantime, he acquired lasting fame as lover to a certain courtesan called Rupmati and as a great patron of music. Already a romantic icon to the Mughals, Baz Bahadur may be taken to represent certain key parameters of the distinctive Indo-Islamic culture of Malwa, including its visually striking Afghan orientation.[36] In 1561, the Mughal emperor Akbar personally led the conquest of Malwa, chasing the unfortunate Baz Bahadur away and causing the demise of his consort. Malwa was settled as a *sūba* or province of the Mughal empire, with most simmering resistance being subdued by 1570.[37] The ancient city of Ujjain, titled Dar al-Fath (Abode of Victory), became the new capital of the province.

## Routes and Nodes

The Mughal province of Malwa produced some very important cash crops, including the famous Malwa opium, which, the *Ā'īn* reported, was a common pacifier given to all children up to the age of three.[38] In a later period, international trade in opium would become the economic mainstay of important post-Mughal Maratha states formed in the region, especially that of the Sindhias of Gwalior; the English East India Company would struggle to control this trade.[39]

35 'An inscription on the Surya-Kund at Tarapur', in Lele, *Parmar Inscriptions*, p. 86.

36 Abul Fazl narrated their tragic romance, including Rupmati's suicide to resist capture by Adham Khan, in *Akbar Nāma of Abu'l Fazl*, translated H. Beveridge (3 vols., Calcutta: Asiatic Society, 1907–39), Vol. II, pp. 213–14; also see the inside cover of the album containing specimens of Persian calligraphy and Mughal paintings, 18th century, Royal Collection, RCIN1005068.a, which depicts Baz Bahadur and Rupmati hunting in a fictional landscape.

37 Ferishta, *History*, IV, pp. 166–8; John Malcolm, *A Memoir of Central India* (Calcutta: Thacker & Spink, 1880), Vol. I, pp. 39–40.

38 Abul Fazl, *Ain-i Akbari*, p. 196.

39 Amar Farooqui, 'Opium Enterprise and Colonial Intervention in Malwa and Western India, 1800–1824', *IESHR*; 32: 4 (1995), 447–74; Amar Farooqui, *Sindhias and the Raj: Princely Gwalior c. 1800–1850* (Delhi: Primus Books, 2011), pp. 112–32.

The province also included internationally significant cloth-production centres, such as Sironj[40] and Chanderi,[41] still famous for its *sārīs*, and was crisscrossed by trade and military routes that connected the Hindustan with the Dakhin and the great ports of the western coast. Those who would travel from Agra to the Indian Ocean port of Surat were prevented from taking a direct route by mountains and forests – the feasible routes were all arcs that swung east before turning west from Burhanpur en route. Of those travellers going from Agra to Surat, those who travelled further south from Burhanpur before turning west usually had some special reason for doing so. In the seventeenth century, an important commercial route was via eastern Malwa, running Agra-Sironj-Burhanpur-Surat and skirting Dhar and Mandu. An alternative, slightly westerly route, favoured by the famous North African traveller Ibn Batuta in the fourteenth century, and by military campaigners including emperor Aurangzeb in the seventeenth, ran via Dhar – the headquarters of our story's heroes.[42] As a result, the area saw both a great deal of mobile imperial presence and the activities of local military entrepreneurs who attempted to milk the commercial traffic for protection money.

These north-south-west routes were marked by significant nodes of administration and state presence – in terms of both personnel and architecture. The most significant of these nodes for the protagonists of this story were Ujjain, Asirgarh and Burhanpur, besides Dhar and Mandu. All these locations were marked by significant forts; Asirgarh being purely a fort. Dar al-Fath Ujjain, the capital of the Mughal province, was an old city of both commercial and religious significance, site of the famed Mahakaleshwara temple, which may have been destroyed in the twelfth century by the Delhi Sultan Iltutmish (it would be eventually rebuilt by the Marathas in the eighteenth century). Caravans carrying cloth and other merchandise from Agra, or nearer home, from Chanderi, travelled south-westwards towards Ujjain. From Ujjain, a further move south-westwards brought one to the city of Dhar, and further south-west, to Mandu. Both Dhar and Mandu had major forts; Mandu, the capital of the old Malwa Sultanate, was replete with Indo-Afghan architecture. After Mandu, the major natural barrier was presented by the river Narmada, which was difficult to impossible to cross during the monsoons. After crossing Narmada, however, commercial routes to Surat arced out south-eastwards, to avoid a heavily forested region whose threats are still coded in the district name 'Nimar' (Arabic for tiger). The next major stop is the fort of Asirgarh, at the edge of the forested region, and already in the southern district of Burhanpur.

40 Niccolao Manucci, *Storia do Mogor*, translated William Irvine (London: John Murrary, 1907), Vol. I, pp. 67–8.

41 Jean-Baptiste Tavernier, *Travels in India*, translated V. Ball (London: Macmillan, 1889), Vol. I, pp. 56–7.

42 Manucci, *Storia do Mogor*, Vol. I, p. 67.

This was a pre-Mughal fort, wrested from the Faruqi kings of Khandesh by emperor Akbar around 1600 and formidable enough to hold a part of the imperial Mughal treasury, under the supervision of well-appointed nobles.[43] More than a hundred years after the British traveller Mundy passed the fort, it played an important role in the Anglo-Maratha wars of the early nineteenth century and was used as a prison for several decades afterwards.[44] From Asirgarh and Burhanpur, caravans turned westwards, moving via Nandurbar towards the 'blessed port' of Surat.

Wars pegged out routes that overlapped with, as well as supplemented, the commercial paths mentioned; spiritual travellers accompanied these armies and caravans. In 1305, Sultan Alauddin Khalji's general Ain al-Mulk 'Mahru' led an invasion that conquered Chanderi, Ujjain, Dhar and Mandu, reaching up to Devgiri (later renamed Daulatabad). The general brought along with him a Chisti Sufi deputed by Nizam al-Din Auliya, who settled in Chanderi and came to be known as Yusuf Chanderi. The great Nizam al-Din is also said to have despatched Kamal al-Din, later known as Malawi, for the guidance of the people of Malwa;[45] presumably, he travelled by a similar route.

Chanderi, Dhar and Ujjain also figured in the route taken later in the same century by Ibn Batuta, when travelling from Delhi to the Malabar with a commission from the eccentric Sultan Muhammad bin Tughlaq.[46] In 1399, when the Chisti saint Muhammad Gisu Daraz, fled from Delhi about to be attacked by Amir Timur, his route from Delhi to Daulatabad via Gwalior and Chanderi must have passed through or close by Ujjain, Dhar and Mandu.[47] Around two hundred years later, in 1534, the Mughal emperor Humayun passed through Raisin, Sarangpur, Nalcha and Mandu, capturing the fort of Mandu before proceeding to Gujarat in pursuit of the Gujarati sultan.[48] Ujjain, the capital of the Mughal province of Malwa, was also an important node in this martial/commercial route; in 1658, the future emperor Aurangzeb, moving

[43] Several items in the prints and drawing sections of the Asia, Africa and Pacific Collections (APAC), British Library, offer a glimpse of the fort. Mundy, the commercial traveller, described the fort: Peter Mundy, *The Travels of Peter Mundy in Europe and Asia, 1608–1667,* Vol. II, *Travels in Asia*, Richard C . Temple (ed.) (London: Hakluyt Society, 1913), pp. 51–2; *Imperial Gazetteer of India* (new ed., Oxford: Clarendon, 1908), Vol. XIX, p. 108; Irfan Habib, *An Atlas of the Mughal Empire* (Delhi: Oxford University Press, 1982).

[44] See the entry in the index for Z/E/4/16/F401 (1839–1842) (APAC), British Library.

[45] Carl W. Ernst, *Eternal Garden: Mysticism, History and Politics at a South Asian Sufi Center* (New York: SUNY, 1992), p. 114; Mandavi, *Azkār-i Abrār*, p. 581.

[46] *The Travels of Ibn Batuta, 1304–1377*, translated Samuel Lee (London: J. Murray, 1829), pp. 155–64.

[47] Richard M. Eaton, *A Social History of the Deccan, 1300–1761: Eight Indian Lives* (Cambridge: Cambridge University Press, 2005), p. 37.

[48] Abu'l Fazl, *The Akbarnāma of Abu'l Fazl,* Vol. I, pp. 300–7.

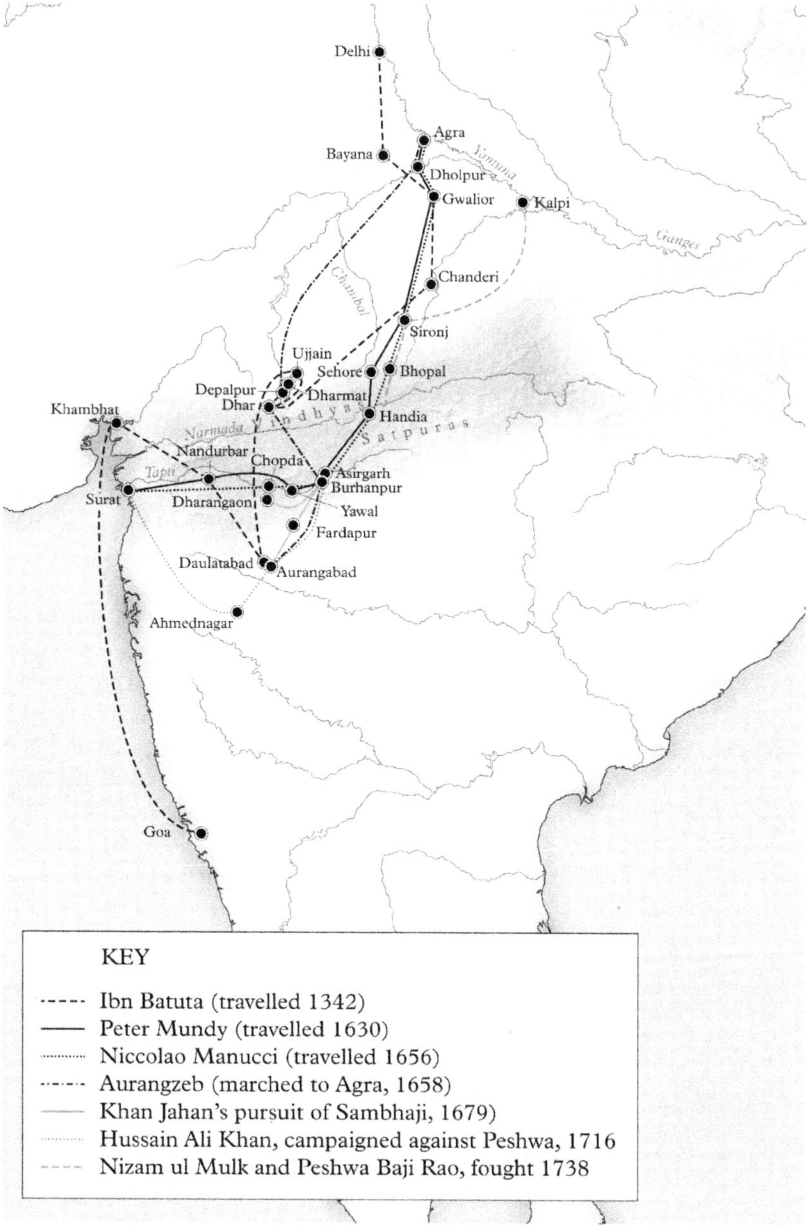


Map 1.2 Commercial and military routes across Malwa

Agra-wards from Burhanpur, defeated Maharaja Jaswant Singh and despatched by his brother Dara Shukoh at Dharmat, a few miles from Ujjain city.[49]

In the interstices of these great commercial and military movements ran the trade routes of the nomadic *banjāras*, their trade oriented towards the rural hinterland but substantial in scale nevertheless, carrying grain between villages and offering loans on the way, to be recouped on the return leg of the journey, or in subsequent cycles. The *banjāras* moved slowly in packs, grazing their cattle as they went, stopping at villages to procure marketable food grains and to sell other goods in return.[50] Persian-language historians from the thirteenth century referred to them as 'people of the caravan' (*karvānīs*) and occasionally, Delhi-based regimes undertook interventionist measures to control their marketing practices in order to lower and stabilise the price of grain in the capital city. Besides dealing in grain, they frequently accompanied armies, even on very long journeys such Jahangir's expedition to Qandahar. Presumably, the women and children that the East India Company agent, Peter Mundy, observed when travelling through Malwa,[51] went along even on those perilous journeys as part of the *tanda*, as their caravans tended to be called in India.[52] John Malcolm, appointed Resident in Malwa in the early nineteenth century, noted that, although illiterate, *banjāras* were known for their capacity of retaining the details of extremely complex transactions in memory.[53]

These acute, itinerant traders were looked down upon by members of more settled castes, and shared the in-between status of several low-ranking 'service' castes, such as Dom, Dhanuk and Pasi, who hovered on the outer peripheries of villages, sustaining the village but never quite of it themselves. An encyclopaedic Persian-language ethnographic project[54] commissioned in the early nineteenth century by a man who was himself of amphibious standing,[55] noted that *banjāras* never lived in the towns or villages, coming and going as they needed. Ethnographic details in James Skinner's *Tashriḥ al-aqwām* are not always plausible; the book itself is a curiously artificial effort to align social

[49] Saqi Mustad Khan, *Maasir-i Alamgiri*, translated Jadunath Sarkar (Calcutta: Asiatic Society, 1947, reprinted 2008), pp. 1–3.

[50] On transport costs for these caravans, see Habib, *Agrarian System*, p. 70 (nn 9–10).

[51] Mundy, *Travels*, II, 95–6.

[52] Irfan Habib, 'Merchant Communities in Precolonial India', in James D. Tracy (ed.) *The Rise of Merchant Empires: Long-Distance Trade in the Early Modern World, 1350–1750* (Cambridge: Cambridge University Press, 1990), p. 374.

[53] Malcolm, *Memoir of Central India*, II, 152–3.

[54] James Skinner, *Tahsriḥ al-aqwām*; Add. 27255, ff. 143 r-v; British Library.

[55] James Skinner was the son of a Scottish soldier and a Rajput woman, who called himself Sikander and raised a cavalry of 'irregulars' which he first rented out to the Marathas and then the East India Company. Patronised by John Malcolm, he produced two encyclopedic works in Persian, one about the kings and princes of India *Tazkira al-umarā-i Hind*, and the other the ethnography which we are discussing now. On Skinner and his complex family, see Nandini Chatterjee, 'Muslim or Christian?'

observations with Brahmanical caste theory of society. Skinner suggested that *banjāras* were the commercial branch of the community (qaum) of Charans (bards), descended from an instance of miscegenation (varṇasaṃkara) between a Bhat woman and a trader (*baqqāl*), and also that some *banjāras* worshipped a goddess named Sri Devi, while others were Muslims. Whatever their precise sociological and ritual dispensation, *banjāras* make several fleeting appearances in this story.

## The Rajputs of Malwa

The conjunction of war-filled landscape, difficult terrain and busy routes carrying valuable merchandise as well as competing armies led to the social entrenchment and, hence, administrative and military function of a range of local chieftains, many of whom identified as Rajputs. All supra-local regimes that jostled each other in Malwa had to contend with these suppliers of armed manpower and with aspirants to royalty. These warlords used the difficulties of the terrain as their resources, inhabiting forts marking key nodes in the martial and commercial routes that traversed those terrains. This was a process of political formation that rested simultaneously on territory and mobility; all empires that wanted to control Malwa had to control these nodes. The process was wobbly, because these local powerholders were simultaneously oriented towards multiple arcs of power and deference; they need constant wooing and awing.

As they offered their services to multiple regimes, these Rajput warlords of Malwa, especially those famous as the 'Purbiya Rajputs' – struggled for equivalence with Turko-Afghan Muslim aristocrats, emulating their lifestyles and households, while also seeking translocal marriage alliances with more successful Rajput groups[56] and genealogical self-aggrandisement, specifically through the patronage of bardic groups known as *charans* and *bhāṭs*.[57] For their part, the Malwa sultans appeared to fully endorse the claim attributed to one famous Purbiya Rajput of Malwa – Silhadi Purbiya – that 'for generations we have de facto enjoyed the essence of the *sultanat*'.[58] But the Rajputs held back from seizing sovereign authority themselves, recognising that this would mobilise internal and external resistance; it appeared to them wiser to keep the Malwa sultans on the throne. And in this way, a prolonged, intense but mutually cautious courtship was initiated.

When the second Malwa sultan, Hoshang Shah, was captured from the fort of Dhar and taken away to Gujarat in 1407, the Malwa 'chiefs' (possibly

56 Kolff, *Naukar, Rajput, Sepoy*, p. 85.
57 Norman P. Ziegler, 'Marvari Historical Chronicles: Sources for the Social and Cultural History of Rajasthan', *Indian Social and Economic History Review*, 13: 2 (1976), 219–50.
58 Kolff, *Naukar, Rajput, Sepoy*, p. 90.

Muslim and Hindu) rose in rebellion against the governor appointed by Gujarat, chasing him away and killing a part of his army, before ensconcing themselves in the fort of Mandu. This display of support led to Hoshang Shah's release; back in Malwa, he was able to secure the support of some soldiers immediately but that of others only after fighting them. When the restless Gujarati sultan attacked the tiny Rajput principality of Jhalawar in 1413, on the north-western boundary of Malwa, the chief appealed to Hoshang for help, providing him with an excuse for counter-aggression. Rajput loyalty was untrustworthy still, and so Hoshang found himself beating a hasty retreat when the *rāja* of Jhalawar made no effort to assist him. In 1418, however, when Gujarat started ravaging Junagadh, Hoshang's support appeared more valuable to these principalities, and the *rājas* (Rajput chiefs) of Jhalawar, Champaner, Nadot and Idar, that is, in a full arc on the north-western borders of Malwa, appealed to him, shamefaced for their 'neglect and dilatoriness' in the first occasion, but promising full support in the current campaign against Gujarat. Clearly, they knew the value of local knowledge, for they offered to take him through such a route to Gujarat that the Sultan of Gujarat wouldn't know what hit him. However, even this time, the *rājas* did not quite deliver on their promise, leading to an ignominious retreat for Hoshang.[59] Some of these *rājas* were capable of raising formidable armies of their own, and had access to crucial war animals, especially elephants. Such *rājas* continued to be self-serving allies, changing overlords whenever suitable, and extending their effective territories as soon as such overlords appeared distracted or weakened. The Sultanates of Malwa, Gujarat and the Bahmanis remained constantly subject to their capricious loyalty.

The Afghan Surs and the Mughals continued the same process of co-option and attrition with the local *rājas* in their subsequent efforts to control Malwa. Humayun marched through Malwa in 1535 on his way to Gujarat, apparently with the support, or at least acquiescence of the *rājas* of Raisin, and had the Rajput *qila'dār* of Mandu opening the gates of that formidable fort for him. Thus strengthened, he met the Gujarat army at Mandsaur, and won Malwa for the Mughal dynasty but apparently with a restricted social base of support, requiring a general massacre in Mandu.[60] Rivers of blood were an inadequate foundation for permanent rule, and Humayun soon found himself out of Malwa. Following Humayun's expulsion, the Surs entered Malwa, and this time the *rājas* of Raisin appeared to be less hospitable. In Sher Shah's violent battle in Raisin in 1543 against the Chanderi *rāja*, Puran Mal, there was

[59] Day, *Medieval Malwa*, pp. 26–37; Ferishta, *History of the Rise of Mahomedan Power*, Vol. IV, pp. 103–13 discusses Hoshang's career.

[60] William Erskine, *A History of India under the Two First Sovereigns of the House of Timur*, 2 vols (London: Longmans, 1854), Vol. II, p. 46–56; Hasan, *State and Locality in Mughal India*, pp. 16–19.

a certain amount of spectacular carnage directed against this powerful clan, justified by an *'alīm* who offered a convenient *fatwā* justifying the breaking of safe-passage promises and the slaughter of infidels.[61] Soon afterwards, however, Sher Shah was able to detach a section of the Rajput followers of Maldeo, the ruler of Jodhpur, prior to a crucial battle.[62]

The Mughals continued and refined this policy. Certain clans of Rajputs were raised by the Mughals to the highest non-princely imperial service ranks, or *mansabs*, granted special privileges such as service land-grants in their home countries (*waṭan jāgīrs*) and even anointed with the title Mirza, which purported kinship with Timur and hence the Mughal royal house. Thus, a select few among these warrior clans developed a resource-base and identity that was inseparable from the Mughal power and courtly culture.[63] For the majority, however, the Mughal technique was a combination of reconfirming old grants made by previous regimes, but also social engineering; for example, by moving branches of Rajput clans from Rajputana into the *sūba* of Malwa through service grants, specifically awarded to such recruits that managed to defeat other Rajput leaders less amenable to imperial absorption.[64] In the interstices of these imperial efforts, there took place the formation of little polities. Looking at these processes of political crystallisation offers us an additional perspective beyond that of the dynamics of the military labour market. It is worth looking at a few such examples of Rajput principalities surrounding the region in which our story is set in order to map out the political and social geography of the region.

The best-known of such sub-imperial Rajput principalities in the region lay just outside Malwa, in the area known as Bundelkhand. The Bundela principality of Orccha appeared on the political map in the early fifteenth century. Incompletely subdued and eventually killed in 1592, Madhukar Shah of Orccha remained a problematic recruit for Emperor Akbar. Constantly bickering and land-grabbing, his many sons and purported heirs were no better tamed.[65] Eventually one of these sons, Bir Singh Bundela, when pressed into imperial service in the Deccan, would abscond and take himself to the rebellious crown-prince Salim's camp in Allahabad, and purchase the latter's patronage by murdering Akbar's *wazīr*, Abul Fazl. In these years, the road between

61 Erskine, *History of India*, Vol. II, p. 434. 62 Ibid., p. 437–8.

63 Norman P. Ziegler, 'Some Notes on Rajput Loyalties in the Mughal Period', in John F. Richards (ed.) *Kingship and Authority in South Asia* (Madison: University of Wisconsin South Asia Publication Series, no. 3, 1978), pp. 215–52; John F. Richards, 'Norms of Comportment among Imperial Mughal Officials', in Barbara Metcalf (ed.) *Moral Conduct and Authority: The Place of Adab in South Asia* (Berkeley: University of California Press, 1984), pp. 255–90.

64 Raghubir Sinh, *Malwa in Transition, First Phase 1698–1765* (Bombay: D.B. Taraporevala, 1936), pp. 12–13, 15; Stewart Gordon, 'The Slow Conquest: Administrative Integration of Malwa into the Maratha Empire, 1720–1760', *IESHR*, 11: 1 (1977), 1–40, at p. 5.

65 Kolff, *Naukar, Rajput, Sepoy*, p. 124.

Gwalior and Ujjain was said to be so dangerous, that even imperial agents felt nervous, and brave Rajputs allied with the imperial court chose to travel by the cover of night and hide during the day.[66]

However sordid the origins of his prosperity may have been, with Mughal blessing, Bir Singh built himself up as a great king, and offered valuable patronage to litterateurs. Such patronage turned Orccha into a centre of courtly Hindi (Braj) poetry, which the classically (i.e., Sanskrit-trained) court poet Keshavdas used to put new wine in old bottles – producing a Braj *praśastī* of emperor Jahangir in good old Sanskrit style in *Jahāngīrrasacandrikā*.[67] However, continued loyalty during the next succession battle led Bir Singh into the wrong side, and his son and heir Jujhar Singh found himself and his estates under severe scrutiny by the once-rebel Khurram, now emperor Shah Jahan. Pushed to rebellion, Jujhar Singh and his son fled to their home territories, pursued by a huge imperial force. The fort of Orccha was stormed, and when Jujhar Singh fled with his injured son into the jungles to the east of his dominions, the neighbouring Gond tribes revealed that there was no love lost between them and the Rajput chiefs by killing the men.[68] The conquering general Khanjahan's secretary, Jalal Hisari, wrote a terse 'sociological' history of this clan-turned-kingdom-turned rebels, noting that the *qaum* of Bundelas had came from Bundi, reproducing what might have been a common trope of attributing locational origin and lineage based on phonetic rather than substantive genealogical connections. Hisari continued by recounting that the Bundelas had grabbed possession and dominance in many villages and towns, and some had declared themselves *rājas*, including Madhukar. The relation with the Mughals remained patchy, leading to almost inevitable rebellion and destruction by Mughal forces.[69]

We have less-detailed accounts of other such kingdoms, but the glimpses we are offered confirm that same pattern of warlordism and functional alliance with empire builders, occasioning inadvertent cultural intermingling. Another

[66] *Waqāi' Asad Beg Qazwinī*, Or. 1996, British Library, published, by collating several manuscripts, as *Waqāi' Asad Beg* (ed. Chander Shekhar) (Delhi: National Mission for Manuscripts and Dilli Kitab Ghar, 2017). Asad Beg, a former servant of Abul Fazl, was incorporated into royal service by Akbar and sent on various diplomatic missions to the south; he crossed Malwa several times. For a discussion, see Muzaffar Alam and Sanjay Subrahmanyam, *Writing the Mughal World: Studies on Culture and Politics* (New York: Columbia University Press, 2012), pp. 165–203.

[67] Allison Busch, *Poetry of Kings: The Classical Hindi Literature of Mughal India* (New York: Oxford University Press, 2011); Alison Busch, 'The Classical Past in the Mughal Present: The Braj Bhasha Riti Tradition', in Yigal Bronner, David Shulman and Gary Tubb (eds.) *Innovations and Turning Points: Towards a History of Kavya Literature* (New Delhi: Oxford University Press, 2014), pp. 648–90.

[68] Abdul Hamid Lahori, *King of the World: the Padshahnāma* (eds.) Milo Cleveland Beach and Ebba Koch, translation of text by Wheeler Thackston (London: Azimuth, 1997), Images 35 and 36, pp. 88–91; corresponding text on p. 38.

[69] Add 16859, British Library, London, ff. 137–46.

Bundela, Chhatrasal, formed the breakaway kingdom of Panna in 1657, and eventually rebelled against the Mughals to ally with the arch-rebels, the Marathas. The connection with the Marathas was substantiated by a significant marital alliance – Chhatrasal's daughter 'Mastani', now with a Bollywood blockbuster to her name, was married (or gifted) to Peshwa Baji Rao I, who brought the fight to the doorstep of the Mughals.[70] In his own lifetime, and contrary to current Bollywood imagination, however, the Bundela king proved as susceptible to the lure of imperial service as any other military entrepreneur, and was found in the imperial army led by Jai Singh in Malwa, in 1714.[71]

On the western edges of Malwa lay Bundi – the reputed original homeland of the Bundelas. Its ruler, Budh Singh, made significant progress towards the latter part of the Aurangzeb's reign. Playing his cards carefully, he sided with Prince Muazzam during key moments and, through the latter's recommendation, gained the districts of Patan and Tonk. He, too, was part of Jai Singh's anti-Maratha army in 1714.[72] In central Malwa, Sitamau was an outright imperial creation, rising on the ruins of Ratlam – through confiscations and grants made by Aurangzeb to a loyal member of a *Rāthoḍ* clan that was otherwise prone to disaffection.[73] Baglana, to the south of Tapti, was also a principality created by long-ensconced hill-chiefs who acquired a 'Rajput', specifically *Rāthoḍ*, genealogy in the sixteenth century. Buoyed for a period by Mughal support, they attacked their neighbours and expanded their own realm, until they were annexed by a southward thrust by the prince Aurangzeb. This annexation let loose a host of subordinates who were eventually overrun by the rising Maratha empire in the late seventeenth century.[74]

Thus, Rajput warlord kingdoms ranged all over north-western, northern and central India, forming a left-leaning C-arc around the heartland of the Delhi Sultanate and, later, the Mughals. Clans branched, migrated and formed multiple small and large principalities, which would only much later be connected through genealogical exercises. In the eighteenth century, with the faltering of Mughal control and patronage, and the rise of the Maratha empire, all such sub-imperial polities in Malwa were incorporated into one or another of the states established by the Maratha generals. After the 1730s, even the grand Rajput kingdoms of Jodhpur, Jaipur and Mewar were dominated by the Marathas, who

[70] Ravindra K. Jain, *Between History and Legend: Status and Power in Bundelkhand* (Delhi: Orient Longman, 2002), pp. 73–4.; Eugenia Vanina, 'Bajirao and Mastani: a Family Tragedy in Eighteenth-Century Maharashtra', in Glushkova and Vora (eds.) *Home, Family and Kinship in Maharashtra*, pp. 101–12.

[71] Jadunath Sarkar, *History of Jaipur* (New Delhi: Orient Longman, 1984) p. 164.

[72] Sinh, *Malwa in Transition*, p. 76 [73] Ibid., pp. 79–80

[74] Sumit Guha, *Environment and Ethnicity in India, 1200–1991* (Cambridge: Cambridge University Press, 1999), pp. 64–6, 70–4.

used the Mughal policy of undercutting them by participating in factional squabbles and encouraging the next rung of feudatories.[75]

Only in the nineteenth century, through British romanticisation, as well as the circumscription of political and military power, did Rajputs become specifically associated with Rajasthan (literally, Hindi/Persian: the land of kings) – putative homeland for Rajputs. Tod, first Resident at the court and camp of the Maratha general Daulat Rao Sindhia, and then political agent to the Western Rajput States from 1818, celebrated British achievement in separating the various warrior groups and breaking their kinship and patronage networks, all of which he framed in a nation-centric narrative of freeing the Rajputs from the control of the foreign Marathas.[76]

Thus, until the nineteenth century, Malwa was an integral part of that mobile and martial political geography, which was marked as the land of Rajputs (western Rajasthan) through the pan–north Indian folk epic of *Dholā-Māru*.[77] The Rajasthani-language versions tell the story of Prince Dhola's two wives, Maru (or Marvani, of Marwar) and Malwani. His journey from one to the other and back represented the twinning of the two Rajput sub-regions, as well as the circulation of martial males between them. In the seventeenth century, when the *Dholā-Māru* story was achieving a stable manuscript form in connection of Rajput courts of Marwar, the story of the derivative nature of Malwi Rajputs, and their de-racination through assimilation with local customs appears to have been popularised by Rajput nobles who had recently moved into the Malwa, backed by Mughal imperial appointments and grants.[78]

### *Raṇbaṇkā Rāthoḍ*

Among all these Rajputs clan-kingdoms, those that claimed *Rāthoḍ* genealogies have a significant role to play in this story. Right next to the district of Dhar were the principalities of Jhabua and Amjhera – both ruled by *Rāthoḍ* clans.

[75] G. N. Sharma, *Rajasthan through the Ages: Vol. II from 1300 to 1761 A.D.* (Bikaner: Rajasthan State Archives, 2014), pp. 147–67.

[76] James Tod, *Annals and Antiquities of Rajasthan, or the Central and Western Rajpoot States of India* (London: Smith & Elder, 1829–1832); Norbert Peabody, 'Tod's Rajasthan and the Boundaries of Imperial Rule in Nineteenth-Century India', *Modern Asian Studies*, 30: 1 (1996), 185–220; for an old challenge to Tod's thesis of Rajput 'feudalism' see Alfred Lyall, 'The Rajput States of India', in *Asiatic Studies: Religious and Social* (London: J. Murray, 1882); Norbert Peabody, *Hindu Kingship and Polity in Precolonial India* (Cambridge: Cambridge University Press, 2003).

[77] Aleksandra Szyszko, *The Three Jewels of the Desert: the Dhola-Maru Story: a Living Narrative Tradition of Northern India* (Warsaw: Elipsa, 2012); Charlotte Vaudeville, 'Leaves from the Desert: The Dhola-Maru-ra-Duha – An Ancient Ballad of Rajasthan', in Vaudeville, *Myths, Saints and Legends in Medieval India* (Calcutta: Oxford University Press, 1996), pp. 273–334.

[78] Sinh, *Malwa in Transition.*

The ruler of Jhabua had been reinstated by Shah Jahan in 1634, after a period of disturbance.[79]

The kingdom of Amjhera claims as its *mūlpurūsh*, Rao Ram (1529–74 CE), who, following a dispute over succession, invited emperor Akbar to intervene in Jodhpur. Rao Ram's grandson, Rao Jaswant Singh is said to have moved to Malwa, to (a now untraceable) fort called Morigarh, and his son, Keshavdas, received a host of grants in south-west Malwa, leading to the effective establishment of the state of Amjhera.[80] Several generations later, Jagrup Rathor provided active service to the governor Nawazish Khan in clearing the area, and was rewarded with a *mansab*.[81] This man's son, Jasrup Rathor, will make a rather sanguinary appearance on our story.

Of these typically fissive groups, whose common motto (*virad*) is the claim of being unflinching in war (*raṇbaṇkā*), those that settled in Marwar,[82] and especially the Jodhpur branch, rose the highest within the Mughal nobility and royal family. This line is now unsurprisingly the claimant of the highest genealogical status among *Rāthoḍ* – considered a kind of mother house.[83] Success within the Mughal imperium appears to have gone hand in hand with the production of chronicles by court-sponsored bards known by the caste name of *charan* and *bhāṭ*, which, again predictably, erased as much of the feudal dependency as possible, in creating the story of these autochthonous royal houses.[84]

Together, such processes blur any border that we might now imagine between the modern Indian states of Madhya Pradesh and Rajasthan.[85] They also, unsurprisingly, blur the boundaries between state and society, for such local recruits and implants were essentially warlords whose loyalties depended on the balance between the relative benefits of imperial service and local autonomy, which in turn depended on the size of their retainer armies and hence the possibility of military success. As constant shoppers for better deals, they represent that persistent turbulence but also a source of state-formation, which André Wink has called *fitna*.[86]

79 Ibid., p. 78
80 Thakur Raghunath Rathor Sandla, *Amjhera Rājya ka Itihās* (Jodhpur: Maharaja Mansingh Pustak Prakash Kendra, 2007), pp. 91–9, 102–3, 106–7.
81 Sinh, *Malwa in Transition*, p. 78; citing *Nawazish Khan's letter book*, ff 10a; 11b–12a.
82 Norman Ziegler, 'Evolution of the Rathor State of Marwar: Horses, Structural Change and Warfare', in Schomer, *Idea*, Vol. 2, pp. 193–201, talks about the centralisation of the Marwar state.
83 Genealogy, always a crucial exercise with royal aspirants, is now a more popular activity because of its combination of cultural-identity pursuits and digital technologies, including the World Wide Web. See www.indianrajputs.com/history/rathore.php.
84 *Rathōḍān ri Khyāt*, (ed.) Hukm Singh Bhatti, 3 vols. (Jodhpur: Itihas Anusandhan Sansthan, 2007).
85 Indeed, the idea of a national and absolute distinction between Marathas and Rajput is one that has been shown to be one of Tod's inventions. Peabody, 'Tod's Rajasthan', pp. 208–9.
86 André Wink, *Land and Sovereignty in India: Agrarian Society and Politics under the Eighteenth Century Maratha Swarajya* (Cambridge: Cambridge University Press, 1988).

## *Girāsiyas* and Afghans

There were other martially oriented corporate groups that thrived in the ecology of Malwa but were less successful in turning their war zones into polities. Among these were armed groups such as *girāsiyas* claiming mixed Bhil (hill-based warrior groups) and Rajput ancestry. Scholars have long been confused about the precise ethnic connotation of the term *girāsiya*, which occurs several times in the documents of our collection. The military historian Irvine considered them hill tribes, but Raghuvir Sinh, based on Malcolm, asserted that these were outlaw Rajputs.[87] Malcolm himself noted unequivocally that the 'Grassiah' chiefs were all Rajputs, but of the category that had been dispossessed and thus eked out a living through predatory raids.[88] The connection with Rajputs and landed power also held in the neighbouring region and province of Gujarat, which also shared the common story of *girāsiya* stemming from a derivative of *grās* – a mouthful – implying a share in land rights. In the eighteenth century, the term, and the group named by it, became associated with robbery and protection rackets.[89] Despite such decline in fortunes, at least some of the *girāsiya* chiefs were significant enough even in the early nineteenth century for the East India Company to conclude treaties with them, protecting their claims on major princely states such as the Holkars.[90]

This was one of the inner frontiers of any empire that claimed the region, including those of the Mughals. Quite like the Sahyadri hills (Western Ghats), about which Sumit Guha has written, the turbulence of Malwa, north of the Narmada river, implied both an endless source of cheap military labour and subversive sources of alternative royal legitimacy, with its own kings, bards and genealogical myths.[91] The professions and fortunes of such militarised marginal groups changed for the worse during the processes of colonial and national sedentarisation; an unimaginative postcolonial anthropological study took the view that these were people of 'backward' tribes, bearing no possible connection with the Rajputs.[92]

Afghans were another locally significant martial group whose occupations and status extended towards royalty on one side and robbery on the other, albeit with a wider geographical and social range than the *girāsiyas*. At least some Afghan chiefs saw their identities of a piece with that of the Rajputs, demonstrated through their choice of titles such as *rāwat*, and their

87 Sinh, *Malwa in Transition*, p. 92.

88 Malcolm, *Memoir of Central India*, Vol. I, pp. 508–11.

89 Samira Sheikh, *Forging a Region,* p. x, citing M. S. Commissariat, *History of Gujarat*, Vol. I, pp. 80–1 and others.

90 Malcolm, *Memoir of Central India*, Vol. II, Appendix XVI: M, pp. 415–16.

91 Kolff, *Naukar, Rajput, Sepoy*, pp. 17–18 – on *girāsiyas*; Guha, *Environment and Ethnicity in India.*

92 B. I. Meharda, *History and Culture of the Girasias* (Jaipur: Jawahar Nagar, 1985).

genealogical stories.[93] The first Afghan kingdoms in Malwa were formed as the offshoots of the dynasty and polity of the Delhi Sultanate, especially the Khaljis. The term 'military market' applies particularly well to Afghans, who maintained a dominance over the supplies of military war horses for several centuries, and also supplied a constant flow of recruitable soldiers, frequently aspiring for more than '*naukarī*'. Derived from a Mongol word – *nökör* – implying retainer/faithful companion/friend, *naukarī* itself was always more than service anyway. It was a concept of political ability and loyalty, popularised around the fifteenth century, which continued to jostle with other concepts that it was related to – especially *bandagī* (servitude), which under the Delhi sultans and their provincial counterparts had lent itself to the politically elevated *bandagī-yi khās* or the specially favoured slave, ex-slave or quasi-slave retainer. Afghan kings struggled with warbands and their leaders, all determined to assert brotherhood and equivalence; certain Afghan warlords were known to have addressed the emperor Bahlol Lodi, himself descended from horse-traders, endearingly (or threateningly) as Ballu.[94] In Malwa, the eastern Afghan Sur empire held sway for brief period in the mid-sixteenth century before Akbar, and the Mughals, took over in the 1570s.

The next political resurgence of Afghans in Malwa, albeit a limited one, coincided with imperialist invasions from the north-west, that of the Durranis, in the 1760s. As with previous conflicts between mobile martial groups, the temporary damage caused to the Maratha empire by that Afghan invasion did not constitute any permanent ethnic opposition. Afghan soldiers flourished under the Maratha *sardārs* (warlords-turned-kings), and, as the Maratha polities crumbled, at least some of them formed part of that motley bunch of freebooters the British called the *Pindārīs*. The campaign against the *Pindārīs*, which brought the British into power in central India, was equally directed against their sponsors, the Marathas.[95] Some parts of this mercenary mass congealed into more stable polities, most importantly, at Tonk, with an Afghan dynasty at the helm.[96] The kingdom of Tonk was particularly connected with Malwa, given the founder, Amir Khan's

93 Digby mentions the instance of Jamal al-Din Rawat, disciple of fourteenth-century Sufi Shaykh Ashraf Jahangir of Jaunpur; Digby, 'Before Timur came', p. 324.

94 Sunil Kumar, '*Bandagī* and *Naukarī*: Studying Transitions in Political Culture and Service under the North Indian Sultanates, Thirteenth-Sixteenth Centuries', in Francesca Orsini and Samira Sheikh (eds.) *After Timur Left: Culture and Circulation in Fifteenth-Century North India* (New Delhi: Oxford University Press, 2014), pp. 60–108.

95 *The Mahratta and Pindari War* (Simla: Government Press, 1910); Stewart Gordon, 'Scarf and Sword: Thugs, Marauders and State Formation in 18th century Malwa', *IESHR*, 6: 4 (1969), 403–29.

96 Gommans, *Rise of the Indo-Afghan Empire*; Jos Gommans, 'Afghans in India', *Encyclopaedia of Islam*, THREE, 2007.

vassalage of the Maratha general Jaswant Rao Holkar, whose state was headquartered at Indore.[97]

Not all Afghans in Malwa were kings, soldiers or even military horse-traders; there was a small but significant settlement around the tomb of Kamal al-Din Chisti, whose legacy, and that of other Chisti and Shattari Sufis, graced the city with the name *Dar al-anwar pirān-i Dhar.*[98] Soldiers and religious adepts were often part of the same migratory episodes; such a family, associated with Dhar and other central Indian Afghan Sufi centres, might even have produced a Bollywood superstar.[99]

## Other Empires: Marathas and British

By the early eighteenth century, this south-western district of Malwa was subjected to repeated Maratha invasions, whose empire spread all over the province and incorporated it after the Mughal *farmāns* (royal orders) of 1741 formally appointed Peshwa Balaji Rao deputy-governor of Malwa.[100] Mughal recognition lagged behind political realities: Malwa had been subjected to periodic Maratha raids from the 1690s, and, in practical terms, passed under the control of Maratha *sardārs* in the early eighteenth century. Three generals and their dynasties established the most significant Maratha kingdoms in Malwa – the Holkars, with the headquarters in Indore; the Sindhias, headquartered in Gwalior; and the Puwars with their dominion in Dhar and Dewas. The substance of these new polities was a matter of prolonged battles and negotiation, with competing and mutually contradictory grants from the sovereigns of competing sides (the Mughals and the Marathas).

As a corollary of this process, Rajput clans in the region changed loyalties, but some of the new Maratha overlords also began to claim to be Rajputs. Such was the case with the Puwars of Dhar, as well as the genealogically associated states of Dewas Senior and Junior.[101]

It was from the fragmented Maratha kingdoms of the region that the British eventually formed the Central Indian Agency in the early nineteenth century.

[97] 'The Pindaris were not a tribe, but a military system of bandits of all races and religions'. *The Mahratta and Pindari War* (Simla: Government Press, 1910), pp. 4–5; Malcolm, *Memoir of Central India,* Vol. I, pp. 325–48; *Memoirs of the Puthan Soldier of Fortune: The Nuwab Ameer-ud-doulah Mohummud Ameer Khan*, compiled in Persian by Busawan Lal, translated H. T. Prinsep (Calcutta: Orphan Press, 1832).

[98] Syed Bashir Hasan, 'Chisti and Shattari Saints of Malwa: Relations with the State', *Journal of Business Management and Social Science Research*, 3: 3 (2014), 51–4; based principally on Muhammad Ghausi Shattari's sixteenth-century text, *Gulzar-i Abrar.*

[99] Jasim Khan, *Being Salman* (Penguin, 2015).

[100] Sinh, *Malwa in Transition*, pp. 268–9; also Malcolm, *Memoir of Central India*, I, pp. 94–5, in which Malcolm provides a translation of the terms of the engagement given by the Peshwa.

[101] Malcolm, *Memoir of Central India*, I, pp. 97–115; Manohar Malgonkar, *The Puars of Dewas Senior* (Bombay, 1963).

Appointed its political and military head for four years from 1818, John Malcolm would produce the most comprehensive political survey of the region, which revealed the area as a shatter-zone in the clash of empires.[102] Dhar emerged as one of the princely states in the region, under the control of the Puwar dynasty, its territories braided with the much larger possessions of the Holkars of Indore and Sindhias of Gwalior.

## Conclusion

Malwa was a land of layered empires from long before the advent of the Mughals in the Indian subcontinent. The family whose story this book tells was distinctive in surviving several changes of regimes: claiming to be present in the region even during the Malwa Sultanates, they outlasted the Mughals, the Marathas as well as the British, retaining documentation of their rights until the present day. Through those documents we can approach the working of empires from underneath, and discover how significant rights-holders situated just beneath the shifting imperial structures entered and extracted themselves from those polities, and what notions of selfhood and entitlements they retained throughout that process of shifting loyalties.

[102] On Dhar state, see *Central India State Gazetteers* (Bombay, 1908), Vol. V, Western States, pp. 389–515. In 1819, a treaty was signed between the Raja Ramchandra Rao Puar (represented by Raghunath) and the East India Company (represented by John Malcolm), which is reproduced in Malcolm, *Memoir of Central India*, II, Appendix XVI: F, pp. 408–9.

# 2 *Zamīndārs*: Lords of the Marches

The earliest extant document pertaining to this family is a *parvāna* dated 1574, and so, from the reign of emperor Akbar. This *parvāna*, issued by an unidentified noble/officer, recited that since 'obedient to Islam' (*muti' al-Islam*) Jayanti Das and Narhar Das had made great efforts in the settling and ordering of *pargana* Dhar, they were granted 200 *bīghas*[1] of fallow (*uftāda*) land as *'inām* (that is, tax-free) in the *mauza'* (village, as a taxation unit) of Gardawad and others, so that, having brought it under cultivation (*marzu' namūde*) they use collections from that land for their livelihood and pray for the enduring good fortune of the 'slaves of the Lord' (i.e., the high-ranking Mughal official who made the grant). Officials of the tax department were instructed not to bother the grantees for taxes of any kind. On the grantees was imposed the rather broad obligation of continuing to make such efforts for the populating and regulating the district of Dhar and that their loyalty remained obvious, that is, to continue being useful in controlling the countryside and making it pay. The verso of the document listed five *mālik-i zamīn*: Jayanti Das and four others, each given lands in a particular village, of which only Mohanpur and Gardawad (both in Dhar district) are still identifiable on Google. This document, then, recorded a cluster of mutually associated *zamīndārs* in the district of Dhar.[2] The lead grantee, Jayanti Das, was the lineal ancestor of Mohan Das and the family at the core of this book. The lands granted specifically to him per this document were in Gardawad, about eleven miles from the town of Dhar.[3]

In rewarding the enterprise of 'clan communities' for expanding the agricultural, and hence revenue frontiers of the empire, and using the reward itself to encourage further enterprise along the same lines, this document records a particular instance of a well-known process. In some regions, especially Bengal, the expanding agrarian frontier became associated with that of confessional Islam.

[1] A measure of land, varying widely across the subcontinent. The Akbari *bigha* was defined as 3600 *Ilāhī-gaz*, or 3025 square yards. Wilson, *A Glossary of Revenue and Judicial Terms*, p. 85.

[2] The synonym for *zamīndār* used most often was *mālik*. In some documents, a *zamīndār* is alternatively termed as *mālik*.' Habib, *Agrarian System*, p. 173, using mostly Mughal documents from the seventeenth century, held at the Uttar Pradesh State Archives, Allahabad.

[3] LNS MS 235 (a), DAI, Kuwait.

Religious and agrarian pioneering proceeded hand in hand through the agency of Sufi *pīrs*, and was only subsequently rewarded by the Mughal regime.[4] This was not the case in all other regions, and definitely not Malwa. Jayanti Das's title '*muti' al-Islām*' indicated, as it did in other more eminent instances,[5] functional rather than confessional concordance with the Mughal regime. In this chapter, we shall see how Jayanti Das, his kinsmen and associates built themselves up as rural powerholders and service-providers to the regime, with particular attention to the role of royal and subroyal grants – *farmāns*, *nishāns* and *parvānas*.

As noted in the introduction, *farmāns*, *nishāns* and *parvānas* were self-nominating Mughal documentary forms, partially shared with the wider Persianate world. They belonged to a world of orders. The language of all such documents was always directive – somebody was told to do something. That action could simply be taking possession of certain rights; for associated others, it could be just taking note of that fact and/or facilitating that transfer. In Jayanti Das's case, the *parvāna* noted that certain villages had been allocated (*muqarrar shud*) as *'inām*; he and his associates were to be occupied (*mashghūl bāshand*) in keeping up the good work and praying for the good fortune of the grantee; imperial officers in the region were told to transfer the named villages into their possession (*ba-taṣarruf-i ishān wā guzāshta*) and not to trouble the grantees for taxes.

While orders could of course be one-off (e.g., Come to court!), they could, in some cases, create powerful titles of right which were about 'property' in the broad and active sense. They did not simply hand out a finite movable or immovable unit to be possessed, but created the right to make money or enjoy power over other people – through strenuous activities constrained by several conditions. These rights could be, as with Jayanti Das's grant, a right to collect a portion of the peasants' produce in named villages, without paying taxes – a right whose fruitfulness depended on keeping the area inhabited, cultivated and under control.

In this and other royal grants, then, property rights were inextricably connected with military prowess and control of the local population. In other instances, such military prowess could be farmed out to the regime, bringing in further rights. Yet other grants could consist of appointment to services with more defined obligations, to be delivered over a longer duration. Looking upon royal orders as rights-creating legal documents, and doing so over a period of time within a continuous collection allows us to enter into the multi-pronged

[4] Richard Eaton, *The Rise of Islam and the Bengal Frontier, 1204–1760* (Berkeley: University of California Press, 1993)

[5] Such as Jai Singh Kachhwaha; see Shujauddin Khan Naqshbandi (ed.) *Fārsi Farmānon ke Prakāsh mein Mughalkālin Bhārat ewaṃ Rājput Śāsak* (Bikaner: Rajasthan State Archives, n. d.), Vol. II pp. 89–90; a *farmān* from Aurangzeb, dated 12 Rabi I, regnal year 13 (1081 AH/ 1670 CE).

portfolio that inevitably went into the creation of the ubiquitous but elusive *zamīndārs*. It also allows us to see that entity as the lynchpin of agrarian society but also imperial polity; because this is where empire was actuated in rural India.

But orders were not simply received and obeyed by their recipients. They were actively consumed, among other things by being repeatedly confirmed, rerecorded, disputed and transferred by members of Jayanti Das's family. One source of right led to another; ad hoc military services leading to the acquisition of an office of record-keeping, for example, bringing its own perks, but also further business opportunities, such as contracting for taxes. As the fortunes and contacts of the family grew, charity provided yet another route, ostensibly of attracting and redistributing royal munificence, but incidentally of adding to family assets. Neither the documents nor the rights it recorded could assure permanence of position or of access to resources; important documents were therefore incessantly copied, authenticated and reconfirmed, drawing in a variety of authorities. Rights were questioned, lost and encroached upon; documents were disputed, lost and destroyed: royal grace was thus turned into property along a complex and proliferating paper trail.

In seeking to establish a contextually sensitive vocabulary to describe the nature of these documents of order (*farmāns, nishāns* and *parvānas*) and of the rights they conferred, it is necessary to transcend the limitations of modern usage of English words that once had much wider implications, even, and especially, in the English medieval and early modern context. If we choose to call what Jayanti Das received by this *parvāna* a 'grant', it is useful not to think of it simply as money or property given by the government to individuals, in the nature of the research grants, for example. Quite like royal grants in medieval and early modern England, *farmāns*, *nishāns* and *parvānas* could give the receiver a very large range of things – from perpetual rights to certain lands, to the right to hold fairs and markets in particular places, to pardons for crimes.[6] It is perhaps most illuminating to conceive of all these things, which we would now classify in very different groups, as emanations from royal grace. The entire point of such grace was that it did not have to be justified with reference to an abstract body of law in the sense of doctrine; it was transcendent, sudden, and reflected the pure will of the sovereign.[7]

Recognition of the transformative potential of royal power does not require us to conceive of the countryside as a blank slate, empty of any rights, over which the unbridled will of the Oriental despot romped unfettered. Neither is it very productive to evaluate whether the *zamīndārs* were the 'true proprietors'

[6] TNA, 'Royal Grants in Letters Patent and Charters from 1199' www.nationalarchives.gov.uk/help-with-your-research/research-guides/royal-grants-letters-patent-charters-from-1199/.

[7] Lucien Febvre, 'La Sensibilité et l'Histoire: Comment Reconstituer La Vie Affective d'Autrefois?', *Annales d'Histoire Sociale*, 3: 1/2 (1941), 5–20.

of land in Mughal times; given that *zamīndārīs* could evidently be transferred, gifted, bought and sold, but were nested within superior and inferior rights in land.[8] The nesting of rights persisted in colonial times, and is perhaps inevitable. The point in this chapter is to demonstrate the accretive process whereby rights were created in the countryside. The grant that Jayanti Das and his associates received, for example, recognised them for their local standing: they were recognised as *mālik-i zamīn* even as a specific order of *ʿinām* purported to reward their activities, now rebranded as service to the empire. On the other hand, the grant of *ʿinām* did create a new right, or a new order of right, too: it held back imperial tax officials from certain villages, creating a space of secure access to resources through the withdrawal of the regime's claim and its apparatus for realising it. It also placed the implied weight of the regime behind the claims that Jayanti Das and his associates might make on other less-privileged peasants. This was not quite a carte blanche, for the fiction of imperial service entailed serious restraints: Jayanti Das and his kinsmen/friends had the obligation to treat the local peasants well enough to keep the area populated and cultivated, for that is what would demonstrate their loyalty, and in turn, ensure the continuance of the *ʿinām*. This entire bundle of entitlements and obligations was clearly inheritable, but also expandable, for we find several subsequent generations *in situ* in the same area, referring to *ʿinām* grants received in Emperor Akbar and Jahangir's time, but also naming several other villages in which rights must have been acquired subsequently.

In reconstructing that process, we chance upon matters related to some of the most persistent legal concerns of post-Mughal, especially colonial, India: land law, with all its variety of tenures; the laws of inheritance and succession, and their relationship to patterns of kinship and norms related to religion. Here we have an exciting opportunity to explore those matters, but in a different landscape of entitlements, with its own categories, sensibilities, norms and institutions, in which kinship was intertwined with enterprise, religion with governance. It is by exploring that landscape, led by the papery ghosts of past aspirations rather than conceptual maps tied to our present-day concerns, that we can begin to understand how people like Jayanti Das acquired documents such as those mentioned, why their families preserved them, and what they wanted when they took them along to various authorities, asking for their rights.

## *Chī-st zamīndār?*

'What is a '*zamīndār*'?' This was the burning question of the early days of the English East India Company's rule in eastern India. In the late eighteenth

[8] Habib, *Agrarian System*, pp. 187–91.

century, seeking to find a cost-effective method for extracting wealth from Bengal's countryside,[9] and the most functional agents for facilitating that extraction, the English East India Company, its officials, supporters and detractors found themselves embroiled in highly arcane but utterly un-academic debates over who exactly those people were and whether their entitlements consisted of something that could translate as 'property' in a highly modernist sense of the word.[10] These debates, which extended from determining whether the king or the *zamīndārs* were ultimate owner(s) of the land, to the nature of the Mughal constitution and of British imperium itself, produced a glamorous impeachment trial in London, and socially transformative land law in India. In 1793, the Company-state in India decided that the *zamīndārs* were proprietors, in the sense of absolute owners of the land in their possession.[11] This decision entailed drastic commodification of the land,

[9] The English East India Company was a joint stock trading company, chartered in 1600 and trading in the Mughal empire since the 1610s. Outstanding studies of the first century and half of the Company's activities, focussing mainly on its trade, are Holden Furber, *Rival Empires of Trade in the Orient, 1600–1800* (Oxford: Oxford University Press, 1990); Om Prakash, *European Commercial Enterprise in Pre-Colonial India* (Cambridge: CUP, 1998); and K. N. Chaudhri, *The Trading World of Asia and the English East India Company, 1660–1760* (Cambridge: Cambridge University Press, 1978). More recent studies have pointed to the ambitions, models and techniques of sovereign rule that the Company brought with itself *ab initio*; see Philip Stern, *The Company-State: Corporate Sovereignty and the Early Modern Foundations of the British Empire in India* (Oxford: Oxford University Press, 2011).

[10] It would be careless to suggest that the de-politicised and de-socialised notion of commodity ownership that was imposed on land in eastern India in the eighteenth century was the extension of a 'Western' notion of property. As Jon Wilson has shown, English legal and political thinkers were perfectly aware of the inevitable social enmeshing of property; as in many other cases, the legal developments of colonial India were at the spearhead of modernity, not the recipient of them. Jon E. Wilson, *The Domination of Strangers: Modern Governance in Eastern India, 1780–1835* (Basingstoke: Palgrave, 2009). It has been shown that although since the Middle Ages, English peasants did have the formal legal right to sell or otherwise dispose of their land outside their family, they did so very infrequently. Henry French and R. Doyle, 'English Individualism Refuted and Reasserted: the Land Market of Earls Colne (Essex), 1550–1750', *Economic History Review*, 56: 4 (2003), 595–622. On the persistence of collective and overlapping rights of access to and use of urban 'commons' in sixteenth- to eighteenth-century England, see Henry French, 'The Common Fields of Urban England: Communal Agriculture and the Politics of Entitlement, 1500–1750', in R. W. Hoyle (ed.) *Custom, Improvement and the Landscape in Early Modern Britain* (Ashgate, 2011), pp. 149–74. Sumit Guha alerts us that when we encounter English legal terminology, such as 'estate', in the words and writings of early nineteenth-century colonial administrators, we should be aware of the feudal meanings they themselves would have attached to those terms. Sumit Guha, 'Property Rights, Social Structure and Rural Society in Comparative Perspective: Evidence from Historic South Asia', *International Journal of South Asian Studies*, 5 (2013), pp. 13–22. English land law remains, to this day, a palimpsest of overlapping feudal titles overlaid with statutes.

[11] The classic study on these debates remains Ranajit Guha, *A Rule of Property for Bengal: an Essay on the Idea of Permanent Settlement* (Paris: Mouton, 1967); for a study that situates these debates within the broader context of British debates over the legitimacy of the Company's empire in India, see Robert Travers, *Ideology and Empire in Eighteenth Century India: the British in Bengal* (Cambridge: Cambridge University Press, 2011).

erasure of myriad nested rights in the countryside and demilitarisation of the *zamīndārs* themselves.[12]

This decision was only the beginning of a process; the official interpretation had to be actuated through nearly a century of legal and military interventions, right up to 1857 when, in the aftermath of military–agrarian rebellion, the mud forts of the thankless *zamīndārs* of northern and central India were flattened by British-employed armies.[13] Even so, the *zamīndārs* of India never quite turned into a profit-oriented modern gentry. Failing to give up their spendthrift ways and coddled by the British-established Court of Wards which protected *zamīndārī* estates from insolvency, *zamīndārs* continued to see land as a component of their status as rulers, rather than a resource for commercial entrepreneurship,[14] and were eventually undermined in the twentieth century (in most parts of India) through the combined effects of tenancy protection legislation, global economic depression and the sheer go-getting of enterprising cultivators.[15]

*Zamīndārs* and their rights were not just modified by colonial legislation; they were destined, in turn, to play a transformative role, albeit inadvertently, in the legal history of British-ruled India. Disputes over *zamīndārīs* produced the bulk of litigation in the *Sadr Diwani Adalat* – the revenue-civil courts of the East India Company, established in 1772.[16] Since succession to *zamīndārīs* was adjudged according to the religion of the parties,[17] we might say *zamīndārīs*

12 Among the many studies on these processes, some of the best known are Bernard Cohn, 'Structural Change in Indian Rural Society, 1596–1885', in Robert E. Fryckenberg (ed.) *Land Control and Social Structure in Indian History* (Madison: Wisconsin University Press, 1969), pp. 53–122; Ratnalekha Ray, *Change in Bengal Agrarian Society 1760–1850* (Delhi: Manohar, 1979).

13 Thomas Metcalf, *Land, Landlords, and the British Raj: Northern India in the Nineteenth Century* (Berkeley and Los Angeles: University of California Press, 1979).

14 Walter C. Neale, 'Land Is to Rule', in Fryckenberg (ed.) *Land Control and Social Structure*, pp. 3–15.

15 In Bengal, this entailed the combined rise of the *jōtdārs* and the communalisation of class relations; see Rajat Ray and Ratnalekha Ray, 'Zamīndārs and Jotedars: A Study of the Rural Politics in Bengal', *Modern Asian Studies*, *Modern Asian Studies*, 9: 1 (1975), 81–102; and also Rajat Ray's re-statement in Rajat Ray, 'The Retreat of the Jotedars?', *Indian Economic and Social History Review*, 25: 2 (1988), 237–47.

16 On the history of the *Sadr Diwani* and other courts in the first century of colonial rule in India, see: M. P. Jain, *Outlines of Indian Legal History* (Bombay: N. M. Tripathi, 1966); Mithi Mukherjee, *India in the Shadows of Empire: a Legal and Political History, 1774–1950* (New Delhi: Oxford University Press, 1950). Cases related to *zamīndārīs* formed a very large percentage of all cases heard by the Sadr Diwani Adalat. T. A. Venkasawmy Row (ed.). *Indian Decisions: Old Series* (17 vols., Madras: Law Print, 1911–16), Vols. 6–17.

17 In accordance with several declaratory, re-confirmatory and modificatory regulations, letters-patent colonial and imperial statutes. See 'Plan for the Administration of Justice' in Proceedings of the Committee of Circuit, 15 August 1772 in M. E. Monckton-Jones, *Warren Hastings in Bengal, 1773–74* (Oxford: Clarendon Press, 1918), pp. 324–6. This plan was followed by Regulations passed in 1781 and 1786. See W. H. Morley, *Administration of Justice in British India* (London: 1858), pp. 45–7, 156–7. See also B. S. Cohn, 'Law and the Colonial State in India', in Cohn, *Colonialism and its Forms of Knowledge* (Princeton: Princeton University Press, 1996), pp. 57–75.

were the concrete occasion for the production of what came to be known as Hindu and Muslim personal laws in India.[18]

Given this history, we can reach for an understanding of *zamīndārī* only with the awareness that much of the material, including the ubiquitous Persian manuals that offer glosses of the term, were produced in response to revenue and political imperatives of the British.[19] Perhaps the most 'official' Mughal view was expressed in Persian chronicles, which were themselves of variable standing depending on their patrons. These used the term *zamīndār* – literally landholder in Persian – to indicate a very large range of rural powerholders. As Habib has pointed out, the word *zamīndār* was a distinctively Indo-Persian innovation, which began to appear in Persian language chronicles, dictionaries and formularies (*munshāts*) produced in regions controlled by the Delhi Sultanate from the fourteenth century. These earlier references to the *zamīndārs* also refer to the heterogeneous origins and status of such people, who could be village headmen (*muqaddamān*), those glorified by government appointment (*mafroziān*) and, more vaguely, owners/ lords (*mālikān*).[20] The picture becomes more complex as legal documents (such as ours) are brought into play to create a usage-based definition of the term – local terms abound for what appears to be a range of village powerholders, such as *muqaddam*, *khōt, bhūmia, pātil, dēśmukh*, only some of whom managed to make it to being regarded a '*zamīndār*' in the regime's view.[21] Based on their size, function and relationship with the imperial structure, Nurul Hasan posited a typology consisting of three levels of *zamīndārs*: autonomous chieftains (substantial *rājas*,

[18] The Anglo-Indian legal system recognised and applied a portion of Islamic law and Hindu laws, in a limited set of areas, mainly pertaining to family matters, including inheritance and succession. These preserved laws came to be known as personal (status) laws; their application depended on the legally recognised religious affiliation of the parties. These laws were sourced from a small body of jurisprudential texts from the respective traditions, which were translated into English, and from precedents produced in the British Indian courts. In effect, what was called Hindu and Muhammadan laws, were significantly different from the classical legal traditions they referred to, and are better referred to as 'Anglo-Hindu' and 'Anglo-Muhammadan' laws. For a short introduction to the subject of personal laws and their history, see N. Chatterjee, 'Law, Culture and History: Amir Ali's Interpretation of Islamic Tradition', in Shaunnagh Dorsett and John McLaren (eds.) *Legal Histories of the British Empire: Laws, Engagements and Legacies* (London: Routledge, 2014), pp. 46–8; for consequent transformation of the Islamic legal system, see Kugle, 'Framed, Blamed and Renamed', pp. 257–313; Michael Anderson, 'Islamic Law and the Colonial Encounter' in Peter Robb and David Arnold (eds.) *Institutions and Ideologies: a SOAS South Asia Reader* (Richmond, 1993), pp. 165–85; Gregory Kozlowski, *Muslim Endowments and Society in British India* (Cambridge, 1985); Zaman, *The Ulama in Contemporary Islam*, pp. 17–37; for Hindu law, see J. D. M. Derrett, 'The Administration of Hindu Law by the British', *Comparative Studies in Society and History*, 4: 1 (1961), 10–52.

[19] See, for example, James Grant, *An Inquiry into the Nature of Zemindary Tenures in the Landed Property of Bengal* (London: J. Debrett, 1790).

[20] Habib, *Agrarian System*, pp. 169–70. [21] Ibid., pp. 160–6.

generally absorbed into the Mughal regime as *mansabdārs*); intermediary *zamīndārs*; and primary *zamīndārs* (land-owning cultivators).[22]

If the term *zamīndār* could apply to highest ranking Rajput nobles of the Mughal empire down to the petty village chieftain, what we are left with is the awareness of the amorphousness of the category, and the methodological problems created by intense interest of successive regimes in precisely this social category. Perhaps what remains is the notion of *milkiyat*, derived from the Arabic *mulk*, equivalent to the Latin *dominium*, which ranged from property to kingship.[23] Such are the men whom peasants would address as *mālik*, their hands folded. The Mughals did not create most of them, they took them as they found them, provided they were effective enough and compliant enough, used them to collect taxes and manage the countryside, through a carrot-and-stick policy, replacing them with other similarly placed candidates when needed. The process of incorporation, however, wrought changes in these men; their aspirations evolving from local power to greater things – in some exceptional cases, to universal sovereignty.[24]

*Zamīndārs* were inevitably armed, maintaining significant armies of their own, consisting mostly of foot soldiers, with a small number of more expensive horsemen and a tiny sprinkling of elephants. This capacity for arms-bearing is what made them useful to the Mughals, as well as to other regimes who competitively wooed them. In its account of the twelve provinces (*sūbas*) of the Mughal empire, the *Ā'īn-i Akbarī* enumerated the number of soldiers maintained by *zamīndārs* in each subdivision of the *sūba* (*sarkār*), and, where data was available, for every district (*maḥāl*, which was the fiscal equivalent of the *pargana*).[25] The *zamīndārs* of *sarkār* Mandu, in which the district of Dhar was located, were reported by Abul Fazl as maintaining 1,180 horsemen to 2,526 foot soldiers,[26] the proportion of horsemen being significantly above the average for the empire as a whole. Dhar sported an even higher ratio, 120 horsemen to 150 foot soldiers. The *zamīndārs* of Dhar were small, but had some elite troops.

Such armed retainers had many uses; from the point of view of the regime, they were to be supplied for action when called upon to do so. Such calls for action would come, not directly from the imperial court, but from the *mansabdār*, who was the imperial official holding an official rank (*mansab*), which carried with it a cash salary and an allocation of taxes (*jāgir*) from a certain number of revenue units, or *maḥāls*. Now although the *mansabdār-jāgīrdār* was allocated his cash salary and/or *jāgīr* so that he might maintain a

[22] Hasan, 'Zamīndārs under the Mughals.'
[23] Richard Tuck, *Natural Rights Theories* (Cambridge: Cambridge University Press, 1979).
[24] Wink, *Land and Sovereignty*.
[25] 'Account of the Twelve Sūbas', in Abul Fazl, *Ain-i Akbari*, pp. 116–413.
[26] Abul Fazl, *Ain-i Akbari*, pp. 206–7.

dedicated army of horsemen, and although most *mansabdārs* recruited their 'followers' (*tābinān*) along clan networks,[27] they might call upon the *zamīndārs* to supply additional local troops, especially to suppress local rebellion. However, the same local armies could also be used by the *zamīndār* to self-aggrandise by waging war against other *zamīndārs*, to hold off imperial tax officials when necessary, and in very ambitious and/or desperate moments, to fight the imperial army itself. This was both the turbulent 'interior' frontier of the Mughal empire and its crucial source of military labour.[28] In following the adventures of Jayanti Das and his descendants, we shall see how the conduct of warfare – self-directed or at the empire's behest – remained a constant feature of their activities. The office/service (*khidmat*) of *zamīndārī* entailed other obligations, which also required military capacity. This included law-and-order responsibilities, including acceptance of liability for all thefts in their domains (or at least those thefts about which imperial officials chose to make a fuss) and apprehension of thieves. The British order to *zamīndārs* in Bengal to dismiss their police force and the Cornwallis' Police Regulations of 1792 formed the beginning of that *longue-durée* and ultimately incomplete effort to demilitarise the Indian countryside.[29]

Mughal terminology was variable and may appear inconsistent because of our expectations, formed of colonial and postcolonial legislation. In general, however, Mughal chroniclers and gazetteers used *zamīndārī* as a general descriptor of social status (sometimes in order to make moral judgements); whereas in formal documents, such as our *parvānas*, the term was used refer to the specific kinds of service (*khidmat*) that we know to have been associated with *zamīndārs*, most commonly, that of being a *chaudhrī*.[30] As we shall see, many other kinds of offices could also be held by people counted as *zamīndārs*. *Zamīndārs* retained such offices due to their evident loyalty (*daulatkhwāhī*) and goodwill of the emperor and his representatives, although clearly the documents themselves recorded several other conditions that established a claim to *zamīndārī* – such as agrarian pioneering, past grants, inheritance and customary rights.

What makes *zamīndārs* an additionally elusive entity – apart from their clearly heterogeneous origins, status and functions – is the fact that, despite the claim of appointing them, official manuals of the empire, the *Ā'īn-i Akbarī* onwards, did not list them among imperial officials. Official orders and other supplementary documents confirming a *zamīndārī* did however refer to a predictable bundle of functions. It is by these functions that *zamīndārs* have

27 Athar Ali, *Mughal Nobility*, pp. 163–4.
28 Gommans, *Mughal Warfare*; Kolff, *Naukar, Rajput and Sepoy*.
29 A. S. Aspinall, *Cornwallis in Bengal* (Manchester: Manchester University Press, 1931), pp. 112–13.
30 As we see in several of our documents; the post is described as *khidmat-i chaudhrāī*.

to be identified – Mughal documents often preferring to refer to them not as *zamīndārs* per se, but according to their contextually specific status, designation or even simply their names.[31] And it is also through documents such as the one recognising Jayanti Das's tenure, and through many others acquired and preserved by subsequent generations, that we begin to form a picture of who these men were, what they did in order to acquire their rights and how they used law in order to secure those rights.

## Royal Grace and Rural Eminence

John Malcolm, the first 'Political Agent' or British military-political administrator of Central India (which incorporated Malwa) noted in the early nineteenth century how several of the principal families in Malwa owed their origins to grants made by Muslim rulers, backed by those of the Rajas of Jaipur, Jodhpur and Udaipur.[32] Grants of the kind that Jayanti Das and his four associates received, as well as the higher-end ones Malcolm discussed (such as those of Kishangarh, Jhabua and Ratlam) all sat within the broad spectrum of operations by which rural grandees were incorporated into successive regimes: the Malwa Sultanate and the Mughals, but then also the Marathas and the British.

Paperwork played a crucial part in that process of incorporation. Documents written on expensive paper and bearing elaborate seals and ciphers bore imperial orders (*farmāns*), princely orders (*nishāns*) and sub-royal orders (*parvānas*), turned people like Jayanti Das into the Mughal *zamīndārs*, awarding them rights to resources that they may have possessed to some extent already, but which were now clothed with the fiction of imperial service and consequent perquisites, and backed up with the weight or threat of imperial force, if needed. Not all was window-dressing, for clearly some people, such as members of Jayanti Das's family, found such recognition through grants led to additional opportunities for imperial service and further grants.

Despite claims in other, later documents in this family's collection, that such rights as they possessed had been granted by imperial *farmāns*, the majority of documents in the collection are in fact *parvānas*, that is, issued by high-ranking nobles/officials, often identifiably the *jāgirdār* of the area. The closest this family got to the emperor was through *nishāns* of royal princes, of which there

[31] Farhat Hasan, 'Indigenous Cooperation and the Birth of a Colonial City, Calcutta c. 1698–1750', *Modern Asian Studies*, 26: 1 (1993), 711–18; the document of sale of the *zamīndārī* of Dehi Kalkatta, Sutanuti and Gobindapur to the East India Company, for example, only referred to the current *zamīndārs* by their name and genealogy (*nisba*). '*Naql-i qibāla-yi kharīdgī-yi mauza' dehi Kalkatta waghera* [Copy of the document of purchase of *mauza' dehi* Kalkatta etc.]', Add. 24,039, f. 39, British Library.

[32] Malcolm, *Memoir*, Vol. I, p. 45.

are a small and crucial number in the collection, which, moreover, are further attested to in the associated *parvānas*. There are eighty-two *parvānas* in the collection, and a further thirteen copies of *parvānas*, taking the total to ninety-five, out of a collection of one hundred and ninety. The collection of the DAI, Kuwait, is almost exclusively *parvānas* – thirty-nine out of forty-three documents; the other fifty-six *parvānas* or copies are from the NAI or from the family's private collection. From codicological, paleographic and diplomatic points of view, the *parvānas* are the best-written within the collection, on good paper, properly sealed and following uniform conventions. They are also clustered between the 1650s and 1670s, with a long tail thereafter; a cluster that also reveals a systematic association of this *zamīndār* family with certain specific nobles and members of the imperial dynasty. These grandees did not just give new gifts; more frequently, they reaffirmed what appeared to be existing rights, and sorted out disputes over them. They also demanded general and specific services and reprimanded the recipients for acts of omission or commission. In doing all this, they established themselves as lords of various realms, able to channel royal grace into the countryside and populate it with rights.

The *parvāna* of 1574, with which this chapter began, created a set of rights for Jayanti Das, and his associates. It is not clear why indeed these five men were selected for the privilege, except for some kind of pre-existing entitlement, signalled by the phrase '*mālik-i zamīn*'. Family histories, written and rewritten in Hindi and English in the nineteenth century, preserved a dynastic memory, claiming landed rights possessed from pre-Mughal times, through grants made by the Malwa sultans, in particular Hoshang Shah.[33] As far as the Persian documentary collection is concerned, there is no direct evidence to support this belief, but there are two bilingual documents of pawn/mortgage that purport to be from the fifteenth century.[34] Both documents date themselves to 21 Rabi II 867 (1463 CE); the first document records that a person called Manji, *mandloī* of *tappa* Sadilpur in *pargana* Dhar mortgaged (*girwī guẕāsht*) several hereditarily owned villages for 18,505 Muzaffari rupees to *chaudhrī* Bhagwan Das, Gopal Das and Jit (or Jayanti) Das, sons of Ganesh Das, son of Gunraj. The other document is nearly identical in content as well as appearance; it is an inexact copy. Both are sealed with the same multiple seals; of the two large circular seals right above the main text of the document (the most authoritative position on the page) one reads '. . . *ma'rūf Suhravardy*' and bears the date 945; the other reads '*qāẕī muhyi sarāf* (?) *khādim-i shari'a*'. There are five smaller seals of witnesses on the right margin, with the superscript *gawāh shud* (it was witnessed). They both include Hindi writing; in one document, the

[33] These will be discussed in Chapter 7.
[34] Choudhary Family Collection, Bada Rāolā Dhar (BRD), 29 and 30.

Hindi element is on the reverse,[35] in the other, on the right-hand margin.[36] Despite all this adherence to form, however, these documents are clearly elaborate forgeries – the handwriting is quite modern, as is the poor-quality, transparent paper, the terms *mandloī* and *tappa* derive from the post-Maratha period. While it is difficult to reconstruct the specific context in which these would have been produced, they are parallel indications of the family's strong belief of their pre-Mughal establishment in the area. There may indeed have been some truth in that belief; given the *parvāna* awarding or recognising rights in 1574, so soon after the Mughal conquest of Malwa.

### *State Office as Property: the* Qānūngōī *of* Pargana *Dhar*

In almost all subsequent *parvānas* and the handful of *nishāns* in the collection, references to *asnād-i sābiq* (old documents) and *dastūr-i sābiq* (old, i.e., long-established rules/customs) is a constant refrain. This is true even of the highest-status documents in the collection; the three documents that purport to be copies of *nishāns*, two of these from Prince Khurram (later Emperor Shah Jahan) and one from Prince Murad Baksh, Shah Jahan's son, who was executed by his brother Aurangzeb in 1658. Murad Baksh's *nishān*, issued some time in 1657, is better evidenced; this princely order clearly generated a series of knock-on effects which generated supplementary documentation that appears authentic.

Two (copies of) *nishāns* of Prince Khurram (enthroned as Emperor Shahjahan, 1628–1658) confirmed Mohan Das, a descendant of Jayanti Das, in the post of *qānūngō* of *pargana* Dhar, and described his entitlements in connection with that post. The first of these is the document that this book opened with; it is held at the National Archives of India, and does not bear a date of issue, but refers to itself as *naql-i nishān-i Khurram Shāh*. The document we have today is a copy of this nishān as authenticated by *qāẕī* Muhammad Mustafa, a regular acquaintance of this family for a long period at the very end of the seventeenth century and the beginning of the eighteenth, with a seal bearing the date 1103 (1690 CE). The contents this document hint at the manner in which the fortunes of the family had grown – the descendant of agrarian pioneers acclaimed by the imperial order, Mohan Das had discovered yet another way of making the state work for him. He had acquired the 'office' of '*qānūngō*' in the district of Dhar. Since being a *qānūngō* entailed being the officially recognised repository of local tax information,[37] it required the ability to memorise and compute local tax information, and usually to read and write to some extent. So Mohan Das, descendant of the *mālik* Jayanti Das, may well

[35] BRD 29, Dhar family collection. [36] BRD 30, Dhar family collection.

[37] Habib, *Agrarian System*, p. 333; Saiyid Zaheer Hussain Jafri, 'The Sarkar Qānūngō 16th-17th century documents', *Proceedings of the Indian History Congress*, 46th session (Delhi: Indian History Congress, 1986), 253–64; Siddiqi, *Land Revenue Administration*, pp. 87–91.

have undergone some self-improvement. That did not seem to have damaged his capacity for military action (as we shall see), and in fact, his appointment to *qānūngō*-ship may have had less to do with his computing skills than his prowess with horse and sword.[38]

Military prowess was naturally paired with a penchant for getting into trouble with one's imperial superiors. The document said in a rather cryptic fashion that Mohan Das had been appointed the *qānūngō* of the (unnamed) *pargana* (but) had subsequently been taken to the fort of Asir (the formidable Asirgarh – which is quite some way from Dhar) and the (unnamed) village had been taken under the administration of the *khalṣa* (the directly administered and taxed imperial domains). Now that Mohan Das had demonstrated his loyalty (which had become suspect for a period, and we shall see why later in the book) and had been reappointed to the *qānūngō*-ship of Dhar *ba-dastūr-i sābiq* (according to old custom), the exalted order was issued that said village, which was excluded from the salary of the (local) *jāgirdār*, was appointed as *ʿinām* to him[39] There are so many intertwined entitlements mentioned in this scrappy little document, written in ambiguous Persian legalese, that it is difficult to say exactly what was granted. For example, *dastūr-i sābiq* literally meant 'as per old rule/customs', so it could be saying that Mohan Das was made *qānūngō* 'as of old', but it could also be saying that he was made *qānūngō*, together with the customary rights to collect local taxes as his perks.[40] If the latter, then this document may be indicating two sets of rights – the first, the *dastūr* (customary rights) associated with the post of the *qānūngō*, and the other, the *ʿinām* additionally granted to him on this occasion by the clearly impressed prince. Prince Khurram was *sūbadār* of Malwa in 1614[41] and had been in Asirgarh several times in the 1620s, but Mohan Das must have been an enterprising man to have caught his eye; one suspects that he did not do that just by balancing the books. Family histories preserved by the descendants propose a military adventure as an explanation; we shall discuss that narrative later in this book, in Chapter 7.

There was also at least another powerful stakeholder in the story – the noble who held the *jāgir* in the region, and in whose area of claims the village granted as *ʿinām* would make a little financial/fiscal hole. The family would naturally need a good relationship with the local *jāgirdārs* as they came and went in order to realise the dues from this village. And this is indeed what we see in the many subsequent *parvānas* in the collection.

[38] NAI 2668/6, 1661 (or 1662) – this is a *maḥẕar-nāma,* a testimonial document produced in the context of a later dispute; which will be discussed in the following section.

[39] NAI 2703/31, purportedly pre-1628, date in the seal on the copy 1693.

[40] As it did in Gujarat, see M. P. Singh, *Town, Market, Mint and Port in the Mughal Empire (1556–1707)* (New Delhi: Adam Publishers, 2015), p. 213.

[41] M. Athar Ali, *The Apparatus of Empire: Awards of Ranks, Offices and Titles to the Mughal Nobility, 1574–1658* (Delhi: Oxford University Press, 1985), p. 56.

But which exactly was the village that was granted to Mohan Das? There is another document, now held in the family's collection, which also purports to be a copy of a *nishān*, issued on 12 Muharram 1026 (1617 CE) which would make it emperor Jahangir's reign.[42] Although the document does not bear any seals, even of validation of the copy, and the handwriting is no older than the nineteenth century, the existence of this copy, together with the notarised copy from the National Archives, does suggest a very strong memory of a grant received from Prince Khurram.[43] The document says that *mauza*ʿ (village) Ahu in *pargana* Dhar, was given as *ʻinām* to Mohan Das, the *qānūngō* of the same district, on condition of *khidmatkārī* (service) and *daultakhwāhī* (loyalty). Ahu is currently a tiny village a few miles from the city of Dhar, close to the villages of Gardawad and Mohanpur, where Jayanti Das and his kinsmen had received a grant of land in 1574. Present-day descendants also confirmed that, until recently, the family had owned land in the village. Thus the family were not just *māliks* in the area, but also regime-recognised keepers of tax for the district, with additional land rights derived from that office.

State office, tax-collection in particular, formed a key source of income as well as prestige for the family. The *zamīndār* as *chaudhrī* was a local tax-collector in the Mughal view, but members of this family held the more professionally oriented position of *qānūngō*, or village-level keeper of taxes. In fact, the *qānūngōī* of Dhar, and later other districts, formed an important source of entitlements for Jayanti Das's family, which returned, tautologically, to rights in land, and its produce. Moreover, these position and rights could be acquired and extended not just through training and heredity-based selection, but also through rewards upon military service and interpersonal transactions. Chapter 3 will discuss the processes of tax-collection and the family's role in it in more detail; here we approach their holding of *qānūngōī* – of Dhar, and other districts – as another form of title to property. As such, this is intended as a beginning of the argument whereby I propose modifications to the concept of 'service communities' detached from land and violence, and point instead to multi-pronged strategies of self-aggrandisement that could work for those that could marshal both pen and arms in Mughal villages.

### *Military Services*

Besides government service and landholding, the family derived its prominence from another source: military prowess. It is this capacity and function that allows us to securely identify this shape-shifting family as *zamīndārs*,

42 1617 BRD 4.

43 And in what is often a giveaway with forgeries, here we have a perfect concordance between the regnal year and the Hijri year.

given, as we have said, that the documents do not always refer to them as such. And it tells us something about the mental world of Jayanti Das and his descendants when we note that whenever it came to making 'over-view' declarations of their status and entitlements, it is this source of privilege that leading members of the family stated most frequently and insistently.

Military service could be rendered proactively, and used as a route into the good books of powerful nobles/imperial officials, and from thence, into public office and associated gains. For instance, in a *maḥẕar-nāma* sealed by *qāẕī* Fath Ilyas, with the date on the seal being 1072 AH (1661–2 CE),[44] *chaudhrī* Purshottam Das, son of Mohan Das, recited how his father had hugely expanded the family's fortunes. There was once, he said, a *rahzan* or highway robber called Bira, who also happened to be a *rāna*, that is, a Rajput chieftain, of the neighbouring *pargana* of Hindola. Because of his '*looting*', the *parganas* of Dhar, Nalcha, Digthan and Amjhera, and even the royal highway that passed through these districts, could not remain *abādān* (inhabited) and *rawān* (moving/working). After a few years of this, a knight in shining armour showed up – his father, Mohan Das – who, looking to repopulate the area, undertook war and struggle (*jang va jaddal*) with Bira.

Despite Mohan Das's valour, Bira was not defeated easily. At some point, the *sūba* of Malwa was given as *jāgir* to the (since deceased) Nawab Mirza Sultan,[45] who graced the fort at Mandu by visiting it in person. Around this time, matters came to a head as a caravan of merchants travelling with fine gold-woven clothes and unstitched cloth (*rakhūt va parcha zarīn*)[46] from Akbarabad (Agra) to Burhanpur, were looted on the highway at Jahangirabad (Orchha),[47] Bira making off with all the expensive wares. Worse, he even attacked, killed and looted the sons of a certain Saiyyid Jamal al-din Hussain who were '*Mughaliān*'.[48] Jamal al-din Hussain may have been none other than

[44] NAI 2668/6, 1661 (or 1662).

[45] This generic name and title combination suggests a royal prince, but it impossible to say who exactly.

[46] Irfan Habib mentions several types of cloths manufactured in India (but not Agra), in 'Non-Agricultural Production and Urban Economy', in Habib and Raychaudhrī (eds.) *Cambridge Economic History of India*, Vol. I, pp. 79–80.

[47] The merchants would have been following a crucial trade route, from Agra to Surat, that passed through Bundela territory. In 1630–1, Peter Mundy took a route from Surat that took him through Burhanpur and Asirgarh, north-eastwards through Narwar (close to where Bir Singh Bundela had assassinated Abul Fazl), to Gwalior and from there to Agra. Mundy, *Travels*, II, pp. 39–67 and map opposite p. 39. Orccha, the stronghold of Bundela Rajput chiefs, had been renamed Jahangirpur in honour of the alliance between Prince Salim-turned-Jahangir and the Bundelas. See Busch, *Poetry of Kings*, p. 51.

[48] 'Mughal' generally referred to Turkish nobles; Jamal al-din was Hindustani. However, the term may have been used to refer to an imperial official. Recently, Mana Kia has suggested that the term applied to Iranis in India.

the then-governor of Malwa, appointed in 1616,[49] and if so, then Bira had indeed overstretched himself.

The appeal (*faryād*) of the merchants, and the grandchildren of Jamal al-din Hussain reached Emperor Jahangir's court, and an imperial order reached Mirza *ṣāḥib 'jīū'* (an Indic honorific suffix frequently used in our documents), the *jāgirdār*, to arrange for the return of the clothes stolen from the merchants in his area, and to expel the miscreant from the region. Thus prodded, the Mirza *'jīū'* called up the *faujdār* of district Nalcha, Iwaz Muhammad Khan, to deal with the matter, but the troublemaker could not be overcome. On receiving this bad news, Mirza *'jīū'* declared in some desperation: 'How is that damned [Bira] to be cured (managed) (*'ilāj-i ān bad-bakht chi-taur mi āyad*)?' Now, luckily for every one, in those days a wise old religious scholar (*mard-i 'ulamā*) called Maulana Ghausi used to live in the fort of Mandu. The *maulāna* sent a petition saying that the matter had to be entrusted to *zamīndārs*. When consulted, the *maulāna* said that Mohan Das of *pargana* Dhar was the best at getting things done (*'umda ba taraddud ast*). And so Mohan Das got his career break.

Mirza *ṣāḥib* promptly summoned Mohan Das, bestowed on him a *saropā*,[50] tied a sword to his waist and gifted him with an excellent large mare.[51] Thus incorporated as the government's agent, Mohan Das was also put in charge of fifty horsemen, together with a certain Khwaja Dilawar *jiū*, and instructed remove all traces of the *maqhūr* (loser; i.e., Bira). Together they attacked some villages of the Bhils but clearly to no avail, because Mohan Das then reasoned with the Khwaja that they needed to go further, beyond the *thāna*, in order to really cure, that is eliminate, the *mufsid* (mischief-maker).

Having achieved permission to search further afield for Bira, Mohan Das then recruited a Rajput called Bharmal, an old *naukar* (retainer) of Raja Keshav Das, whom we know to have been the ruler of the petty Rajput principality of

49 This could be Mir Jamal al-din Hussain, appointed to Bihar and then removed to Malwa in 1616. Ali, *Apparatus of Empire*, p. 60. As source of information, Athar Ali refers to the published memoires of Thomas Roe, the East India Company envoy to the Mughal court. Jamal al-din Hussain was one of the very few Mughal nobles the normally irascible Roe liked. *The Embassy of Sir Thomas Roe to India, 1618–1619* (ed.) (London: Hakluyt Society, 1899), Vol. I, pp. 238–9; 245. If Roe is to be trusted, Jamal al-din was grumpy about the way Mughal administration was run, and gave him his own memoirs in which he noted down all instances of royal willfulness and other such failings. This manuscript may be available at Berlin.

50 On *sarōpā* – the head-to-foot attire – and its role in the classic Mughal ceremony of investiture, see Harbans Mukhia, *The Mughals of India* (Oxford: Blackwell, 2004), p. 104; Bernard S. Cohn, 'Cloth, Clothes, and Colonialism: India in the Nineteenth Century' in *Colonialism and Its Forms of Knowledge* (Princeton: Princeton University Press, 1996), pp. 106–62; Richards, 'Norms of Comportment', p. 255–90.

51 On the symbolism of the mare, see Shahid Amin, *Conquest and Community: the After-Life of Warrior Saint Ghazi Miyan* (Chicago: Chicago University Press, 2017), pp. 91–7.

Jhabua in the early seventeenth century.[52] Since Keshav Das had just died, Bharmal was between jobs, so Mohan Das retained him. Mohan Das then established a *thāna* called Sultanpur, named after the *jāgirdār*, who expressed satisfaction when this was reported to him. The mission was a success; the *harāmkhōr*[53] Bira was found and hounded out of the country. The *pargana* (not sure which) which had become *ghair ʿamalī mawās* (totally ungoverned) was taken into the *khālṣa sharīf* of the government (i.e., turned into crown lands). As reward, the Rajput Bharmal received no less than an imperial *mansab* and three *parganas* – Hindola, Jamli and Bawani – as his *jāgir*, besides the *thānadārī* of the royal highway of Jahangirpur. And Mohan Das appointed him his own *gumāshta* (agent) for the office of the *chaudhrāī* and *qānūngoī* in the *qasba* of Sultanpur, himself receiving the *dastūr* (rights to collect certain taxes) of the *pargana* and five villages including Ajnai as *ʿinām*.

Years passed, and the families that were once allies, fell out with each other. Paras Ram, Bharmal's son, tried to take over the other family's perquisites, and even had Mohan Das assassinated. Mohan Das's brother Chandar Bhan, and later his son Purshottam Das inherited his position, salaries and allotments. Purshottam Das's position must have remained unstable, since he appealed for testimony from all those in the know, that there were no sharers in the *dastūr* and the villages of *ʿinām*. The reason for the instability appeared to be that Bharmal's descendants, having turned to robbery themselves and lost their *mansab*, had established themselves in the hills on the boundaries of Jhabua and wanted to grab the *zamīndārīs* of Dhar, Hindola, Sultanpur, Jamli and Nalcha. In the typical style of a *maḥẓar-nāma*, the testimony was witnessed by various individuals: there was a certain Nasirullah, 'resident of Dhar'; Abdul Fatah, son of Abdul Hamid Sadr Jahan; a Shaikh Kani or Kali who claimed to be the grandson of no less that Hazrat Shah Kamal of Malwa (see Chapter 1): and a Sayyid whose name I cannot read – their names were written in the Perso-Arabic script. Besides theirs, was the name of a certain Paras Ram (clearly not of the Bharmal family, and possibly Purshottam Das's long-standing associate), written in a very difficult archaic Nagri script. Paras Ram also added an interesting symbol: that of the *katār*, the short Indian push dagger, which was both a symbol of military courage and status – frequently associated with Rajputs, as well as the Mughals.[54] It

[52] Keshav Das had risen to some prominence in the retinue of Prince Salim, later emperor Jahangir, and deputed, just after Jahangir's accession in 1605, to deal with the troublesome Jhabua Naik and various other associates who had made the region difficult to govern. Keshav Das killed Jhabua Naik and was granted his territories, but was murdered by his own son soon afterwards. C. E. Luard, *The Central India State Gazetteer Series: Western States (Malwa) Gazetteer*, Vol. V, Part A (Bombay: British India Press, 1908), p. 518.

[53] A swear word – one who eats what is *harām* (i.e., forbidden to him).

[54] For an instance of the *katar* being incorporated into Mughal iconography, see the MSS of the *Hamza nāma*, commissioned by emperor Akbar. John Seyller, *The Adventures of Hamza: Painting and Storytelling in Mughal India* (London: Azimuth, 2002), cover.

appears that there was no getting away from martial symbols, and the people they represented, in this south-western corner of Malwa.

The story of the rise and fall of Mohan Das maps onto the political geography of Malwa, outlined in Chapter 1. A landscape crisscrossed by trade routes but also dotted with military encampments, formal and informal, created a dangerous environment, which also provided opportunities for military entrepreneurs. Some such entrepreneurs formed little and frequently ephemeral warrior-polities (such as Jhabua), alternately hounded and patronised by imperial regimes. Others did not progress to that stage, but remained service providers to various regimes, but always on the brink of slipping over to the other side themselves. Mohan Das may not have been Rajput himself, but there is no discussion of his precise caste status in the document; this was a land of Rajput-ness. To that heterogeneous spectrum belonged various kinds of individuals and groups, including the Bhils, who lived in the forests and hills of west-central India, were familiar faces in the Mughal army and continued to be recruited by *zamīndārs* as strong-arm men even in the nineteenth century. While their social superiors never managed to stop thinking of them as thieves,[55] several of them managed to replicate the techniques of small-scale war and aspirational marriage in order to rebrand themselves as similarly 'spurious' Rajputs. The relationship between Bhils and Rajputs continues to be fraught as well as intimate to the present day.[56]

In behaving like boundary-keepers or 'lords of the marches' – *marzbān* – and consequently a militarised landed gentry,[57] while also seeking the *jāgirdār's* patronage for his confrontation with Bira, Mohan Das, his protégé Bharmal, and their descendants exemplified the dynamics of incorporation of local military groups into the Mughal regime. The persistent militarisation of the Indian countryside and the development of certain zones as simultaneously hotbeds of rebellion but also centres of military recruitment has been studied by military historians.[58] This well-recognised interplay between forces of disorder and order has been extended by Wink to a broader thesis about the constantly contested nature of sovereignty in India – where any would-be sovereign had to not only suppress insubordinate inferiors, but compete with peers and superiors in order to recruit them to his own flag rather than theirs.[59] Mohan Das and Bira were both potential foot soldiers of the empire; they established their market

[55] Kolff, *Naukar, Rajput, Sepoy*, p. 117–19; William Irvine, *The Army of the Indian Moghuls: Its Organization and Administration* (London: Luzac & co., 1983), p. 170.

[56] Janet Kamphorst, *In Praise of Death: History and Poetry in Medieval* (Leiden: Leiden University Press, 2008), pp. 199–202, offers the historical sociology of this relationship; the entire book is an examination of the tension through written and oral literary sources.

[57] Gommans, *Mughal Warfare*, p. 15; the idea of *marzbān* as *zamīndār* is based on Habib, *Agrarian System*, p. 169.

[58] Kolff, *Naukar, Rajput and Sepoy*; Gommans, *Mughal Warfare*.

[59] Wink, *Land and Sovereignty in India*, p. 386; also Peabody, *Hindu Kingship and Polity*.

value through the conspicuous display of force, and in doing so, they dipped into the seemingly bottomless military labour market – the Bhils and the *girāsiyas* – until order and disorder melted into each other. Bira, Mohan Das and their descendants were all locked in an embrace of mutual as well as collective violence, all inspired by visions of upward mobility.

Exactly like their European contemporaries, whether they would be deemed privateers/state agents or pirates/highwaymen depended on their success in attaching themselves to the state apparatus at the right time. But what turned their temporary gains into entitlements, and part of the *dastūr* of the area was the recording of those rights on paper, and repeated deployment and/or refreshing of those magic scraps of paper at crucial points.

### *Brushes with Greatness: Princes and Their Gifts*

Although we have seen shadowy references to Prince Khurram in connection with Mohan Das's career, the member of the Mughal dynasty who is mentioned most frequently in the documents of this family is his son, Prince Murad Baksh. This ill-fated prince, who was executed by his younger brother Aurangzeb during the succession battles of 1658, remained a long-remembered source of royal munificence for this family. Several later documents in the collection, while airily and vaguely claiming older *farmāns* and *asnād* as sources of the family's rights, referred very specifically to a *nishān* of Murad Baskh. While this *nishān* (if it ever existed) has disappeared, we do have three or four other documents in the collection that attest to this family's brush with royalty, and specifically, with the sons of Shah Jahan. Some of these documents have been noticed by Munis Faruqui as an illustration of the process by which an imperial prince took charge of the revenues of his *jāgir* through the offices of a deputed representative – in this case Dianat Khan – and, in that process, interacted and clashed with the local *zamīndārs* in the inevitable tussle to extract resources from the *jāgir*.[60] While Faruqui's reading helps us confirm the presence of both Murad and his appointee Dianat Khan in the story of this family's fortunes,[61] there are some important inaccuracies which, when corrected, reveal a more complex process, with more than one prince and noble involved.

[60] Faruqui, *Princes of the Mughal Empire*, p. 96.

[61] Although he does not, in this case, cross-reference to any other source of information, such as an *Akhbarat*, so it is difficult to see how he established these facts. The documents cited are LNS MS 235 (b) DAI, and (c), (d), (i), (j), (k), (l) and (mm) from the same series. I have not been able to trace the last document (mm), the others are in the calendar in the Appendix. There seems to be some misreading on Faruqui's part, for document LNS MS 235 (i) DAI refers to Dara Shukoh, not Murad Baksh.

Prince Murad Baksh was governor of Malwa between 1651 and 1654.[62] The earliest document within the collection to mention him directly was a *parvāna* sealed by a noble who styled himself 'Abd al-Salam, son of [. . .] Khan, *banda-yi* (slave of) Sultan Murad Baksh'. The seal bore the date 1054 (1644 CE), but the document could be from later, and from during Murad Baksh's incumbency, because non-royal seals were not necessarily renewed every year. The document introduces two other active characters into the history of our family – Purshottam Das and Paras Ram – both referred to as *chaudhrīs*. As we know from the later *maḥẓar-nāma*, just discussed, Purshottam Das was Mohan Das's son and indirect heir; Paras Ram appears to have been Purshottam Das's constant associate, and witness to the crucial *maḥẓar-nāma* just discussed. Together, documents pertaining to these two men, active in tandem in the middle of the seventeenth century, made up nearly half of the entire collection. In this case, Abd al-Salam, the servant of Murad Baksh, who may have been a noble himself, instructed the two men to send the corrected record of *siyāhā-yi roznāmcha* (account of daily activities) and *āmadan va jamaʿ* (taxes) *ba-zūdi-yi zūd* (ASAP), because he had none of these records in front of him. Appended instructions consisted of forwarding news of Gujarat if anybody arrived from there.[63]

Although the writing in this document is particularly difficult to read, it still indicates the difficulties faced by the entourage of a new *jāgīrdār* who moved into his new *jāgīr* and attempted to find out how much it could pay. Records needed to be extracted from those in the know; and in being the appropriate repository of such information Purshottam Das revealed that he was in fact a *qānūngō*, a record keeper, not just in name, even if he may have been proud of his father having won his state offices and grants through military adventure. As for Abd al-Salam, as Faruqui has eloquently explained, as soon as a prince was allocated *jāgīrs* in a region, he sent his own men to take charge of the revenue collection. These men were frequently high-ranking nobles themselves; incorporated, through that mix of politics and administration that characterises everything about Mughal governance, into the prince's team, or household. The same noble possibly occurs in at least one other document from 1658, and if so, had done a rather rapid change of affiliations after Murad Baksh's death and Aurangzeb's coronation.[64]

Another person who appears in a series of documents in the mid-1650s, and about whom we have much more information, is Dianat Khan, who is known to have worked as Murad Baksh's *divān*. Several of these were *parvānas* issued in the twenty-eighth regnal year of Shah Jahan (1655 CE) and pertain to the

[62] Ali, *Apparatus*, pp. xxxix–xv, 262, 279, based on *Waris*, *Pādshāhnāma* 114(b), 179(a), Ethé 329. Faruqui suggests that Dhar was within Murad Baksh's *jāgir* between 1653 and 1657, but his sources are not evident.

[63] 1644 (?) BRD 16. [64] 1658 BRD 18, dated 6 Ramzan RY1.

confirming of Purshottam Das's title to the *qanūngōī* of Dhar and other entitlements after the death of his uncle and predecessor, Chandar Bhan.[65]

But the most striking documents in the collection that refer to an imperial prince do not pertain to Murad Baksh, but to Dara Shukoh, known by the title Shah Buland Iqbal. There is a brief flurry of such documents issued between 1656 and 1658, when the *jagīr* of Malwa was taken from Murad Baksh and given to Dara Shukoh. The first of these is a letter bearing the seal of a certain *banda-yi* (slave of) *Shāh Buland Iqbāl* (Dara's title), and the date RY 29 (1656). In this, an employee of Dara's acknowledged the secret information that Purshottam Das and Paras Ram had supplied, about the depredations of Audi *girāsiya* and about counter-measures taken by Muhammad Aqil, Harnath Singh and Nand Lal (possibly nobles and/or imperial officials) and by Purshottam Das himself. The letter writer instructed Purshottam Das to take agreements (*muchalkas*) from the local village headmen, that they would not let the 'ill-fated monster' pass through their area, at the pain of committing a crime. For all this effort, however, Purshottam Das did not even qualify for a discount in the taxes he was supposed to collect, for after all, there had been good rains and no natural disasters, and the order only grudgingly suggested some minor adjustments for the difficulties caused by the *girāsiya*.[66]

We also have a copy of a *nishān*, dated 1657, preserved in the National Archives of India, addressed to the local Chandrawat Rajput noble, Rao Amar Singh, informing him about the transfer of the districts from the *jāgīr* of Prince Murad Baksh to the 'representative of the government' (i.e., the current *jāgīrdār*), and instructing him to make his way to the *maḥāls* (revenue areas) with twenty horsemen, to make sure that nobody created a disturbance while the new *amīns* and *karorīs* arrived.[67] The document had an elaborate list on the verso and bore the seal of Rao Amar Singh Chandrawat.

This copied *nishān* was referred to, and complemented by, a *parvāna* dated 24 *Safar* 1068 (29 November 1657), this time issued by Rao Amar Singh on his own authority – now the striking lotus-crested Nagri-script seal was placed on the front.[68] Amar Singh's *parvāna* declared:

> Since now the exalted *nishān,* necessitating respect and obedience, has been glorified by being issued, [ordering] that the *pargana* Sanawar (?) etc. according to the details on the reverse [of this document], due to the transfer of the representative of the celestially-titled

[65] LNS MS 235 (b) DAI, dated 9 Rabi I RY 28 (January 1655); 1655 BRD 1, dated 10 Rabi II RY 28 (February 1655).

[66] LNS MS 235 (i) DAI, (RY 29 on seal; 1066 AH = 1656). This document appears to have been misconstrued by Munis Faruqui, who sees in it evidence of rebellion by *zamīndārs* of Dhar due to enhanced tax collection led by Dianat Khan, Murad Baksh's agent. Faruqui, *Princes of the Mughal Empire*, p. 96, note 78.

[67] NAI 2703/6 (6 Safar 1068/13 November 1657)

[68] LNS MS 235 (l) DAI, (R +V) 11 Safar 1068 (29 November 1657).

Nawab Murad Baksh, according to the order that the world obeys, has been allocated to the *jāgīr* of the representative of the Nawab of [glorious deeds] of the exalted government from the beginning of the Kharif harvest of the [Turkish duodenary year] Qawi-Il . . .

Hence, the writer said, 'We have made a copy of the *nishān* and brought it into action, so that the servants of the court protect the subjects and their property' and more importantly, that 'no one pays any attention to the old officials (*ahdi ba-ʿamalān sābiq ʿamal na dahand*)'.

As for Amar Singh's precise role, this may be an instance of princes, princesses and *mansabdārs* making subordinate *jāgīr* grants within their own *jāgīrs*, which has been noticed elsewhere,[69] but it was also a case of a low-ranking *mansabdār* (with nearby but distinct *jāgīrs*) being deputed to manage a prince's *jāgirs*, quite like Dianat Khan. In any case, these two documents bring to light a network of interlocking authorities and derivative documentary orders which confirmed and created, as well as displaced local rights. Amar Singh used a striking lotus-crested seal, which bore the Nagri-script legend 'Sri Ram Upasak (Worshipper of Ram) Chandrawat Rao Amar Singh'.

This worshipper of the Hindu Vaishnava god Ram most likely belonged to Chandrawat branch of the Sisodia Rajputs of Udaipur, who were settled in Antri, at the northern edge of Malwa in the fifteenth century by the patronage of the Malwa Sultans. Their capital was Rampura.[70] Rescued from the control of Udaipur by Akbar and favoured with *waṭan jāgīrs*, that is, *jāgīrs* within one's 'homeland' or power-base, as only Rajputs were, this clan became rebellious towards the end of the seventeenth century, because of one of those several succession crises badly handed by Aurangzeb.[71] In the mid-seventeenth century, the family seemed to be doing well. In 1060/1650, Amar Singh had received a *mansab* of 1000 *z̲āt* and 900 *sawār* and the title Rao; the next year, he received a small promotion and went up to 1000/1000 *z̲āt/sawār*; the following year, he was raised to 1500/1000 *z̲āt/sawār*; and in 1655–6, he was on 2000/800 *z̲āt/sawār*.[72]

So in 1657, we see this member of a Mughal-sponsored Malwa Rajput clan being drawn into Prince Dara Shukoh's entourage either with the grant of a derivative *jāgīr* or deputation to handle the prince's *jāgīrs* close to his *thikāna*.

69 Habib, *Agrarian System*, referring to Princess Jahanara's grants within her *jāgīr* in Surat. The copy of this order is in the collection Suppl. Pers. 482, ff.33a-34a, Bibliotheque Nationale de France; it refers to these sub-grants as *tankhwā jāgīr*.

70 *Imperial Gazetteer of India*, DSAL Vol. 21, p. 191 (Sheo Singh Chandrawat, settled in Antri by Dilawar Khan, capital Rampura); Mellia Belli Bose, *Royal Umbrellas of Stone: Memory, Politics and Royal Identity in Rajput Funerary Art* (Leiden: Brill, 2015), offers a genealogy; Sinh, *Malwa in Transition*, pp. 48–9.

71 Gopal Singh Chandrawat of Rampura rebelled against his son's conversion to Islam; the Kacchwaha noble Jai Singh II effected a reconciliation between father and son after Aurangzeb's death. Sarkar, *History of Jaipur*, pp. 164–5; Kolff, *Naukar, Rajput, Sepoy*, p. 127.

72 Ali, *Apparatus*, pp. 257, 264, 271.

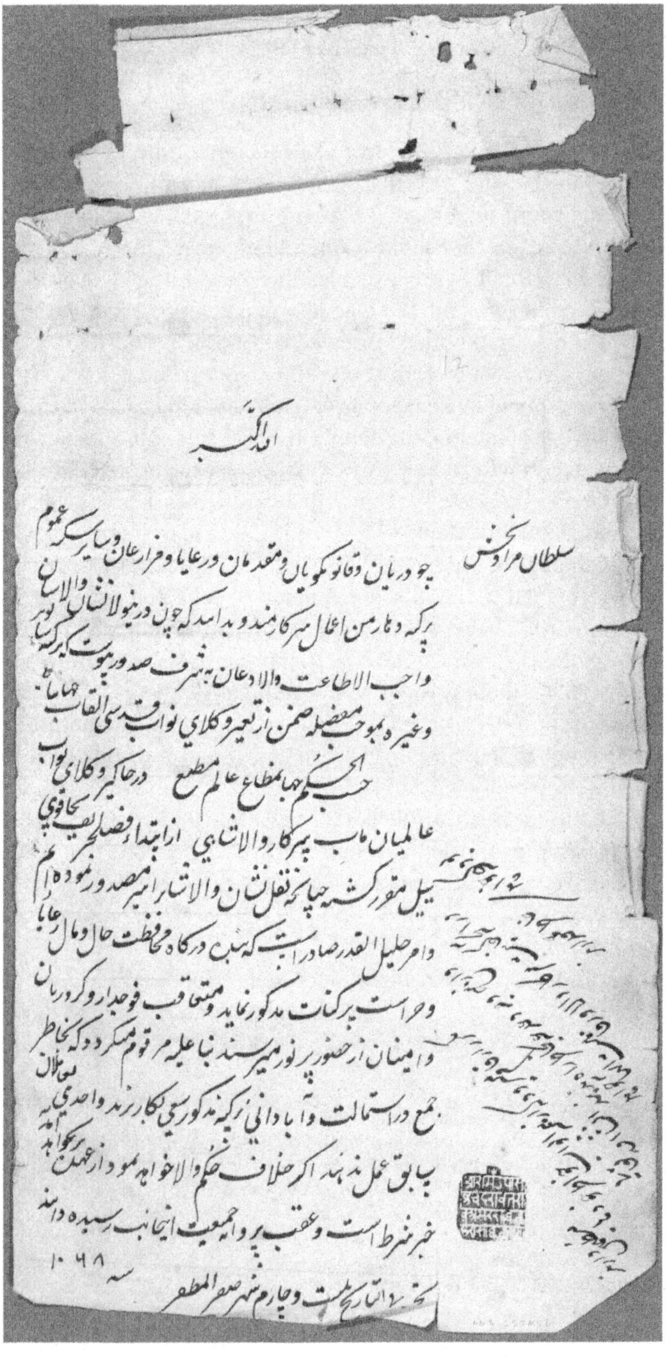

Figure 2.1 *Parvāna of Rao Amar Singh Chandrawat*, 1658 DAI LNS MS 235 (l); © The Al-Sabah Collection, Dar al-Athar al-Islamiyyah, Kuwait

But we also see this grant leading to an immediate effort to displace older officials, those of Murad Baksh, and to forge a relationship of deference with the local rural powerholders. The addressees of this *parvāna* were the *chaudhrīs*, *qānūngōs*, *ria'ia* (peasants), *muzari'ān* (agriculturists) and general inhabitants of the *pargana* of Dhar, which was within the *jāgīr*. And so, just as Mohan Das had picked up a retainer of a neighbouring Mughal-sponsored Rajput kingdom for his military adventure, his son Purshottam Das was drawn into subordinate service by yet another Rajput noble – the intertwining of empire and warrior groups continuing to create the local state machinery as well as local polities in a constant dance.

As for members of our *zamīndār* family, these documents, issued by nobles in the entourage of imperial princes, reveal both their entrenchment and the precariousness of their position. The claims of multi-generational occupation, of good service and past grant, as the transactions through which these confirmatory grants were extracted, will be discussed further in the subsection on inheritance. It is worth noting here, however, that despite both Murad Baksh and Dara Shikoh dying at their brother Aurangzeb's behest, orders given by them and their officers were upheld later. For example, a *parvāna* dated 1674 confirmed Purshottam Das's title to Ahu and nine other villages, 3,300 *bighas* of land and several mango trees, due to, it said explicitly, a *nishān* of Murad Baksh, as well as other *asnād*. The verso of this document produced a detailed and categorised list of all his rights – villages Ahu, Chandwada, Balwada, Dhamanda, Aguthia, Sindhawda, Phulwada, Taliwada and others forming a phonetically similar and surprisingly long arc stretching across several districts.[73] Mughal emperors and their nobles respected the orders of rulers of the past, even those that they had killed.

### *Noble Language*

Besides the matter of martiality, honour and rights, we may also pause here for a brief reflection on the use of languages and script. The use of Nagri-script seals in Persian documents is unusual; we have only one other such example in our collection, from the later, Maratha-ruled period (1735 CE, to be precise). I will discuss that document in Chapter 4, because it is a transactional document, of a type called *fārigh-khaṭṭī* (a deed of release).[74] The opposite, that is, Persian seals in Hindi or other regional Indic language documents being a far more common practice, continued by landed families and princely states well into the twentieth century. As the symbolic display of power, seals are significant artefacts for studying the deployment of scripts in early modern South Asia. I

[73] LNS MS 235(i1) DAI (R+V), 8 Shaban 17 and 1085 AH (both dates given) 6 November 1674.
[74] NAI 2668/27 (1735).

intend to do this in a future project; for now I note the possibility of a precocious, that is, a Mughal-era Malwa Rajput tradition of the use of Hindi and Nagri in official documentation. We have two unsealed copies of *parvānas* in our collection, both issued in the summer of 1671 CE by the then-*jagirdār* of Amjhera, a Jujhar Singh. Jujhar Singh was very likely of the *Rāthoḍ* family that became entrenched in Amjhera as a result of service to the Mughals from the sixteenth century; he acquired the seat of power after his father's death in a battle with Shivaji around the family's fort at Morigarg in 1678.[75] Prince Jujhar Singh was already issuing orders a few years prior to that; his first order in our collection entailed informing the officials and landlords of the district of Amjhera that some parts of the *qānūngōī* of the district had been sold to Purshottam Das and his son Nathmal.[76] By the second *parvāna*, Rao Jujhar Singh granted 101 *bīghas* of fallow but arable land to Nathmal, for the setting up of a garden in the town of Amjhera, together with wells and mango trees. Both documents began: '*Naql-i parvāna ba-mazmun-i Hindī ba-muhr-i Rao Jujhar Singh, jāgīrdār-i* Amjhera . . . (Copy of a *parvāna* of contents/text in Hindi, bearing the seal of Rao Jujhar Singh, *jāgīrdār* of Amjhera . . .'[77] It does appear that at least some Rajput *jāgīrdārs* felt free to develop their own epistolary styles in Hindi (which may mean a range of languages, including variations of Rajasthani). But the recipients of such orders found it most useful to store only the Persian translations in their household archives. Such a finding should push us to reconsider the clean ethno-linguistic boundaries that we may anachronistically impose on the past by explaining bilinguality in documents on the basis of variable reading skills alone. People may simply prefer to keep Persian documents, even if they did not read them very well, because those appeared to be more authentically 'legal' to them.

It is frustrating to not be able to see what Jujhar Singh's original Hindi/Hindvi *parvānas* were like, and compare them to what purported to be their Persian translations. As we shall see with bilingual tax contracts and legal deeds (in Chapters 3 and 4), such 'translations' often included significant variations, both in the formulaic opening and closing sections and in content that was considered relevant. Also, given the availability of a mass of Kacchwaha *parvānas* from the sixteenth through to the nineteenth centuries, with relation to the temples at Mathura, Vrindavan and later Jaipur, it would offer us the possibility of comparing the development of epistolary styles across various Rajput noble households.[78]

[75] Sandla, *Amjhera Rājya kā Itihās*, p.111. [76] NAI 2733/17 (1671). [77] NAI 2733/18 (1671)

[78] For published examples of these, see Horstmann, *In Favour of Govinddevji*. The Jaipur royal house moved over to Rajasthani-only *parvanās* in the 1710s, although the usage of Persian in other kinds of documentation, for example, diplomatic correspondence, continued until much later.

We do have, however, a very intriguing Rajasthani document in our collection, which I gathered from the residual documents at the family's household. The document is unsealed, but bears a decorative dagger-like symbol used like a cypher (as the Kacchwaha documents also do), and the date 1723 Saṃvat, which is 1667 CE. The invocation is 'Shri Gopal Satya'. The document's language, undifferentiated words and an eccentric archaic Nagri script make it very difficult to read, even with the assistance of experts from the region. In summary, however, it seems to be a letter written by a certain Maharajadhiraja Maha Singh to Nathmal *qānungō*, acknowledging the receipt of news about Hari Ram *qānungō* of *pargana* Amjhera. Thereafter, matters become a bit unclear, but the recipient is assured that his *watan* has been given him by Gopalji (i.e., Krishna; god), that the writer was pleased with him, and that Nathmal would always have a place in the writer's court. Thus, Nathmal should remain content, work well and keep reporting.[79]

While much remains unclear about the sender of this letter/order, it is clearly related to two other documents in the collection, both issued in the Regnal Year 9 of Aurangzeb or 1666–7, one currently at DAI, Kuwait, and the other at the NAI, New Delhi. The first document is a *parvāna* bearing the faint but clear seal of a high-ranking *mansabdār*, Wazīr Khan, ordering confiscation of the *chaudhrāī* of Hari Ram and *qānungōī* of Bulandar (name unclear) of Amjhera in favour of Purshottam Das and Paras Ram of Dhar and some other associates, who had stood *ẓāmin* for him.[80] The second is a copy of a *yād-dāsht* (literally, memory; in Mughal usage, a register entry) recording the ordered transfer.[81] Wazīr Khan was none other than the provincial governor or *ṣūbadār* of Malwa from 1664;[82] he appears at least twice in our documentary collections, both times in relation to confiscation of *chaudhrāīs* and *qānungoīs*. We shall discuss this episode in more detail in Chapter 3. Suffice here to note that while these transactions were recorded in Persian, somebody, perhaps the Rajput *jāgirdār* of Amjhera with a longer-term relationship with our landlord family, wrote to them in Rajasthani, congratulating them on their good fortune, and asking them to keep up the chain of communication that clearly proliferated in several languages alongside the Persian.

### *Jāgīrdār* and *Zamīndār*

There was an unavoidable love-hate relationship between these two points of the Mughal spectrum of state. In theory, the *jāgīr* was an assignment of revenue from a specific jurisdiction – *maḥāl* – or several of them. Most *maḥāls* were territorial, but there were also important non-territorial jurisdictions, such as customs dues.

[79] P Das 1667 Hin NCD, Choudhary Family Collection, Baḍā Rāolā, Dhar. I thank Elizabeth Thelen for helping me understand this document.
[80] LNS MS 235(f). [81] NAI 2733/15 (1667). [82] Khan, *Ma'āsir-i 'Ālamgiri*, p. 31.

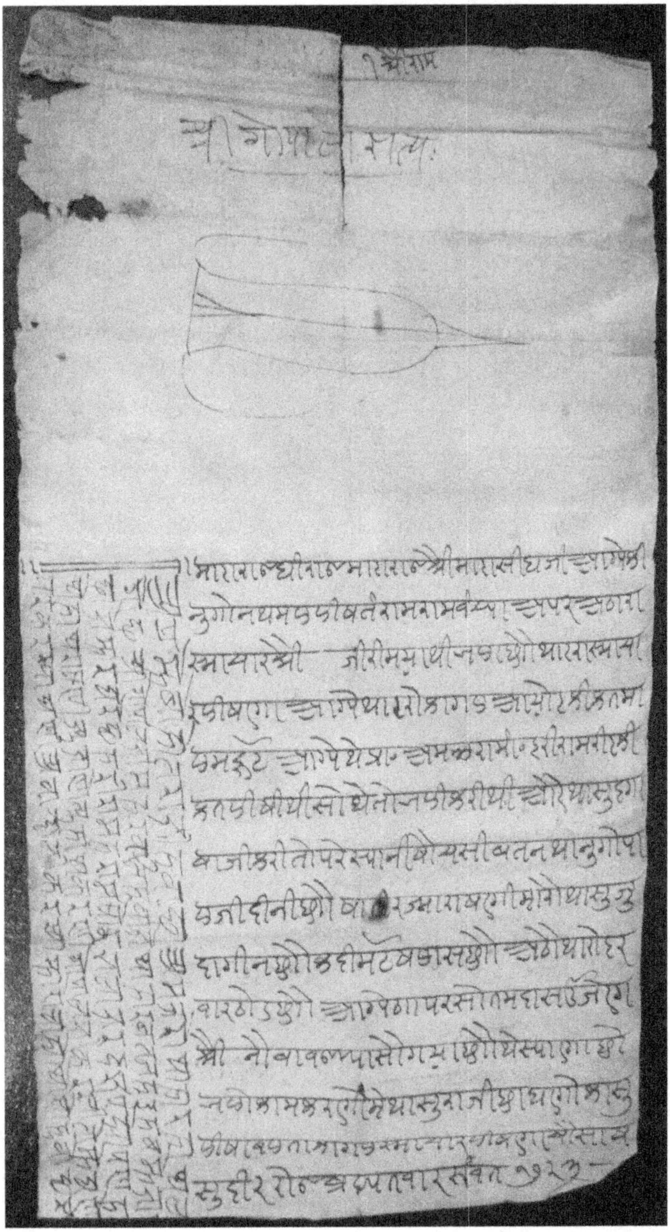

Figure 2.2 *Parvāna of* unknown Rajput noble, possibly of Amjhera, P Das 1667 Hin NCD

Such assignments – the right to collect taxes from designated *maḥāls* – was the Mughal method of paying a centrally conceived military bureaucracy, without the necessity or ability of channeling all taxes to the centre and redistributing them again. Thus the highest-ranking imperial officers, called *mansabdārs* (holders of *mansabs* or positions) were assigned, besides the occasional and very partial cash salary, the right to collect taxes from a number of *maḥāls* – which formed their *jāgīr*. Again, while in theory there was a separate and autonomous revenue bureaucracy which would just deliver the taxes as collected to the relevant *jāgīrdār*, in most cases the *jāgirdār* was expected to supervise and even organise the collection of taxes. This then brought them into contact with those lynchpins of rural society – the *zamīndārs* – who held the keys to the wealth of the countryside. The extent to which a *jāgīrdār* was successful in extracting that wealth, depended on his military might, which, tautologically, depended on the funds he had available for recruiting his soldiers.

Even so, the relationship between *jāgirdārs* and *zamīndārs* was not persistently adversarial. Although the *jāgīrdār's* demands for his share of the revenue pie squeezed what the *zamīndār* could retain for himself, the *jāgīrdār* also represented a ladder into the imperial system, and consequently, a route for the acquisition and legitimation of further resources. Documents within our collection indicate specific lines of mutual dependence, as well as stress between our *zamīndārs* of Dhar and the many imperial *jāgīrdārs* who came and went.

Mohan Das and his descendants – his son Purshottam Das and grandson Nathmal – reveal their incorporation into the regime by the regular summons they received from the incumbent *jāgīrdār* to render military and other services. In particular, a not-very successful *mansabdār-jāgīrdār* called Nawazish Khan developed a long-standing relationship with the family: at least twenty-six out of the ninety-five *parvānas* or their copies were issued under his seal, or that of his servants. Nawazish Khan was appointed *qila' dār* and *faujdār* of Mandsaur in the thirtieth year of Aurangzeb's reign, or 1687, and then of Mandu until the forty-eighth year of Aurangzeb's reign, or 1704.[83] He also appears in documentary collections related to other landed families in the region, especially the *qānūngō* of Dharampuri, Nandlal.[84] He is mentioned several times as fairly ineffective against Maratha invasions in a collection of

[83] Khan, *Maāsir-i-'Ālamgiri*, pp. 170, 286.
[84] S. K. Bhatt, 'Five Persian Documents of Aurangzeb's Reign from Malwa', *Proceedings of the Indian History Congress*, 39: 1 (1978), 398–401. These documents were taken at random from the Mandu Daftar of Natnagar Shodh Samsthan, Sitamau. Thanks again to the help of Dominic Vendell, I have been able to access these records in full. The records of the Mandu Daftar are numerous, and I am still analysing them, but there is a partial list with Hindi summaries in Manohar Singh Ranawat, *Mālwa Itihās ke Phārsī Kāgaz-Patroṇ kā Vivaranātmak Sūchī-Patra* (Sitamau: Shri Natnagar Shodh-Samsthan, 2000), pp. 84–100. Of these, the very first *parvāna*, from 1700 CE, addressed to Nandlal, *qānungō* of *pargana* Dharampuri (about 50 miles south of Dhar), is sealed by Nawazish Khan.

Aurangzeb's orders known as the *Kalimāt-i Tayyibāt.*[85] He struggled throughout his career, recording his woes in an unhappy little notebook of which a single, highly damaged contemporary manuscript copy survives in the National Library, Kolkata, as part of Jadunath Sarkar's collection. Fortunately for us, there is a pristine copy at Sitamau, commissioned by Jadunath Sarkar's princely scholar-disciple, Raghubir Sinh. It is a small codex, consisting of a compilation of letters (*ruqa'āt*) addressed to nobody in particular (i.e., anonymised), and completed, according to the final folio, on 24 Zil-Hijjah 1115 (1704 CE). The letters mention several characters in our story – the *Rāthoḍ jāgirdār* based in Amjhera, Jagrup; Wazir Khan, an important *mansabdār* and *sūbadār* of Malwa for a period from 1664; as well as Purshottam Das himself. In his letters, Nawazish Khan complains incessantly – of the weather, his poor health, undue punishments from the emperor and Maratha invasions.[86] Plaintive as he may seem in his letters, in the documents in our family's collection, Nawazish Khan comes across as an intimidating man and a formidable, if occasionally benevolent patron, in whose *dā'ira* lay, for a period, the work and fortunes of our family of landlords.

Of the twenty-five *parvānas* in our collection that are clearly associated with Nawazish Khan, several are issued under the seal of a certain Asadullah, who designates himself in the legend on the seal as '*murīd-i khāṣ*' (special servant/disciple) of Nawazish Khan. The *parvānas* range in date from 1659 CE to 1675 CE, that is, from an earlier period of his career than evidenced by the imperial chronicles. This noble was clearly deeply, if unhappily, entrenched in the region. Most of the *parvānas* are written in what appears to me to be a similar hand, and bear marginal notes in a very distinctive handwriting, written with a thicker pen than the main text. It would be a plausible speculation that these marginal notes were written by Nawazish Khan in his own hand, adding a further layer to what we know about corporeality and authenticity/authority in Mughal documents. It was not just emperors whose palm-prints could render orders more valuable;[87] the 'sign of the hand' of nobles could do similar, if smaller tricks.

The first three *parvānas* we have under the seal of Nawazish Khan bear dates ranging from April to May 1659 and clearly relate to a tense period when the imperial throne was still in dispute. It is striking that, although by this time Shah Jahan had been imprisoned and Dara Shukoh in flight, this noble hung on to his

[85] On the *Kalimāt-i Tayyibāt*, ascribed to Inayatullah Khan Kashmiri, also the author of *Ahkām-i 'Alamgīrī*, see S. M. Azizuddin Hussain, '*Kalimat-i-Aurangzeb*: a Source of Aurangzeb's Reign', *Proceedings of the Indian History Congress*, 40 (1979), 314–18.

[86] *Letterbook of Nawazish Khan* – No. 14 under 'Aurangzib Histories' in handlist of Natnagar Shod Samsthan, Sitamau. I am extremely grateful to Dominic Vendell for procuring this copy for me.

[87] We see such *farmāns* in Mahendra Khadgawat, *Phārsī farmānọ ke Prakāsh mein Mughalkālīn Bhārat evaṃ Rājput Shāshak*, Vol. IV (Bikaner: Rajasthan State Archives, 2018).

old seal, according to which he was '*murīd* (disciple)' of Hazrat Shah Jahan. The first of these *parvānas* was written in response to a petition from Purshottam *chaudhrī* and his long-term associate Paras Ram *qānūngō* of Dhar about their *nānkār* villages, that is, villages whose revenues were given as payment to *chaudhrīs* for their tax-collection duties.[88] Nawazish Khan said dismissively that the matter had already been raised by an unnamed *qāẕī* '*jīū*' and would be decided according to the recommendations of the same *qāẕī*.[89] The marginal note merely summarised what the main text had said. The next two orders from Nawazish Khan were strict instructions to pay up; the first said that the arrears of the year 1065 Hijri (1654–5 CE) must be paid up, and that anything Purshottam Das or Paras Ram had to say in the matter could be sent in writing to the *wizārat panāh* (the *wazīr*?). A marginal note summarised the order and then said: Whatever the petitioners had to say could be said to the *qāẕī* '*jīū*' when he reached the area.[90] The second document backs up the first with a generally intimidating order to Purshottam Das and Paras Ram to make sure that the cultivation of the area was improved significantly, because their welfare lay in achieving these goals.[91]

In the next year, 1660 CE, Nawazish Khan was cracking his whip again. Nawazish Khan's '*murīd-i khāṣ*' (therefore, probably Asadullah), wrote to Purshottam Das and Paras Ram reporting that a camel of *Khalīfa jīū* had been stolen from the town of Dhar. It is not clear who this *Khalīfa*, literally 'successor' may have been; perhaps it was being used as a *laqāb* (honorific title) for the *jāgirdār* himself, nicely indigenised through twinning with the Indic honorific '*jīū*', as the *qāẕī's* title had been in the first set of *parvānas*. Whoever it was that had a camel stolen, he was important enough for Purshottam Das and his colleague to be set scurrying. 'Search, and make such efforts', the *parvāna* said, 'Such that the camel may be found. Certainly do not consider yourself forgiven/exempt (*ma'āf*) in this matter'.[92] It was a spree of highway robberies, including the looting of the caravan of a rich merchant, which had offered Mohan Das his career break sometime in the early seventeenth century. Now, maybe forty years later, his son found himself ordered to catch thieves as a routine matter.

Again, in the very hot months of the 1664, a clearly harried Nawazish Khan, still taking tax proceeds from the same *jāgīr*, urged Purshottam Das: 'It is necessary that [you] appoint and engage [your] own son in the collection of revenues, [and] come with [your] collection of horsemen and foot soldiers.' However, military exigency did not excuse sloppiness in maintaining the cash

[88] Habib, *Agrarian System*, pp. 182, 213.
[89] LNS MS 235 (e), DAI, Kuwait; dated 30 Rajab 1069 (21 April 1659).
[90] LNS MS 235 (f), DAI, Kuwait; dated 7 Shaaban 1069 (28 April 1659).
[91] LNS MS 235 (g), DAI, Kuwait; dated 8 Ramzan 1069 (30 May 1659).
[92] LNS MS 235 (11), DAI, Kuwait.

flow, so the *jāgīrdār* warned darkly, 'If there occurs any laziness in the collection (of revenues), the results will not be good and his excuses will not be heard, the arrears will be seized.'[93] We can only speculate what the urgency was about.

On other occasions, Nawazish Khan could be more helpful to Purshottam Das and his associates. In 1660, for example, Nawazish Khan granted the possession of two houses to Purshottam Das. The first *parvāna* was addressed to a certain (again anonymous) *qāẕī 'jīū'*, informing him that he (Nawazish Khan) had given a house, formerly belonging to Muhammad Hashim Shiqdar, to Purshottam Das. This order also said that the wood and tiles of the house, should be dispatched to Nawazish Khan himself and the land made over Purshottam Das, on payment of 150 rupees as *pīshkash* (tribute).[94] Then there were two other *parvānas*, issued within two days of each other, both about a house formerly belonging to a certain Bulaqi Chand. The first of these spoke of an architect called Hamid who had done some good work. After this, the order gets somewhat difficult to interpret because of the poor use of pronouns that plagues Persian documents. According to 'his' request, 'he' was gifted the house on condition that the wood be sent to 'the Lord' along with a *pīshkash* of 150 rupees.[95] The second of these two *parvānas* was clearer; here Bulaqi Chand's house was granted unequivocally to Purshottam Das 'out of kindness'. The instruction that the house be destroyed (*mismār*) and the wood sent to His Lord (the noble who issued the *parvāna*, i.e., Nawazish Khan himself) was repeated.[96] It is not clear what Nawazish Khan was going to do with all that wood, but this was a regular pattern.

Handing over a mansion or two were important acts of self-interested benevolence; in some cases such transfers helped not just aggrandise Purshottam Das's family, but discipline unruly relatives. As we shall see in greater detail in the following section, Nawazish Khan also played an important role in sorting out disputes relating to inheritance within the family. In these matters, Nawazish Khan's responses could vary – sometimes he helped sideline and excise difficult or nonconformist members of the family, and on others, he insisted on the respecting of the proper distribution of inherited rights.

In addition to *parvānas*, we also have *qaul-qarār* documents (tax contracts, to be discussed in Chapter 3) sealed by servants of Nawazish Khan. For example, we have a bilingual *qaul-qarār*, dated 1664, whereby Gambhir Chand, another son of Purshottam Das, took on the *ijāra* of the village Nalawada for 894 rupees for the year.[97] There are also multiple collective

[93] LNS MS 235 (d1), DAI dated 13 Shawwal 1074 and RY 7 (9 May 1664).
[94] P Das 1660 AC-BRD ii (Dhar family collection), dated 6 Muhrram 1071 (11 September 1660).
[95] P Das 1660 (Dhar family collection), dated 28 Zil-Hijjah 1070 (28 September 1660).
[96] P Das 1660 BRD 8 (Dhar family collection), dated 26 Zil-Hijjah 1070 (26 September 1660).
[97] NAI (1664) 2703/15.

*qaul-qarārs* covering the entire district, for example, one for Dhar in 1659, for the amount of 109,571 rupees. This agreement, which involved many *chaudhrīs*, also had a very clear seal of Nawazish Khan, and also a characteristic superscript.[98]

Such engagements led to further difficulties, negotiations and orders. A final *parvāna* we have from Nawazish Khan dates from the thirtieth year of an unnamed emperor, most likely Aurangzeb, that is, the year 1675 CE.[99] This is a response to a petition that Purshottam Das and Paras Ram had written, complaining about the 'setting aside' of certain villages by two men called Abdul Hamid and Khuda Dost. The *parvāna* ordered these men to withdraw their soldiers, and as a compensation, exempted Purshottam Das and his associate from a payment of 3000 rupees, possibly from the taxes they had agreed to collect. In a rambling and plaintive marginal note that circled around the main text, a clearly desperate hand wrote with a thick pen, 'It is strange that you have not sent me a part of mine [my dues]. Now, it is suitable that you send the money here, and you make a little effort to please me'. A second note added: 'Entrust my money, with speed, to the person selected by me, so that he can send it', continuing, somewhat contradictorily: 'Allah, Allah, *zar che khwāhad būd*', which could mean 'God, what will happen of the money', or indeed, 'God, what good is such money!'

The *jāgīrdār's* frustration, in conjunction with his willingness to be flexible, reining in imperial officials and offering discounts, demonstrates the constant negotiation that structured the relationship between the *jāgīrdār* and the *zamindār*. The episodes described in this section also highlight the crucial role of the *jāgīrdār* in representing the 'state' in the Mughal empire. Here we see not a state–society binary, but in fact a three-way formation: the *mansabdār-jāgīrdār*, the *faujdār* and the *zamīndār*. The *jāgīrdār* could hardly hope for an automatic smooth flow of taxes towards his salary; what flowed in depended on the relationships he could cultivate, which included both intimidation and negotiation. Also, what the *jāgīrdār* could achieve, in terms of his duties, depended on such local ties – the *faujdār* of Nalcha had been helpless to maintain law and order or protect highways without the help of *zamindārs* such as Mohan Das; Nawazish Khan needed to turn to Mohan Das's son Purshottam Das to deal with thefts of property belonging to important people. At times, this negotiation approached a breaking point, and we can sense a figurative throwing up of hands by either side or both. But in most cases, difficult terrains, interrupted cash flows and endemic violence served to establish symbiotic relationships between *jāgīrdār* and the *zamindār* – two points on the spectrum of martiality that constituted the Mughal state – and ensured the continuance of landed patrilineages such as ours.

[98] NAI (1659) 2703/7. [99] LNS MS 235 (q1) (1675), DAI.

### *Passing the Mantle: Death, Incorporation and Succession*

Deaths of incumbent patriarchs inevitably led to a flurry of documentary activity, recording negotiations of the family with outside authorities as well as efforts to re-define the boundaries of kinship and associated entitlements. This was so when the family mantle passed to Purshottam Das. We observe this in high focus during the period of Prince Murad Baksh's holding of Dhar as *jāgīr*.

In January 1655, a *parvāna* was issued, possibly under the seal of Dianat Khan, officially affirming Purshottam Das's status as *chaudhrī* of *pargana* Dhar, and also helpfully tracing the genealogical and historical route by which the office and its perquisites were inherited by him. '*Muti*' *al-Islam* Purshottam Das', said the *parvāna*, 'son of the elder brother of Chandar Bhan, *chaudhrī* of *pargana* Dhar, know that the petition you had sent, has reached, and from its contents, we learnt that Chandar Bhan has died . . . according to [i. e. conditional upon] good service, you will receive the *sanad* of *chaudhrāī*'. The *parvāna* also noted that the family was in some difficulty at this juncture, with 4,000 rupees of dues remaining outstanding. However, it noted that a certain *sādat* and *iqbāl panāh* (Refuge of blessings and glory) Mir Ibrahim had written in, no doubt to encourage leniency, hence, it was loftily declared: 'investigations in this regard would [only] lead to exile [of the defaulters] and nothing would be achieved'.[100] Mir Ibrahim's recommendation appears to have hit the mark, thus in the following month, Rabi II, an order was issued, forgiving the outstanding dues, confirming Purshottam Das in place of his uncle and, per form, admonishing him to stay loyal and work hard, or else. Here, the source of authority was clearly spelled out: the *madār al-mahām* Dianat Khan had agreed to excuse the *pīshkash* of 4,000, the document said.[101]

While the position of the *chaudhrī* and *qānūngō* tended to be hereditary, they clearly had to be negotiated at generational borders, and this involved hefty exchanges that modelled themselves on imperial ones. *Pīshkash* is most commonly translated as tribute, and indeed conquerors from around the Persianate world made claims to it from defeated kings, especially when they were principally interested in a quick raid-and-return operation.[102] But it always included a spectrum of implications ranging from tribute to tax to gift.[103] In

[100] LNS MS 235 (b), DAI, dated 9 Rabi I RY 28 (17 January 1655); (parts of the seal impression are too blurred to be legible, but appear similar to perfectly clear impression on LNS 235 MS c), dated 20 Muharram RY 28 (8 Dec 1654).

[101] 1655 BRD 1, Baḍā Rāolā Dhar.

[102] For example, Nadir Shah's claim to *pīshkash* during his 1739 raid of Delhi and north-western India. Sanjay Subrahmanyam, *Europe's India: Words, People, Empires, 1500–1800* (Harvard: Harvard University Press, 2017), pp. 202, 205

[103] Ann Lambton, '"Pīshkash": Present or Tribute?', *Bulletin of the School of Oriental and African Studies*, 57: 1 (1994), 145–58.

post-conquest Golconda in the late seventeenth century – that is, a few decades after Purshottam Das's succession to his uncle's estate – Naiks, semi-independent warlords, paid *pīshkash* as they formally acknowledge the overlordship of the Mughal empire and their own transformation into *zamīndārs*.[104] However, the payment of *pīshkash* was not necessarily attached to the immediate aftermath of conquest and change in regimes; in the early eighteenth century, the *dēśmukh* (southern equivalent of *chaudhrī*) of *pargana* Pathri in erstwhile Bijapur paid a hefty *pīshkash* in order to receive an imperial *farmān* confirming his succession.[105] Before the consolidation of Anglo-Hindu law from the late eighteenth century, succession to *zamīndāri* titles was more a process of royal incorporation than reference to abstract doctrine of any kind. Scholarship on courtly gift-giving[106] points us towards understanding the simultaneity of royal incorporation, economic transaction and assertion of entitlement that is contained in this moment when *pīshkash* was demanded of Purshottam Das, but also graciously excused, as royalty can always do. In this case, such grace may have been exercised by a noble who had a penchant for appropriating royal jurisdiction; for instance, by granting *jāgīrs* of his own accord.[107]

Purshottam Das's father, as we know, was Mohan Das, the brave man who had defeated the highwayman Bira. Why had Mohan Das not passed on the *chaudhrāī* of *pargana* Dhar to his son, but to his younger brother, Chandar Bhan, leaving him to make the transfer in turn? Was it because his son had been too young? Or was it a case of co-parcenery title, which was being affirmed on the death of a senior co-parcener? Or maybe it a bit of both: the position of *chaudhrī*, while inheritable, entailed certain specific services relating to tax-collection and administration, and could not be passed on to an unsuitable family member at will, since it required affirmation by the senior provincial officials. With Purshottam Das having demonstrated his worth for nearly thirty years, and his uncle, perhaps the oldest male member of the family, now dead,

[104] M. A. Nayeem, 'Mughal Documents Relating to the Pīshkash of Zamīndārs of South India, 1694–1752 A.D.', *IESHR*, 12: 4 (1975), 425–32.

[105] W. H. Moreland, 'The Pargana Headman (Chaudhrī) in the Mogul Empire', *The Journal of the Royal Asiatic Society of Great Britain and Ireland*, 4 (1938), 511–21, at page 514, discussing Document E.

[106] Bernard Cohn posited a stark cultural opposition between transactional Europeans and incorporationist Indians; William Pinch strongly disagreed with this opposition especially for the early modern period, when Europeans were equally located in courtly cultures. The latter view appears strengthened, without direct reference, by Kim Siebenhüner in 'Approaching Diplomatic and Courtly Gift-Giving in Europe and Mughal India: Shared Practices and Cultural Diversity', *Medieval History Journal*, 16: 2 (2013), 525–46.

[107] Dianat Khan, when *diwān* of Dakhin towards the end of Aurangzeb's reign, may have granted *jāgirs* under his own seal, without the usual validation by the emperor or the imperial *diwān*. P. Saran, *The Provincial Government of the Mughals, 1526–1658*, 2nd ed. (Bombay: Asia Publishing House 1973), p. 263, *Maasir al-Umara*, translated Beveridge and Prashad, Vol. I, pp. 472–5, at 473.

the provincial governor willingly confirmed his title, despite the evident glitch during the period of transition.

However, as generally happens with large propertied families, matters were not quite as smooth as this suggests. Purshottam Das may have been an obvious successor, and clearly the documentary record the dominant line of the family preserved made him look that way, but he was not the only claimant to Chandar Bhan's legacy. Almost immediately after Purshottam Das was confirmed in his position, Chandar Bhan's own son, Suraj Bhan, turned up to assert his claims. Now this cousin was one who has been systematically erased from the family's documentary records (more about which in later chapters), and we only know about him (and his line) because of their occasional disruptive appearances, always to make complaints about rights that they were being denied. In doing so, they reveal to us the multiple bases of entitlements in the villages of Mughal India, and the variety of authorities that could (or had to) be mobilised in order to claim them.

In 1660, Purshottam Das wrote an *'arzdāsht* (petition) to this patron, Nawazish Khan, which led to the latter seizing Suraj Bhan's *havelī* (mansion), which was attached to that of Purshottam Das's own, for reasons unknown. In any case, the mansion as handed over to Purshottam Das, subject to the payment of a substantial sum of money – two hundred rupees.[108]

As we have already seen, there was a long-term relationship between Purshottam Das and the not-so-eminent *jāgīrdār*, Nawazish Khan. However, in the next few years, this relationship failed to shield all of Purshottam Das's wheeling and dealing. August 1664, Purshottam Das received a rather stern *parvāna* from the provincial governor (*sūbadār*), Najabat Khan.[109] 'Purshottam Das', it said, 'you should know that Suraj Bhan had come as a petitioner (*mustaghas̱-i shud*) complaining that the *chaudhrāī* of *pargana* Hindola (which had been gained by the family by defeating Bira) belonged to the plaintiff, as co-owner with him (*ba-sharkat-i ū, ba-rafe' ta'aluq dārad)* [but] at present, he had no control over the *dastūr* (customary due) of *chaudhrāī*, [for] by oppression and force [Purshottam Das] had himself taken possession of these. Apart from this, there was also the matter of the eighteen villages which had been allocated to the family as *'inām*, from ancient times. Of these *'ināmī* villages, Suraj Bhan had populated one village called Ajnai.[110] Out of malice, the partner [i.e., Purshottam

[108] BRD 2 (1660).

[109] LNS MS 235 (m) DAI, 19 Muharram RY 7 (22 August 1664). The name of the official is unfortunately unclear on the seal, but Najabat Khan had been appointed governor of Malwa in August or September 1663. Khan, *Ma'āsir-i 'Ālamgiri,* p. 29. Najabat Khan is also mentioned as the authority issuing the *parvāna* that is cited in the document recording the continuance of the dispute in the *qāẓī's* court.

[110] The *parvāna* misses out the final 'noon' but comparing this document with the next one helps us identify this village, which is probably the same as the one now called Anjan Kheda, in district Dhar.

Das] had desolated the peasants of that village'. Now, while familial squabbling was something that all aristocratic families were used to, destroying the revenue capacity of a village was not something that a *jāgirdār* would put up with. So, he wrote rather crossly to Purshottam Das that he should not interfere with the plaintiff, but above all, that none of them should cause disturbance to the population of the village (*dar abādānī-yi mauza*ʿ *khallal nakunad*), or else. After this general instruction from the governor, the local *qāẕī* was set to work out the details of the two cousins' respective entitlements, which clearly spilled beyond the district of Dhar into the neighbouring district of Hindola and towns such as Sultanpur.[111]

Suraj Bhan appears to have fared much the worse in this conflict. In 1673, he turned up, practically begging, at the door of the *kotwāl* of the *pargana*, Sheikh Ghulam Muhammad, asking for a house to live in. He declared himself currently resident in the village of Kharpura, in the same *pargana*, but clearly life was intolerable in the village, and he wished to move to the town of Dhar. The *kotwāl* was sympathetic, and so he called for Bardman and Bhagwati Das, who appear to be members of the same extended family, and asked them to arrange things. A suitable empty townhouse was found – it had belonged to someone called Santokni, who was now dead, and before her (?), to Sundar Das, resident of Sultanpur. The house, together with some goods left therein, was made over to Suraj Bhan, who, let us hope, was able to end his days in peace in there.[112] Forty years later, somebody in the family found it necessary to have a copy of this document – which must have functioned like a kind of conveyance deed – made, and *Qāẕī* Muhammad Mustafa dutifully affixed his seal, bearing the date 1123 (1711 CE) noting that it was a 'true copy'.

The cycle of disputing and recording was repeated in the next generation. Around 1684, for example, Purshottam Das died, and his heirs immediately fell upon each other to gain bigger shares for themselves. In that year, an unsealed *maḥẕar-nāma* was produced in favour of Purshottam Das's son, Narsingh Das. The document again told the rollicking tale of exploits of their illustrious ancestor, Mohan Das, but also narrated how the cycle of order and disorder had been repeated in the next generation. Because his own sons were too young, the title had passed from Mohan Das to his brother Chandar Bhan. When Purshottam Das came of age, he had secured his title by seeking and receiving various confirmatory orders from *jāgīrdār*. But because he had not been able to keep up a sufficient armed contingent, the Bhils and *girāsiyas* had again surfaced as a major problem, blocking the trade route to Gujarat. The merchants, peasants and general inhabitants now testified that after Purshottam

[111] NAI 2703/17 (1665), attested in 1692.
[112] NAI 2668/25 (1684); date on seal attesting the copy 1123 (1711); NAI incorrectly catalogues it as dated 1732.

Das, his son Narsingh Das was the best man to be granted the titles and dues, so that he could protect the area and make life and trade possible again.[113]

Narsingh Das was not the only claimant, in fact, he may have been the weaker party, for in 1683, it had been decided in a court (it is not clear whose) that Hamir Chand, the eldest brother, had exclusive right to certain villages, because they were associated with the office of the *chaudhrī*; the rest of the family estate had been shared out.[114] But Narsingh Das had clearly not been satisfied, for he kept seeking and securing specific grants giving him titles to lands and rights,[115] while probably also battling more distant cousins, such as Kanwal Das and Tilok Chand, whose claims had to be warded off with yet another *maḥẓar-nāma*, repeating a variant of the Mohan Das story, and favouring the main line of the family.[116]

It is worth noting in this connection that in none of these documents is there any reference to an entity such as 'Hindu law'. Inheritable property, which included offices and associated perks travelled downwards along the male agnatic line, but not according to any of the *dharmaśāstric* rules that came to dominate the legal fortunes of Hindu *zamīndāri* families under British rule. What appeared to apply instead was a conjunction of documented possession of specific shares and remaining within the family's affective circle and in the good books of incumbent *jāgirdārs*. Having said that, there was at least a sense of long-established custom, repeatedly referenced as *dastūr*, and the sense that property and offices that had remained in the family for generations may not be lightly disposed of, even within the same family. Hence the *sūbadār's* stern intervention in 1663, when Purshottam Das tried to cut out Suraj Bhan from his *dastūr* (customary entitlements). But here, too, it was no *śāstrī* that made the decision, but an imperial *mansabdār*, aided by a *qāẓī*.

### *Local Patronage*

*Noblesse oblige* required that members of a wealthy family such as this one also undertake charitable activities, with enlightened self-interest at work. Conspicuous giving, especially associated with permanent and popular structures, was an effective way of stamping one's status on the landscape, from emperors down to rural grandees. Especially where such architectural interjections could rest on, and feed off, existing lines of worship and/or commerce, it also offered opportunities for dialogue or, more cynically speaking, transaction, between lower and higher rungs of the imperial hierarchy. The seeking and granting of royal and sub-royal grants, inevitably out of the same pool of

[113] NAI 2703/61 (1684). [114] NAI 2703/27 (1683).
[115] NAI 2733/108 (1684); undated, unsealed, much-later copy.
[116] NAI 2703/62 (1684?); the document is undated and unsealed; the date is contextually guessed by the cataloguer of the National Archives of India.

agrarian resources, was yet another mode of creating spaces of entitlements, but it was also a way of demonstrating the power of benevolence of several powerholders at the same time.

In 1662 (1073 AH) a certain Kishan Das managed to secure a grant from Muhammad Hussain of twenty *bīghas* of *banjar pokhta* (fallow) land in Sultanpur, the *thāna*-town in the neighbouring *pargana* of Hindola which Mohan Das had established, for setting up a much-needed garden and rest-house for travellers.[117] A remarkably accurate, although scrappily scribed copy of this *parvāna* was also produced and authenticated at some point, and preserved within the collection before it was dispersed.[118] Since this is the only instance in which Kishan Das is mentioned in our collection of documents, it is hard to say what exactly his relationship was with the other protagonists, whom we have come to know better. It is possible that he was an individual unrelated to the family. Since in the 1655 dispute between Suraj Bhan and Purshottam Das, the latter had secured control over the well-bearing towns and villages of Sultanpur, Kishan Das's grant would have impinged upon the holdings of the dominant family faction, and this maybe why the document was preserved in the family collection. The family would have looked upon the building of said garden and rest-house as an effective way of attracting potentially toll-paying commercial traffic through their areas. In other instances, it is clear that such percolation was facilitated by recognisable members of the family. The official called Muhammad Hussain made more than one grant in the month of Rabi I, year 1073/1662, this too for the establishment of gardens in which travellers could rest. A few days before the grant to Kishan Das, another grant of 25 *bīghas* of fallow land, located in the village of Sindhauri had been made to Nathmal, son of Purshottam Das *chaudhrī*.[119]

Muhammad Hussain himself declared the grant a *taṣadduq* – that is, a virtuous act of charity. Quite like Kishan Das and Nathmal, his piety was no doubt along the lines of enlightened self-interest, for, as he said, the garden would be for the *ārām-i musāfirān* (comfort of the travellers). Such grants may be connected with similar awards made in the same period by higher-ranking noble/officials of Malwa to the temple complexes of Ujjain and their keepers.[120] In recent and ongoing studies of the Rajput Kacchwaha dynasty, their channelling of imperial grants and redistribution of their own empire-derived resources have much to tell

117 LNS MS 235 a1 (1662).

118 NAI 2703/11 (wrongly dated as 1665 by the archivist; based on a misinterpretation of the word '*amali*', which follows the date; date of copying not known).

119 LMS MS 235 s (1662).

120 Jnan Chandra, 'Alamgir's Grants to Hindu Pujaris', *Journal of the Pakistan Historical Society*, 6: 1 (1958), 54–65. The grants were made by Najabat Khan and Khan-i Azam, successive *sūbadars* of Malwa in the 1660s, to a family of priests who served at the Mahakaleshwar temple of Ujjain.

us about layered efforts at capturing sacred geographies; that can take us beyond the stale and inaccurate stories of Mughal 'tolerance' or its obverse.[121] Of course all these grants were made in Emperor Aurangzeb Alamgir's time; but they were not all his own, and as such are poor evidence for his tolerance or bigotry. As in earlier periods in south-central India, the creation of resources providing water supply and facilitating travel were an established form of charity in which locally deputed officials and local gentry could cooperate.[122] Just as the neighbouring Bijapuri nobles had been, Mughal nobles-officers were provided with opportunities for patronage; *zamīndārs* such as this family witnessed the drawing of the apparatus of the Mughal state into rural pockets, and managed to haul themselves up into it, bit by it.

As Mughal nobles-officers themselves, local Rajput families with *jāgīrs* did not hold back from making similar charitable grants. We have already seen how Nathmal, son of Purshottam Das, was able to benefit from one such grant in 1672, when the Amjhera-based *Rāthoḍ* noble Jujhar Singh granted 101 *bīghas* of land, tax-free, for the setting up of a garden in Amjhera town. This order did not call the grant anything specific; it was just said that a certain amount of land 'was given'. The order had a certain earthiness about it – it declared that anybody who interfered with the grant would be judged *nāmak-harām* or unfaithful, and appended some kind of specific curse/threat towards such Hindu and Muslim interlopers.[123]

Finally, all these grants were repeatedly reconfirmed by additional confirmations. In 1671, Purshottam Das's son Nathmal appears to have been on a spree of organising gardens; he secured another *parvāna*, this time from the district tax official (*amīn*) Sheikh Ibrahim, confirming 50 *bighas* of land in the village of Gondhra, *pargana* Dhar, on the basis of old custom (*ba-dastūr-i sābiq*) and unspecified old documents.[124]

Here, it is worth commenting on the terminology used in the making and recording of grants such as these. The endowment of lands or property for the establishment and upkeep of charitable institutions is recorded across the Islamicate world with the legal device of *waqf*, which derives from the Arabic root w-q-f, implying stopping, bringing to a standstill. For centuries, the making of *waqf* has been a method for taking property out of the fiscal reach

121 Catherine Asher, 'Kacchavaha Pride and Prestige: the Temple Patronage of Raja Mana Simha, in Margaret H. Case (ed.) *Govindadeva: a Dialogue in Stone* (New Delhi: IGNCA, 1996), pp. 215–40.

122 A. A. Kaderi, 'A Mahdar from Hukeri in Karnataka', in *Epigraphica Indica: Arabic and Persian Supplement* (Delhi: Archaeological Survey, 1972), pp. 51–77. The bilingual Persian–Marathi inscription studied here recorded the endowment of lands to support the maintenance of a *karanja* (water-tank) and a *mehmān-khāna* (guesthouse). Unlike the later Mughal grants, however, the Bijapuri grant was collectively made by a range of local individuals, from a *qāẕī* down to the a humble *mehtar* (cleaner).

123 NAI 2733/18 (1671). 124 NAI 2703/24 (1671).

of the state and beyond the ordinary distributive rules of Islamic inheritance laws. Within the Persianate sphere, deeds creating *waqfs* – *waqf-nāmas* – were prolific well into the twentieth century.[125] In South Asia, despite acrid politics over the validity of specific types of *waqfs*, and their significance for Muslim identity formation under British colonial rule and afterwards,[126] the legal device of *waqf* and *waqf-nāma* documents appear to be startlingly absent until the nineteenth century.[127] The situation may have been somewhat different in the Deccan Sultanates,[128] but this was certainly the case in the Mughal empire. None of the collections of documents associated with charitable grants that I have seen, these including grants to Hindu temples and monasteries as well as Muslim scholarly families, contain any *waqf-nāmas*. The term of choice for charitable grants in the sixteenth and seventeenth centuries is *madad-i ma'ash* (lit. 'help with livelihood expenses'). Such grants are made using documentary forms for royal and sub-royal orders – *farmāns, parvānas* – and so on.

In the first two documents discussed, the officer-noble Muhammad Hussain uses a particular set phrase '*taṣadduq-i farq-i mubārak-i bandegān-i haẕrat Suleimān martabat*', which is best translated as 'charitable donation on the part of the servants of His Solomonic Majesty'. The phrase is followed by a gap in the text which is the usually the indication of *elevatio*, or a name respectfully elevated. Here one is clearly meant to read the name of the donor, Muhammad Hussain himself, as written within the seal. Looking at the formulaic phrase more closely, however, one finds elaborations of Indo-Persianate legal terminology that occupied the lexical space for '*waqf*'. The phrase '*tasadduq-i farq-i mubārak*' was pan-Mughal; it also occurs in a *parvāna* issued by a Mughal governor, which granted a regular levy from certain villages to a group of ascetics associated with the temple complex at Vṛndavan. '*Farq-i mubārak*' is difficult to translate; Habib has suggested 'For His Majesty's good fortune'.[129] Another scholar proposed that the literal meaning of 'blessed head' may

[125] Christoph Werner, *Vaqf en Iran: Aspects Culturels, Religieux et Sociaux* (Paris: Association pour l'Avancement des Études Iraniennes, 2015); on *waqfs* created in the Qajar period for the establishment of allopathic (i.e., western medicine based hospitals), see Fabrizio Speciale, *Hospitals in India and Iran, 1500–1950* (Leiden: Brill, 2010), pp. 4–5.

[126] Kozlowski, *Muslim Endowments.*

[127] Although Irfan Habib mentions *waqf* as a type of grant, he refers only to the text of jurists such as Barani and Badauni, rather than any of the vast numbers of documents he has surveyed. Habib, *Agrarian System*, p. 359.

[128] There is a photocopy of a purported Qutb Shahi *farmān*, dated 1672, making a *waqf* for the upkeep of a resthouse for Indian pilgrims to the shrine of Imam Reza in Mashhad in Iran; even for this, the original document in not traceable. Omid Rezai, '*Dilbastagī mazhabī angize-yi dīgar barā-yi muhājirāt az shabe qare be falāt Iran*', in Iraj Afshar and Karim Isfahani (eds.) *Pazūhesh-hā-yi Irānshanashī* [Iranian Studies] (Tehran: Chapkhane-yi Tarana, 2014), pp. 198–213.

[129] Habib, 'A Documentary History', p. 135.

indicate the cultural practice of twirling a donation above the recipient's head before handing over.[130] It may also mean that that all such donations were theoretically made on the behalf of the emperor. In any case, Muhammad Hussain aimed, by making this *taṣadduq* or charitable grant, to enact the royalty through generosity, just as Solomon the Great had done in his legendary charitableness.

### *Copies, Lists and Assertion of Rights*

However successful one might be, in the Mughal empire it was essential to be proactive about one's entitlements, and the family was well aware of this need, demonstrating this awareness by acquiring authenticated copies *nishāns* issued by imperial princes. In this section, we will consider the possibility that the making and validating of such copies reveals an active approach to recording rights, and excluding those of others. And in doing so, I shall consciously depart from standard practice in Mughal historiography, in which historians display great care in detecting forgeries but treat what appears to them as plausible copies as the equivalent of originals.[131]

Reconfirmation could take place through the instrumentality of a documentary form specifically intended for this purpose, called *taṣdīq* (derived from the Arabic root *ṣa-da-qa*, related to truth). We have one such *taṣdīq*, said to be issued under the seal of a certain Mirza Khan, which noted that since *farmāns* of *Arsh Āshiyānī* (Akbar) and *Jannat Makānī* (Jahangir) and other documents of past governors, [granting] village Ahu and others as *ʿinām* and *nānkār*, in the name of Mohan Das, Chandar Bhan and Purshottam Das, had reached the office [of the verifying authority] and had been found correct after checking, 'For this reason, these two words were written in the manner of *taṣdīq* (*li-hazā, in dō kalme tarīq-i taṣdīq tahrīr yāft*)'. There followed a list of fifteen villages,

[130] Dan Sheffield, personal communication, 30 August 2019.

[131] Two examples will suffice here: the use of the set of copied documents in the Bibliotheque National de France (BNF), referred to by many historians as MS. Blochet Supplementary Pers. 482; and the use of the copied documents in the British Library, London, shelfmark Add. 24039. The BNF codex is referred to as 'a collection of contemporary documents, mostly concerning Surat, compiled in the mid-seventeenth century, by an anonymous Mughal official in Surat' from Surat, and used several times in the book; by Hasan, *State and Locality*, Bibliography, p. 132, and as 'Documents Mostly Relating to Surat, Ranging over the Period 1583–1648', by Shireen Moosvi, in her *People, Taxation and Trade in Mughal India* (New Delhi: Oxford University Press, 2008), Bibliography, 440. The British Library codex relating to Calcutta, shelfmark Add. 24,039 is treated by Hasan as if they were original documents, when in fact, they are copies of unclear provenance bound in a notebook. See Hasan, 'Indigenous Cooperation', 65–82. Both sets however, are copies; as per a note on the first page, the Surat collection was clearly produced for the collection of the Orientalist A. H. Anquetil-Duperron. The location and exact contents of the originals is unknown in both cases.

grouped into two categories: ten in their entirety (*mawāzī dah mauza'*) and five in which some *bīghas* of land were claimed.[132]

Although by content alone, it would appear that the *taṣdīq* was issued to Purshottam Das, the document we have is itself a copy. This *naql* of the *taṣdīq* was validated by the seal of the familiar *qāẕī*, Muhammad Mustafa, who, as we know, worked in the area between the 1690s and 1710s. Thus, rather mind-bogglingly, what we have is a validated copy of a verificatory document confirming older orders; which shows, if nothing else, how the family's claims on various villages and their produce, on the basis of *'inām* and *nānkār* (that is, non-specific and specifically office-related grants) had expanded. The making of this copy also hints that, towards the end of the seventeenth century, a certain line of the family was obsessively recording and rerecording those rights, to establish a seemingly uncomplicated line of succession to those rights.

Reconfirmation could also be achieved through declarative orders. In 1672, for example, Islam Khan, the *jāgīrdār* who appears to have replaced Nawazish Khan as principal patron of the family, declared that since several villages including Ahu, further arable land and several mango trees belonged to Purshottam Das as a result of *nishāns* and *asnād* (generally, documents), their possession was reconfirmed.[133] By 1693, by which time Purshottam Das was dead and gone, a serious division of spoils needed to be achieved. On that occasion, the then-*jāgīrdār* Asad Khan, possibly a well-known noble of Aurangzeb's reign, together with the *Qāẕī* Muhammad Mustafa sealed a *taqsīm-nāma* (partition deed) pertaining to no fewer than 178 villages. Three major lines, related to the five original *māliks* emerge from the divisions – and so fifty-two villages went to Tilokchand, Lalchand and others, heirs of Gopal Das; fifty-six villages to the descendants of Bhagwant, and fifty-six to the descendants of Jayanti Das.[134]

In 1731, the family secured a *parvāna* from none other than the *wazīr al-mumālik* Qamar al-Din Khan, 'Asaf Jah', who had by this time established a practically autonomous kingdom of his own, the Nizamat of Hyderabad.[135] But a breakaway provincial governor still respected old imperial documents. When Hamir Chand and Nihal Chand, two sons of Purshottam Das, who did not quite get along with their other brothers, petitioned the governor, stating the *chaudhrāī* of the *pargana* Dhar belonged to them, noting their loyalty (to whom, one wonders) and the fact that they possessed copies of *farmāns* and a *nishān* of Murad Baksh in support of their rights, their claims were upheld and confirmed. In the twilight of the Mughal empire, there was a clear case of

[132] NAI 2733/60 [date unclear; archive dates it incorrectly as 1637–38]
[133] LNS MS 235 (x) DAI (1672). [134] NAI 2668/15 (1693)
[135] Avril Powell, *Muslims and Missionaries in Pre-mutiny India* (London: Routledge, 1993), p. 45.

authentication inflation – and so a copy of this order was sealed by none less than the Chief *Qāẕī* – the *Qāẕī al-Quẕẕāt*.[136]

Ironically, these efforts at recording and erasing assist us in recreating the family tree, tracking the genealogical, but even more importantly, personal and consequently legal relationships of various men and women with each other. Conceiving of the family as a fluid matrix of emotional and material resources[137] complements our concept of law and an interlocking field of orders, transactions, obligations and entitlements. As we shall see in subsequent chapters, the documents in our collection played an active role in the evolution of the matrix of kinship and entitlements within this family – and bear clear signs of having been deployed as instruments for the consolidation of certain familial knots, paired with the exclusion of certain other lines.

## *Conclusion*

Orders issued by emperors, princes and nobles co-created enforceable rights in the countryside, which rested on multiple references, most importantly to pre-existing titles, custom and written documents. Custom, or customary dues, while being references to antiquity, could themselves derive from older written orders conferring rights – of office-holding, collecting taxes or exemption from them. These rights were acquired and expanded through a capacious portfolio of enterprise by families such as ours; clan-based landholding, military enterprise and literacy- and numeracy-based state services all fed into the building of rural eminence that made the *zamīndār*. The entitlements all broadly consisted of the rights to share in the produce of the land – whether one calls that landowning with right to rent, office-holding with right to tax, or tax exemption. And so it is to tax – the state's extraction of resources from its subjects, and its potential as a business opportunity – that we turn in the next chapter.

[136] NAI 2703/44 (1731).

[137] Margot Finn, 'Family Formations: Anglo India and the Familial Proto-State', in David Feldman and Jon Lawrence (eds.) *Structures and Transformations in Modern British History* (Cambridge, 2011), 100–17; Leonore Davidoff, Megan Doolittle, Janet Fink and Katherine Holden, *The Family Story: Blood, Contract and Intimacy, 1830–1960* (London: Longman, 1999), Introduction, pp. 3–51.

# 3 Contractors: Engaging the State

Of course, no book on Mughal history can be written without a chapter, or more, on taxation.[1] Within the historiography of the Mughals, tax has served as code for the state – its mechanisms, personnel and extractive capacity and effect on 'the economy', as well as its mirror. For our protagonists, however, tax – the specific arrangements for extracting and recording it – was a key source of entitlements. Tax brought armed and locally entrenched rural bosses into the purview of the state; it gave them opportunities for engagement with the system, and for substantiating it. Such engagements produced documents that, in their contractual form but executive intent, blurred the line between interpersonal transactions and royal/subroyal orders. They also generated a variety of obligations and entitlements, which could be disputed, transacted and reordered; they produced law.

In talking about law in connection with Mughal taxes, we could be pulled towards Islamic jurisprudence, which is loquacious on the subject. Hanafi jurists from classical times (the 8th–10th century CE) had been concerned with explaining, justifying and categorising taxation, that is, the ruler's claim to a share of the peasant's production. The Mughals were Sunni Muslims and, due to their Central Asian heritage, Hanafis. The greatest compilation of Islamic jurisprudence in India, the imperially sponsored *Fatāwá-yi ʿAlamgīrī* (completed 1692; henceforth *FA*), had a long section on taxes.[2] Since Emperor

1 Two classics of Mughal historiography, Habib's *Agrarian System* and Shireen Moosvi's *The Economy of the Mughal Empire c. 1595* (2nd edn. New Delhi: Oxford University Press, 2015) are essentially works on the Mughal fiscal system. Other tax-centric or tax-derived discussions of the 'state' are Chetan Singh, 'Centre and Periphery in the Mughal State: The Case of Seventeenth-Century Panjab', *Modern Asian Studies*, 22: 2 (1988), 299–318; which led to his *Region and Empire: Panjab in the Seventeenth Century* (Delhi: Oxford University Press, 1991); Farhat Hasan, 'The Mughal Fiscal System in Surat and the English East India Company', *Modern Asian Studies*, 27: 4 (1993), 711–18, which led to his *State and Locality*, especially pp. 110–25. Additionally, there are innumerable descriptive works, such as Siddiqi, *Land Revenue Administration*. For a survey of the historiography on the Mughal state, see Sanjay Subrahmanyam, 'The Mughal State: Structure or Process? Reflections on Recent Western Historiography', *IESHR*, 29: 3 (1992), 291–321.

2 The 'book' or *Kitāb al- muzāraʿāt* in the *Fatāwá-yi ʿAlamgīrī*, translated to Urdu by Amir Ali, 10 vols (Lahore: Maktaba-yi Rahmaniya, n.d.), Vol. 8, pp. 287–355.

Aurangzeb Alamgir had a penchant for referring to *sharīʿa* in connection with his orders, it is tempting to see this section of the *FA* as part of a concerted effort to give 'Islamic legal interpretation . . . to a widening agrarian tax base', as many historians have done.[3] In fact, the effort to align the documented practice of Mughal tax collection, allocation and exemption with the contents of *fiqh* books derives from an abortive mid-nineteenth century British Orientalist effort.[4] In 1853, the Scottish Orientalist Neil Baillie, remonstrating against the established tendency to seek the legal limits of taxation in the 'opinions of the people and the practices of subordinate governors', proposed instead that the 'written records of the law', that is, *fiqh* books such as the *Fatāwá-yi ʿAlamgīrī*, be consulted. He produced an amalgam of extracts of juristic argumentation from *fiqh* books and commentaries highly regarded in India, together with key imperial and sub-imperial orders related to taxation. Some of the latter, especially those issued by Aurangzeb, used terms recognisable from the jurisprudential corpus; others did not. Baillie's effort was to produce a conceptual grid of the Islamic (largely Hanafi) theory of taxation, and then fit Mughal usage onto it. So, having established first that there were two kinds of agricultural tax – that which involved a sharing of produce and hence varied with output (*kharāj muqāsima*), and that which was obligatory (*kharāj waẓīfa*) – he recited how, historically, non-Muslims in lands conquered by Muslims were always subject to the latter. From here he proceeded to survey Persian chronicles to trace taxation practices in the Delhi Sultanate, and then Emperor Akbar's sixteenth-century innovations. Wading through the *Āʾīn's* classification of lands with various taxation rates, all in Indic terms (*pulij, paḍaotī, chāchar, banjar*, etc.), he declared having 'little hesitation in saying that the impost levied by Akbar was the *Wuzeefa Khiraj* of the Mohammedan law'.[5]

Although interested in how taxation produced a significant arena for the instantiation of law, specifically Islamic law in Mughal India, this chapter will not follow Baillie in his forced conflation, for a number of reasons. The simplest of these is the unconvincing assumption that Islamic regimes must have a given law of taxation, and therefore, all that is observed must be a version of those laws. Islamic law is, quite simply, not reducible to books of Islamic jurisprudence. Such books contained sections and content for multiple reasons, including scholastic traditions of literal textual reproduction.[6]

[3] Hayden Bellenoit, *Formation of the Colonial State: Scribes, Paper and Taxes* (London: Routledge, 2017), p. 24.

[4] Neil Baillie, *The Land Tax of India, According to the Moohummudan Law, translated from the Futuwa Alumgeeree* (2nd ed., London: Smith, Elder & Co., 1873, first published 1853).

[5] Ibid., p. xxx.

[6] The section on documentation – *mahāẓir va sijillāt* – in the *FA* is bodily reproduced from the *Hedaya*. I am grateful to Ofir Haim for pointing this out to me.

Given such textual reproduction across centuries, and the frequent absence of local referents in the *fiqh* texts, one has to be very careful when explaining any section of texts such as the *Fatāwá-yi Alamgīrī* with reference to contemporary political or social concerns. The other objection is that Persianate imperial traditions – not necessarily Islamic, and frequently claiming their grandeur from Persia's pre-Islamic past – clearly supplied a large body of precedent, if not doctrine, for imperial practices in South Asia. Thus a practice, such as *pīshkash* or tribute, which we have encountered in Chapter 2 as a familiar mode of *zamindār* to *jagirdār* extractions, may in fact derive from a Persianate,[7] rather than an Islamic legal norm, and the distinction is significant when we are tracing textual and intellectual genealogies. Finally, the proliferation of Indic terminology, especially in Mughal tax administration cannot be dismissed as detritus dragged along in a system whose concepts were completely insulated from its own vocabulary. Instead, this chapter will remain alert to lexical intertwinings, with the aim of tracing the evolution of legal concepts across languages and empires, and discovering what the Islamicate might have looked like in rural South Asia.

This chapter will use that portion of our family archive which deals explicitly with extraction of taxes (as opposed to allocation of its proceeds and exemption from its demands, which we have already seen in Chapter 2). The documentary type that forms the core of the source base here called itself *qaul qarār.*[8] We shall read these 'words of declaration' together other documents, including records of loans taken or sureties given in connection with the tax contracts, and petitions to higher authorities during moments of dispute. This documented transactional spectrum will be placed alongside manuals of two kinds: 'rules of governance' – *dastūr al-ʿamal* – books, which described how much tax was to be collected, and by which officials; and *munshāts/siyāqnāmas*, which taught potential scribes and accountants how to produce the necessary documents appointing such officials and recording their activities. While such manuals were completely silent as far as Islamic legal doctrine is concerned, they nevertheless offered a highly coherent vision of the Mughal state, one that continues to beguile us even today, obscuring the people and processes that constituted this state in its everyday form.

So this is an effort to the trace the substantiation of imperial theory in the reality of governance. It is also aimed at mapping the ideational matrix within which Mughal warlords-turned-tax officials functioned. The formal 'apparatus' of the Mughal empire consisted of *mansabdārs* – nobles ranked as officials – who

[7] Lambton, 'Pīshkash': Lambton concluded that *pīshkash* was representative of the 'ethos of Persian society' and a manner of protection money given to the powerful.

[8] The documents, in their characteristic top 'title' line, write *qaul qarār patta-yi ijāra*, but the cataloguers have tended to refer to them as '*qaul-o-qarār*'. Since a *vao* is not visible between the first two words, I have omitted it.

took their pay by appropriating the taxes on areas allocated to them as *jāgirs*; the armies they maintained by those funds; and a teeming army of tax officials aimed at enabling the collection of those taxes. Despite alternative genealogies and regional variations, this theory, which was repeatedly articulated and elaborated in the innumerable *dastūr al-ʿamals*, represented a system which the protagonists of our book would have recognised, because they inhabited it. In this book, it is of little importance whether Emperor Akbar invented that system or it grew out of precedents and kept growing (naturally, it did), and whether or not the *mansabdārs* were really a perfectly pliable bureaucracy (unsurprisingly, they were not). What matters is how this recognisable pattern of resource extraction led to a series of claims, some overlapping, some nested, some competing, and how some of those claims were turned to entitlements. This sociopolitical context offers us a rich opportunity for tracing the uses and evolution of legal forms and concepts, and for substantiating the concept of Islamicate law which inspires this book.

Playing multiple roles lay at the heart of the Mughal system. Just as nobles were also officials, *zamīndārs* were also functionaries, and all of them were tax speculators and eager contractors for the state. Success at the top as well as the bottom of the spectrum depended on a combination of warlordism and entrepreneurship, in a manner that makes the separation of state and economy meaningless. The founder of the family's fortunes, a certain Jayanti Das, we recall, had gained his grant of *ʿinām* villages for having worked for the populating and settling of *pargana* Dhar. He and his descendants had built up their little kingdom in the district by providing a combination of military and administrative services to the imperial regime, which led to further tax-free grants of land. As such, he was a sort of agrarian pioneer who, together with his kinsmen, ensconced himself among the ranks local powerholders, and could be counted among the 'intermediate *zamīndār*s' – not a direct cultivator, but despite occasional brushes with greatness, not quite an autonomous chieftain, either.[9]

As *zamīndārs*, or to refer to them by their Mughal office, *chaudhrīs*, Jayanti Das's descendants of course played an important role in the collection of taxes – land revenue and other cesses – that formed the financial foundation of the Mughal empire. But Jayanti Das's descendants, at least from the early seventeenth century onwards, were also noted as *qānūngōs* or revenue record keepers of *pargana* Dhar.[10] So said the copy of Prince Khurram's *nishān* that was notarised in the 1690s by Qāẕī Muhammad Mustafa, then district *qāẕī* of *pargana* Dhar. Muhammad Mustafa also verified quite a few other documents, which recorded the antecedents, status, rights and, broadly speaking, *dāʾira* or

[9] Hasan, 'Zamīndārs under the Mughals'.
[10] On the office of the *qānūngō*, Jafri, 'The Sarkar Qānūngō 16th-17th century documents'.

area of influence and authority, of the powerful local family of Mohan Das of *pargana* Dhar. These documents collectively point to a composite power and resource base, which combined control over records, revenues and roads and presents a gritty, detailed picture of how to use the coercive and extractive mechanisms of government on the one hand and legitimating and disputing functions of law on the other, in order to make a success of oneself in rural and small-town Mughal India.

## Administration, Extraction and Outsourcing

Despite all its turbulence, Malwa was known to be an exceptionally fertile and prosperous province, remarkably free of the disastrous famines that periodically afflicted other parts of the Mughal empire.[11] The *Ā'īn* described it as a temperate country with parts as pretty as fairyland, endowed with a very long sacred and secular history, including that of an alchemic *paras* stone having once been discovered there, although unfortunately lost due to human frailty. Ujjain, the provincial capital, abounded in Hindu places of worship and produced contemporary miracles for Abul Fazl to report. On his way to the Deccan March 1599 CE (month *Farwardin,* regnal year 46), Abul Fazl apparently witnessed the Shipra River, on which Ujjain was situated, flowing with streams of milk. Not all was necessarily milk and honey in this province, however, since the *Ā'īn* also noted that this was a highly militarised populace – apparently there was nobody, including the peasants and grain dealers, who were without weapons.[12] Getting taxes out of such a populace, then, was a venture that was inseparable from military operations.

For purposes of administration and taxation, the *sūba* of Malwa was divided into twelve *sarkārs*, of which Mandu was one.[13] Unlike in several of the other *sarkārs*, the caste of the *zamīndārs* of Mandu was not noted, being too varied for enumeration.[14] The total revenues collected from the province rose rapidly from the time of its conquest by the Mughals until the mid-seventeenth century, then dipping, but not precipitously, during the battle of succession leading to Aurangzeb's coronation and during the Deccan wars. But our aim here is not to assess the province's contribution to a gross national (or imperial) product, but to show how the intertwining of regulation and outsourcing, related to the main military-cum-administrative spine of the regime, proved fecund with entrepreneurial possibilities for our protagonists.

In order to understand the dynamics of this family's multiple entrepreneurial ventures, we should begin with a quick review of what we know about the

[11] Habib, *Agrarian System*, p. 20.
[12] Abul Fazl, *Ain-i Akbari*, trans. Blochman, Vol. I, pp. 195–6. [13] Ibid., pp. 198–209.
[14] Ibid., pp. 206–7.

dispensation of tax-related institutions, offices and paperwork in Mughal India. Experts of Mughal history may wish to skip this section, although a quick skim would help clarify how I see the structural features described relating to the specific dynamics of the family's fortunes.

The Mughals had a highly systematic view of the rural order that they presided over, and one that was relevant principally because it financed the imperial military–administrative hierarchy. The nobles, who in the official view were mere officers of state, were designated *mansabdārs*. Abul Fazl's *Ā'īn* had no section on 'nobility' as such; *mansabdārs* appeared in the 'book' or section on the army.[15] In a clear expression of the military ethos of the Mughal regime, all *mansabdārs*, no matter whether they were provincial governors or heads of treasury, were designated military officers; this was only partly fiction. The *mansabdārs*'s pay was graded accorded to their rank, and Abul Fazl provided a rather complex table outlining what was due to *mansabdārs* on forty-nine grades, ranging from the middling 600 to the princely 10,000.[16] The implications of the table were fervently debated by historians for several decades from the beginning of the twentieth century, until poring over pay scales in Persian manuscripts went out of academic fashion.

As we all know, however, pay scales, then as now, are highly contentious texts. They declare and record entitlements, but frame these with so many caveats and conditions that it takes an expert to decode them. And of course, they change, or their interpretation changes, fairly frequently. Already in Abul Fazl's table, there wasn't just one salary figure corresponding to one rank; for each rank several species of animals, each of multiple grades, were listed, together with the corresponding costs of maintenance of each such animal. Each rank also included three salary points – first, second and third class. The *mansabdārī* system of ranks was introduced in that form and under that name by Emperor Akbar; the idea was that commanders recruit and supply an agreed number of equipped soldiers and the equipment, including horses and other animals. At its simplest, the *mansabdār's* rank corresponded to the number of equipped horsemen he was obliged to supply, so a *mansabdār* with the rank of 500 was obliged to supply 500 horsemen on demand.

However, already in Akbar's reign and by the time of the completion of the *Ā'īn-i Akbarī* (1592), it was recognised that not all *mansabdārs* could match the number of their recruits to their rank. The *Ā'īn* provided three columns for every *mansab* rank, those who could supply the full number of horsemen being of the of the first class of that rank, those who could bring at least half that number or more were second class, and others, third class.[17] This table in the *Ā'īn* has been the source of a fair amount of confusion and debate, because it does not help us trace the emergence of the 'two-part' *mansab* rank, which most

15 Ibid., pp. 236–47. 16 Ibid., p. 248. 17 Ibid., table on p. 248.

scholars agree had already taken place in Akbar's reign, and possibly, before the *Ā'īn* was completed. In the full-blown Mughal *mansabdārī* system, the difference between the *mansabdār's* rank and the number of troopers he supplied (and was paid for) was formalised into a two-part rank – the *z̲āt* or personal rank, and *sawār*, or the number of troopers to be supplied.[18] In the two subsequent reigns – Shah Jahan's and Aurangzeb's – a further complication was introduced in that the equipage of the horsemen were taken into account – with different rates of pay being disbursed depending on whether the horsemen in question were equipped with single horses, or with two or three (very useful for forced marches).

This was a system of salary calculation comprised of multiple caveats which can be summarised as follows. A *mansabdār's* rank was split into two parts, the personal rank or '*z̲āt*', which entailed a certain allowance associated with the rank itself, regardless of any specific services, and the other part consisting of the number of horsemen or '*sawār*' they were supposed to equip, maintain and provide. The *sawār* rank was associated with a certain rate of pay per horseman. Since a *mansabdār's* contingent might include some one-horse soldiers and some two- or three-horse soldiers, his *sawār* pay would correspond to a formula that took into account the different rates payable for these differently equipped soldiers.

For all such intricate formulae for calculating salaries, most of the *mansabdārī* pay was in fact not disbursed in cash, but allocated as the right to take the taxes of designated regions. These allocations were known as *jāgīrs*, and the right-holder, the *jāgīrdār*, was the *mansabdār* seen from the vantage point of the tax office. Barring *khālṣa* lands, whose taxes were reserved for the emperor, the rest of the empire was parcelled out in *jāgīrs*. To make things even more complicated, a *mansabdār* received *jāgīrs* scattered all over the empire, which, moreover, where frequently changed – all to prevent them from slipping back to the kings they had once been, or aspiring to sovereignty. The value of the *jāgīr* naturally depended on the taxes that could be collected from the villages – *mauza'̔s* – within the *jāgir*. Some parts of the Mughal empire had been formally measured and assessed for their tax-paying capacity; these parts were called *ẓ̈ābtī*. In others, a round figure of tribute had been imposed on the clearly unsubjugated landlords. In all cases, the official revenue demand of any unit of taxation was termed *jama'̔* (from the Arabic word for collection), later *jama'̔dāmī* – referring to the collection of copper coin, *dām*, in which the taxes were paid. The officials assigning

[18] And Moreland used a series of appointment orders from the 1620s, related to the highest-ranking Rajput *mansabdārs*, to show how the salaries were in fact calculated under this system. Moreland, 'Ranks (mansab) in the Mughal Service'. Habib, 'The Mansab System' and Moosvi, 'Evolution of the Mansab System' disagreed with Moreland, but mainly over the precise date of this development.

*jāgīrs* simply had to match up the recorded tax-paying capacity of certain regions with the *mansabdār*'s salary, applying fractions if needed.

While this sounded very transparent on paper, it was already officially recognised in Akbar's time that the official tax demand was hugely inflated – a sort of imperial flourish than a reliable source of information on how much money the *mansabdār-jāgīrdār* might actually expect to receive from his *jāgīrs*. By Emperor Shah Jahan's reign, *jāgīrs* were assigned taking a 'month-ratio' into account, that is, a *jāgīr's* worth was taken to be equal to that fraction of the year, and so expressed as a twelfth. If, on the other hand, shortfalls were significant and unexpected, a *takhfīf* (from the Arabic for 'lightening') was applied to compensate.[19] The infamous *jāgīrdārī* crisis beset the Mughal empire during Aurangzeb's reign, because as more and more elites were incorporated into the empire with *mansabs*, there were fewer and fewer fully paying *jāgīrs* to go around. Collection in the newly conquered regions naturally depended on the extent of subjugation, which in turn depended on the military capacity of the *jāgīrdār* in question. Imperial surveys, in such a context, could be conventional hyperbole geared to be displays of power, rather than the collation of precise information.[20] However, the vast stores of documents across household archives, recording the minutiae of transactions, offer a different kind of source base, not just for correcting the imperial statistics, but for understanding how the system really functioned. Tax lay on the seams of the Mughal empire, where warfare met rule-referenced negotiation.

## Taxmen in the Countryside

Whatever the dues of a certain *mansabdār-jāgīrdār*, there had to be an administrative structure in place to actually collect a share of what the peasants in the allocated *jāgīr* produced. And here is where some confusion begins to enter the picture, because earlier historians produced descriptions of 'provincial administration' that offered a picture of a centrally appointed hierarchy, of which the fiscal and administrative wings were, moreover, separately managed. The fiscal side consisted of the provincial *diwān*, answering directly to the imperial *diwān*, and managing a staff of tax-recorders and collectors, and a regularly replenished store of paperwork, which was transmitted to the centre. Notably, this highly coherent picture was based primarily on manuals – the great *Ā'īn-i Akbarī* itself, and also the later, mainly eighteenth-century *dastūr*

19 Ali, *The Mughal Nobility*, pp. 74–8, is the clearest exposition of this complex system. His description of such seventeenth-century modifications are based on contemporary letters, including those of Aurangzeb, when still prince, collected in the *Ruqa'āt-i 'Alamgīrī*, documents of order and *Akhbarat* or newsletters.

20 Guha, 'Rethinking the Mughal Economy'.

*al-ʿamals*.[21] On the other hand, from the 1960s, historians, who combined their knowledge of manuals with detailed study of administrative documents similar in nature to our archive, began to emphasise the key role of the *jāgīrdārs*, and the fact that they had to appoint their own tax officials.[22] The trouble of course is that no manual of governance actually states how this was to be done: who appointed and controlled whom. We are therefore left with a blurred image, consisting of multiple alternatives. We could imagine a centrally appointed tax bureaucracy, always *in situ*, which would pass on the collected tax revenues to the current *jāgīrdār* with minimal or no intervention from him; judging even from contemporary accounts, we can be sure that this did not happen. We could also speculate on the possibility of a completely noble household-centred tax collection structure that entered and left regions together with the noble. This too, seems implausible, because we certainly have records of the post of the provincial *diwān*, including a very well-known account produced by just such a *diwān*, albeit one who was deprived of access to the *diwānī* records himself.[23] The notion of complete administrative portability also does not match the picture of long-term entrenchment at the very lowest levels, in posts such as *chaudhrīs* and *qānūngōs*, as presented by our archive and all comparable collections. The tension, then, would have been somewhere at the middle of the spectrum, around the region of the *ʿamalguzār* – the equivalent of the still-crucial post of the district magistrate – where overlapping structures wove into each other.

In his classic work, Irfan Habib focussed on an imperial system that extended from the centre down to the villages, with standard administrative personnel whose offices evolved over time. However, Habib combined this picture of uniformity, best realised in the *khālṣa* or crown lands, with the variability of the *jāgirdār's* mobile tax-office. Habib seems to suggests that in non-crown lands (that is, up to four-fifths of the empire), there was no permanent tax administration except the men that each new *jāgīrdār* brought in, their job titles mirroring offices in the *khālṣa*, and their work following imperial regulations. The only offices that were indeed local and unchanging (with *jāgīr* assignments) in all this were those of the *chaudhrī* and *qānūngō*,[24] which places the protagonists of this book at the crux of the Mughal apparatus.

More recently, Faruqui has proposed a more interlaced picture, based on his studies of the households of Mughal princes, who were also the highest-ranking nobles. Faruqui shows examples where the princes, especially Aurangzeb and

[21] Saran, *The Provincial Government of the Mughals*, pp. 174–82; 249–316.
[22] Ali, *The Mughal Nobility*, p. 82; Faruqui, *Princes*, pp. 93–9.
[23] Ali Muhammad Khan, *Mirat-i Ahmadi*, translated M. F. Lokhandwala (2 vols., Baroda: Oriental Institute, 1965), pp. 7–8, for the story of this failed search. Most administrative details are in *Mirat-i Ahmadi Supplement*, translated Syed Nawab Ali (Baroda: Oriental Institute, 1928).
[24] Habib, *Agrarian System*, pp. 316–41.

his sons, incorporated lower-ranking nobles, also holding significant administrative offices, into their household and loyalty network, and conversely, how long-standing members of the princely household were appointed to administrative posts from which they would be in a position to assist the prince in managing and milking their *jāgīrs*. We have already seen in the Chapter 2 how the petty locally based Sisodia Rajput noble, Amar Singh, was recruited by Dara Shukoh into his household to assist with the collection of taxes when Dhar was transferred from the *jāgīr* of Murad Baksh into his, in 1657. So Faruqui's suggestion of an ethnic–confessional divide, such that the only local men in the picture were the village-based Hindu officials (i.e. the *chaudhrī* and *qānūngō*),[25] possibly needs modification. Petty Rajput *mansabdārs* of local roots could equally be recruited to service the tax-collecting needs of a *jāgīr* grantee. Overall, however, all these findings point towards the crucial administrative role of the noble's household, and its interlacing, or indeed co-formation with the Mughal state, which was 'patrimonial-bureaucratic' not just at the imperial centre, but also at its lower levels.[26] The current archive offers us an unusually detailed view into the instantiation of such a system, especially through the crucial function of tax extraction, and from the vantage point of its lowest-level functionaries.

## The Mughal Vision of the Agrarian System

Although it is the everyday Mughal state and its functionaries that is our main interest in this book, it is still useful to start with Abul Fazl, like everybody else. We will then proceed to the manuals that began proliferating towards the end of the seventeenth century, in order to trace an outline of the personnel structure that was meant to structure tax-extraction in the countryside. Abul Fazl called the main imperial tax official in the district: the *'amalguzār*, alternatively known as the *'āmil*.[27] This man, said Abul Fazl, was meant to be a friend to the peasant, advancing him loans on soft terms when needed and collecting taxes flexibly, through a variety of measures, in cash as well as kind, depending on the area under cultivation and the value of the crops. Assessing taxes payable was a major part of his duties. He was supposed to deal with every agriculturist's case on an individual basis, be aware of past assessments and correct any errors therein, and make adjustments for changes in usage of land, for example, for animal husbandry rather than cultivation of crops. He was to keep stock of tax-free grants of land and check for the accuracy of land boundaries, work on abolishing illegal taxes and submit a monthly report on

[25] Faruqui, *Princes*, pp. 94–7. [26] Blake, 'The Patrimonial-Bureaucratic Empire'.

[27] *Ā'īn-i Akbarī* (Persian) ed. H. Blochmann (Calcutta: Printed for the Asiatic Society of Bengal by the Baptist Mission Press, 1872), Vol. I, pp. 285–8. I have used the Persian edition here in order to check the exact terms used.

the general conditions of the district. In addition, he was supposed to keep an eye on law and order in the area, apprehending and punishing thieves and highwaymen, and even taking on the role of the *kotwāl*, or police officer, if required.[28]

Since, however achieving all this would have been impossible for an outside appointee without the benefit of local knowledge, Abul Fazl indicated the range of extra-local and local officials who could assist the *amalguẕār*. These included specially appointed survey officers (*jarībkash* and *paimanda*), and clerks (*bitikchī* and *karkūn*), all of whom appeared to accompany him. The *amalguẕār*'s entourage also incorporated eminent villagers. All procedures of measuring, collecting and recording, while apparently administrative, included contractual elements. It began with the surveyors – the *amalguẕār* was encouraged to take *ẕamānat* (surety) from these officials – no doubt to ensure that they did not cheat. From the *kalantar* – literally biggest man (i.e. village head man) – too, a *muchalka* (agreement) was to be taken that no lands would be hidden. Then, as the official called *karkūn* kept writing the *sawānih-i ẕabtī* (record of assessment), village officials called *muqaddam* and *patwārī* would write along. It is not clear what *ham-qalam bāshand* implies, since it could mean both keeping their own records and writing on the same document. But it is clear that mutual checking, validation and signing to indicate such validation was an essential part of the process. At the end of the assessment process, the *amalguẕār* would compare the documents, seal them with his own seal, and give a copy to the *bitikchī*. This detailed record – called *khasra* – would be sent by the *bitikchī* to the court, but an abstract would be entered into the village accounts, which would be reverified by the *karkūn* and the *patwarī*, and then forwarded to the imperial centre.

When it came to actual collection of the taxes, the official called *bitikchī*, a constant companion of the *amalguẕār*, appeared to be the accountant who would interact with the villagers paying the taxes and the *pargana* and villager record keepers, the *muqaddam* and *patwārī*, most intensively. *Bitikchī* and *karkūn* may have been alternative ways of referring to the same accountant always accompanying the *amalguẕār*, because Abul Fazl assigns the same tasks to one and then the other, and only defines the post of *bitikchī*. In any case the *bitikchī/karkūn* would maintain a *roznāmcha* (day-ledger) of collections and periodically send these ledgers to the court. It is in connection with the *bitikchī*'s office that the tasks of a host of village officials, and the papers they would regularly generate, are slightly elaborated: the *qānūngō* would maintain and supply the *muwāzana dah-sāla* (ten-year rent records),[29] the

[28] Abul Fazl, *Ain-i Akbari*, English, Vol. II, pp. 43–7.

[29] For samples and analysis of *taqsīm* and *muwāzana dah-sāla* documents from the eastern Rajasthani district of Udehi, which was given as *jāgir* to the Rajas of Jodhpur and then Jaipur, see Satya Prakash Gupta and Sumbul Halim Khan, *Mughal Documents: Taqsim (c. 1649–c. 1800)* (Jaipur: Publication Scheme, 1993).

*patwārī* would also maintain rent rolls called *taujīh*, according to which the *muqaddam* would collect the taxes. Copies of the *patwārī's* rent rolls had to be supplied to the *bitikchī* for cross-checking with his own collection records, along with the *sarkhat* or *yad-dāshti* documents that had been given to the cultivators, perhaps as a receipt. Periodically, the *bitikchī* would send his ledgers, countersigned by the treasurer and the *'āmīl*, to the court.[30] The *muqaddam* would retain, for his pains, the collections of one *biswa* per *bīgha* of land, that is, 1/20 of the collections. But the *muqaddams* were constantly suspect: Abul Fazl warned the *amalguzār* not to allow the *muqaddams* to make their own tax assessments, lest they oppress the peasants.

Abul Fazl's description left a lot unclear about these several officials, their exact duties, the length of their office-holding, and their mutual hierarchy. Among other things, there is no mention of the office of *chaudhrī* – which, in combination with *qānūngō*, kept our protagonists in business over so many generations. Things are both clarified and complicated with reference to the proliferating manuals of governance and related enumeration and documentation – the *dastūr al-'amal*, *munshāts* and *siyāqnāmas* – that became very popular in the early eighteenth century, many bearing dedicative titles naming the Emperor Alamgir. Taken together, these overlapping genres offered further details by providing model forms of appointment to various posts, including the lower-ranking ones that did not quite make the cut with Abul Fazl.

## *Dastūr al-'amal* – Rules for Doing Things

Despite their abundance, the *dastūrs* are difficult sources. One source of difficulty is the variety in nomenclature for what appears to be the same posts; while some of the differences arise from regional conventions, in other cases we can only speculate why one title is used rather than another. The village-level tax-collecting officer whom Abul Fazl called *muqaddam*, for example, appears to be the same as the *chaudhrī* of Hindustan (northern and central India), the *desāī* of Gujarat and some parts of the Marathi-writing areas and the *dēśmukh* or *munīwar* of Dakhin (western and southern India). At the neatest conceptualisation, the *muqaddam/chaudhrī/dēśmukh/desāī* was a man co-opted by the regime from among several village headmen and, by his standing, inevitably a *zamīndār*.[31] The Sikh empire, which retained and

[30] Abul Fazl, *Ain-i Akbari*, English, Vol. II, pp. 47–9; *Ā'īn-i Akbarī* (Persian), p. 288.

[31] Habib, *Agrarian System*, p. 335; J. F. Richards, *Mughal Administration in Golconda* (Oxford: Clarendon Press, 1975), p. 141. Habib bases this conflation on Khwaja Yasin's dictionary, Add. 6603, which was produced for the British, Charles Alfred Elliott, *The Chronicles of Oonao, A District in Oudh* (Allahabad: Allahabad Mission Press, 1862), and his extensive study of documents similar to ours; Richards bases it on his analysis of the huge store of documents from Mughal Golconda, which is the Inayat Jung Collection, NAI, New Delhi.

elaborated the Mughal administrative posts and terms, and was most closely observed *in vivo* by the British, had one or more *muqaddams* in every village, but only some of them were *chaudhrīs* whose hereditary job was to collect taxes, taking a share of the collections as commission. But the extent of overlap between (even) these north Indian terms – *chaudhrī, muqaddam* – remains murky, because contemporary documents reveal that both *chaudhrī* and *muqaddam* could also be termed *panch*, thus also associating this position with that of the legendary five elders of village governance.[32]

The other, and rather serious difficulty arises from what we can surmise about the context of production of these *dastūr al-ʿamal* manuals. Some of the most elaborate of these, frequently used by historians, were clearly produced under British pressure and patronage. In fact, the form was so popular with eighteenth-century Company officials, that there were British *dastūr al-ʿamals* produced, to explain the workings of the undeniably novel Company courts in familiar Persianate idiom, perhaps to the Indian personnel of these courts.[33] And while accessing the Mughal system via the accounts of carried-over personnel is a logical idea, there are risks of ignoring the possible interests such people would have had in representing things in a certain way. And in this connection, it is rather crucial that, in elaborating the office of the *chaudhrī,* these eighteenth-century manuals were commenting on the status of *zamīndār* – perhaps the single most contentious policy issue of eighteenth-century colonial India.

Before we take a look at these manuals then, we have to take note of the other position that brought rewards and tax-free lands to our protagonists – that of the *qānūngō*. Mohan Das had been a *qānūngō*, and his grandson, Purshottam Das, himself styled *chaudhrī*, appeared to work in constant conjunction with individuals called Paras Ram and Parmanand, both *qānūngōs*. The *qānūngō*, if we remember our Abul Fazl, was the first point of contact in the district for the imperial *bitikchī* – supplying him with ten years worth of revenue records on demand. Unlike British observers of the eighteenth and nineteenth century, historians are generally of the opinion that the classic Mughal system consisted of two entirely distinct offices. The *qānūngō* was a hereditary accountant and record keeper, drawn predominantly from literacy- and numeracy-oriented castes, such as *Kāyasth* or Brahmin,[34] and therefore both institutionally and sociologically distinct from the martial *zamīndār* who worked as *chaudhrī*. The

[32] Indu Banga, *Agrarian System of the Sikhs: Late Eighteenth and Early Nineteenth Centuries* (Delhi: Manohar, 1978), pp. 83–6, citing Ghulam Muhammad, *Dastūr al-ʿAmal*, Or. 1690 British Library, f. 15a; *Munshī* Bakhtawar Lal, *Tarikh-i Montgomery*, Ganesh Das, *Char Bagh*, British reports and Khalsa records.

[33] *Dastūr al-ʿamal mutażammin bar navad va panj āʾīn barā-yi intiẓām-i umūr-i ʿadālathā-yi dīvānī-i ṣadr va mufaṣṣal* (A Persian Translation of the Regulations for the Administration of Justice in the Courts of Suddur and Mofussil Dewannee Adauluts) (Calcutta: Charles Wilkins, 1782).

[34] Siddiqi, *Land Revenue Administration*, pp. 87–91.

fact that distinguished *qānūngōs* acquired extensive grants of land, and even *mansabs*, building up huge *zamīndārīs* in the process,[35] is seen as an unintended outcome, and actual Mughal grants appointing individuals simultaneously to the posts of *chaudhrī* and *qānūngō* as a symptom of imperial decline. Indeed, historians may be echoing a colonial commonplace: British colonial officials in the early nineteenth century were convinced that, with the decline of previously centralised imperial power, there was an epidemic of land-grabbing, facilitated by the connivance of lower-level record keepers, especially *qānungōs*,[36] or worse still, by the clubbing of official positions with portfolio investment.[37] But what did the manuals say?

In the late eighteenth and early nineteenth centuries, when the East India Company was expanding its claims on the revenues of the various parts of the now-crumbling Mughal empire, there was something of a minor Orientalist craze for acquiring guides that would explain just how Mughal administration and its Indo-Persian paperwork functioned, and would open the caves of treasure that lurked just beyond reach. An internally diverse genre of Persian-language manuals began to pour into the collections of specific individuals, particularly, those involved with the supervision of the perpetually suspect Indian administrative officials.

One such collector was James Grant, the first British *sarishtadār* (record keeper), appointed in Bengal in 1786.[38] Grant's contribution to the India Office's and, ultimately, the British Library's collection of Persian manuscripts, many identifiable by the large Persian-language seal he used, was decidedly functional in scope. It included a *dastūr al-ʿamal* which has been frequently cited by historians of the Mughal empire.[39] This text purported to have been composed in the third year of Aurangzeb's reign, under his orders. All this was rendered rather untrustworthy by the fact that the unnamed author got the Hijri date for the regnal year wrong, taking it to be AH1065 rather than AH1070, as no near-contemporary would. This quite-likely late-eighteenth-century composition offered detailed instructions on enumeration and calculation in the context of tax-collection, using various locations in northern India to

[35] Richards, *Mughal Administration*, pp. 162–7, discussing the career of Babu Pandit, the Brahmin *dēśpāndē* (southern *qānūngō*) of Hyderabad, who was also classified as *zamīndār*.

[36] See, for example, cases discussed in the Enclosures to the Resolution, Government of India, Revenue Department, 2 April 1824, on points connected with the Special Commission appointed under Regulation I of 1821; and Minutes of the Members of the Sudder Commission, in *Selections from the Revenue Records, North-West Provinces* (Allahabad: Government Press, 1873), pp. 124–9.

[37] Elliott, *The Chronicles of Oonao*, pp. 112–13, discussing the gradual takeover by wily *qānungōs*.

[38] P. J. Marshall, 'Indian Officials under the East India Company in Eighteenth-Century Bengal', *Bengal Past and Present*, 84, Part II, 158 (1965), pp. 95–120.

[39] *Dastūr al-ʿamal-i ʿAlamgīrī*, Add. 6598, ff. 1a–128b and Add. 6599, ff. For instance, Irfan Habib cites this text several times in *Agrarian System*.

Afghanistan as realistic locales for the various sample revenue accounts that should be written, and the associated procedures that had to be followed. For all its detail, it did not actually descend to officers at the village level and their functions, and instead offered generalities about the *khidmat-i diwāngirī* (office of diwan), for example, that all officers associated with it, down to the *zamīndārs*, should be well adjusted to each other, collect and forward all paperwork generated by *'amils* to the office of the *diwān*, so that the rights of the Lord were respected and nobody was oppressed.[40]

There are several *dastūr al-'amals*, in James Grant's and several other late-eighteenth-century collections, all with various imperial dedications.[41] The contents can vary widely: some are only light-touch surveys of provinces and districts therein, without any mention of offices, posts or procedures and united only by a neo-imperial interest in administration.[42] The codices in which these *dastūrs* are bound contain a second kind of manual, called *khulāṣat al-siyāq*, which elaborated further on the method of writing the cryptic accountancy numbers which were the stock-in-trade of tax officials.[43] These numerals were logographs based on abbreviations of Arabic words for numbers, and were predictably used in documents that needed to record exact numbers, such as tax records, or indeed, transactional documents. Naturally, cracking the code for such numerals became a serious concern for the East India Company.[44] The manuals that we may think of as 'Mughal' were very likely the product of that colonial effort to access the Ali Baba's cave of Indian taxes.

Dictionaries were a third kind of guide into this intricate world, once again produced in abundance during the long colonial transition.[45] In the early nineteenth century, Khwaja Yasin, resident of Daha, in Karnal district (about seventy miles from Delhi), wrote a dictionary for the use of British officials. Khwaja Yasin's short Persian-language dictionary was focussed on administrative terminology and, in particular, on Indian words – *lafẓ-i Hindī* – as well as regional usages. For example, it offered the word *chākarān* but explained

[40] *Dastūr al-'amal-i 'Alamgīrī*, Add. 6598, ff. 108a-109a and Add. 6599, ff. 1b-132a.

[41] For example, *Dastūr al-'amal Shāhjahānī* Add. 6588, ff. 15–47, which is another of James Grant's.

[42] *Munshī* Thakur Lal, *Dastūr al-'amal-i Shāhenshāhī*, Add. 22831, completed in 1778 and purchased in an auction.

[43] Anon., *Khulāṣat al-siyāq*, British Library, Add. 6588 (Ibid.), ff. 64–94. Najaf Haider uses this manuscript, among others, in his 'Norms of Professional Excellence and Good Conduct in Accountancy Manuals of the Mughal Empire', *International Review of Social History*, 56 (2011), 263–74.

[44] 'Figures called rukkum' in Charles Stewart, *Original Persian Letters and Other Documents* (London: William Nicol, 1825), facing p. viii.

[45] Walter Hakala, *Negotiating Languages: Urdu, Hindi and the Definition of Modern South Asia* (New York: Columbia University Press, 2016). Hakala focusses mainly on lexicons produced in literary contexts.

that it belonged to the *muhāwara* (idiom or usage) of Bengal.[46] It also included variations of word meanings, offering a much larger range of offices for the administrative term *ʿāmil*, than that envisaged by Abul Fazal. According to Yasin, the term could be applied to anybody who held a position of trust (*amānī*), which could well include officials of law courts.[47] With regards to *chaudhrī*, he had an interesting sociological explanation preceding the administrative one: '*chaudhrī sardār-i firqa rā guyand . . . har kasī ke az zamīndāran muaʿtamad alaīhū bāshad ū-rā az sarkār khitāb-i chaudhrāī dehand* (the leader of a sect is called *chaudhrī* . . . all those among the *zamīndārs* who are reliable are given the title of *chaudhrāī* by the government)'. The gloss continued, in a rather ungrammatical sentence: 'Working as the helper of the *ḥākim* in everything, his task is *mālguzārī* (collecting taxes). The other, smaller *zamīndārs* were given a *ẕāminī* (bond) by the *ḥākim*, contracting them to pay the taxes. And the custom was that everyone of the *ẕāminī mālguzārs* took 5 per cent (of the collections) as the right of *nānkār*'. Towards the end of the definition, Khwaja Yasin noted that all groups had *chaudhrīs*, even the artisans, for example.[48] This definition, which combined social eminence, reliability from point of view of the regime, and one or more contracts, offered a satisfactorily rounded view of a post that derived from status and was formalised by agreement.

The last type of manual written by Indian authors that we should consider here are forms of appointment orders. This was indisputably based on an older genre and shaded into the broader area of Persian-language formularies, or *munshāts*. These, too, were extremely popular among Company Orientalists, and were among the first Persian texts to be translated to English. One such formulary of appointment orders was produced in the early eighteenth century, by an individual who was surmised by the historian John F. Richards to have been a junior official in a central or provincial revenue department during Aurangzeb's reign. This text describes the posts of *chaudhrī* and *qānūngō* in tandem, thus: 'at this time, according to the exalted order, *falān* (so-and-so) is appointed to the *khidmat* (service/office) of *chaudhrāī* and *qānūngōi* of *pargana* so-and-so due to the transfer of so-and-so upon payment of (amount) *pīshkash* (tribute)'. The 'so-and-so' form of anonymising documents points to a modular standard, one intended to be copied without much introspection. The officer thus appointed was then instructed to both maintain and despatch tax records to the provincial *diwān*, as well as maintain law and order and refrain from illegal extractions.[49] Based on his extensive research, especially into the administrative system in Golconda,

[46] Add. 6603, British Library, ff. 58a [47] Ibid., ff. 72b–73a. [48] Ibid., ff.

[49] John F. Richards, *Document Forms for Official Orders of Appointment in the Mughal Empire* (Cambridge: E. J. W. Gibb, 1986), which introduced, translated and produced facsimiles of the eighteenth century *dastūr al-ʿamal* previously described. The text can be seen in the reproduction of folio 220a and Richards' translation on p. 41; I have translated the text slightly differently.

Richards deemed such conflation of posts exceptional,[50] but there are further such conflations suggested even within this manual – the military and fiscal posts of *faujdār* and *amīn* (referred to as *amānat*) are co-awarded in a single model appointment form.[51] At least by the early eighteenth century, then, the writers of formularies expected such conflations. In case of the *chaudhrī-qānūngō*, the demand of *pīshkash* (which we have also come across in Chapter 2) identified such appointments as part of a process of attrition and incorporation of rural notables, rather than unilateral imperial appointment.[52]

Historians of the Mughal empire have used these manuals intensively and in conjunction with sources they consider entirely distinct, if useful, namely, accounts of East India Company officials looking to understand the system. In fact, although separated by language and authorial identity, the Persian and English accounts were both products of the same process of colonial investigation into the Mughal system, and in using them, it is important to be aware that we are following a well-trodden path of colonial discovery. Thus the famous 'Amini Report' of Bengal, produced in 1778, under direct orders of Warren Hastings, was part of that effort to settle the revenues of Bengal (i.e., establish how much taxes were to be paid and by whom). It classified the taxes and the tax-payers, in the process defining a *zamīndār* as the 'superior of a district, of which . . . he collects the rent for which he pays a revenue to the government', but also, rather confusingly given what we have seen before, as superior to a *chaudhrī*.[53] This may have been Bengal-specific usage or an error, but the Amini Report did offer useful definitions of the *zamīndārs'* rights, such as the *nānkār*, the proceeds of land set apart revenue-free to support him.[54] It also described the types of documents and subordinate offices a *zamīndārī* required. Around the same time, there was a report produced on the post of the *qānūngō*, with an aim to assessing the usefulness of this office. This report included long lists of the kind of documents a *qānūngō* was supposed to maintain, including rent rolls and copies of *qabūliyats* (deeds of acceptance entered into by *zamīndārs*).[55] No rent roll documents have been found in the reconstructed archives of the protagonists of this book. Nor do we see the papers related to *zamīndārī* administration in Bengal in the early nineteenth century. We have to provisionally conclude, therefore, that either the regional traditions were significantly different or the kinds of documents considered essential to preserve in early colonial Bengal were different from those in Mughal Malwa.[56]

50 Ibid., p. 41, note 1. 51 Ibid., pp. 35–6. 52 Ibid., pp. 41–2, note 2.

53 'The Amini Report', in R. B. Ramsbotham, *Studies in the Land Revenue History of Bengal, 1769–1787* (Bombay: Humphrey Milford, 1926), pp. 99–134; at p. 102–3.

54 Ibid., p. 107

55 'Report on the Office of the Kanungo', produced in 1787 and reproduced in Ibid., pp. 162–97.

56 D. Carmichael Smyth, *Original Bengalese Zumeendaree Accounts, accompanied with a translation* (Calcutta, 1829).

Despite their detail, and hence their usefulness in opening up the underbelly of *zamīndārī*, what these British-commissioned manuals and surveys lacked was a sense of politics that so characterises the documents in our collection; the constant negotiation between village strongmen and imperial nobles, and all who passed in between. It was that negotiation that contextualises the contractually toned documents, as well as the pleadings and receipt of royal grace. In decapitating the Mughal and post-Mughal polities, the Company Raj, despite its name and ceremonial, aimed to reduce systematic jostling to routinised administration. And in working through colonial-era Persian materials, historians may have been distracted by the language and misled into taking colonial ambition for description of precolonial reality.

## Contractual Incorporation: the Reality of Governance

The Mughals had such a vision of perfect order themselves. As we have seen, the *chaudhrī* and *qānūngō* were supposed to be locally co-opted officials, their roles clearly distinguished: military ability made a good *chaudhrī* and accountancy skills made a good *qānūngō*. The offices also mapped on to what are now seen as caste-specific skills. In reality, however, things were more blurred, and precisely because of the necessity of collaboration between the *chaudhrī* and the *qānūngō*. Whether or not this was a symptom of imperial decline, such overlap in posts was also the case with our family. But it was not just Purshottam Das's family that concentrated these posts among kinsmen, or even in the same hands.

In the neighbouring *sarkār* of Chanderi, a family of *qānūngōs* had built up substantial fortunes, based on initial direct contact with a prince and the imperial court and sustained reaffirmation of their position and perquisites by repeated imperial orders. They gained control over several villages, tax-free, as *ʿinām*, bestowed their names on some of these villages and established marts blessed by the imperial court.[57] In comparison, Mohan Das's family dealt in a smaller territory, only a district or two, as opposed to an entire *sarkār*.

As we know from John Richards's detailed work of Mughal administration in Golconda using the largest extant collection of Mughal administrative documents, the *chaudhrī* (*dēśmukh* in the Deccan) gave an undertaking or *qabūliyat* whereby he promised to collect and deposit an agreed sum of money in the provincial treasury. Such agreements were made every two or three years, and in some cases, especially during times of transition, involved the payment of an enormous 'fee' for the privilege, whether to the locally deputed *mansabdār* (noble) or to the imperial court directly.[58] From the point

[57] Jafri, 'Sarkar Qānūngō'.

[58] Richards, *Mughal Administration*, provides a detailed description of this process of incorporation, which documented instances of the payment of such special fees. See especially pp. 110–34.

of view of the regime, this process of give and take and mutual attrition was part of incorporating the local aristocracy into the state apparatus; from the point of view of *zamīndārs*-turned-*chaudhrīs*, it was a risky investment, whose success depended on their military as well as diplomatic skills, for they had to extract the taxes engaged for (plus make a profit) from the peasants, while maintaining some kind of alignment with the bureaucratic ideal of objective surveys, transparent and accurate records and bloodless tax-collection. Maintaining that alignment depended a great deal on collaboration with the other official named by Abul Fazl, the *qānūngō*; it was therefore most convenient for the *zamīndār*-contractor when he, or his family members, could hold both offices at once.

The association of the rural warlords with the tax-extracting state is well documented first and foremost in a type of document called *qaul qarār*, of which we have fifteen in our collection, all from the National Archives of India, except two, which are from the family's household in Dhar. They range in date from 1626 to 1726, which could point to this being a Mughal form abandoned by the Marathas, or it could simply be a function of the sparseness of surviving documents for the family after the second quarter of the eighteenth century.

The earliest *qaul* in the collection, dated 1626, began the Persian section thus: '*Qaul qarār patta-yi ijāra-yi mauza ͑ Mohanpur fī ͑amal-i pargana Dhar sarkār Mandu gīrad* [?] *az qabūliyat-i Purshottam Das* . . . ' (A *qaul qarār* document of lease of the village of Mohannpur in the administration of district Dhar, *sarkār* Mandu, was taken by the agreement of Purshottam Das . . .). The document detailed the amount of *māl-jihāt* (land tax) and *sāyirjāt* (other taxes) that Purshottam Das would pay for the three years of 1034 to 1036: 46 rupees in the first year, and 52 rupees per year thereafter. The amounts of money payable are written in the *siyāq* numbers that we touched upon earlier in this chapter, as well as Hindi numerals. The calendar used is a combination of Islamic months (13 *Zu al-qa ͑da*, in this case) and Faslī years.[59] The document bore two seals, the more legible one saying '*Banda* (slave/slave of) Sundar Das *jīū*' in Persian script. The identity of Sundar Das is not clear: he may have been an ancestor whom members of the family venerated in their personal seals, or he may have been a revenue official, possibly also a relative. The Hindi version, in the bottom half of the document, followed the Persian text closely but not entirely. While the first four lines followed the Persian so closely that nearly all the words were identical although written in the Nagri, rather than Perso-Arabic script, the next three lines added elaborations not provided in the Persian section. It also ended with instructions in a different formula. The Persian portion ended with '*mublagh maẕkūr rā sāl besāl faṣl befaṣl bi lā ͑ujar jawāb gūyand*' (he will answer for the

[59] In fact, the calendar is not indicated in the document; I have chosen to follow the cataloguer's judgement.

said amount from year to year and season to season, without excuse), whereas the Hindi added a bit of declarative flourish and a pat on the back '*sahī hamāra kaul bōle hai, khātir jama kar kamāī karṇā. Bidi*' (A true/valid *kaul* has been uttered. Earn with a settled mind).[60] The *shikasta* of the Persian section is particularly difficult to read but the words are distinguished; the Hindi, on the other hand, is even harder because of the absence of word breaks and the incursion of graphemes now associated with other languages, such as the character for 'ja' in Marathi/Modi and Gujarati. The use of the retroflex nasal in the imperative verb endings, as in *karṇā* indicates a Rajasthani phonology, which accords well with the Malwi/Rangri later observed in use in the region.

*Qauls* were the most persistently bilingual and bi-scribal of all document types encountered in this family's archives – typically, with Persian in the upper half of the document and Hindi in the lower. Examining similarly bilingual legal and administrative documents from sixteenth-century south-western India, Sumit Guha has suggested that these were the result of greater state penetration into the countryside and its resources. Even in the seventeenth century, after self-conscious efforts in the Maratha empire to create a Sanskrit-derived administrative and diplomatic vocabulary, the Marathi used in the substantive portion of the documents continued to abound in vernacularised Persian words. As Guha suggests, such language use attests to a specific kind of plurilingual skill set possessed by administrative functionaries, who knew some Persian administrative terms and formulae by heart and found it easiest to use these in the Marathi/Moḍi script when writing out formal orders that were dictated by kings and commanders. Such scribes may not have been able to write the Perso-Arabic script, at all, or very well.[61] If this was indeed so, then this is very similar to the social context that produced the Judaeo-Arabic documents of the Cairo Genizah, and possibly the Judaeo-Persian documents of the Afghan Genizah, in which, incidentally, the writers demonstrate at least some facility in writing the Arabic script, too.[62]

The villages and places named in these documents map out the area of operations and influence – *dā'ira* – for Purshottam Das, his descendants and his associates. Ten of these *qauls* are for individual *mauza'̒s* – Mohanpur (twice), Nalawada (three times), Antrai, Nekpur (twice), Ekalduna and one unidentifiable[63] – for sums that range from 35 rupees (Mohanpur, 1654) to nearly 900 rupees (Nalawada, 1664). The villages are arranged in a tight circle

[60] NAI 2703/2, 1626.

[61] Sumit Guha, *Mārgī, Deśī and Yāvanī: High Language and Ethnic Speech in Mahrarashtra*, in *Mārga: Ways of Liberation, Empowerment and Social Change in Maharashtra* (Delhi: Manohar, 2008), pp. 129–46.

[62] Ofir Haim, 'An Early Judeo-Persian Letter Sent from Ghazna to Bāmiyān (Ms. Heb. 4° 8333.29)', *Bulletin of the Asia Institute*, 26 (2012), 103–19.

[63] NAI 2703/2 (1626); 2668/2 (1643); 2703/3 (1654); BRD 28 (1662); NAI 2668/5 (1663); 2703/15 (1664); P Das 1664ii NCD (1664); 2668/2 (1693); 2703/33 (1693); 2703/40 (1717) and 2703/43 (1726).

around the city of Dhar, and I do not have information to judge why one of these villages would be viewed as so much more valuable to a contractor for revenue than the others. There are also *qauls* of higher value and for larger regions – Purshottam Das took on *ijāra* the entire neighbouring *pargana* of Jamli in 1659, for what appears to be a paltry sum of 901 rupees.[64] In 1655, that is, in the same year that he was confirmed in his *chaudhrī*-ship of *pargana* Dhar, Purshottam Das joined several others in a collective *qaul* for the entire *pargana* of Dhar, for the amount of 89,501 rupees,[65] which offered a discount in case of locust attacks; in 1659, he was party to another collective *qaul*, worth 109,571 rupees.[66] In two of these three district *qauls*, the seal is that of Nawazish Khan, the long-time *jāgirdār* of the area, and the marginal notes are in the bold hand associated with his *parvānas*. Clearly, at some point, this *jāgirdār* felt it most convenient to deal with the entire district rather than for one village at a time; Purshottam Das, the recently elevated patriarch of the family, was ready to step up to provide the lead. The two collective *qaul* documents are very useful for mapping out a range of associates for the core line of the family – we see Purshottam Das *chaudhrī* in the lead, followed by his most long-standing partner, Paras Ram *qānūngō*, and a host of others who are later glossed as the *muqaddamān* and *ijāradarān* of the *pargana*. Many of these were Purshottam Das's relatives, near and far: there was his cousin Suraj Bhan in both cases, and in the second there were also Tilok Chand and Kanwal Das, more distant cousins with whom he had disputed over hereditary entitlements.

Thus although the *qaul* of 1626, just discussed, was a contract with an individual, for one village and bilingual, this is not true of all the *qauls* in the collection. Seven of them, that is, nearly half the number, are only in Persian. There does not appear to be any identifiable pattern to the use of languages – Persian-only *qauls* appear throughout the date range, for individual as well as collective *qauls*.

Since the usage of documents changes their meaning, it is unproductive to offer a single definition of what a *qaul* was. However, this was a prolific documentary form that shared linguistic space with Persian, Indic languages and Arabic, each language-zone introducing its own phonetic and semantic variations. To take some examples, in the Marathi (and Persian)-writing areas, *kaul* or *kaulnāma* indicated a document of assurance, which was renamed *abhayapatra* in the Sanskritising later seventeenth century.[67] Possibly first produced in the fourteenth century, some of these *kaulnāmas* were bilingual (Marathi and Persian), but the majority in Persianised Marathi continued to be produced well into the colonial period and were used to record a range of dealings which required assurances.[68] Meanwhile

[64] NAI 2703/9 (1659). [65] NAI 2703/4 (1655). [66] NAI 2703/7 (1659).
[67] Guha, *Mārgī, Deśī and Yāvanī*, p. 140.
[68] Prachi Deshpande, 'Property, Sovereignty and Documentation: Marathi *Kaulnāmas* from Persianate to Colonial Eras', Unpublished MSS shared kindly by the author.

in the Telugu- and Tamil-writing region, and especially the warrior-state of Pudokottai, which came into existence in the seventeenth century, '*kaval*' indicated protection, while the king assumed '*patikkaval*' rights which entailed the right/duty to protect a '*pati*' or place.[69] In the nineteenth century, Indian Ocean mariners referred to safe-conduct passes as *qawls*, and used these in combination with flags of various regimes that might afford them protection against capture at sea.[70]

Thirteen of the fifteen documents in our collection all begin with the words *Qaul qarār patta-yi ijāra*; the four words making up this titular phrase presenting a wonderful example of linguistic hybridisation across Arabic, Persian and Hindi through administrative practice. The word *qaul*, means 'speech' or 'utterance' in Arabic, and derives from the Arabic root *q-w-l*, which is related to a spectrum of meanings related to the speech act. Conventionally, all *hadith* began with '*Qala* .. (He said/reported)'. *Qarār* was another common Arabic word, meaning a resolution or settlement, derived from the root *q-r-r*, which in turn generates a range of words associated with the sense of stability, finality, settling. A word derived from that complex is *iqrār*, which is a technical legal term in Islamic law, implying a binding declaration, which counts as the best evidence in an Islamic tribunal. Together, then, *qaul* and *qarār* referred to an Arabic vocabulary, and implied an utterance that settled matters, ironically, encoded in writing in Persian and Hindi.

But the next two words took the mixing of vocabularies and concepts several stages further: *paṭṭā*, with its characteristic retroflex consonants is a Sanskrit word that bears a range of meanings from tablet or plate for writing on, a document written on that plate, or a diadem (similarly indicating title). Interchangeable with *patra*, the word is very similar to the Persian *nāma*, in indicating textual genres that ranged from personal letters to royal edicts and official reports. In Persian documents that use the word *paṭṭā* itself (as in the one we have just seen), the retroflex sound, characteristic of the Indic soundscape is not indicated, and indeed, this is the orthographic pattern well into the nineteenth century. In colonial India, *paṭṭās* were ubiquitous, and referred to a range of title-deeds pertaining to property and entitlements related to land, but also more abstract rights, such as employment. In his dictionary, Khwaja Yasin produced a definition of the term, explaining that it was a *lafẓ-i Hindī*, and provided alongside a model which defined the rights and responsibilities of a revenue-paying *zamīndār*.[71] The states of Marwar from the nineteenth century compiled registers of such deeds in *paṭṭā-bahīs* which are still a major object of interest for landowners in those areas.

69 Dirks, *The Hollow Crown*, p. 145.
70 Fahad Ahmad Bishara, '"No country but the ocean": Reading International Law from the Deck of an Indian Ocean Dhow, ca. 1900', *Comparative Studies in Society and History*, 60: 2 (2018), 338–66, at 350, 360–2.
71 Add. 6603, ff. 52b-53, British Library.

Finally, *ijāra*. This Arabic word, implying lease, was the only unambiguously legal word in the quartet of terms that made up the name of this document. Today known worldwide as a device used to achieve *sharīʿa*-compliant mortgages, there is an extensive jurisprudential literature associated with *ijāra*, much of which concerns the risks of usury or *ribaʿ*, which is prohibited in Islamic law. In the Mughal context, it was most commonly associated with revenue farming, that is, a contract undertaken to collect taxes in an area and pay in a fixed sum – whether to the imperial tax office or a *jāgirdār*. Although it appears that the method was frowned upon, it was still widespread.[72] Colonial surveys in northern India in the early nineteenth century tried to distinguish the real ownership rights of the *zamindār*, from a mere contractor or *mustājir* (one who had taken on an *ijāra* contract), but found that things were often too tangled to separate.[73] In the *qaul qarār paṭṭā-yi ijāra* documents, we see direct record of that complex transactional bundle that combined local power with tax contracting.

The protracted late-eighteenth-century process of colonial ethnography and archival hunts uncovered a vast amount of documentation related to rural landholding, including several *qauls*. Some of these were from the Northern Circars (or the northern *sarkārs*) which were ceded to the English East India Company in 1765 by the embarrassed Mughal Emperor Shah Alam, out of the area controlled by the provincial governor-turned-ruler of the Hyderabad state, Nizam ul-Mulk Asaf Jah, and only gradually wrested by the British from the latter's control.[74] The detritus of the colonial machinery-in-formation was analysed by an Orientalist named Charles Frances Greville, who had never been to India but had very strong views about its governance.[75] Greville advocated careful scanning of *sanads* (documents) of various *zamīndārs* and an effective land registry, believing, like the James Grant he quoted approvingly, that much revenue was being lost to the state otherwise.[76]

Among these crucial documents were 'cowles' that, according to Greville, used to be given to *zamīndārs* every year by the Mughal district revenue officer, the *ʿāmil*, based on a rent roll prepared by the great accountant Todar Mal in 1592. Naturally, that rent roll had to be locally updated with more recent information about *hustobood* (*hast-o-būd*, that which is and was), based on

[72] Habib, *Agrarian System*, pp. 274–5.

[73] *Selections from the Revenue Records, North-West Provinces*, p. 18, 128–9.

[74] For a history of these events, see Karen Leonard, 'The Hyderabad Political System and Its Participants', *Journal of Asian Studies*, 20: 3 (1971), 569–82.

[75] Charles Frances Greville, *British India Analyzed: the Provincial and Revenue Establishment of Tippoo Sultan and of Mahomedan and British Conquerors of Hindostan* (London: R. Faulder, 1795), p. xiii.

[76] James Grant, 'Political Survey of the Northern Circars', in W. K. Firminger (ed.) *Fifth Report From the Select Committee of the House of Commons on the* Affaris *of the East India Company* (Calcutta: R. Cambray & Co., 1918), pp. 1–118; Greville, *British India Analyzed*, pp. 148–9.

the *daul* or more specific documents in the possession of the *zamīndārs*.[77] Our *qaul*, then, would become the next year's *daul* – and form part of the *kāghaz̠-i khām* (rough papers) in Hindavi that Emperor Aurangzeb supposedly demanded be acquired from every village, translated and their contents or summary entered into the official Persian rent roll or *tumār*, all in the interest of more transparent and efficient revenue administration.[78] Believing in the truth of its findings, the Company government continued to hand out 'cowles' to *zamindārs* well into the nineteenth century, giving Mughal terminology and forms an extended lease of life. That formal extension, however, flattened out a political process into an image of free-market contracting. Fortunately, in our collection, we have documents that reveal to us the multiple negotiations that surrounded the contracts of the *qaul qarār* in Mughal-era Malwa.

## Conflicts and Resolution

The *mansabdār-jagīrdār* Nawazish Khan had developed a symbiotic relationship with our *zamindār* family, as we have seen in Chapter 2. The noble was able to order Purshottam Das to look for camel thieves, run up to court for unstated emergencies and send along valuable supplies, in turn confirming their titles and intervening in family disputes to sort out the errant relative Suraj Bhan. But when it came to taxes, his own salary depended on it, and there was no room for a soft touch. In a peremptory *parvāna* dated 13 *Z̠u al-qaʿda* 1073 AH (18 June 1663), Nawazish Khan noted that Purshottam Das *chaudhrī* and Paras Ram *qānūngō*, both of Dhar, had sent in a petition about the collection of taxes. Whatever the duo had requested, it was summarily swept aside; it is necessary, said Nawazish Khan, that whatever had been written about (i.e., agreed), taxes in the *qabūliyat* should collected, and no excuses were to be made. In fact, such efforts should be made that the district was cleared of arrears (*bī bāqī shavad*). The same message was repeated in summary on the right margin of the document, in a characteristic bold hand we see in many of Nawazish Khan's *parvānas*, perhaps his own.

We can only imagine that Purshottam Das and his work partner backed down in the face of this dismissal. But sometimes the demands of superiors did become too much to bear. Two documents in our family collection point to

[77] Greville, *British India Analyzed*, pp. 220–1; Jadunath Sarkar, 'The Revenue Regulations of Aurangzeb' (with the Persian texts of two unique farmāns from a Berlin manuscript', in *Journal and Proceedings of the Asiatic Society of Bengal*, New Series (1906), pp. 225–55, at 236 on enquiry required into *hast-o-būd* and at 234 on the need for proper *qauls*. Although this is a frequently cited source in Mughal history, its provenance is unclear, since the said *farmāns* only occur as copies within a bound 'collection' in the Staatsbiblioteek, Berlin, The codex contains various other materials of colonial interest, such as Maratha-Afghan wars and Chait Singh of Banaras.

[78] Sarkar, 'The Revenue Regulations of Aurangzeb', p. 236; Persian text at p. 255.

such an episode. These documents, which were collected from two different repositories – the National Archives of India and the family's mansion in Dhar – point towards outright conflict between three crucial officials whom we can recognise from the *dastūr al-ʿamals* – *faujdār, amīn* and *karōrī* – and Purshottam Das, by this time *chaudhrī* of several *parganas*, including Dhar, Nalcha and Hindola. One of the documents offers the year for a key incident, which, if we take to be a Faslī year, as the NAI archivist has done, is 1669; the conflicts described in the other document are either the same one or associated and similar. In any case, they together point to the complex nature of overlaps that we have been attempting to reconstruct, and are particularly illuminating because they indicate conflict.

The first document is an account or record of a series of incidents, made in a general *maḥẓar-nāma* form, beginning with the formula '*bāiʿs-i tahrīr-i īn sutūr*' (the reason for writing these words), and appears to be a recitation of antecedents backing up a petition, the crux of which was alleged inability to pay the agreed taxes. Purshottam Das *chaudhrī* and Parmanand, describing themselves as *mutasaddiān* (officials) of *parganas* Dhar and Nalcha, said the position was this: because of the *taʿādī* and *sitam* (oppression) of the *faujdār* Ahmad Beg, *amīn* Barbek and *karōrī* Nimatullah, they had been forced to take their complaints and leave their districts and go to the exalted court on 10 Muharram 1072 (1661 CE) whereby these three officials were replaced by men more acceptable to themselves. However, through counter-lobbying, the displaced *faujdār* attempted to have the areas allocated to himself in *jāgīr*. Although this effort was foiled by the protests of Purshottam Das and company, they returned to their villages to find that the imperial tax officials had collected taxes according to the harsh assessments of the previous officials, causing havoc and depopulation. As such, Purshottam Das and his associates claimed inability to pay the taxes and requested a fresh assessment so that the charges could be handed over to the *karōrī*.[79]

The second document is a *parvāna*, issued by a noble unidentifiable by the seal, but whose scribe had very similar handwriting to the person writing several of the *parvānas* issued by Nawazish Khan. In this undated document, the noble assured Purshottam Das, referred to as *chaudhrī* of the *parganas* Jamli and Hindola, that his *ʿarzdāsht* had reached its destination. Purshottam Das's complaint, about the displacement (*bi-jā shudan*) of the *mardam-i mahājan* and *khushbāsh* (worthy and well off) of *qasba* Sultanpur, due to the *bī-sulūkī* (bad manners) of the *karōrī* of that area, had been noted. Purshottam Das was directed to pass on the enclosed note, accompanying the *parvāna*, to the offending *karōrī*, and work together with him to conciliate and soothe the locals, so that they returned to their places. The noble, annoyed by the

[79] NAI 2703/21 (1669).

dislocation caused by the left-footed *karōri*, encouraged him and everybody else to thereafter engage themselves in the improvement of agriculture to ensure increase in tax collections.[80]

The rebuked *karōrī* may have been the Nimatullah against whom Purshottam Das had complained, and the incidents as well as their dates are close enough for us to speculate that the two documents were related to a single protracted episode of conflict, over the appropriate mode of tax-collection, between imperial officials and our *zamīndār* family. But the nature of Purshottam Das's complaint points to more entangled relationships; here, the collusion of the *faujdār* with the *amīn* and *karōrī* appears to have produced an oppressive local clique. Even when effectively challenged, such officials, or at least those with military ranks, could attempt to cling to those rural revenues through alternative ways, and not necessarily for the benefit of the regime – the effort of the *faujdār* to get the area allocated in his *jāgīr* is telling. However, large *zamīndārs* such as Purshottam Das and his associates preferred certain imperial officers over others. Also, there were multiple routes for expressing that preference – from approaching the *mansabdār-jāgīrdār* through petitions, up to a direct personal petition to the imperial court.

## Tax Contracts and Law

The majority of documents explicitly related to the collection of taxes are contractual without making any explicit references to a body of law. However, it is also within this subset of documents that we have the few explicit references to 'law' as an abstract entity. These references occur in a protracted set of complex transactions, where a tax contract is underwritten by Purshottam Das, and subsequently transferred to him as guarantor.

In 1662, Purshottam Das and his associate Paras Ram paid 1,600 rupees to a servant of the *jāgīrdār* Wazir Khan, as surety for Hari Ram *chaudhrī*.[81] It is not clear whether their willingness to do so was due to family connections or an astute business move; in any case, this was not an isolated instance, for in 1666, Purshottam Das again stood surety for *chaudhrī* Kanpil of Amjhera, which was the neighbouring district to the west of Dhar, which, as we know, was a *Rāthoḍ* Rajput base with which the family had been involved.[82] This time, the *jāgirdār* reminded Purshottam Das that Kanpil had defaulted.

Defaulting was serious business, and the bonds taken and given were in dead earnest, for in the same year, 1666, a copy of an entry in a register – an *yād-dāsht* – noted that Hari Ram *chaudhrī*'s *dastūr* was confiscated in favour

[80] NCD 1669, Choudhary Family Collection, *Baḍa Rāolā* Dhar. [81] NAI 2703/13 (1662).
[82] NAI 2733/14 (1666) and LNS MS 235 (v) dated 27 Muharram RY 9 (30 July 1666).

of Purshottam Das.[83] The resulting order, a *parvāna* under the seal of Wazir Khan, made clear reference to bodies of law – according to *sharī'a* and *'urf*, it said, Purshottam Das was the rightful owner of the *dastūr*, which Hari Ram had forfeited by not being able to pay up in time.[84]

At the time of this order, Wazir Khan was the *ṣūbadār* of Malwa, having been appointed to that position after the death of the previous *ṣūbadār*, Najabat Khan.[85] In 1664, Najabat Khan had stepped in to prevent Suraj Bhan being deprived of his share of inheritance due to his unpopularity with his kinsmen. Now in 1666, Wazir Khan had to decide that Hari Ram *chaudhrī*'s defaulting and absconding was a serious enough failure to deprive him of his *dastūr* – customary rights.

It does not seem to be a coincidence that when it came a question of potential deprivation of inherited rights – of office-holding and associated rewards – the *ṣūbadār* involved himself in making the decision. *'Urf* was the traditional classical Islamic term for custom. Islamic legal scholars were generally sympathetic to *'urf* provided it did not conflict with core doctrines; it is striking that this explicit reference to legal adjustments with local custom occurs, not in a document issued by a *qāẓī*, but an order issued by a noble concerned about the source of his salary, and dealing with complex outsourcing of tax-collection under his banner. Was the stray reference to *'urf* in this document a relatively unusual effort by a perhaps exceptionally *sharī'a*-literate *mansabdār* to translate the ubiquitous *dastūr* into a technical language recognisable within the wider Islamic world? If so, who was that translation for the benefit of? We are inevitably left with some questions that we cannot as yet answer.

## Conclusion: Tax and War

A flush of recent literature on scribes serving various precolonial regimes reveals a spectrum of social statuses and functionaries, united by the common skills of writing and record keeping: the arts of *inshā* and *siyāq*. Collectively, the professional group was deemed *munshīs* in Indo-Persian vocabulary. At the highest end of the spectrum were ministers and diplomats who, while proud of the powers of the pen, were not entirely averse to or immune from wielding the sword when called upon to do so by their kings.[86] Such men sported Persian titles, savoured Persian poetry and were fully *au courant* with the Indo-Persianate courtly culture or *adab*. At the lower end of the spectrum were

[83] NAI 2733/15 dated 17 Rabi II 1077 (15 October 1666).
[84] LNS MS 235(f1) 7 ZQ RY 9 (11 May 1666).
[85] Saqi Mustad Khan, *Maāsir-i-'Ālamgiri*, p. 31.
[86] Alam and Subrahmanyam, 'The Making of a Munshī'; Kinra, 'Master and *Munshī*'; Chatterjee, 'Scribal elites in Sultanate and Mughal Bengal', *IESHR*, 47 (2010), 445–72; Rosalind O'Hanlon and Christopher Minkowski, 'What Makes People Who They Are? Pandit Networks and the Problem of Livelihood in Early Modern Western India', *Indian Economic and Social History Review*, 45: 3 (2008), 381–416.

village-level scribes, who dealt more in numbers and vernacular languages and scripts. In north India or Mughal lands, these men, generally of the *Kāyasth* or *Khatrī* caste groupings, acquired a culturally shallow level of Persianisation, with lesser investment in Persian classical poetry and more in legal and tax jargon – the vocabulary of which tended to be shared across multiple languages.[87] When various areas came under British control, these lower-level functionaries typified the information bottlenecks that came to be denounced as sources of corruption, whereas, of course, they were also the conduits that made the colonial regime possible by making money and information flow, by whatever means. In Bengal, the post of the *qānūngō* was abolished in 1793, when the Governor-General's council decided that embodied local knowledge was redundant if the amount of tax due was agreed through written contracts.[88] Thus, while popular lore depicted *munshīs* (and *qānūngōs* among them) as essentially a bunch of pen-pushing scribes with their secret bundles of crucial information that could make or break tough men and honest soldiers,[89] in fact, information, landholding and force may not have been such distinct areas of expertise. Multitasking could extend to religion, too: a future imperial *ṣadr* – supervisor of charities and so of charity-enjoying *ʿulāma* and *qāẕīs* – made his mark as the secretary of a Mughal princess.[90]

The story of *qānūngōs*-cum-*chaudhrīs* that this book tells is meant to query the assumed line between the pen and the sword and propose that *munshīs* and *thākurs* did not necessarily have to be completely different kinds of people in Mughal India. There were a variety of routes to acquiring visibility and, in select cases, utility in the Mughal regime; in the countryside this almost necessarily included the ability to manage violence. Tax-collection, however systematised on paper, was only one step away from minor warfare; combinations of skills therefore made good entrepreneurial sense, at least in some cases. On the other hand, successful office-holding led to acquisition of lands and tax privileges, pulling the proto-bureaucrat into the militarised world of landlordism. The Mughal regime ruled by riding this process, and the story of our family of landlords illustrates how. What is feared across the world today as 'state capture'[91] was actually how the state operated in early modern South Asia.

[87] Bellenoit, 'From Qānūngōs to Clerks'. [88] Wilson, *The Domination of Strangers*, p. 71.

[89] In this vein, see the story about the clerk who forced a soldier to knock out his own teeth in order to claim his salary, reported by Crooke and reproduced by Bellenoit.

[90] Sayyid Rizvi Khan Bukhari was *diwān* of Jahan Ara Begam in the 1660s. Bhatia, *The Ulama*, p. 131.

[91] Alex Hertel-Fernandez, *State Capture: How Conservative Activists, Big Businesses and Wealthy Donors and Reshaped the American States – and the Nation* (New York: Oxford University Press, 2019).

# 4 Transactions: Recording Deals

Pirates, as Lauren Benton has shown us, could be as law-savvy as lawyers.[1] Early modern oceans were violent places, but they were not lawless in the sense of being empty of law. When they were done with their swashbuckling, or were put in a tight corner, especially by the unsystematic reach of rising imperial states, the most terrifying of pirates fished out their legal documents with which they declared loyalty to specific sovereigns and the legality of their actions. Even if a vital letter of marque, which could turn a pirate into a privateer with a magical swish, failed to make its appearance in court, whether because it was lost, or because it had never existed, pirates who had had the gall to capture Mughal ships, threaten the trading status of the East India Company and chance the wrath of both, still argued until the end that such papers existed, and all they had done, had been done within the law.[2]

It was no different in the land-locked Mughal province of Malwa. There, in the district of Dhar, the descendants of Jayanti Das had clearly built up an interlocking resource base by clearing land, being headmen of villages, assisting the state in tax-collection and maintaining order and receiving various grants of tax-free lands in return. In their own view, the entitlements of the family and its individual members derived from their military prowess and service, and imperial grants and the reiteration thereof, which produced their very own ancient custom or right (*dastūr-i sābiq*), specifically, to collect taxes.[3] Being local strongmen partially recruited by the Mughal military-administrative structure did not, however, stop them from constantly transacting with a variety of local actors, and meticulously recording such transactions within a predictable range of legal deeds.

These legal deeds, which include documents of sale and purchase, rent, mortgage, gift, debt, repayment and, more exotically – blood-money, open up for us a world of commercial transactions, charitable activities and interpersonal

[1] Benton, *A Search for Sovereignty*.

[2] As William Kidd did, albeit unsuccessfully, when he was tried in the Old Bailey in 1701 in connection with his capture of the ship *Queddah Merchant*. Robert C. Ritchie, *Captain Kidd and the War against the Pirates* (Cambridge, MA: Harvard University Press, 1986).

[3] See Introduction and Chapter 2.

exchange of property and obligations. As we have already seen, the modernist divisions of private and public, state and society are not particularly helpful in analysing the location and functions of our heroes and their activities. It is also important to relax the conceptual constraints of a term embedded in English law, in which a deed implies a record of property transfer. In our case, we have a much wider range of transactions recorded in the non-imperative documents of our collection. These documents are therefore best considered as written and authenticated record of transfers of entitlements and/or obligations, including, but not limited to, those involving physical property or money.

As the record of transactions voluntarily entered into by individuals and actors without direct pressure from or direct reference to the state, they offer us a particularly fertile source-base from which to explore everyman's engagements with law in the Mughal empire. In scholarship on other Islamicate contexts, legal deeds (typically of sale, purchase, endowment, gift, rent, mortgage, debt, marriage and so on) have been used to construct the social history of a region, or of a specific community, producing the 'human side' of broader political and commercial histories.[4] In a comparable fashion, such documents in Mughal India have been used to excavate the local structures of power, the workings of the local government structures and formation of wealthy religious complexes, the last also serving to illustrate the complex patronage patterns of Indo-Islamic kingship.[5] In the Indian case, the status of such records as historical sources remains distinctly secondary to royal and sub-royal orders and chronicle histories, and several of the works listed in Footnote 4 are in the nature of valuable source-books, rather than historical arguments.

Recent historiography, especially in the burgeoning and diverse field of Islamic law, has added several new angles of enquiry that can be pursued using legal deeds as sources. One approach that I find particularly useful is the one suggested by Brinkley Messick, who, while exploring the *textual habitus* in nineteenth- and twentieth-century Yemen, suggested that legal documents stand in front of a world of transactions, and represent a reality filtered and codified through legal principles and categories.[6] This idea has recently been applied by Fahad Bishara to the world of Indian Ocean

[4] Nobuaki, *Persian Documents*; Shaul Shaked, 'Early Persian Documents from Khorasan', *Journal of Persianate Studies*, 6 (2013), 153–62; Fatiha Loualich, 'In the Regency of Algiers: The Human Side of the Algerian Corso', in Maria Fusaro, Colin Heywood and Mohamed-Salah Omri (eds.) *Trade and Cultural Exchange in the Early Modern Mediterranean: Braudel's Maritime Legacy* (London: I.B. Tauris, 2010), pp. 69–96; Christoph Werner, *An Iranian Town in Transition: A Social and Economic History of the Elites of Tabriz, 1747–1848* (Wiesbaden: Harrasowitz, 2000); Werner, *Vaqf en Iran.*

[5] Goswamy and Grewal (eds.), *The Mughals and the Jogis of Jakhbar*; Grewal, *In the By-Lanes of History*; Habib, 'From Ariṭh to Rādhākund'; Horstmann, *In Favour of Govinddevji.*

[6] Brinkley Messick, *The Calligraphic State: Textual Domination and History in a Muslim Society* (Berkeley: University of California Press, 1993), p. 227.

commerce. Bishara's work is centred on the instruments for recording obligations of debt, generically known as *waraqa* (paper), that merchants from all around the ocean used in their transactions. Bishara showed both how the scribes (*kātibs*) who penned these documents used recognisable formula that codified the intensely diverse world of oceanic commerce within the recognisable, and legally cognisable Islamic legal language of contracts.[7]

The terminology used in the documents cited by Bishara, Messick, Werner and all scholars working on Islamic legal deeds is one that is instantly recognisable far beyond their immediate provenance. That is because they were written using a truly global vocabulary, whose key terms for describing transactions, such as: sale (*bai'*), mortgage (*rahn*), lease (*ijāra*), gift (*hiba*); or legal actions, such as: declaration/confession (*iqrār*), denial (*inkār*), witnessing (*shahada*); or legal actors, such as: claimant (*mudda'*), respondent (*mudda' 'alai-hi*), deponent (*mukhbir*) were largely identical, whether the documents were scribed in Morocco or Bengal. That similarity derived from the connection of such legal deeds with a long-established genre, that of Islamic legal formularies, known as *shurūṭ* or *wathāiq*. Works of *shurūṭ* were first produced around the ninth century CE, and written by eminent Islamic jurists, who, with the expansion of Islamic empires and the consequent elaboration of administrative and adjudicative institutions, were concerned to guide people on how to produce legally cognisable documents.[8] Books of *shurūṭ*, which dealt with the sort of 'private contracts' that we are dealing with here, were often combined with books on *maḥẓars* and *sijills* (Arabic plurals: *maḥāẓir va sijillāt*), that is, documents recording adjudication proceedings in *qāẓī*'s courts. And both these kind of formularies often formed part of even larger works: compendia on Islamic jurisprudence or *fiqh*.[9] Given Islamic law's formal insistence on the superiority of oral testimony over documentary evidence, there is an unresolved debate among scholars about the significance of this prolific genre; older scholarship suggested a pragmatic but doctrinally incoherent effort to associate doctrine with practice,[10] whereas more recent works suggest that the formulary literature was a logical outcome of the

[7] Bishara, *A Sea of Debt*.

[8] Jeanette Wakin, ed. and trans. *The Function of Documents in Islamic Law: The Chapters on Sales from Ṭaḥāwī's Kitāb al-shurūṭ al-kabīr* (Albany: State University of New York Press, 1972), 9–29; Wael Hallaq, 'Model *Shurūṭ* Works and the Dialectic of Doctrine and Practice', *Islamic Law and Society*, 2: 2 (1995), 109–34.

[9] For an introduction to *fiqh*, see Wael Hallaq, 'From *Fatwās to Furū'*: Growth and Change in Islamic Substantive Law', *Islamic Law and Society*, 1, 1994, 29–65; for a more detailed exposition, see his *Sharī'a : Theory, Practice, Transformations*.

[10] On this conflict, see N. J. Coulson, 'Doctrine and Practice in Islamic Law: One Aspect of the Problem', *Bulletin of the School of Oriental and African Studies*, 18: 2 (1956), 211–26; N. J. Coulson, *Conflicts and Tensions in Islamic Jurisprudence* (Chicago: University of Chicago Press, 1969)

efforts of jurists and evidence of the alignment of jurisprudence with the processes of adjudication.[11]

Bishara's study of legal documents used in Indian Ocean commerce shows that the conflict between doctrine and practice could arise from several other sources. At the most superficial, this may be a matter of form, for example, the need for an appropriate family name or *nisba,* which could require a cosmetic re-coding of the names of the parties involved in order to cater for non-Arab and non-Muslim protagonists. Thus the Gujarati Bania merchant Ladha Damji would be called Ladha bin Damah Al-Banyani in a document from nineteenth-century Zanzibar, which recorded complex credit transactions. 'To trace back the ancestry of'– *nasaba* – was an active and meaningful verb for jurists who wrote Arabic-language formularies, as well as scribes who actually penned these Indian Ocean commercial documents.[12]

More seriously, Bishara's documents reveal a host of legal fictions, used to contain a huge range of property transactions within the doctrinally valid limits of Islamic law. In fact, Bishara shows that while 'jurists suspected that alliance between commercial actors and *kātibs*, could potentially conceal illicit gains', they were powerless to stop just such transactions being recorded, because they were simply too far away from the site of commercial activity and recording. Many jurists ended up taking an actively permissive view towards legal devices, such as the *khiyār* or 'delayed' sale, which could be suspected of circumventing Islamic injunctions against usury.[13] In their 'creative thinking', such jurists used analogies to expansively interpret that doctrines of Islamic law to fit current realities. Devices permitted through such analogical reasoning are very similar to the 'legal fictions' of English law. These are not fabrications in the lay sense but professionally shared and legitimate devices for representing a reality that was particularly unwieldy, and which would otherwise not be amenable to legal action.[14] Law does indeed make a certain reality for its own use; a reality that is not just fiction because it determines how people and things are disposed of. The vocabulary of Islamic *shurūṭ* just made legal reality in a certain form. It is rather sterile to be pushed by such discoveries into the debate over the gap between doctrine and practice in Islamic law, for wider scholarship reveals that law's need, as well as ability to sublimate unique and

[11] Joseph Schacht, *An Introduction to Islamic Law* (Oxford: Clarendon, 1964), 82; see also Wakin, *Function of Documents*, pp. 4–10; Hallaq argues against these formulations.

[12] Bishara, *A Sea of Debt*, pp. 69–70.

[13] Ibid., pp. 90–9; in doing so, Bishara took Patricia Risso's suggestive proposition that a shared understanding of Islamic commercial law undergirded Indian Ocean commerce much further. Patricia Risso, *Merchants and Faith: Muslim Commerce and Culture in the Indian Ocean* (Boulder, CO: Westview Press, 1995) pp. 104–6.

[14] That is, until they fell prey to the reformist drives of nineteenth-century English law reformers.

eccentric social reality into legally cognisable records, universally involves creativity as well as distortion.[15]

The question for us really is what form that creativity takes in specific contexts, and why. Asking that question allows us to approach legal deeds as cultural artefacts, in the sense of being products of a specific institutional, doctrinal, textual and scribal milieu. In early modern Islamic empires, such as that of the Mughals, such milieux were inevitably multi-confessional and multi-lingual with distinct regional dispensations of those pluralities. In characterising legal documents produced by and for this family of landholders in Malwa, we need to use a number of nominative categories, such as Islamicate, Persianate, Mughal and Indic, and do so while reflecting on the accuracy and explanatory value of each. As we shall see, despite the recognisable legal vocabulary, many of the Persian documents produced by this family had no exact counterpart in Arabic-language *shurūṭs*. Instead, they were most directly modelled on Indo-Persianate formularies called *munshāts*, which were a prose genre whose contents owed at least as much to the chancellery practices of Persianate empires, as to the doctrines of Arabic-writing jurists.[16]

But we shall not retreat into dealing with legal documents as pure texts, and instead attempt to reconstruct (through what is bound to be fragmentary evidence), the social locus in which they were produced. I am working with the idea that understanding the legal and formulary culture from which these documents were derived, is necessary for understanding how and why people represented themselves and their interests in a certain way.[17] Properly viewed, these legal deeds are fragments of a historical mirror which offers us inevitably distorted glimpses of the lives they record. They are episodic and in a particular fashion.[18] Just as archives of criminal justice record instances of deviation and/or dispute over what is good and what is not, and are thereby useful if letting us discover what people thought was normative,[19] these legal deeds record smaller moments – of engagement, disengagement and dispute over the terms of the making of such social and economic relations.

[15] Kathryn Burns, *Into the Archive: Writing and Power in Colonial Peru* (Durham, NC: Duke University Press, 2010); Kathryn Burns, 'Notaries, Truth, and Consequences', *American Historical Review*, 110 (2005): 350–79; Chatterjee, 'Maḥẕar-nāmas in the Mughal and British Empires.

[16] And thus here I differ from Paolo Sartori regarding the sources of such legal formulae; Sartori, 'Colonial Lgislation Meets Sharī'a', 43–60, note 56.

[17] Paolo Sartori, 'Introduction: On the Social in Central Asian History: Notes in the Margins of Legal Records', in P. Sartori, ed., *Explorations in the Social History of Modern Central Asia (19th–Early 20th Century)* (Leiden: Brill, 2013), 1–22.

[18] E. P. Thompson's well-known formulation: 'History is made up of episodes' in his 'The Peculiarities of the English', in *The Poverty of Theory and Other Essays* (New York and London: Monthly Review Press, 1978), p. 275.

[19] Christopher Brooks and Michael Lobban (eds.), *Communities and Courts in Britain, 1150–1900* (London: Hambledon, 1997).

The specific transactional moments that these legal deeds record peg out the matrices of the social and commercial life of people captured therein, such as this family of landholders–tax officials–strongmen. Quite like the Indian Ocean mercantile documents discussed by Bishara, these documents from Malwa also map onto the recognisable terminology and formulae of Islamic law, but they also relate to their geographic and social location. Consequently, while the collection of papers related to families of merchants from the port cites Surat and Khamabayat are replete with deeds of sale, purchase and rent agreements, the contract most often entered into by members of this family of landholders-cum-officials-cum-strongmen was in fact that of revenue farming, or *ijāra*, which we have discussed in Chapter 3. In this chapter, we shall deal with the other kinds of property transaction evidenced in this collection, such as gift-giving, loan-taking and repayment, which involved less direct engagement with mechanisms of the state. However, such debts were sometimes secured on projected revenue collections, closing the circle of taxation and transactions and revealing the fluid boundary between state action and social exchanges at the lowest, that is, village level in Mughal India. Following the trajectory of such circles allows us to think carefully about the category of law, and the place of the state within it.

Legal deeds also happen to be the only sub-set within this collection where one is able to catch a glimpse of women in what might otherwise appear to be a highly militarised world swarming with macho men. Gifts and transfers effected and recorded by such women alert us to the mutual enmeshing of statecraft, property-holding and kinship. However, this is not harem politics writ small; women of this family who executed such legal deeds did so within a shared world structured by tax, rent and Islamic legal categories, as much as marriage and reproduction. Moreover, it so happens that women of the Purshottam Das family appear not as appendages to transactions negotiated to men, but as agents in their own rights, with surprisingly loud and clear voices of their own.

When people transacted among themselves, as opposed to receiving the fruits of grace of the great and mighty, they liked to do so in a way that would make the transaction binding and secure in law. But they also liked to make an additional effort to make sure that they understood what they were signing. We have seen how the Mughal's contractual approach to tax-collection lent itself to a vibrant multi-linguality in the associated contracts – the *qaul qarār paṭṭa-yi ijāra* that collectively formed the *kāghaẕ-i khām*, the lowest level of rental records in Mughal India. People's various and variable facility in multiple languages also made itself felt in legal deeds, typically through marginal comments, attestations and seals and validation symbols in a variety of languages and scripts. And so these documents offer us not only a substantive corpus of non-literary evidence for studying the history of development of languages in India, but also offer us a rare opportunity for reconstructing the social context of multi-linguality in early modern India, with an eye on those little experts, the scribes, who have drawn so much attention from scholars in recent times, and among whose ranks our *qānūngōs* may have belonged. When such men (and women) wanted something written down, what would it be?

## Gifts – and Curses

Unsurprisingly, it was most frequently about money or property changing hands. This could include transfers within the extended family, including its female members, which indicates a high level of formal individuation of titles, as well as the perceived need to legally record alterations, even within the affective and kinship matrix. Gifts are a favourite with anthropologists for their ostensibly non-transactional format, which epitomises the creation, iteration and modification of what purports to be extra-economic relationships. Islamic jurists, on the other hand, always classified them together with other transactions of property such as sale and pawn, naming it '*hiba*' and prescribing elaborate rules for completing such a transaction validly, and recording it securely. In the one document in our collection that records the making of a gift by a female member of the this extended family, we are offered a tantalising glimpse of its kinship and property dynamics, and also a rather striking picture of how Islamic legal terminology and forms circulated and combined with other forms and means of validating such transactions on paper.

In 1690, the thirty-third year of Emperor Aurangzeb's reign, a woman called Puran gifted eight villages, a garden and two houses to Narsingh Das and Gambhir Chand, the sons of Purshottam Das.[20] She called herself the 'legally wedded wife (*mankūḥa*)' of Gharib Das, son of Dinkar Das, son of Jayanti (?) Das and uncle of Purshottam Das. In her own words, Puran made over these properties, which had been in her sole title (*patta bilā sharkat*) to her cousins-in -law of her own accord (*ba-raẕāmandī-yi khūd*), considering them her children (*ba-jā-yi farzand dānishte*). This assumption of generational superiority and generosity came with some conditions attached, for she noted that the beneficiaries had 'performed the duties of children (*khidmat-i farzand-i ba-jā āwarde*)'. Given their dutifulness, whatever that may have consisted of, she gave them a 'rational deed (*sanad nāṭiq*)' (i.e. created in the legally necessary state of rationality), warning off anybody who may make claims on these properties in future.

The cryptic contents of this gift deed suggest that there was rather a lot going on in the background. How did this woman come to acquire sole title or *paṭṭās* of eight villages, and what did those titles consist of in terms of her

[20] NAI 2733/29 (1690).

entitlements? The inventory beneath the main text of the document grouped the villages into *muqadammī* and *dāmī* – which, as we have seen before, pertained to the rights of *chaudhrīs* (alternatively, *muqaddams*) to collect a share of the peasant's produce, as a putative salary for their work for the revenue machinery of the Mughals. We know already that while in theory *chaudhrīs* were state officials, they were also co-opted village headmen, their positions normally inheritable, although subject to ratification, and occasional alteration, within the family, by the *jāgirdārs*, with whom negotiations were constant, and tense. Puran was likely to have been childless, or at least son-less, and perhaps her husband and father-in-law had died. If so, then despite inheriting the *paṭṭās* of their *chaudhrāīs*, she may have been constrained by her gender and unable to undertake the full range of *zamīndārī* duties, especially the occasional military and policing services. There were of course a small number of notable women *zamīndārs*; some were encountered by the British in late eighteenth-century Bengal,[21] but by then the need to provide military duties had disappeared; strong-arm men could do the rest. It was probably harder to manage that in late seventeenth-century Malwa. If she had, in fact, become isolated through a combination of unfortunate life-cycle events, Puran may not have made the transfer entirely of her own free will, but document still made a note of mutual obligations. We do not know what exactly the 'duties of children' were, but she may have negotiated for a maintenance. In any case, as a result of this transfer, villages located further north, in what would later become the princely state of Sitamau, came into possession of the main and most successful line of the family.

Puran's deed of gift, of which we only have a copy, is a striking example of both the penetration of law into the interstices of rural society and family life in Mughal Malwa and a record of the variety of influences that went into shaping the language and valences of that law. The original deed had been sealed by '*shari'at panāh qāẕī Muhammad Muhsin*' and bore two dates – the regnal year, as well as the Faslī year, that is, the solar Hijri year invented by Akbar and used in all revenue-related documentation. The lunar Hijri year was absent, as was the word '*hiba*' itself, but the document reproduced the necessary Islamic legal formulae for making valid gifts, such as noting the absence of co-sharers, and the presence of free will. The donor, Puran, referred to herself as '*mankūḥa*', specifically using the Islamic legal term *nikāḥ* for marriage, in place of possible alternatives: the more generic *jauza* in Arabic or *zan* in Persian. No doubt she chose '*mankūḥa*' to record her unassailable legal status, and hence unquestionable right to the *paṭṭās* she had inherited. But in the end, she stepped beyond

21 For example Rani Rashmoni; later women *zamīndārs* were essentially regents for minor male heirs. See Sonia Nishat Amin, *The World of Muslim Women in Colonial Bengal, 1896–1939* (Leiden: Brill, 1996), p. 15.

mere formulae, and had it recorded, 'If [anybody] makes a claim [on this property], I will seize their skirt on the day of judgement (*Wa agar da'va nūmāyad, roz-i qayāmat dāmangīr-i-ū shavam*)!'

Curses, and their more passive form, imprecatory prayers (asking God to punish someone), have been studied as legal devices in various ancient Middle Eastern contexts.[22] These uses are very similar to instances from Mughal and pre-Mughal India, in which curses are included in stone inscriptions recording the dedication of property, to support resthouses for travellers, for example, and intended to protect against encroachment. Islamic jurisprudence provided for specific procedures for using curses in legal disputes.[23] But nothing we learn from that scholarship can fully prepare us for this evocative curse, recorded by a Hindu widow in a *zamīndār* family, as a guarantee for a legal transaction.

## Credit and Obligation

Despite their diverse resource base, people like Purshottam Das and his family were sometimes desperately short of money. As we have seen, the rates of taxation were variable year-to-year and subject to negotiation on various bases, despite Malwa being a *ẕābtī* or regulation province in which clear rates of taxation, based on a systematic survey were supposed to be the norm. Such negotiation was reliant on a series of exchanges up and down a social and official ladder, all of them involving coercion. Although actors at the middle to lower end of the scale, such as Purshottam Das as his family, were not passive recipients of either coercion or magnanimity, occasionally the balance of negotiation tipped against them. We have seen in Chapter 3 how Purshottam Das was able to benefit from the discomfiture of his peers; when another *chaudhrī-cum-qānūngō* failed to deliver the taxes as promised, he had to abscond in order to escape the wrath of the *jāgīrdār*, and Purshottam Das was able to buy up that *qānūngōī*. At other times, however, the Purshottam Das clan suffered from a lack of liquidity themselves. The surviving documents recording their debts and repayments offer us some insights into the sources of rural credit supply, the other key social actors that this family dealt with, and also the tangling of taxation and credit at the base of the structure of the Mughal empire.

Mohan Das, the state-approved vigilante who brought down a fearsome landlord-turned-highwayman, ran short of money at some point in his career, and was obliged to look for a loan. Either because they were all short of money, or because theirs was really a family enterprise which required collective acceptance of liability, Mohan Das, together with his brothers, Chandar Bhan

[22] H. G. L. Peel, *The Vengeance of God* (Leiden: Brill, 1995), pp. 236–8; K. van der Toorn, *Sin and Sanction in Israel and Mesopotamia: a Comparative Study* (Assen/Maastricht, 1985), pp. 45 ff.

[23] Guy Bochor, *God in the Courtroom: the Transformation of Courtroom Oath and Perjury between Islamic and Franco-Egyptian Law* (Leiden: Brill, 2012), pp. 129–35.

and Dinkar Das, approached a man called Nayak Khandha, said to be of the '*banjāra*' caste. We do not really know how much Mohan Das was compelled to borrow, but it was a hefty amount, and possibly one that built up through several loans on separate occasions. Despite establishing the family and its resource base, Mohan Das and his brothers did not manage to pay off his debt, whether because they remained cash-strapped, or because they did not feel adequately pressured to prioritise repayment. In any case, in 1660, a couple of years after Aurangzeb made himself emperor, Mohan Das's son, *chaudhrī* Purshottam Das, decided to repay the outstanding amounts, to the brother of Nayak Khandha, called Nayak Sundar, and to his sons, Haridas and Ramdas. The document called *fārigh-khaṭṭī* in which this transaction was recorded noted that all dues were cleared except a remaining bond (*tamassuk*) for twenty-five rupees.[24]

Purshottam Das, who begun contracting for revenue with Mughal tax officials at least in the 1620s, was an elderly man by this time. He was also quite wealthy by rural standards. But even a substantial rural magnate such as this became periodically strapped for cash. Nayak (headman) Khandha, from whom Purshottam Das's father Mohan Das had taken a significant loan, belonged to that ubiquitous group of pastoralist-traders called *banjāras* whose mobile histories lay intertwined with the martial histories of groups associated with the great north-western desert, such as the Rajputs.[25] In the nineteenth century, the mobility and amphibiousness of groups such as the *banjāras* came to be legally associated with criminality by the colonial state keen on a pacified, immobilised agrarian population.[26]

In the Mughal empire, however, such men performed the essential service of moving grain across long distances, provisioning urban centres as well as armies. For this reason, no doubt, we see a very clear *dastak* (passport), issued under the seal of a servant of the *jāgirdār* Nawazish Khan, to Nayak Singha and other *banjāras*, assuring them that they may purchase grain without the need to pay *pīshkash* or other taxes.[27] One can only imagine how such a document may

[24] NAI 2668/4 (1660).

[25] Habib, 'Mercant Communities', p. 373–4, quoting Zia Barani, *Tarīkh-i Firūz Shāhī* (ed.) Saiyid Ahmad Khan (Calcutta: Bibliotheca Indica, 1862), pp. 305–7; and a *dōhā* of the mystic poet, Kabir; Henry M. Elliot, *Memoirs on the History, Folklore and Distribution of the Races of the Northwestern Provinces of India* (ed.) J. Beames (2 vols., London: Hertford, 1869), Vol. I, p. 56; and R. V. Russell and Hira Lal, *Tribes and Castes of the Central Provinces of India* (Delhi reprint, 1975), II, 188.

[26] Radhika Singha, 'Providential' Circumstances: The Thuggee Campaign of the 1830s and Legal Innovation', *Modern Asian Studies*, 27: 1 (1993), 83–146; the suspicion of early nineteenth-century commentators, such as William Sleeman, persisted into the twentieth. Thus Russell and Lal, *Tribes and Castes of the Central Provinces*, Vol. IV, p. 561: 'it seems probable that many of the Thugs were originally Banjaras'.

[27] LNS MS 235 (n1) DAI, dated 1 Ramzan 1073 (1663).

have been preserved carefully by the leader of a caravan, who almost certainly would not have been able to read it, but knew to display it at checkpoints.

It is not clear why this *dastak* should have made its way into our family's archive, but it may have been because the family had long-standing financial entanglements with the *banjāras*. In any case, the *dastak* is additional evidence of the ability of these itinerant and usually illiterate traders to negotiate Persian-language legal documentation and its associated judicial processes.

When recovering their brother and father's money, for example, Nayak Sundar, Haridas and Ramdas would have appeared in front of the district *qāẕī*, a certain Sheikh Ilyas, who affixed his seal to the document, and wrote: 'sealed with the confession/declaration (*ʿitrāf*) of Nayak Sundar'. Others would have turned up to complete the transaction, for the document was witnessed and signed by recognisable associates of the family – Parasram and Parmanand, *qānūngōs* of Dhar; Madhav Das and Girdhar Das, possibly also kinsmen; and also a certain Daud Khan and Shaikh Hussain. These last two may have been men whom the *qāẕī* considered respectable and dependable as witnesses; Shaikh Hussain may even have been his own relative. And thus people of at least three social circles – upper caste Hindu landlord and tax officials, the illiterate itinerant merchants and Muslim *ʿulamā* – all converged in the court of the *qāẕī* to record a small economic episode, that of the return of a loaned amount, thus leaving a paper trail of the pattern of their mutual relationship. Such episodes and their institutional location (the *qāẕī*'s office) serve to substantiate a key point of this book: the deep imbrication of Persianate and Islamic legal forms into the economic and social fabric of Mughal India, encompassing people of social groups who did not write or read in Persian (or indeed, in any language), but believed in its authenticating capacity.

Further loans, their repayment and the recording of such transactions, caught other social groups and actors within the net of historical records generated and preserved by Purshottam Das's family. Substantial and multigenerational loans were raised by Purshottam Das's sons, Narsingh Das and Gambhir Chand, this time from a certain Ganesh Sahu and his associate, Kale Afghan.[28] We may speculate that in moving on from itinerant traders, the *banjāras*, to the sources of their capital, higher status Hindu *bania*[29] and Afghan moneylenders, the family revealed its own rise in social status in two generations. Kale Afghan is rather more elusive; he may have been part of the small community of migratory traders visible all over India even in the nineteenth century and immortalised by the Bengali poet and novelist Rabindranath Thakur in *Kabuliwala*, or he may have been of the many soldiering families Malwa, dabbling in some

[28] NAI 2668/22 (1710)

[29] 'Sahu' being the Hindi term, recorded in use between the fifteenth to eighteenth centuries, to indicate big bankers, typically of *bania* caste. Habib, 'Merchant Communities', pp. 375, 379, 382, 390.

moneylending on the side. In case we needed confirmation that such inter-community commercial ventures worked admirably, Kale had indeed made a good investment. Like the *banjāras*, the *bania* moneylenders kept meticulous intergenerational accounts, but this time in writing, noting all giving and taking (*dād sitād*) in their account books (*bahī va afrād-i ḥisāb*). After Ganesh Sahu's death, his son Sangram took charge of the business, and having checked through all accounts and deducted all receipts, recovered the remaining money from Narsingh Das's brother Hamir Chand, and the latter's son, Nihal Chand, who were clearly deemed liable for the financial obligations of their relative. Sangram honestly handed over Kale Afghan's share to his son, Muhammad Jafar. The transaction was once again recorded in the court of the *qāẓī* in the year 1711, by which time the era of the great Mughals was finished and Emperor Aurangzeb Alamgir's son Bahadur Shah was in the fourth year of his short reign. The *qāẓī* in Dhar was a man called Muhammad Mustafa, who would notarise many important documents for the family during his tenure. On this occasion, details of the repayment were written down, and the document sealed by the *qāẓī,* who superscribed a note: 'A valid declaration (*iqrār muʿatabar*) was made by Musamma Muhammaad Jaʿfar, the declarant (*muqīr*)'. Once again, the *qāẓī*'s court and Persianate legal documentation netted diverse social groups, reinforcing and recording their mutual economic and social relationships in black and white.

There is much that of course remains unclear from these records. With the loans taken from the *banjāras* and the *bania*-Afghan partners, we cannot tell what the loaned amount was, neither can we tell whether the lenders took some kind of security,[30] or were confident enough about their ability to recover their loan through community knowledge and the *qāẓī*'s authority. As we know, Hamir Chand had once been taken to court by his younger brother Narsingh Das over disputes related to inheritance.[31] We do not also know whether, in discharging his (presumably dead) elder brother's loan, he, together with his son, was acting as Hindu coparceners, as required a by *dharmaśāstric* norms that would become law under the colonial government in the late eighteenth century,[32] or whether they were merely acting out of sense of family honour. What we can see is that the people undertaking such transactions looked upon the local *qāẓī*'s court and his notarisation services as useful, if not necessarily exclusive, tools for securing their interests.

In 1721, the same *qāẓī*, Muhammad Mustafa, recorded a more complex transaction between Hamir Chand *chaudhrī* and another man, possibly a noble called Mir Muhib Allah, referred to in the document by the hyperbolic

[30] For example, through the mortgaging of certain properties, for which we have a instance studied by Habib, in 'Aspects of Agrarian Relations and Economy'.
[31] NAI 2703/29 (1684), discussed in Chapter 2.
[32] Wilson, *The Domination of Strangers*, pp. 75–103; Derrett, 'The Administration of Hindu Law'.

title 'Refuge of happiness (*sa'ādat panāh*)'.[33] In this self-described *tamassuk*, Hamir Chand recorded taking 2,240 rupees in loan, and took the cash from the [account of the] villages listed beneath (*tankhwāh az mazkūr ba mawazī'-yi zīl mī namūdam*). He promised to return the money within the year 1128 AH/1726 CE, after gathering the harvest. The villages in question were the *'ināmī* village of Dhamanda, and the *dāmī* village of Ahu; Hamir Chand was therefore securing this loan against the tax-collecting rights that were important sources of the family's income.

## *Tamassuks* and *Fārigh-Khaṭṭīs*: Law and Taxation

As we have seen, when taking loans from various people, members of Purshottam Das's family created *tamassuks*. While all documents in the collection relating to debt and repayment mention them, there are two surviving *tamassuks* in this collection. These show this was a documentary form based on the recording of an *iqrār* or 'confession'. The document which recorded *chaudhrī* Hamir Chand taking a loan from a certain aristocrat called Mir Muhib Allah, for example, contained a short superscription above the seal of the *qāẓī*, which said '*iqrār 'aindī*' (I have a confession; or There is a confession *chez moi*).

The standard translation of *iqrār* as 'confession' creates certain semantic difficulties with those not cognisant of the vocabulary of Islamic legal studies. *Iqrārs* may indeed be acknowledgements of guilt, but unlike this more restricted modern English connotation, *iqrār* relates to a broader range of meanings. *Iqrār* is a key category in the Islamic law of evidence: it is a unilateral declaration made by a person, which creates a binding legal obligation. Although subject to various conditions of validity, classical jurists considered *iqrārs* to be of the highest evidentiary value, and 'binding in itself' *(mūjib bi-nafsihi)*. Thus, an *iqrār* did not have to be put down in writing, let alone authenticated through notarisation in order to be valid. In practice, however, jurists recommended a documentary form which recorded to the *iqrār* using the correct terminology which would also be attested to (not notarised) by a legal expert, acting in this case as a reliable witness.[34] An *iqrār* did not have to be about a loan or a property transaction, or about guilt; it was simply a legally valid declaration that could be made in any of these contexts, but an endless number of others, too. There are innumerable *iqrār* documents available in various collections from around the Islamic world.

[33] NAI, 2668/20 (1726?)

[34] Christian H. O. Müller, 'Acknowledgement', *Encyclopaedia of Islam*, 3rd edition (eds.), Kate Fleet, Gudrun Krämer, Denis Matringe, John Nawas and Everett Rowson. Brill Online, 2015. 11 July 2015, http://0-www.brillonline.nl.lib.exeter.ac.uk/entries/encyclopaedia-of-islam-3/acknowledgement-COM_0166

As it happens, Hamir Chand's *iqrār* was recorded in a very specific documentary form, called a *tamassuk*, which derived more directly from Indo-Persian revenue administration practices, and only indirectly from Islamic jurisprudence. As such, while the fact of Hamir Chand's acknowledgement, that he had taken a certain amount of money on loan, had taken possession of the cash and was committing himself to repay it within a given period of time, was recorded, together with the details of his name and genealogy as well as the name of the beneficiary, as a standard *iqrār* should, its vocabulary did not fully correspond with the forms recommended by the jurists, or with *iqrār* documents specifically acknowledging debts from other parts of the Islamicate world, especially from earlier periods. Thus Arabic-language *iqrār* documents, whether from the twelfth century and stored in the Cairo Genizah, or from the fourteenth century and stored in the Haram al-Sharif in Jerusalem, all began with the *Bismillah* (In the name of God . . .) and continued '*aqara/aqarat* X bin/bint Y' (X son of/daughter of Y declared'.[35] They invariably had witness clauses, such as, in the Cairo documents ' *'aind shahud hadha al-kitāb*' (in the presence of witnesses to this writing) or '*shahīd 'ala al-X ba-dhalika*' (witness on X with regard to this), in the Jerusalem documents.

Hamir Chand's *tamassuk* on the other hand, said much more directly, and in the first person:

*Manke Hamir Chand chaudhrī-yi pargana Dhar Sarkar Mandu muẕāf ba-sūba Malwa am, mublagh dō hazār rūpiye . . . az nazd-i sa'ādat panāh Mir Muhib Allah ba-ṭariq-i qarz girafte, dar qabz wa taṣarruf-i khūd āwardam.*

I, who am Hamir Chand, chaudhrī of pargana Dhar Sarkar Mandu sūba Malwa, having taken 2,240 Rupees, of which the half would be 1120 Rupees, from the refuge of goodness Mir Muhib Allah, in the manner of loan, have brought it into my possession.

He then continued to explain how he would return the money within the year, and said at the end:

*Īn chand kalme ba-ṭariq-i tamassuk nawishte dādam, ke s̱anī al-hal sanad bāshad.*

I give these few words in writing in the manner of a *tamassuk*, so that it can be/act as a document in the future.

There were no witness clauses to the document. We do have a superscription '*aqara 'aindī*' (I have an *iqrār*) written by the *qāẕī* together with his seal above

[35] Khan, *Arabic Legal and Administrative Documents*, Documents 35–47, pp. 208–38; Huda Lutfi, 'A Study of Six Fourteenth Century Iqrārs from Al-Quds Relating to Muslim Women', *Journal of the Economic and Social History of the Orient*, 26: 3 (1983), pp. 246–94.

the body of the text.[36] Hamir Chand's name was written in the document in Hindi on the right-hand margin.[37]

Thus the legal specialist, the *qāẓī*, was certainly part of the process of creating a legal deed recording a debt, affixing his seal to the document as also noting that it was an *iqrār*; the India form omitted the typical opening formula in which the *qāẓī* or another suitable notary recorded that the parties had made a declaration. Instead, these documents proceeded straight to a declaration in the first person. To spell this out, whereas the standard Islamic legal formula read, 'He declared that, I . . . ', Indian documents ran, 'I declare that . . . ' It is tempting to speculate whether this abbreviation of the formula, omitting the framing voice of the *qāẓī*, indicates a difference in procedure, personnel and location in terms of the drafting of legal deeds in India. Were such documents of debts written by people themselves, or more likely, by hired scribes, the archetypical *munshīs*, rather than legally trained *qāẓīs*? Was the document presented to the *qāẓī* post-preparation, thus somewhat defeating the original purpose of the *iqrār*, which was to record a direct declaration in the presence of respectable witnesses, ideally the *qāẓī* himself? Such a conclusion is difficult to arrive at based on these documents alone, and awaits the discovery of an adequate text describing the procedure for drafting such everyday legal deeds.

Whatever the social and institutional reasons for this deviation in form, we can explore the wider context of the word *tamassuk*, with which these documents of debt identified themselves. And thus we find ourselves back in the realm of the Mughal tax-collection juggernaut, for this was a term shared with revenue administration. A documentary form called *tamassuk-i ẓāminī* was used in the *Khālṣa* or treasury department to record security bonds given by 'workmen', and state loans.[38] It was probably used by Purshottam Das to record his bond, underwriting other *chaudhrī's* commitments, which we have discussed in Chapter 3.

This was an interplay between taxation, administration and law, mediated through a Persianate culture of which chancellery procedure was an essential part. Thus it was particularly apt that Hamir Chand's loan was sourced from the taxes of the villages which he himself was charged to collect. Call it a government loan authorised by the *jāgīrdār*, call it cooking the books plain and simple – in *pargana* Dhar taxation and credit were inseparable parts of essential cash flows, and hence recorded in a shared documentary form.

This interplay between revenue and credit or taxation and transaction, and consequently between Islamic legal forms and Persianate chancellery

[36] This is similar to the inscription on the Haram 108 document, cited in Lutfi, 'A Study', pp. 267–8.
[37] NAI 2668/20.
[38] Jadunath Sarkar, *Mughal Administration* (Patna: Patna University, 1920), pp. 63–4.

procedure, was even stronger in the documentary form that complemented the *tamassuk* – the *fārigh-khaṭṭī*. *Fārigh* is an Arabic word, which means 'empty;' in Persian and Urdu, the meaning shifts slightly, to imply 'free' (of obligations, work, etc.). Thus, the term *fārigh-khaṭṭī*, which is a specifically Indian innovation, can be translated as the writing/record of freeing. The functions of such documents demonstrated that these were deeds of quittance, or written release from some specific obligation, on the fulfilment of the obligation, or its removal.[39] British officials writing in the nineteenth century noted that such quittance documents were issued by *zamīndārs* to peasants at the end of the revenue year, to record that all dues had been paid. They also noted who would scribe such a document – the village revenue record keeper or *patwārī*, who might charge a specific fee called *fārigh khatāna* for this service.[40]

The *fārigh-khaṭṭīs* in the Purshottam Das family collection served a wider range of functions, also related to the emptying of claims. When in 1660, Purshottam Das, together with his uncles Chandar Bhan and Dinkar Das, repaid the *banjāra* traders for the loan his father had taken, he used a *fārigh-khaṭṭī* to record this transaction. When, in 1690, his son Hamir Chand did the same for his brothers, he too used a *fārigh-khaṭṭī*. *Fārigh-khaṭṭīs* were thus the necessary documentary complement to *tamassuks* – one inscribed obligations, and the other released them.

Such obligations were not limited to loans. In 1735, we find an elderly Hamir Chand, accompanied by his son, Nihal Chand, using a *fārigh-khaṭṭī* again, this time to record the fulfilment of his obligations towards his own servants.[41] A man called Jagannath, self-described son-in-law of Anandi and Bhagirath Dhangar, declared that he had two documents in his possession, both inherited from his now-dead in-laws. One of these was a *tamassuk* of debt, and the other, a *patta-yi naukrī* (employment deed) which promised the fairly impressive sum of Rs. 8 per month. It is impossible to tell what work this *naukrī* really entailed; *dhangars* were listed by nineteenth-century British ethnographers as shepherds, many of whom had been amalgamated into the generic central and western Indian agricultural caste called *kunbī*.[42] Given the sum of money involved, and term *naukrī* itself – Bhagirath may have been among the retainer that a *chaudhrī* such as Hamir Chand would be expected to recruit in considerable numbers. Given that this was now the early eighteenth century, these men would be even more in the nature of private militias than before; Mughal claims of military service having become ineffective and non-existent. What is rather

[39] Despite the similarity in name, and the occasional use by certain nineteenth-century British lexicographers, a *fārigh-khaṭṭī* is not a 'quit-claim deed', which, in English law, is a deed used to transfer title to property without checks on the status of the property, unlike ordinary conveyancing.
[40] Elliot, *Memoirs*, p. 147 [41] NAI 2668/27 (1735).
[42] Russell and Lal, *Tribes and Castes of the Central Provinces of India*, Vol. II, p. 480.

more noticeable in Jagannath's claim and the documents he furnished, is the specific reference to his mother-in-law, Anandi. This woman appears to have been named in the *tamassuk* as one of the two creditors, and even been one of those named on the *paṭṭā* of *naukrī*. Whether we have here an eighteenth-century bandit queen, or a woman who kept the family finances and papers well under control, her son-in-law must have impressed the *zamīndārs* rather less, and that must have been why he needed to press a legal claim rather than continue in the position that his *paṭṭā* clearly allowed him to inherit.

In any case, either Hamir Chand did not need any more men, or Jagannath was an unsuitable candidate, or this family of employees, who had started advancing loans to the bosses, had become a bit too big for their boots and needed shaking off. Clearly Jagannath was too strong to be brushed aside, so a certain Hira Chand and Shaikh Ghulam Muhammad, the *kotwāl* of *qasba* Dhar, had to be appointed arbitrators to the dispute (*Hira Chand va Shaikh Ghulam Muhammad, kotwāl-i qasba Dhar, ba s̱ālisī īn muqaddama pardākhte*). Jagannath was given hundred rupees to clear all dues. At this point, this slippery character revealed that he had actually lost the vital *paṭṭā* of *naukrī*, but he was made to declare that if it turned up later, or indeed, if any more *tamassuks* surfaced, these would be void and not worth considering (*bāṭil wa na-masmu'*); and he said: 'after this, there does not remain with me any claim on Hamir Chand *chaudhrī* and Nihal Chand, nor any claim or quarrel'.

This time, the local *qāẕī*[43] was not called to grace the proceedings. Someone summarised the whole matter in formulaic Persian in a brief three-line note on the bottom of the right-hand margin – '*Bana bar ān in chand kalme ba ṭariq-i fārigh-khaṭṭī lā-dā'va-yi nawishte dāde shud* (On this basis a *fārigh-khaṭṭī* [and] no-claims was written)'; Jagannath's name, and some other matters were written in three lines of obscure Nagri, next to which a small Persian seal, reading 'Jagannath' was affixed twice. The main difference with earlier *fārigh-khaṭṭīs* was the presence of two other brief marginal notes which appears to be in Moḍi, or the 'twisted' Marathi script. The largest and most official looking seal in the document, positioned where the most authoritative seal in a document would usually, be, that is, above the main body of text, was square in shape. I have not been able to read the text in Nagri in this seal, but it begins with 'Śrī . . .'. It is impossible not to see these features as symptomatic of the fracturing of Mughal administration and the rapid encroachment of Maratha warlords. If so, this is rather rapid institutional change, and evidence of creation of an alternative dispute resolution and recording machinery, for the Persian marginal note in the document puts the date at 2 Muharram, RY 17. If the reference is to Muhammad Shah's reign, this would make the year 1734,[44] and

[43] We know that there was one in office, from the seal on the document NAI 2668/25 (1732).
[44] The conversion by the NAI cataloguer is wrong.

Malwa would be officially ceded to the Peshwa by the Mughal emperor only in 1738.[45] It was not regime change that caused the absence of the *qāẓī* and the use of arbitrators; this had happened in disputes resolved and recorded in the family archive even in the mid-seventeenth-century. For example, in 1658, on the bidding of the *jāgīrdār*, Purshottam Das and Paras Ram had arbitrated and resolved a boundary dispute between two villages; the document recording the resolution only had notes in the Nagri script on the margins, two plough symbols and a small, Persian seal of an unidentified officer. Now, however, there was a document that looked official and bore an official seal, only in a different script and bearing different pieties. This seal was very similar in appearance to those on later documents in the collection, written entirely in Nagri and referring to the raising of soldiers by Maratha '*mōkāsadārs*'.[46] The form of the document, however, remained the same; it was still a classic *iqrār* or binding declaration, narrating the facts, claims and resolution, self-nominated as *fārigh-khaṭṭī* in the Indo-Persian style.

The *fārigh-khaṭṭī* had an extended life, and lived well into the twentieth century. Within this collection, the most recent *fārigh-khaṭṭī* dates itself from 1195/1776.[47] In this document, a certain Anwar Beg and Syed Azam noted that they had made a claim on the mango trees in the garden of Sahib Rai, but after a resolution in court, they were relinquishing the claims. By this time, Dhar was well-established as a Maratha state under a branch of the Puwar dynasty. Regime change thus did not necessarily indicate a complete change in the forms of documents used to record disputes and resolutions. This should give us pause and encourage us to think more closely about the content of 'law' across regimes.

## Transacting Lives

The *qāẓī*'s court in the city of Dhar remained important for the pressing of various claims, well into the 1730s. These claims and their resolution continued to be recorded through the *fārigh-khaṭṭīs*, but the nature of some of these transactions makes it important to remind ourselves of the expanded meaning of 'legal deed' with which this chapter is working. We have seen how debt and obligation melted into taxation; in this section we shall discuss two documents which recorded exchanges over human lives, and their assessed money value.

The events recorded in these two documents, both of them *iqrārs*, and both sealed by Qāẓī Muhammad Mustafa, appear to have taken place sometime

[45] Amar Farooqui, *Smuggling as Subversion: Colonialism, Indian Merchants and the Politics of Opium, 1790–1843* (Lanham: Lexington, 2005), pp. 34–70.

[46] P Das 1750 Hin NCD (Private+Author). [47] P Das 1785 NCD.

between 1703 and 1709.[48] In what appears to be the earlier document, a man called Kalyan, the son of Nathu, turned up at the *qāẕī*'s court, together with his son Dalu and his wife Ganga. They identified themselves as of the *qaum* of *khyāṭī*, tailors. They were not exactly local, since they described themselves as inhabitants of the town of Kharkun, in *sarkār* Bijagarh.[49] They had come to complain about the disappearance of a Kalyan's son, Hira, during a major quest in which he had been accompanying Rupa *chaudhrī* of the town of Dhar, in the capacity of Rupa's servant. Hira had gone with Rupa to Shahjahanabad (Delhi) to lodge a petition (*mustaghasa*) against the oppression of the *jāgīrdār* of *pargana* Amjhera – Rao Jasrup.

Now this *Rāthoḍ* Rajput noble[50] was not an easy man to deal with. Although an elite soldier (*ahdī*)[51] called Muhammad Ashiq was despatched from Delhi, and he accompanied Hira to Rao Jasrup's court, despite days of arguing, nothing was achieved. In fact, as soon as the soldier gave up and left, Jasrup imprisoned Hira. For three months, his family received no news of whether he was alive or dead. Desperate, they lodged a claim against Bardman, Dev Chand, Ratan Chand, Kalyan Chand, Nihal Chand and Aman Chand – sons of Rupa, who appears to have died by this time. In their claim, the claimants demanded that Hira be found, and to their credit, their employer's sons made a great deal of effort to find the missing man. The proud and oppressive Rao Jasrup did not even deign to respond to such queries, and the search had to be eventually called off.

Hira's old father, son and wife now took their appeal to Nawab Marhamat Khan, the *faujdār* of *sarkar* Mandu. The *faujdār* decided that it was pointless to pick a quarrel with the *Rāthoḍ jāgīrdār*, and instead summoned the sons of Rupa *chaudhrī*. Having made his investigations, he decided that the equivalent of eight month's salary for Hira, which amounted to 32 rupees, would be an adequate compensation for the loss suffered by his family. The poor people must have felt that this was the best outcome they could hope for under the circumstances, and so, the money being handed over to them, they made a declaration (*iqrār*) in writing, that they had no further claims, and that if, due to quarrelsomeness or naughtiness they made any demands related to Hira

[48] NAI 2668/23 has two seals, one clearly 1115 (1703) and the qāẕī's seal possibly 1116 (1704); the other document, NAI 2703/42 has three seals: the clearly backdated 1100 (1689), 1113 (1701) and the qāẕī's seal 1121 (1709).

[49] William Irvine, *Later Mughals* (ed.) Jadunath Sarkar, Reprint (New Delhi: Oriental Books Reprint Corporation, 1971), pp. 161–2.

[50] Mehrangarh Museum Trust, 'Rathore Dynasty Tree', http://freepages.genealogy.rootsweb.ancestry.com/~princelystates/states/r/rathore.html.

[51] *Aḥdīs* (literally: sole, alone) were elite gentlemen soldiers directly recruited by the imperial government, often forming the personal guard of the emperor. See Irvine, *The Army of the Indian Moghuls*, pp. 43–4; and I. H. Qureshi, 'The Army of the Great Mughals', *Pakistan Historical Society*, 6: 1 (1958), 34–54 at 37–8.

in future, such claims would be void and non-cognisable. Somebody called Muhammad Hussain, who had a proper Persian seal, witnessed the document, as did five others, writing in the Nagri script. One of these was *chaudhrī* Hamir Chand of *pargana* Dhar, and the other *qānūngō* Jaswant Rao, also of Dhar. The claimants did not write their names, and instead drew symbols – Hira's mother, Ganga, drew a shaky *swastika*, while his father and brother drew symbols that looked like large scissors – which corresponds rather neatly with their stated profession of barbers. All these symbols were superscribed with their names, in the Persian script. The *qāẕī* superscribed a little note on the document, summarising the case – that Kalyan and others had recorded their relinquishing their claims (*lā-da'va*) on Rupa's heirs, and the fact of their having taken possession (*qabẕ al-waṣūl*) [of the compensatory sum]. Then he sealed it, and that was that.

These were troubled times in Malwa. From 1681, Mughal and Maratha armies had been criss-crossing the province, and from as early as the 1690s, Maratha war bands had begun raiding Malwa in search of tribute.[52] Then Emperor Aurangzeb Alamgir died in 1707, leading to a vicious succession battle between his sons and grandsons. Before Prince Mua'zzam emerged victorious as Bahadur Shah, several armies followed the obligatory path through Malwa, on their way towards the imperial capital, testing the loyalties of *mansabdārs* posted in the region but also all measures of *zamīndārs* ensconced in the regions they traversed. An entrenched clan of middle-sized Rajput *zamīndārs*, big enough to have acquired a *jāgīr*, possibly on privileged non-transferable terms, made the *Rāthōḍ*s of Amjhera a difficult entity to handle for imperial Mughal officials – whether a commando despatched from Delhi, or the local *faujdār*, or the *qāẕī*. Under such circumstances, one can see why the *faujdār* would propose a settlement in cash, and why indeed, the bereft family would accept it.[53]

This family was not the only one to have been affected by Rao Jasrup's manner of dealing with the servants of troublesome but weaker rivals, for in 1709 (1121 A.H.), *Qāẕī* Muhammad Mustafa recorded yet another *iqrār*, this time of five women.[54] These distressed women included Nanho, daughter of a learned man – a certain Shaikh Pesar Muhammad, but more importantly, the widow of a man called Daulat Khan. She came to the *qāẕī* with her daughters – Nur Bibi, Taj Bibi,

52 Irvine, *Later Mughals*, p. 164; also see Chapter 7.

53 Discussing cases of homicide decided in the Benares magistrate's and later Resident's court, during the earliest years of British supremacy in the late eighteenth century, Radhika Singha discusses several such instances of acceptance of 'blood-money', especially by impoverished kin, for whom the money made a more positive difference than the execution of the murderer would. Of course, in this case, there was no possibility of the murderer being punished in any way, let alone executed. Radhika Singha, *A Despotism of Law: Crime and Justice in Early Colonial India* (Delhi: Oxford University Press, 1998).

54 NAI 2703/42 (1709 – by date on seal).

Chand Bibi and Hayati, and described her family as weavers (*qaum-i mū'min safīd bāf*)[55] and residents of the town of Dhar. It turned out that Bardman and the other sons of Rupa *chaudhrī*, had hired Daulat Khan to go to Jasrup in *pargana* Amjhera and get news about the missing Hira. Rao Jasrup predictably imprisoned the scout. After some time, his family learnt that he had died in Jasrup's prison. The family, as heirs (*wāris̱ūn*) of Daulat Khan demanded of Bardman that he produce the man he had hired, and since (naturally) Bardman failed to do so, having no other option (*lā-chār*), the claimants declared their situation in the court of this very *qāẕī*.

Hearing their complaint, Qāẕī Muhammad Mustafa had felt it necessary to seek a legal opinion (*riwāyat*), and sent for one from the *muftī* of the city (*balda*) of Ujjain. Whatever the *riwāyat*, a set of arbitrators were appointed, through whose mediation it was decided that fifty-five rupees would be an adequate compensation. Bardman and his kinsmen paid the sum so decided, and the women of Daulat Khan's family declared that they had no further claims on the successors of Rupa. They did so in a document that self-described itself as a *lā-da'va* and *sulḥ-nāma*. Three men who could read Persian witnessed the document – of these Lutfullah Suhrawardi and Sabir Muhammad also added seals, Muhammad Baqir did not. Hamir Chand *chaudhrī* witnessed it in the Nagri script. The women plaintiffs drew what looks like leaf-symbols, their names were written in Persian above these marks. And of course, the *qāẕī* Muhammad Mustafa added his summary as superscription, and sealed the document.

Social groups abound in this brief episode of violence and law. We have encountered a violent Rajput *Rāthoḍ* sub-clan, an imperial crack-soldier, a frustrated imperial *faujdār*, a *qāẕī* who had performed the Haj, and poor people of tailor and weaver castes who hired themselves out on dangerous missions. What about their employers? Here we have some confusing angles – Rupa *chaudhrī* appears only in these two documents, but Bardman is also named as a *chaudhrī* who engaged to collect and pay the revenue of village Bhaghdi, in *pargana* Dhar.[56] It is quite likely therefore, that the employers of Hira and Daulat Khan were indeed descendants of Purshottam Das, or of another line of the family. However, the declarants in both documents said that Rupa *chaudhrī* was of the *qaum* of *ahl-i hirfa*.[57] This latter term normally referred to artisans; it could perhaps be an awkward reference to their *Kāyasth* status. We do not have any clear indication of the caste status of this family of *zamīndārs*; an associate or

55 Muzaffar Alam, 'The Mughals, the Sufi Shaikhs and the formation of the Akbari Dispensation', in Richard Eaton, David Gilmartin, Munis Faruqui and Sunil Kumar (eds.), *Expanding Frontiers in South Asian and World History: Essays in Honour of John F. Richards* (Cambridge: Cambridge University Press, 2013), pp. 124–63 at 127.

56 NAI 2703/43 (1726)

57 John Shakespear, *A Dictionary of Hindustani and English* (1834), p. 179.

kinsman is referred to in one document as a Brahmin (*zunnardār*), and two later documents, purporting to be copies of *farmāns*, designate them *Kāyasth Nigam*. They were clearly powerful players in a local economy of violence and order.

## *Munshāts* and *Munshīs*

As we have seen, the specific kind of legal deeds that survive from the activities of the Purshottam Das family are documents of *tamassuk* (obligation), *fārigh-khaṭṭī* (quittance/no-claims deed) and *hiba-nāma* (gift deed). All of these conform in structure and composition to documentary forms that were well known and widely used, not only in Mughal India, but until much later, well within the colonial period. The standardised format of these documents point to manuals of legal writing, or legal formularies, which scribes in Mughal India, quite like scribes in many other parts of the world,[58] would have used in their day-to-day work. In these tremendously unexciting manuals, however, lies an unexplored domain of cultural interaction and creativity, which we can explore to uncover the language in which ordinary people in Mughal India knew to express their entitlements and obligations. If *farmāns* and *parvānas* expressed the ideology of dynastic royal power, these scrappy documents of petty transactions bear evidence for what villagers in Malwa thought of their rights. They also tell us much about the language in which they expressed those entitlements and obligations, and conversely, about the multiple sources – linguistic and disciplinary – from which the languages of India developed specific functional forms, in this case, that of law.

As in all other contexts, legal deeds from Mughal India, recording the transfer of property rights, are extremely formulaic. They make repeated use of predictable phrases, which are specific to the kinds of documents in question. The formulae are also shared, although with uneven overlaps across the Islamic and Persianate world. Thus, any documentary form recording a certain amount of cash being transferred or promised, stated the amount being transacted first in full, and then halved, in order to securely clarify the amount being transacted, for the same reason that the value of a cheque in the present day is written both in words and in numbers. The actual transfer of property or cash was always recorded in such documents with a declaration of possession, such that, for example, a person borrowing money always states that amount in question ' . . . *ba-ṭariq-i qarẕ dar qabẕ wa tasarruf-i khūd āwardam* (I brought the [money] into my possession, in the manner of a debt)'. Following a full description of the transaction, the document closed with a phrase that revealed its own type:

[58] For example, *The Formularies of Angers and Marculf: Two Merovingian Legal Handbooks* (translated) Alice Rio (Liverpool: Liverpool University Press, 2008).

'... *īn chand qalme ba ṭariq-e* [whatever is the documentary form] *nawishte dādam ke s̱ānī al-ḥāl sanad bāshad* (I give these few words in writing in the manner of ... so that later on, they can act as a legal deed)'.[59]

This was indeed the language of rights, and as we know, rights are always coded affairs. On the one hand, this was the language of lawyers, and as a specialist jargon, it bore all the marks of a specialist vocabulary, which included exclusiveness, opacity to outsiders or non-specialists, and specific functional value.[60] Lawyers, alongside merchants and criminals, are among social groups frequently associated with the production and utilisation of highly developed jargons, whose impenetrability always produced in outsiders the suspicion of meaninglessness and fraud. Jargons are also frequently associated with linguistic creativity (or eclecticism and bowdlerisation, depending on one's taste), and specifically, with multiple linguistic sources. This was certainly the case with legal deeds produced in Mughal India, with their multiple sources of vocabulary and phraseology – which ranged from Islamic jurisprudence and Arabic terminology to Indo-Persianate governance to vernacular-medium corporate assertion. Legal deeds were a site par excellence for the proliferation of heteroglossia, in which the boundaries between vocabularies and grammars moved along a fluid spectrum of registers, rather than in neatly compartmentalised boxes.[61]

Indian books of *fiqh* contained very large sections of legal formularies or *shurūṭ*, the most outstanding example of this being the imperially sponsored *Fatāwá-yi ʿAlamgīrī*, commissioned by the Mughal emperor Aurangzeb Alamgir, which was completed by a team of Islamic jurisprudents or *fuqāha*, led by a scholar from Burhanpur.[62] The *FA* included a large Book of Shurūṭ (*Kitāb al-shurūṭ*),[63] which included models and instructions for writing, among other things, deeds of marriage, divorce, manumission, sale, pre-emption, lease, endowment, mortgage, and significantly for us, gifts and declarations. There was no specific document recommended for the recording of debts.

*Shurūṭ* were not, however, the only source of models for legal deeds written in Mughal India. While scholars working on other contexts have discovered works of jurisprudence specifically addressing local evidentiary and documentation needs, and have thus indeed revealed the bridge between Islamic jurisprudence

59 For example, in NAI 2668/20, which we shall discuss.

60 Peter Burke and Roy Porter, *Languages and Jargons: Contributions to a Social History of Language* (Cambridge: Polity Press, 1995).

61 For a very useful discussion of heteroglossia in connection with Urdu, see Javed Majeed, 'The Jargon of Indostan': An Exploration of Jargon in Urdu and East India Company English', in *Ibid.*, pp. xxxx.

62 Mouez Khalfaoui, 'Al-Fatawa Al-ʿAlamgiriyya (al-Hindiyya)', in *The Encyclopaedia of Islam*, 3rd Edition, Part 3 (Leiden: E.J. Brill), pp. 120–2.

63 Sheikh Nizam and others, *Fatāwá-yi 'Alamgiri*, translated to Urdu by Maulana Saiyid Amir Ali (Lahore: Maktaba Rahmaniya, n.d.), Vol. X, pp. 9–124; the 'Book' or section on *shurūṭ* runs pp. 125–298.

and Islamic legal documentation, in India, this mediation was more complex. Here, Islamic kingdoms and empires reigned over a persistent majority of non-Muslim people for eight hundred years and were particularly united in their use of (legally untrained) non-Muslim scribes, or *munshīs*, whose religious, social and educational make-up utterly distinguished them from the *ulama*, or Islamic jurists. These men were trained in Persian literary forms, including history and diplomatic correspondence, at the upper end of the scale, and account-keeping and revenue-management, often in a combination of (more) local vernaculars and esoteric accountants' scripts, at the lower end.[64] The stalwarts of this pan-imperial scribal class produced books of model prose, *munshāt*, a word derived from *inshā* or prose-writing. From the seventeenth century onwards, *munshāts* produced in Mughal India began to contain a section on legal forms, which was designated *qibālejāt-i sharī'a* or legal deeds.

My current understanding is that the legal sub-sections of *munshāts* happened to precede the first *shurūṭ* written in India, that is, the relevant section in the imperially sponsored *Fatāwá-yi 'Alamgiri*, by about eighty years. Despite its early origins, *munshāt* as an Indo-Persian literary genre, really came into its own under the Mughals. Manuscripts of only three Persian-language *munshāts* composed in India before the Mughal period have survived; the *'Ijāz-i Khusrawī* of the famous poet Amir Khusraw Dehlwi, the *Inshā-yi Mahru*, and the *Riyāz al-Inshā* of Mahmud Gawan.[65] Of these, the first two were courtiers of the Khalji and Tughlaq sultans of Delhi in the fourteenth century, and Gawan (1411–81) was the Persian courtier of the Bahmani sultans of Bidar in north Karnataka.[66] None of these contain any legal formulae; they were essentially epistolaries, that is, formularies of letters, mainly diplomatic and royal but also those of *qāẓīs* and *Shaikhs*, and in Mahru's case, a delightful sprinkling of admonitory letters to his son, who was clearly not keeping up with his peers in his commitment to his studies. It was only with the Mughals that learning to write legal deeds became an essential qualification for *munshīs*.

### Writing in Law

It is now time to take the magnifying glass even closer to our documents, and take a look, not only at their use of multiple languages and scripts, but also the

[64] Alam and Subrahmanyam, 'The Making of a Munshi', 61–72; Rosalind O'Hanlon and David Washbrook (eds.), Special issue on Munshis, Pandits and Record-Keepers: Scribal Communities and Historical Change in India, *IESHR*, 47: 4 (2010): 441–615. For lower-level scribes, who wrote, for example, in Marathi in the Modi script, or even lower, in Tamil, and not on expensive paper, but on palm leaf, see Raman, *Document Raj*.

[65] I. A. Zilli, 'Development of inshā literature to the end of Akbar's reign', in Muzaffar Alam; Francoise 'Nalini' Delvoye; Marc Gaborieau (eds.), *The Making of Indo-Persian Culture: Indian and French Studies* (New Delhi: Manohar, 2000), pp. 309–49.

[66] Eaton, *A Social History of the Deccan*.

patterns of that co-deployment. In general, our documents are outstanding examples of that phenomenon which was the bane of language activists of all hues in mid-nineteenth century India. This was the 'impure' written language(s) of offices and courts, which failed to live up to the literary standards of re-discovered classical literatures, sported notoriously 'mixed' vocabularies abounding in administrative Persian, and were written in a variety of scripts and hands that came to be increasingly condemned as illegible and susceptible to various forms of corruption. It is now time to look beyond that historical indictment, not only to historicise and analyse that modern politics of language, and to understand the modes of early modern language use on its own terms. Why did people write legal documents in more than one language and script? Further on to the mechanisms and sociology of multi-lingualism: did the same hand write both sections; and in what order were they written?

In South Asian studies, these questions have primarily been essayed from the point of view of literary studies. In other contexts, historians have attempted to explain them on the basis of function – related to the requirements of distinct jurisdictions, and to the movement of people between them. Such propositions have been strongly Mediterranean-focussed, and predominantly with reference to the experiences of Jewish individuals, pulled between the claims of Islamic state courts and unofficial but demanding tribunals of their own communities.[67] On the other hand, studies of a recently discovered documentary cache from twelfth-century Bamiyan, in present-day Afghanistan, point to more complex linguistic features in documents evidencing Jewish communities' formal and informal interactions with Islamic law. The Bamiyan documents, for example, appear to be a family archive (quite like our own), and consist of legal documents such as *iqrārs*, but also personal letters, and are all written in Judaeo-Persian, which means Persian written in the Hebrew script. What makes this inter-graphia (to coin a term) even more interesting is that the writers of such letters and documents also combined these scripts, often within the same sentence and the same word! The very plausible rationale for such digraphia that scholars working on these documents have proposed is entirely pragmatic – lack of space at the end of a line and the suitability of the letter from one script rather than another, for example.[68]

It is with these exciting possibilities, which suggest poly-lingual practice, with variable but necessarily combined dexterity in a number of scripts and languages, that I wish to take a closer look at patterns of language and script use, within the archive of the family of Hindu landlords whose story we are

67 Jessica Marglin, *Across the Lines: Jews and Muslims in Modern Morocco* (Yale University Press, 2016); Marglin echoes Khan's introductory comments in *Arabic Legal and Administrative Documents*.

68 Haim, 'An Early Judeo-Persian Letter', Vol. 26, 103–19; example of such digraphia in line 6 and 13, verso of the document presented, p. 105.

pursuing in this book. In this connection, I also propose that, in order to understand the deployment of languages and scripts, we need to understand the different kinds of documents present in the collection, and map linguistic usage onto a context-sensitive formal-cum-functional typology. By formal, I mean the self-nominated form of document: Mughal Persian documents typically named themselves with a formulaic sentence, usually in the first or final lines of the documents. By functional, I mean the substantive directive, petitionary or transactional purpose of the document. In this case, since we already know about the protagonists very well, we do not just have to speculate on the mutual relationships of parties and their interests and aims; we can work from fairly full information about them, and from that starting point we can begin to tell what kinds of language-script use featured in which kinds of documents. This is a provisional typology proposed in order to systematically organise the documents in this family's collection.

The number of documents that demonstrate any form of bilingualism (two languages) and/or digraphia (two scripts) within the collection is limited; 37 out of 195 documents bear such features, that is, around 18 per cent. Moreover, the linguistic and graphic diversity is clearly distributed towards the right-hand side of this typology, with contracts and transactional documents and testimonial records showing a combination of Rajasthani-Hindi and archaic Nagri script, and in some of the later material, Marathi and Modi script.

Table 4.1 *Typology of documents in the Purshottam Das archive*

| Orders | Petitions | Tax contracts | Interpersonal transactions | Documents related to adjudication |
|---|---|---|---|---|
| *Farmān* (only copies) | *Iltimās* | *Qaul qarār-i pattā-yi ijāra* | *Hiba-nāma* (gift deed) | *Sanad* recording *qāẕī's decision* |
| *Nishān* | *'Arzdāsht* | *Muchalka* | *Tamassuk* (deed acknowledging a debt or other obligation) | *Maḥẕar-nāma* |
| *Parvāna* | | *Qabuliyat* | *Fārigh-khaṭṭī* (deed of emptying of obligations) | |
| *Dastak* | | | *Iqrār* or *iqrār-nāma* (generic – binding declaration) | |
| *Khaṭ/Kharīṭa* | | | *Nikāḥ-nāma* (deed of marriage – for Muslims; naturally absent in our collection) | |
| | | | *Rāẕī-nāma* (deed of agreement – of any kind) | |

However, such bilingualism and digraphia was of various types. The clearest full-blown type is the co-situation of two languages in the same document, scribed in two distinct scripts, and located in vertical sections – the Persian/Perso-Arabic above, the Hindi/Nagri beneath. This is almost unfailingly the case with documents that call themselves *qaul qarār*, a kind of tax contract. Although 'tax contract' is an odd term to use today, it made full sense in a context where revenues were a matter of negotiation, usually between individual village headmen and a *jāgīrdār*.

When we examine the first *qaul* in our collection, dated 1626, we see that it is both bilingual and bi-scribal. Although the content of two parts of the text is nearly identical – with very large proportion of Persian words in the lower Hindi section, including the use of the same calendar, there are slight differences. Short phrases, including '*sahī hamārā qaul bolē hai*' (a true declaration has been made) which does give us autonomous Hindi verb-form, together with pronouns and particles, provide the essential template for distinguishing between languages. Also, there is at least one distinct formulaic phrase at the end, '*bidi*', which signifies an order, which one also sees in the *parvānas* issued from the Kacchwaha chancellery with relation to the temples at Mathura.[69]

When talking of grants scribed by Rajput chancelleries, however, it is worth considering the documents whereby grants were made to the Mathura temple by *mansabdārs-jāgīrdārs* of the Kacchwaha house over two centuries. Strikingly, and unlike most other *parvānas*, these documents were bilingual and bi-scribal – the Persian on the left and the Rajasthani on the right. The fact that the two languages are here vertically arranged (rather than one beneath the other) makes a striking visual point about the equivalence of languages. Also, the Rajasthani portion, written in Nagri script is much more linguistically autonomous than the Hindi-Nagri portion in the Dhar *qaul qarār* we just discussed. Thus we can begin to speculate that in some of the noble households, distinct chancellery styles began to develop, which, in certain classes of documents, especially those expressing royalty (so, *parvānas*), made space for the growth of linguistically distinct documentation styles.

## Originals, Summaries, and Copies

The second way in which multilinguality worked is through 'translated copies'. This phrase may appear to be an oxymoron, but this is because of a series of presumptions in our mind with regards to originality, which we implicitly contrast with reproduction on the one hand and transformation of any kind on the other. Situated as we are now in a world of mass reproduction through print and the infinite reproductive as well as transformative capacity of digital media,

69 Horstmann, *In Favour of Govinddevji*.

we fetishise the original artefact. We imagine a unique hand producing the original, all subsequent copies and versions being reductions of the essence of that original. There may also be an implicit chronology in this vision – which valorises and grades all such inevitably deviant versions by antiquity – the older the copy or version, the closer it is assumed to be to the essence of the original. We even transfer some of this fetish value to early short-run print editions of culturally significant books, such as Shakespeare's *Folio*, for example.

In the manuscript world, however, written artefacts were ranked differently, with reference to factors other than faithfulness to the original or antiquity. Based on scholarship related to literary production in the Persianate world, in particular, it appears that texts were valued for the quality their re-worked contents – the debates about the relative value of Nizami's *khamsa* versus Amir Khusrau's appear to be quintessentially modern, for example, and there is no indication that the creative changes introduced by Khusrau were seen by his contemporary audiences as edgy or violative in the way that Shakespeare purists sometimes do.

Translators in that cosmopolitan world should be seen as retellers, and of a piece with Khusrau. Then, as now, their attempt was to make sense to their intended audience, but they appear to have been less restrained by concerns about fidelity to the words and concepts of their source text, and more concerned about the effect they wished to produce. In that process, it may be perceived as perfectly valid to summarise the less interesting portions of a text, and expand upon the parts more relevant to the aims of the author/re-teller. It may also be seen as valid to replace key terms with others, and situate the latter within a conceptual genealogy extrinsic to the text; for instance, when Sanskrit religious texts are translated into Persian by Sufis in order to provide yet another model of conceptualising and accessing the divine. A striking example of this is the Persian *Gītā* of Abd al-Rahman Chisti, a Sufi who died in 1683 CE.[70]

In addition, translation is a rather different exercise when the audience can be assumed to know some elements of all the languages involved. Where present-day authors, especially those dealing with diasporas, sprinkle their texts with untranslated words from a source culture/language in order to evoke alterity and exoticism or authenticity (with tangled politics associated with each approach), Persian writers in India retained words from Indic languages, usually transcribing them in the Perso-Arabic script, for more functional

[70] Roderic Vassie, 'Persian Interpretations of the Bhagavadgīta in the Mughal Period: With special reference to the Sufi version of Abd al-Rahman Chisti'. Unpublished PhD Thesis, SOAS, London, 1988; Ilyse R. Morgenstein Fuerst, 'A Muslim Bhagavad Gita: 'Abd al-Rahman Chisti's interpretative translation and its implications', *Journal of South Asian Religious History*, 1 (2015), pp. 1–29.

reasons. Accuracy with names (of plants, animals, their products, physical conditions, persons and places) was a concern that the writers of medical and legal texts shared. They may also have shared concern about the accurate identification of doctrines and procedures through the precise use of technical terms.

In Chapter 2, we have also seen a grant made by a very low-ranking imperial noble, a Rajput called Jujhar Singh, to the same family of *zamīndārs*. While visually, this might appear monolingual, in fact, it attests to its origin in multilingual practice, because the first line says: *parvāna ba-mazmūn Hindavī ba-muhr-i Rao Jūjhar Singh* (*parvāna* of Hindi content under the seal of Rao Jujhar Singh).[71] It appears that in this case, translation, particularly to Persian, was not seen as a diminution of authenticity of an authoritative document; it may have even captured its essence better than the Hindi original.

## The Marginal Languages

The third mode of marginality is through marginal notes, symbols and signatures. Non-Persian attestations are most frequent in transactional documents (of sale, taking and repaying of debts and so on), and also testimonial documents related to disputes. Here, parties as well as other witnesses had their names written on the right-hand and bottom margins of the document, following the formulaic declaration '*gawāh shud*' or '*sākshī*', both meaning witness(ed) in Persian and Hindi, respectively. It is striking, in this case, that such attestations appeared to reveal a preference for the script one's name is written in; Hindus, including members of our family, seemed to prefer Nagri.

Others, who could not read or write at all, had their consent indicated with graphic symbols, following another set-phrase '*alāmat-i dastkhaṭ*' (sign of the hand). In the choice of symbols, we see a wonderful array of significant images, comprehensibly aligned with castes/professions – Rajputs (including members of our family, who thought of themselves as military entities) preferred the *kaṭār* (the stab-dagger, later associated with Rajput identity), whereas a family of barbers chose scissors.

Together, this mode of multilingualism should encourage us to think beyond the clearly inadequate equation of language and religious identity, but also the notion of a centrally directed Mughal language policy, whereby Hindi is discarded once and for all by imperial decision, and inevitably in Akbar's court, leaving Persian to trickle down to the corners of the empire. Just as English never managed to erase the astonishing diversity of Indian languages and scripts, nor resist the grammatical, lexical and phonetic incursions that made it an Indian language, Persian and the Perso-Arabic script too, were

[71] See Chapter 2.

situated in a complex and creative interplay with other languages and scripts. Legal documents offer us a large corpus of material to study that interplay systematically; this chapter has made some effort to begin that work.

In order to go further, however, we also need to discard the imperial court–centric fantasy of the Mughal empire, and understand the significance of not just princely, but aristocratic households. We also need to re-examine the 'idiomatic' translations of technical terms using early modern English vocabulary, which have obscured rather than illuminated Mughal practice. 'Chancellery' is one of those unfortunate words; the sole book on Mughal documentation practices, while based on the survey of a large number of manuals and documents, is plagued by the notion of a stationary central imperial chancellery, which ignores the persistently peripatetic nature of the Mughal court. Moreover, the vast majority of orders would have been issued not by the emperor, but by the *jāgīrdār-mansabdārs*, implying both multiple sites of document production, but also, potentially, variable documentation and archiving practices. In fact, the linguistic differences between *parvānas* in different private collections even suggest *gharānas* of documentation,[72] with language use tied to the household tradition of great (and small) nobles.

## Conclusion

This chapter, which focussed on the documents recording transactions between members of the family and their kin, associates and rivals, was intended to take the story into the intimate and everyday crevices in which law flowed in Mughal India. Here too, as with orders and tax records, 'law' and 'legal documents' emerged from a combination of authoritative sources in which the royal and the legal were inseparable. Counter-intuitively, or perhaps not, it is at this intimate and everyday level that the Islamic identity of that law becomes most obvious, with several documents revealing the percolation of pan-Islamic legal forms into the Indian countryside.

This is also the level at which we see the most complex interplay of languages and scripts. It as if in the permissive court of the *qāẕī* and the voluntary transactions between individuals, the overwhelming grandeur of classical Persian and the Perso-Arabic script eased up, permitting, on the one hand, the use of Hindi, Marathi and Indic scripts, but also Arabic. All these languages and scripts intertwined, produced a visually and phonetically linguistic sphere within which law was articulated in the lives of this family of Hindu *zamīndārs* from Mughal Malwa.

[72] I am grateful to Syed Akbar Hyder for suggesting this to me.

# 5 Disputes: Judges and Courts

## Law in Many Courts

We only know about all these activities of the family of Mohan Das – agrarian pioneering, military entrepreneurship and so on – because members of this family were adept at legal documentation. They meticulously sought, preserved, re-created and re-validated documentary records of their offices, perquisites and obligations, often utilising the offices of the local *qāẕī* in order to do so. They also disputed their entitlements and obligations with entertaining regularity, and in doing so, once again involved the local *qāẕī*. Documents recording such disputes, and their resolution, push us firmly towards reconsidering the role of *qāẕīs* in Mughal India, and the role of the classic institutions of Islamic law in that complex polity. Furthering what Farhat Hasan has shown, *qāẕīs* in Mughal India can not simply be taken to be judges dealing in Islamic law and with Muslim subjects alone. On the other hand, as Richard Eaton suggested with relation to Bengal,[1] and as scholars from all over the Islamic world have pointed out,[2] law in Islamic empires was clearly not exhausted through its deployment in *qāẕīs*' courts. This book is an effort to build on and extend those formulations by using the concepts of Islamicate law and *dāi'ra* or circles of jurisdiction. This chapter comes to the heart of the matter by showing how *qāẕīs* and their authority coexisted and overlapped with the jurisdictions of several other powers, producing a totality that Mughal subjects like our protagonists understood to be 'law'.

In this corner of the Mughal empire, as princes and *mansabdārs* came and went, armies marched hither and thither and merchants big and small took grain and cloth along the highways, one official remained something of a constant, learning about all the deals and difficulties of Purshottam Das and his family. This was the *qāẕī* – the classical Islamic judge, whose evident imbrication in recording and, on occasion, adjudicating the rights and obligations of this family of Hindu *zamīndārs* urges us to rethink our current understanding of

[1] Eaton, *Rise of Islam*, pp. 180–3.
[2] Baldwin, *Islamic Law and Empire*; Sartori, *Visions of Justice*.

the place of Islamic law in the Indian subcontinent, which was ruled by Muslim kings for eight centuries, but whose population remained predominantly non-Muslim. It remains an implausible, although very widely shared conclusion among historians of the Mughal empire, that *sharīʿa* as a system of jurisprudence (as opposed to pious reference to political and spiritual righteousness) remained unworkable under the obvious demographic conditions of India, and the pragmatic policy of tolerance generally adopted by the regime. This assumption is bolstered by a conception of Islamic law, which, despite the huge progress in research in the last two decades, remains highly *systemic* in a way that makes it impossible to conceive of it being applicable under the conditions of the Mughal empire.

Let us begin by taking stock of that systemic view of the *qāẕī*'s role, and proceed from there to explore the stories that the documents generated by this propertied and highly fractious family tell us.

## The *Qāẕī* in Islamic Law

A systemic conception of Islamic law conceives of a fully coherent legal system, whose corner piece is the jurisprudent, the *muftī*, fully trained in Islamic jurisprudence or *fiqh* under the guidance of experts, in one or more Islamic schools of higher learning: *madrasas*. In any specific case, the officially appointed judge, the *qāẕī*, directs the initial adjudication process by admitting pleas, inviting confession or denial by the accused, selecting acceptable witnesses and recording their testimony, and considering any relevant documents produced by the parties. The facts established, he then calls upon the *muftī* to state the relevant legal doctrines and their contextually sensitive interpretation, through an anonymised question called *istifta*.[3] The *muftī*, in responding, takes into consideration a huge textual corpus, which reaches through the writings of the stalwarts of his preferred school of law, *mazhab*, back to the reported sayings and actions of the Prophet and his companions, *hadith*, and ultimately to the revealed word of God, the Quran. Since there is no system of precedents in Islamic law, this enormous intellectual exercise happens every time, at least in theory.[4] Because there may not be adequate guidance in the textual tradition available for consideration, or more commonly because the ancient jurists, being scholars, had recorded strident disagreements among themselves, the *muftī* is often called upon to exercise juristic preference, *istiḥsān*, in order to arrive at a response that is both doctrinally defensible and socially sensible. The *muftī's* considered response is the *fatwá*, which is no more and no less than

[3] To be accurate: de-specified; the generic names ʻUmar and Fatima are used in *istiftas*.

[4] This account is based on Hallaq, *Sharīʿa* ; Hallaq, 'From *Fatwā*s to *Furū*'; Tucker, *In the House of the Law*.

expert opinion, which the *qāẓī* may follow, disregard, or seek a second or third opinion on before making his judgement. The decision would then be recorded in a register of *sijills*, which would form a corpus of public record, and a sealed copy given to the parties. Specially trained scribes, generally called *kātibs* (from the Arabic verb *kataba*, to write) or possibly even *shurūṭīs* (referring to the manuals of documentation referred to in Chapter 4), would draft all documents, including depositions made by the parties.[5]

The weak points of this hyper-coherent vision are the points of actuation – the disputants, witnesses, the scribes and the enforcement agencies. Among other things, it leaves the king out of the story. A large number of historical studies, focussed exclusively on territories under the Ottoman empire, have shown that people often petitioned the sultan rather than the local *qāẓī* – while in some cases this may simply have been a way of kick-starting the legal process rather than by-passing it, in others – and autonomous royal jurisdiction, threatening the authority of the *qāẓī*, appears to have developed.[6] Kings did not just resolve disputes, they also had a tendency of taking policy decisions and making rules that did not necessarily align with transcendent laws, which, if properly applied, would constrain their power. Such prolific legislation by the Ottomans, known as *kanun name*, came to be eventually accommodated by the jurists working as *muftī* and *qāẓī*.[7]

Reconciliation of the royal and juristic realm may have been achieved in several ways. In the Mediterranean regions, it appears that the concept of a separate, political sphere (*siyāsa sharī'a*) may have helped jurists to deal with such encroachments.[8] The Islamic political-legal doctrine, which considers

5 Hallaq, 'Model *Shurūṭ* Works', pp. 109–34.

6 Baldwin, 'Petitioning the Sultan'; Baldwin's argument is distinct from older arguments, which proposed the existence of a separate jurisdiction of 'bureaucratic justice' from the earliest days of Islam until (at least) the Mamluks, which was only partially explained by juristic writing from the 11th century onwards. See H. F. Amedroz, 'The Mazalim Jurisdiction in the Ahkam Sultaniyya of Mawardi', *Journal of the Royal Asiatic Society*, 2 (1911), 635–74; Jørgen S. Nielsen, *Secular Justice in an Islamic State: Maẓālim under the Baḥrī Mamlūks, 662/1264–789/1387* (Leiden: Nederlands Historisch-Archaeologisch Instituut te Istanbul, 1985); Jørgen S. Nielsen, 'Mazalim', in *Encyclopaedia of Islam*, 2nd edition, Brill Online, 2016, surveys the jurisprudential cognizance and rationalisation of this jurisdiction; Albrecht Fuess, 'Zulm by Mazālim? The Political Implications of the Use of Mazālim Jurisdiction by the Mamluk Sultans', *Mamluk Studies Review*, 13 (2009): 121–47; R. Irwin, 'The Privatization of 'Justice' under the Circassian Mamluks', Mamluk Studies Review 5 (2002): 63–70; Yossef Rapoport, 'Royal Justice and Religious Law: Siyāsah and Shari'ah under the Mamluks', *Mamluk Studies Review* 15 (2012): 71–102.

7 Gerber, *State, Society, and Law in Islam*.

8 Ann K. S. Lambton, *State and Government in Medieval Islam: An Introduction to the Study of Islamic Political Theory: The Jurists* (New York: Routledge/Curzon, 1981), pp. 138–52. For the origins, meaning, and different perceptions of the term, see F. E. Vogel, 'Siyāsah', in C. E. Bosworth, et al. (eds.), *The Encyclopaedia of Islam*, 2nd ed. (Leiden: Brill, 1997), Vol. 9, 693–6; and Bernard Lewis, 'Siyasa', in A. H. Green (ed.), *In Quest of an Islamic Humanism: Arabic and Islamic Studies in Memory of Mohamed al-Nowaihi* (Cairo: American University in Cairo Press, 1984), pp. 3–14.

the king as the fountain of justice, may also have helped,[9] as might have a healthy concern among the jurists for keeping their jobs and lives. Mughal emperors were famously capable of dismissing chief *qāẕīs* if they did not suit their policy imperatives: Akbar dismissed Abd al-Nabi after the execution of a Brahmin for blasphemy, against his express wishes, and his great-grandson Aurangzeb did it to *the qāẕī al-quẕẕāt* (chief *qāẕī*) who refused to convict Dara Shukoh of heresy.[10]

However, we restrict ourselves illogically if we only look to the imperial court and its decisions in order to understand how Islamic jurisprudence may have been intertwined with other sources of justice. As we have seen, Mughal nobles/imperial officers (*mansabdārs*), as representatives of the government (*vukāla-yi sarkār*) constantly took decisions – by making land grants, revoking them, resolving disputes between various functionaries and over access to natural and revenue resources, and directing succession to lucrative positions – many of which would be common areas of litigation in British courts from the late eighteenth century. In making those decisions, however, these *mansabdārs* often associated themselves with the local *qāẕī*, and more rarely, made passing references to the legal bases of their decisions, without a *muftī* in sight. In understanding Mughal law therefore, we may have to relinquish our modern-day distinction between administration and law; and understand how the *qāẕī* was situated within an array of authorities capable of taking normative and effective (i.e., therefore, legal) decisions.

Things also become muddier when we turn to the disputants themselves. In terms of its jurisprudence, Islam, being the latecomer among the Abrahamic religions, possesses a heightened awareness of religious diversity *ab initio*. The need to peaceably reconcile a universal law with a heterogeneous population led two main lines of jurisprudential reasoning, the first being the designation of some categories of people as 'People of the Book', and the other being the consideration of yet others as *z̲immīs*, or protected, provided they accepted the rule of Islam and their own subordinate status without contest.[11] A vast body of research, mainly related to Fatimid Egypt and the Ottoman empire, has shown that there could be considerable flexibility in the ascription of these categories to groups of people, and also that the considerate application of rules by *qāẕīs* and/or the existence of multiple alternative tribunals, some specifically geared to dealing with non-Muslims, could afford substantive justice to people in the formally inferior categories.[12]

[9] For discussions of this idea with reference to India, see, Mohammad Habib and Afsar Umar Salim Khan, *Political Theory of the Delhi Sultanate: Including a Translation of Ziauddin Barani's Fatawa-i Jahandari, Circa, 1358–9 AD*. (Delhi: Kitab Ghar, 1961).

[10] Bhatia, *Ulama, Islamic Ethics and Courts*, pp. 161–2.

[11] Anver M. Emon, *Religious Pluralism and Islamic Law: 'Dhimmīs' and Others in the Empire of Law* (Oxford: Oxford University Press, 2012).

[12] Marina Rustow, 'The Legal Status of Dhimmis in the Fatimid East: a View from the Palace in Cairo', in Maribel Fierro and John Victor Tolan (eds.), *The Legal Status of Dhimmis in the Islamic West* (Turnhout, Belgium: Brepols, 2013), pp. 307–32; Mark R. Cohen, 'A Partnership

None of this research goes far enough to tell us what happened when non-Muslim litigants were not a minority, but nearly the entire clientele of a *qāẕī*'s court; it does not tell us whether referring the case to a *muftī* would still be appropriate; and if so, which jurisprudential texts and traditions the *muftī* might consider applicable. Differentials of power naturally affect the course of justice in all contexts, but the existing literature on Islamic law does not tell us, except with reference to the very different modern European contexts, how Islamic law might work when a *qāẕī* is significantly less powerful and wealthy than most of the non-Muslim landlords, officials, traders and strongmen who took their disputes to his court. And indeed, it tells us nothing about why they should do so in the first place, if they were not required to, and the system was one that weighed against them.

Research using document collections comparable to this book, however, has led scholars to comment on the ubiquity of *qāẕīs* and their involvement in a range of disputes, not purely 'religious' ones.[13] Such comments are still based on the systemic understanding of *sharīʿa* that we have summarised. In this view, in order for a *qāẕī* to handle disputes among Hindu *zamīndārs*, for example, *sharīʿa* would have to take on a completely new meaning, derived from ethical or spiritual discussions outside the realm of jurisprudence, and basically stop being Islamic law. Farhat Hasan, in using yet another set of comparable documents and their copies, those pertaining to the port city of Surat, has noted the presence of Hindu merchant families in the court of the *qāẕī* of Ahmedabad, and also pointed out that the law that such litigants sought was the very recognisable provisions of Islamic law. In explaining these observations, Hasan has suggested that '*Sharīʿa* was a normative system that was shared by all sections of the local society and not just the Muslims'. Less in line with his own observations, however, he suggests that it worked by being 'flexible and ambivalent', closely integrated with 'local customary usages' and plastic enough to be fitted to local contexts by social actors.[14]

This chapter attempts to recreate the role of the *qāẕī*, situating his status and functions in relation to other possible authorities that Purshottam Das and his associates could turn to at various times, and tries to map the manner in which they made these choices.

## The *Qāẕī* and His Range of Authority

As we have seen in Chapter 4, the *qāẕī's* seal and notes appeared in documents that recorded property transactions between private parties, such as the

Gone Bad: Business Relationships and the Evolving Law of the Cairo Geniza Period', *Journal of the Economic and Social History of the Orient*, 56 (2013): 218–63; Al-Qattan, 'Dhimmis in the Muslim Court'; Appelániz, 'Judging the Franks', 350–78.

[13] Alam and Subrahmanyam, *The Mughal State*, pp. 31–2.

[14] Hasan, *State and Locality*, p. 76.

contracting or repayment of debt, the making of gifts or the declaration quittance of claims. It also appeared on copies of documents that recorded orders of high-ranking imperial officials, especially those documents that made or confirmed property-bearing grants. As such, the *qāẕī* appeared to play a role similar to that of the public notary in the early modern European context, or contexts where European legal systems were effective.[15] In this, the role of the *qāẕī* points to a clear difference between the systems based on common law or Roman law, and those based on Islamic law. As Fahad Bishara explains in his work on commercial contracts in the nineteenth-century Indian Ocean world, *katībs*, or scribes of such contracts were 'not expected to guarantee the authenticity of a previously written contract (although they were sometimes called upon to do so) nor were they expected to preserve copies of contracts that they drafted. They were tasked with bridging between the contracting parties and the law, not with furnishing the information necessary to enforce the law'.[16] Comparing our collection of documents with similar, and much larger and better-known caches from several parts of the Islamic world, suggests that it was the role of the *qāẕī* to provide that guarantee of authenticity.[17]

According to strict juristic doctrine, of course, documents, attested and sealed by no matter who, could only have secondary probative value; pride of place in the arena of evidence remained with the personal testimony of reliable and respectable witnesses. We know that this strict and impractical doctrine had been modified in many parts of the Islamic world. Of the four principal Sunni schools of law (*mazhab*, pl. *mazāhib*), the Malikis, followed in North Africa, are said to have gone furthest in accepting the probative value of documents. But the Hanafi school, prevalent in the Mughal empire, may not have been far behind.

A *farmān* of Aurangzeb, dated 20 Muharram, RY35 (1691), appointing the *qāẕī* of the city (*balda*) Pattan, in the province (*sūba*) of Gujarat and neighbouring areas, may have listed what had become established practice in the Mughal empire. After reciting all aspects of the *qāẕī's* service (*khidmat*) and his right to the taxes of certain villages, conditional upon his performance of those services, a crucial final line was added: 'The custom (*ṭariq*) of the inhabitants of the said city is that they consider the letters of attorney ('*khuṭūt-i vukālāt*) . . .

15 Burns, *Into the Archive;* on notaries in early-modern Europe, see Laurie Nussdorfer, Brokers of Public Trust: Notaries in Early Modern Rome (Baltimore, MD: Johns Hopkins University Press, 2009).

16 Bishara, *A Sea of Debt,* p. 126.

17 Khan, *Arabic Legal and Administrative Documents*, pp. 7–8, 29. Khan refers to the professional scribes-cum-witnesses, *'udul*, as 'notaries', but the content of the documents shows that this is another technical mistranslation; through the 'witness clauses' they wrote by their own hand, the *'udul* witnessed the transaction and attested to the accuracy of the document's contents and the fulfilment of various conditions, such as the mental and physical capacity of the parties. These witness clauses did not, of themselves, authenticate the document, although they supported it.

and the records of court judgements (*sijillāt*), in his [the *qāẓī*'s] writing and with his seal, as authentic (*mu'atabar shamarand*)'.[18] Evidence from many parts of the Islamic world suggests that the regard of the people of Patan for deeds and legal records signed and sealed by the *qāẓī* could not have been an eccentric local tradition.[19] Nearer home, the presence of many copies (*naqls*) of important documents in the collection of Purshottam Das's family, nearly every one of these authenticated by the local *qāẓī*, suggests that people in many other parts of Mughal India considered such *qāẓī*-attested documents as authentic.

Such active seeking of the *qāẓī's* seal for the authentication of documents by non-Muslims has been studied most intensively with regard to Jewish communities in various North African sultanates and the Ottoman empire.[20] In these cases, however, there was usually a formal procedure of 'double notarisation', first by communally and sometimes officially recognised Jewish notaries and then by Islamic *qāẓīs*. The reason for such procedure was clear – documents authenticated by the *qāẓī* were more likely to be upheld if disputed in state courts. While taking disputes outside the community was a clear violation of their own authority, in many cases, Jewish rabbis simply recognised reality and sometimes even explicitly recommended that people prepare for such eventuality by acquiring the *qāẓī's* seal on their documents.

Unlike the Jews, of course, Hindus were not a small minority in the Mughal empire. Even more strikingly, therefore, available records reveal no inclination of their part to acquire primary authentication in any kind of 'community court' before approaching the *qāẓī*. Looking at this unusually rich archive created by our family of *qānūngō*-cum-*zamīndārs* over several generations, we are able to map the various authorities that such significant commoners in rural Mughal India were able to appeal to, and detect some patterns of correlation between the types of issues and the kinds authorities appealed to. In doing so, we discover the *qāẓī* occupying a key position that complemented various others, such as the *qānūngōs* and *zamīndārs* themselves, and the imperial *mansabdār-jāgirdārs* whose temporary presence represented the awe-inspiring royal dimension that I have argued was a constant and essential element in the matrix that was imperial law. Within that matrix, the role of the *qāẓī*, or indeed that of the other adjudicative authorities, was not within a strictly defined separate sphere – defined by *sharī'a*

18 'Aurangzeb's *farmān* appointing a *qāẓī*', Or. 11698, British Library.

19 This is particularly, but not exclusively, true of the Jewish communities of Morocco whom Marglin studies, and also of Egypt, whose records, preserved in the Cairo *genizah* or storehouse, were acquired by the Cambridge University library, and is catalogued in Khan, *Arabic Legal and Administrative Documents*. A project that has been developing since the first discovery in 2011, is the Afghan Genizah project, based on an eleventh-century collection of documents from northern Afghanistan, which includes several documents in recognisable Islamic legal forms, but with no seals.

20 Marglin, 'Cooperation and Competition', pp. 111–30; also Haim Gerber, *Jews and Muslims in Ottoman Law, Economy and Society* (Istanbul, 2008).

or anything else – but functioned in a mutually reinforcing mode over a field of entitlements and obligations that encompassed tax contracts, surety and grants, as much as sale, gift, inheritance and endowment.

## The Man Who Would Be *Qāẕī*

In recognisable Islamic legal systems, the *qāẕī* is supposed to be the product of a specialised education as well as social system. He (until recently, a *qāẕī* was inevitably a man) would almost certainly belong to a family of jurisprudents, those who were experts in jurisprudence (*fiqh*). In training to become one of the *fuqahā'* himself, he would pursue a highly personalised course of learning, in which scholarship and personal relationships would be inseparable in the making of the man. He would also work to maintain a solid reputation of respectability and combine book learning with at least some level of spiritual achievement. Eventually, he could expect to acquire a position as *qāẕī*, a judge, in his native district to begin with. Only if he made an outstanding success of his career, by working on his connections and/or attracting the attention of high-ranking officials, possibly the emperor himself, would a *qāẕī* move on to greater things – from district to province to the imperial capital, not necessarily following any given path of promotion.

Our documents cannot really tell us much more about the *qāẕīs* who authenticated them, except their names and the years of their activity in the district of Dhar. We can also trace a small network of associates for each *qāẕī*, based on other signatories on the document, or on the narrative of their actions. But by noting the kinds of business the local *qāẕī* was involved in, and by comparing this with what we know of the role of the *qāẕī* in other Islamic or Islamicate contexts, we have offered some idea about the place of the *qāẕī* in the local administration and, by extension, local society. Now we can begin to use two different bodies of material – collective biographies (*taẕkiras*) and works of jurisprudence (*fiqh*) – in order to recreate the social and mental world, if not of these specific *qāẕīs*, then those of very comparable ones from around the Mughal empire.

A boy destined to become a *qāẕī* in the Mughal empire would spend most of his early student life acquiring intimate knowledge of the Quran, possibly memorising it, and learning the basics of Arabic grammar and rhetoric. A higher level of study would commence with his entry into a *madrasa* (literally: school, or place of learning, in Arabic),[21] where he would typically study a number of disciplines, including those that are classified a *manqulāt* (based on *naql*, or copying, that is, based on revelation) and those called

[21] George Makdisi, *The Rise of Colleges: Institutions of Learning in Islam and the West* (Edinburgh: Edinburgh University Press, 1981).

*ma'aqulāt* (based on human intelligence, *'aqal*). *Manqulāt* disciplines would include exegesis of the Quran (*tafsīr*), theology (*kalām*), traditions (*hadis̱*) and how to study them (*'usul al-hadith*), jurisprudence (*fiqh*) and its principles (*'usul al-fiqh*); and *ma'aqulāt* would include logic, but also medicine.[22] A man looking to make a career in law would be likely to concentrate on *hadith*, *fiqh* and *'usul al-fiqh*, with variable combinations of the other disciplines depending on the curriculum he followed.

In India, until the late nineteenth-century, choice of the content of study as well as the process of learning would be high personalised. The 'colleges', such as they were, were inseparable from the scholars who taught in them; in fact, the seat of learning would usually be the residence of the scholar, which would be a sacral complex combining mosque, (Sufi) shrine and *madrasa*. Pupils would actively seek out teachers famous for their knowledge of particular disciplines, even particular books. The working of the teacher–student relationship would depend almost entirely on personal dynamics, and if all went well, the student would be declared by the teacher to have learnt all that was needed in the particular area, and granted permission (*ijāza*) to teach it. This was effectively a graduation, but an eminent scholar would typically acquire several such permissions/graduations in the course of his learning.[23]

What we know far less about is the process by which this scholar of Islamic law would acquire the knowledge of fiscal rules and procedures on the one hand, and a range of customary laws, dues and obligations on the other, in order to officiate in key moments that occurred regularly in the lives of our protagonists. It seems to have been a case of learning by doing, although high levels of competence may have been achieved thereby.

As for actually acquiring the post of a *qāẕī*, especially at the district level, this appears to have been largely guided by succession, with some need to keep the emperor and his deputies happy. It might be different of course, if one were an illustrious foreign traveller and scholar, such as Ibn Batuta, in which case appearance in the emperor's court might lead to an instant appointment. There is nothing to indicate the presence of such illustrious foreign-born appointees in *pargana* Dhar; *qāẕī* Mustafa, in particular, seems to have been a local man.

When this book was nearly complete, my indefatigable collaborator and correspondent, Amit Choudhary, managed to contact the gentleman who is still regarded as the *shahr* (city) *qāẕī* of Dhar. The small number of Persian *parvānas* shared with me showed that the members of the family held *madad-i mā'ash* (charitable) grants from Emperor Muhammad Shah's period,

22 Hallaq, *Sharī'a*, pp. 125–58.

23 Metcalf, *Islamic Revival in British India*; Francis Robinson, *The 'ulama of Farangi Mahal and Islamic Culture in South Asia* (London: Hurst, 2001).

that is, the eighteenth century.[24] A *shajara* (family tree) claimed an older connection with the area. The connection between persons named in these documents and *Qāẕī* Muhamad Qudratullah, named in the Dhar State Report of 1924–25, is difficult to establish. But Qudratullah had reported descending from a certain Abdul Fateh, who received his *sanad* from Emperor Shah Alam; he also possessed deeds of grants from Maratha times.[25] Changes in regimes did not necessarily uproot the *qāẕīs* nor end their jurisdiction entirely.

## Village Quarrels

Let us begin, however, with the jurisdiction of our protagonists themselves. In 1653, there was a dispute over the usage of water from a pond (*tālāb*) adjoining two villages – Navgaon and Khilchipur. It appeared that villagers from the *mauza*ʿ Tornod had, in recent times, taken it upon themselves to draw water from this pond for their own fields. No doubt complaints were made, although it is not clear by whom exactly. The *jāgīrdār*, who called himself a servant of Prince Murad Baksh (at that time the governor of Malwa) on his seal, issued a *parvāna* saying:

> no one should, for any reason, take possession of the water of the lake other than the subjects, who had since olden times, not been [*sic*] in possession (*mutaṣarraf*) [of the lake], and should not cause obstacles to their [the subjects'] situation and should not count themselves among partners/co-owners of this pond (*khud rā sharīk va ba-ham dar ān tālāb na shamarand*) and not become the reason for chastisement and correction.[26]

While superficially an executive decision, the *jāgīrdār* clearly referred to a pre-existing set of rights, calibrated through notions of possession and partnership. The countryside was not a blank sheet for Mughal officials to stamp their writ on; it was crisscrossed with rights that derived from ancient (*qadīm*) custom and imperial recognition, those of peasants and those of *zamīndārs* that lived off the peasants. Moreover, such rights could clearly be encroached upon, and disputed, requiring adjudication by someone higher in the pecking order of the beneficiaries of the peasants' work and imperial office. In making his decision, power and patronage no doubt swayed the *jāgīrdār*, but when issuing his order, he was constrained to refer to that body of rights.

At other times, there appeared to be fewer stable rights that could be referred to and/or the disputants were more equally balanced in the eyes of the power-holders. In such cases, the 'lord' of the area (the *jāgīrdār*) appeared to call upon *zamīndārs* in their capacity as village officials, to arbitrate. In 1658, for

[24] Dhar *shahr qāẕī* documents, 1724 and 1725. Digital copies in my possession.
[25] *Report of the Administration of the Dhar State 1920–21 to 1925–26* (Dhar, 1926), Table XXXI.
[26] DAI, LNS MSS 235 j.

example, there was a quarrel about the boundaries between the villages of Gondri (currently East Nimar, Burhanpur district) and Bahram Kot (no longer on Google). Gondri deputed one headman, Kalka, and Bahram Kot sent three, Sagu, Kalu and Hassan, to the local *mansabdār-jāgīrdār*, respectfully referred to only by an elaborate title: The Abode of Governance. The noble so approached *appointed* Purshottam Das *chaudhrī*, Paras Ram *qānūngō*, and three other headmen as *s̱ālis* (third-party, arbitrator). In what appears to be an elaborate ceremony, the disputing villagers and all those appointed to resolve the problem arrived at the borders between the villages (the document calls the place '*kankar*' or '*kangar*' – which may mean a pebbly boundary). The noble administered an oath to the arbitrators, who then proceeded to define the boundaries between the villages. It was then declared that if the headmen of the two villages quarrelled again about this matter, they would be held *gunahgār* (guilty) by the government.[27] Under the Persian text, the names of the disputing headmen were written, in two opposing columns, in the Nagri script, their names preceded by the interesting title '*mātang*' – which means 'elephant' in Hindi. If I have read this correctly, this would indicate the circulation of an interesting range of earthy epithets beyond the formulaic Persian *alqāb*. Below the names of the headmen, the plough symbol was drawn, demonstrating, at the very least, a regional tradition shared with the Marathi-writing area next door. The document bore a Persian seal with the pious legend '*'Aliyān rā sharf kamāl az tū* (The saints achieve perfection due to you)', with a note underneath 'His slave, Bhogan Chand *kārkūn*'.

In thus resolving boundary disputes between villages, Purshottam Das *chaudhrī* acted somewhat like *pāṭils* (village headmen) and *muqaddams* (village headmen in northern India) who formed part of community-based local courts – the iconic Maratha *majlis* or the *panch* 'five elders'.[28] On the other hand, *zamindārs* all over the Mughal empire, and even in the neighbouring and rival polities, were expected to exercise a certain measure of adjudicative authority in their own right. Hence, when the East India Company purchased the villages that made up Calcutta at the end of the seventeenth century, they also set up a *zamindārī kacherī* (court). In the early nineteenth century, after the demise of the Maratha empire, the Bombay government even passed a specific legislation recognising such adjucative rights for the most eminent landholders.[29]

27 NAI 2668/3, 1658.

28 For a document recording *pāṭils* forming part of a *majlis* (community court) that decided a dispute over the sharing of a *pāṭil*ship, see V. T. Gune, *The Judicial System of the Marathas* (Pune: Deccan College, 1953), p. 203. Habib provides similar examples of certain *muqaddams* forming part of the iconically Indian *panch* or 'five-elders' system of village tribunals in *Agrarian System*, pp. 148–9.

29 This was the case with the Brahmin lineage of Devs of Cincvad, who controlled a richly endowed religious household/institution near Pune. 'A regulation for vesting certain jagheer-dars, surinjameedars, enamdars with the power of deciding suits within the boundaries of their

However, in this instance, Purshottam Das did not act either as part of a stable community court (a *panchayat*) or as a *zamīndār*-judge in his own right. Moreover, his role was defined with reference to a clear Islamic legal term – the *s̱ālis*. Arbitration abounded across the Islamic world, of course, but scholars locate arbitrators differently with relation to Islamic law and institutions. They also acknowledge that this might have varied significantly from polity to polity; while in the Ottoman empire arbitration by local notables may have formed a distinct domain from that of the *qāẓī's* court, in the Central Asian *khanates* prior to Russian colonisation, arbitrators were frequently *aqsaqals* (white-beards), whose authority derived not just from social eminence but government office, especially as tax officials. Central Asian *aqsaqals* worked under orders from the central government, and in association with the *qāẓī*, to whose court appeals lay.[30] Such layered and braided jurisdictions sound very much like the *dai'ra* within which Purshottam Das exercised his authority. The size of the Mughal empire precluded direction from the imperial centre about every little boundary dispute between villages; the *jāgīrdār* performed that royal role, deputing local landlords, acceptable to the communities, to resolve the matter. Unfortunately, in this case, we cannot tell whether the *qāẓī* of the district may have entered the picture; he did not make an appearance in this document.

## *Zamīndārs* in Court

The picture does become clearer when there was a higher level of rights involved, for example, when the entitlements of *zamīndārs* were in dispute. We have long known, of course, of the existence of transferable and marketable rights in land, individual as well as collective, in Mughal India,[31] even if such rights were inevitably nested and did not correspond to a modernist imagination of absolute and exclusive ownership. Looking closely without expecting an anachronous distinction between public office and personal property, we find every single element of the 'portfolio' of resources of Purshottam Das's family open to possession, inheritance, interpersonal transfer and dispute. The notion that *zamīndārs* possessed a right that was to a great extent independent of the will of the government was not dreamt up by British physiocrats looking to introduce the wonders of private property into the Indian society and polity. In 1772, around the inception of British rule in India, when asked about the rights of succession to *zamīndārīs*, the highest-ranking Indian official in the province of Bengal, the ill-fated *nāib-nizam-cum-nāib-diwān* Muhammad Reza Khan,

respective estates', Bombay Regulation 13 of 1830, in *Parliamentary Papers* 1833, xxv, 276–7. See Preston, *The Devs of Cincvad*, p. 200.

[30] Sartori, 'The Evolution of Third-Party Mediation'.

[31] Habib, *Agrarian System*; also Habib, 'From Arith to Radhakund', 211–24.

had said: 'according to the laws of the Koran' *zamīndārīs* were always inherited and could not be resumed by the government.[32]

Reza Khan may have been exaggerating to some extent, and his reference to the Quran may have been a generic reference to the rules of 'Islamic' government. What is clear from our documents, and ones comparable to them, is that the offices of *chaudhrāī*, bearing with them the right to *nānkār*, and of *qānūngōī*, bearing with it perquisites of the same name, were inheritable, partible and consequently, susceptible to disputes and adjudication. There are also some noticeable patterns to such disputes; they predictably appear at the intergenerational boundaries recorded in the papers of Purshottam Das's family. Looking at the process of adjudication of some such disputes in detail allows us to explore what Reza Khan may indeed have implied about laws pertaining to *zamīndārīs* and discover the tribunals where those laws were enforced.

As we have seen, from 1626, Purshottam Das, referred to as *chaudhrī*, had started taking on revenue farms in the *pargana* of Dhar, and also the nearby *pargana* of Nalawada.[33] By 1658, he had become eminent enough to officiate as arbitrator in boundary disputes between villages. Sometimes, however, he had to beat off rival claimants from the various branches of his own extended family. In 1661, a quarrel with some distant cousins, Kanwal Das and Tilok Chand, led to the production of a *maḥẕar-nāma*, narrating the history of the family's acquisition of rights, with exclusive focus, naturally, on the achievements and therefore entitlements of the complainant's own direct ancestors.[34]

We have also seen how, in 1664, in a serious squabble between the leading men of two agnatic branches of the family – Purshottam Das and Suraj Bhan – the provincial governor had heard petitions from the parties, and sternly admonished both to behave themselves.[35] Which was all very well, but that admonition did not, in itself, resolve the matter of who exactly among the family members was actually entitled to the various villages and to control of their produce. On 5 Rajab 1075, that is, on 21 January 1665, *Qāẕī* Abul Fath noted that Suraj Bhan, son of Chandar Bhan, had turned up in the court of the province (*maḥkama-yi īn sūba*) in the city (*balda*) of Dhar, flourishing a *parvāna* bearing the special seal of the provincial governor Najabat Khan, probably the very *parvāna* that we just mentioned. Suraj Bhan declared that: 'the *dastūr* of the *chaudhrāī* of *pargana* Hindola, together with the village Ajnai, which was part of the five villages currently allocated as *nānkār* to

32 Extracts from the consultations respecting the administration of justice, Add MSS 29079, British Library. For a discussion of this document, see N. Chatterjee, 'Reflections on Religious Difference', 396–415.

33 NAI 2703/2 (1626); NAI 2668/2 (1643). 34 NAI 2668/6 (1661–2).

35 LNS MS 235 (m) 19 Muharram RY 7 (12 August 1664), Dar al-Athar Al-Islamiyya (henceforth DAI), Kuwait and NAI 2703/17 (1665).

*chaudhrī* Purshottam Das, belonged to him, by shared ownership (*ba-sharkat ta'aluq-i ū dārad*)'. *Qāẓī* Abul Fath appeared to be able find a resolution to these tangles, and in accordance with the consent of the two parties (*muvāfiq-i raẓāmandī-yi janībain*), declared that it had been decided that (*muqarrar ānke*): 'After this, the plaintiff will make no claims on the defendant about the *dastūr* incidental upon the *chaudhrāī*, which he had not been in possession of from ancestral times; nor make any claims of shared ownership. He should be satisfied with what had been written as a result of the resolution'. The deal itself was in the fine print; scribbled in three sections under extended lines at the bottom of the page, it was declared: a) *Mauza' Ajnai* in Hindola, belonged to Suraj Bhan; b) In exchange for towns with wells for Sultanpur, the tribute for *mauza'* Chindwara was discounted; and c) The *bhaint* of *pargana* Hindola had no claim or share in the villages and towns which were the dues and customs (*lavāzim va rusūm*) of *chaudhrāī*.[36] All this was written up as a *maḥẓar*, under the seal of *qāẓī* Abul Fath, and nearly thirty years later (1103/1692), a copy was sealed by the then-incumbent *qāẓī*, Muhammad Mustafa.

It is difficult to make sense of all aspects of the deal that was recorded in this document. What is clear is that Suraj Bhan, who had once been able to work together with Purshottam Das,[37] was now being shaken off with token gains. While he got his little village called Ajnai, Suraj Bhan's succession claim to the rights of *chaudhrāī* were annulled under the *qāẓī's* seal. Despite his being Chandar Bhan's son, the *qāẓī*'s judgement could use a formulaic phrase, saying Suraj Bhan had no hereditary claim (*dakhal*) on the perquisites of the *chaudhrāī*, although his nephew, Purshottam Das, did. Something had happened in this family that had made it exclude this otherwise very strong claimant from its circle of entitlements; in the next section, I reveal what that event might have been. It is also notable that in deciding the shares of members of this family, *Qāẓī* Abul Fath made no reference to their religion, or to any entity like 'Hindu law'. Instead, the decision was based on three things: the customary dues (*lavāzim* and *rusūm*) associated with the position of *chaudhrī* of certain districts; secure possession; and succession, the last being subject to intra-familial relationships rather than abstract rules of survivorship derived from jurisprudential texts – whether *fiqh or dharmaśāstra*. This was the kind of decision that necessitated rich local knowledge; the *qāẓī* had to be a local man in more than one sense of the term.

## Which Son? The Limits of Kinship and the Circle of Entitlements

Purshottam Das, clearly the family patriarch for more than half a century, died in 1684. Predictably, the family, with all its immediate and allied agnatic

[36] NAI, 2703/17 (1665). [37] NAI 2703/4 (1655) and NAI 2703/7 (1659); section on *qaul*.

branches, burst into vicious quarrelling to decide who would inherit the by now enormous portfolio of lands and tax-exemption grants he had built up, through inheritance, long office-holding, a sharp business sense and constant disputing before a range of authorities. These disputes made the next generation of male heirs and their mutual relationships, alliances and rivalries immediately visible. It also revealed, albeit briefly, a line of the family that had been resolutely written out of the family's archive. This line had related to the disenfranchised Suraj Bhan, and what had possibly been a youthful indiscretion on his part. The claims put forward by Suraj Bhan's son, and his conflicts with the other male claimants of the family, also explained why the line of inheritance may have skipped Suraj Bhan and passed from Chandar Bhan to his nephew, Purshottam Das. This is because Suraj Bhan's son was called Muhammad Asad.

An undated *maḥẕar* was scribed soon after RY 4, which probably referred to the reign of Bahadur Shah I, and if so, it was produced in 1711. Two copies of that *maḥẕar* were preserved in the family's collection (now at the National Archives, Delhi), both sealed by our friend *Qāẕī* Muhammad Mustafa.[38] The date on his seal is unfortunately smudged, but appears to be 1216 AH (1717 CE), and this would be well within *Qāẕī* Mustafa's years of office in *pargana* Dhar. The document recited that from the time of kings of yore until the time the document was scribed, Hamir Chand, son of Purshottam Das, son of Mohan Das, son of Jayanti Das, son of Ganesh Das, son of Gunraj, was the hereditary *chaudhrī* of *pargana* Dhar, and the *chaudhrī* as well as *qānūngō* of *pargana* Hindola, and had kept the peasants content with his good behaviour. A man called Muhammad Asad, the *pesar baṭanī* (son of the belly of)[39] a woman called Parwar, of the *qaum lūlī*, had declared himself the *farzand* (child) of Suraj Bhan, who was son of Chandar Bhan and nephew of Mohan Das. In Indian usage, *lūlī* indicates a courtesan; clearly Suraj Bhan had committed some serious indiscretions in his youth. However, while consorting with courtesans may not have been an unusual activity for martially oriented landlords, his alleged son claimed that Suraj Bhan had gone further and taken the name of Abd al-Islam, which means that he had converted to Islam.

Whatever was Parwar and Suraj Bhan's personal story – and we have already seen him languishing in poverty and begging local officials for a place to live – Muhammad Asad was a resourceful man. According to this *maḥẕar*, he managed to secure the removal of Narsingh Das and other sons of Purshottam Das from the *chaudhrāī* of pargana Dhar, and made a petition to the *ʿadalat al-ʿalīya* of Ujjain (perhaps for the securing of his title). As a result, a horseman called Yar Khan was sent by the *nāẓim* (governor) of the province, Sher Afghan

[38] NAI 2668/21 and NAI 2703/46, dated by the cataloguer to 1711, based of 'style of writing'.

[39] This is a technical term, frequently used in Islamic legal documents, to indicate biological parentage. See *Sulḥ-nāma bayn Āqa Begam wa farzandānesh*, www.qajarwomen.org/fa/items/15161A24.html.

Khan,[40] to summon Gambhir Chand, the elder brother of Hamir Chand. Gambhir Chand had to turn up at the court, and there he created a *maḥẕar* with the *gawāhī* (evidence) of the *quẕẕāt* (*qāẕīs*), of the nobles and the great men and the *jamhūr al-ayyam* of *pargana* Dhar and other *parganas*. The *arbāb-i ʿadālat* (people of the court, the *qāẕīs*) discussed the matter in three sittings but the claims of Muhammad Asad could not be verified.

These sittings may well have been soon after Purshottam Das's death in 1684, when, as we have already seen, all heirs were squabbling over shares. But Muhammad Asad refused to relinquish his claim. A few years passed, and then he managed to secure a *sanad* from the court of the emperor Bahadur Shah (r. 1707–12, referred to here by his posthumous title, Khuld Manzil). This document ordered the *faujdār* of *Sarkar* Mandu, Murhamat Khan,[41] to secure (for Muhammad Asad) the post (of *chaudhrāī* of Dhar), and, accompanied by a *dastak* (order) to a *gurzbardār* (mace-bearer, who often accompanied orders), reached the town of Dhar on 22 *Zu al-ḥijja*, regnal year 4 (1710 CE). Muhammad Asad had clearly impressed the powers that be, for ominously, even the horsemen of the then-current provincial governor, Raja Jai Singh [II] turned up to intervene in the rights of Hamir Singh.

The *faujdār* could not quite order a displacement of the title-holders, but was pressured to appoint his own deputy, Abu al-Khair, to conduct an investigation. Hamir Chand was allowed to inspect the *sanad*, and he declared that Asad had no claim to inheritance. Thus Muhammad Asad was invited to establish his inheritance right, and Hamir Chand declared that the evidence of the respectable people of the area, who knew the facts about the parties, should be gathered. So Hamir Chand requested all the great and good to offer their evidence in writing, so that the truth (*ḥaq*) might become clear to the *arbāb-i ʿadālat* and *bandegān-i ḥuẕūr muʿala* (slaves of His Highness, i.e., the Mughal officials). Finally, all the Muslims and Hindus reported (*khabar dādand*) that Hamir Chand held the *khidmat* (service/office) of *chaudhrāī* by heredity, and Muhammad Asad was neither the child of Suraj Bhan nor had any claim to inheritance.[42]

This document is not a judgement or an order, so it does not quite record the end of the protracted legal dispute featuring Muhammad Asad and his claims. It was a document of testimony produced at a crucial moment in the process, but because of the support that Hamir Chand had been able to mobilise, there is good reason to conclude that this document may well have decided matters. And it was not just a matter of calling up favours with one's peers, the neighbouring *zamīndārs*. The surviving copies recorded that the original

[40] This was probably Sher Afghan Quli Khan.

[41] Murhamat Khan is known to have been a *faujdār* of Mandu in the early eighteenth century.

[42] The detailed summary offered in the catalogue has some errors, including of the date 22 *Zu al-ḥijja*, regnal year 5.

*maḥẓar* had been sealed by an astonishing number of religious and non-religious functionaries; the former included Sayyid Mirza and Mir Abdullah, *qāẓī* and *muḥtasīb* of *sarkār* Mandu, respectively; Shaikh Lutfullah Suhrawardy, *pīrzāda* and resident of *qasba* Dhar; and the *qāẓīs* of *parganas* Kanpil, Dewas and Dhar (including *Ḥājī* Muhammad Mustafa, who then later validated the copy). Then there was also Muhammad Arif, the *mutaṣaddī* (officer) of Islam Khan (the *jāgīrdār*), Gangaram, *mutaṣaddī* of the *diwān* of the province, and a host of *chaudhrīs*, *qanūngos* and *mandlōīs* from the neighbouring districts.

This startling document, and the protracted dispute it records, offers a tantalising glimpse of the manner in which landed families in Mughal India used the law in order to guard their circle of affiliations and entitlements. It also offers a rich picture of the manner in which three distinct social/institutional circles overlapped to create the infrastructure of Mughal law: the Islamic scholars who formed the *arbāb-i ʿadālat*; the royal sphere from the emperor down to the *faujdār*; and the *zamīndārs* themselves. In the various types of disputes discussed in this chapter thus far, we have seen all three circles in operation, with varying degrees of focus on each, depending on the dispute in question. Muhammad Asad's life and claim was such that it required all three circles to be activated to an unusual extent, creating an intensely illuminated dramatic episode where a Muslim man claimed the right to be the son and successor of a Hindu *zamīndār*, and failed, but not easily. And in doing so, he demonstrated the full extent of the *dā'ira* of Mughal law.

Although too capacious a matter to be duly discussed here, this incident and its records are also a reminder that what we know about imperial religious policies cannot be conflated with the substantiation of law at an everyday level. The culture at the imperial court must have changed to some extent due to emperor Aurangzeb's ostentatious adherence to a doctrinaire form of Islam, although the extent of this may be exaggerated. The emperor's professed support for conversions to Islam did affect some careers and disrupt some landed families, even in the region – Rampura most notoriously.[43] But when conversion consisted of an individual's non-conformism, rather than a politically astute decision, all circles of authority closed ranks to exclude the heir who did not fit. What is perhaps surprising is the extent to which a courtesan's son was able to activate legal processes such that his claims were heard over a prolonged period in court sessions that involved a range of state functionaries, including Islamic judges.

The documents do not tell us on why Muhammad Asad could not be considered a *wariṣ*; if his factual claims about his parentage had been implausible, surely he could not have made the headway that he did at the imperial

[43] Ratan Singh of Rampura converted to Islam in 1698, with the support of the then provincial governor, Mukhtiyar Khan, causing disruptions in the family. Sinh, *Malwa in Transition*, p. 48.

court. Classical Islamic law on religious conversion focusses on apostasy from Islam, which is considered a heinous crime and punishable by death for men; and with imprisonment and correction for women. The implications of conversion into Islam, on the other hand, is scattered throughout the enormous body of jurisprudence, in subjects ranging from taxation to marriage, since becoming Muslim altered a person's legal subjectivity, affording them different (not necessarily always better) rights and obligations. However, the continuance or erasure of rights under Hindu law (or indeed any other non-Islamic law), which is at issue here, is naturally not the subject matter of Islamic jurisprudence. Clearly, Suraj Bhan's own conversion (assuming that Muhammad Asad was right about that, and the matter was public knowledge) had not led to his 'social death' – a *qāẕī* had still been able to hand him his rights with the backing of the provincial governor. But these claims to *dastūr* and *rusūm*, did not appear to extend to Muhammad Asad; we can only speculate whether it was his religious identity or his mother's social status which decided his fate at the end of the day.

This dispute left a trickle of traces in the scattered archive – there are documents, all dated in the 1710s, in all three locations from which I reconstructed the collection. All of them refer to the anxiety of the main line of the family about this unwanted relative and his claims. The two *maḥẕar-nāmas* had already revealed a complex intertwining of authorities; the effort to appeal to political authorities continued. In the National Archives, we have another document, which is a copy of an *iltimās* (petition) in which the *vakīl* (representative) of Hamir Chand reported all that the *maḥẕar* had said, and stated that Hamir Chand had this *maḥẕar* to hand. Clearly, though, Hamir Chand was not satisfied, and his *vakīl* still hoped that the rightful would be rendered their rights and the false claimants punished.[44] An unsealed and poorly scribed *parvāna* still preserved in the family home in Dhar, and dated to regnal year 5, may have been a response to this petition. It declared that the brothers Hamir Chand and Gambhir Chand had appealed to the local *jāgīrdār* about Muhammad Asad referring to himself as *chaudhrī*. The *jāgīrdār* appears to have mediated or imposed an agreement, for a *rāẕī-nāma* is mentioned. The reverse of the document also had the office note – *mulāhaẓa shud* (noted).[45]

## Conclusion

Disputes over entitlements in Mughal India were of different types, scales and levels, depending partly on the social and political status of the persons

[44] 1713 NAI 2733/34. (The document bears no date and is clearly scribed much later; the date is ascribed by the chain of events by the cataloguer.)

[45] 1711 NCD, Choudhary Family Collection, *Baḍā Rāolā* Dhar.

involved. In the case of our protagonists, such disputes could range from conflicts among villagers over the use-rights of water bodies or over the boundaries of villages, in which they acted as arbitrators, to the inheritance rights of *zamīndārs*, in which a braided range of authorities – kings, nobles, *qāẕīs* and their own peers made crucial decisions relating to the limits of family and associated entitlements.

In looking at these disputes together with the transactions that we have discussed in Chapter 4, we find the persistent presence of the local *qāẕī*. Many of the transactions recorded and validated by the *qāẕī* followed in the wake of disputes, which the *qāẕī* must have helped resolve. In all these processes, we see a plethora of Islamic legal terminology being used in the documents – *dīa*, *s̱ālis, wirās̱a*, *pesar baṭanī*, and so on. We also see, in the recording and resolving of these disputes, the use of a number of documentary forms that are fully recognisable across the Islamic world, for reason of their being included in Islamic manuals for documentation.

That familiarity with Islamic vocabulary did not, however, exclude several other sources of right and authority: Purshottam Das was chided by the *jāgīrdār* for trying to cut out other legitimate heirs to the family fortune; Hamir Chand had to deal with orders from the emperor and his delegates, and had to claim his rights with reference to both his impeccable genealogy, his secure possession of his position and his reputation among his peers in order to refute claims that, in turn, referred to biological-emotional relations and royal orders. The *qāẕīs* who heard these disputes appeared to be perfectly able to sift through this range of rights-producing events, artefacts and relations; nobody expected the decisions they made to be final – the royal seal could always reopen matters.

As I said in the Introduction, it does not appear that the protagonists of this story saw their experience has eclectic, comprised of conflicting jurisdictions and legal systems. Indeed, what is striking by its absence in this documentary collection is explicit reference to abstract bodies of 'law' or even legal doctrine related to a jurisprudential tradition which experts – such as the *qāẕī* and *muftī* (or for that matter, the *pandit* or *śāstrī*) – could draw upon in order to come to doctrinally informed decisions about specific matters. In one sole document, there is reference to a *muftī* and his legal opinion – the document recording the transaction of blood-money payment to the family of the Muslim retainers of the family; the corresponding payment to the Hindu retainers makes no such reference. Even in matters such as the validity of conversion (for example of Suraj Bhan's), on which the *Fatāwá-yi ʿAlamgīrī* contained detailed discussions,[46] nobody in Dhar seemed to step beyond possession and reputation in order to evaluate claims.

[46] Mouez Khalfaoui, 'From Religious to Social Conversion: How Muslim Scholars conceived of the *Rites de Passage* from Hinduism to Islam in Seventeenth-Century South Asia', *Journal of Beliefs and Values*, 32: 1 (2011), 85–93.

It is possible that this lack of abstraction may be the function of the nature of the archive. No *qāẕī's dīwān* has been discovered from Mughal India; in fact, the Dhar *shahr qāẕī's* family papers appear to focus on the family's own entitlements rather than the records of others' fortunes. Family papers of other Islamic scholars, collected by the National Archives of India, demonstrate a similar mix of doctrinally indifferent orders, transactions and testimonial records pertaining to their own families. Were a *qāẕī*'s *dīwān* to be discovered from *pargana* Dhar, we may discover that Muhammad Mustafa, for example, had developed highly sophisticated notions of how the family and property of Hindu landholders ought to be managed. We may have to accept, however, that such record keeping was not considered necessary in Mughal India; the *qāẕīs* lacking both the resources and the motivation for doing so. In the absence of such juristically rationalised records, we have to content ourselves with assuming that nobody thought that the doctrines of negotiation needed to be abstracted from everyday practice.

# 6 Invaders: Marathas and the British

In 1656, around the same time that Purshottam Das was picking up the family mantle, Shivaji, the ambitious son of a high-ranking noble of Bijapur, offered his services to the equally ambitious Mughal prince, Aurangzeb.[1] Bijapur was a flourishing kingdom in south-west India, located at the junction between two linguistic zones, Marathi and Kannada, ruled by a dynasty of Shiʿa Muslim rulers and under threat from the Mughals from the early sixteenth century.[2] Shivaji's father, Shahji, held a Bijapuri grant to a *mōkāsa* (equivalent of *jāgīr*) to large areas around Pune, where he already possessed the rights of *dēśmukh* (the regional equivalent of *chaudhrī*). Shivaji was a far more ambitious man, and had taken to conquering areas and forts around this core area of control, leading to Bijapuri wrath. His overture to the Mughals was an effort to strike a deal with the worst enemies of Bijapur, with the aim of securing the beginnings of his own empire.

After negotiations with Aurangzeb did not come to fruition, Shivaji embarked upon an independent career of conquest, vanquishing and recruiting other *dēśmukh*. In 1663, he attacked and maimed a Mughal governor; in 1664, he sacked the Mughal 'blessed port' of Surat. Following significant military deployment led by the Mughal commander, Mirza Raja Jai Singh, Shivaji was defeated, and induced to come to the imperial court. But unlike an

[1] Jadunath Sarkar, *Shivaji and His Times*, 2nd ed. (London: Longmans, Green and Co., 1920), pp. 55–6.

[2] For Mughal–Bijapur relations in the early sixteenth century, see Muzaffar Alam and Sanjay Subrahmanyam, 'The Deccan Frontier and Mughal Expansion, ca. 1600, Contemporary Perspectives', *Journal of the Economic and Social History of the Orient*, 47: 3 (2004), pp. 357–89; this based to a great extent on the account of a Mughal noble sent to the Bijapuri court in 1603, which has been published as Chander Shekhar, *Waqāiʿ Asad Beg* (Delhi: National Mission for Manuscripts and Dilli Kitab Ghar, 2017). More broadly on Bijapur, see Richard Eaton, *Sufis of Bijapur, 1300–1700: Social Role of Sufis in Medieval India* (Princeton: Princeton University Press, 1978). Eaton's theory that Bijapur and its Sufi complex were co-constituted in a 'shatter zone' has been resoundingly critiqued in Ernst, *Eternal Garden*, esp. pp. 99–105. Ernst has discussed the Sufi complex of Khuldabad, near Aurangabad, which is indisputably within a Marathi cultural zone and not on any frontier. He has also pointed out that few of the Sufi saints related to the Khuldabad complex were 'militant' pioneers in any sense of the word.

earlier generation of similarly vanquished Rajput kings, Shivaji could not be turned into a Mughal *mansabdār*, whether due to structural shortage of inducements to offer, cultural clash, or entrenched court politics. Instead, there was a famous falling-out in court, leading to his imprisonment, then daring escape.[3] Thus began a half-century-long battle of mutual aggression between the Mughals and the Marathas, punctuated by efforts at co-option, which eventually led to the creation of the Maratha empire, the most important 'successor state' of eighteenth century India, save, perhaps the state of the East India Company.[4]

The rise of the Maratha empire coincided with a change in the dynamics of military and political recruitments in South Asia. Jos Gommans, in his work on Mughal warfare, proposed a process whereby *zamīndārs* with effective reach into a key zone of military recruitment, were turned into *jamaʿdārs* or military recruiters for any regime that would pay enough. But in the latter half of the seventeenth century, the attraction appeared to be in the opposite direction, with locally entrenched *zamīndārs* flooding the Mughal army, and at the same time, becoming difficult about paying up the taxes, hurting Mughal revenues and making Mughal service less attractive. It may be questionable whether we should characterise this period with the downward imperial arc and local entrenchment (zamīndārisation, as Gommans calls it),[5] or see it as part of a continuous spiral of competitive state formation.[6]

It may be productive to take a step away from that macro-historical question of why the Mughal empire declined, and look at the situation from the other, less dramatic side of the process. What our specific archive allows us to do is trace the fortunes of a non-Maratha *zamīndārī* family that, like the majority of *zamīndārs*, never made the move towards full sovereignty, and observe how it negotiated to remain in the same place, through the transition from Mughal overlordship to that of the Marathas, and eventually, that of the British. In doing so, this chapter would continue to make an oblique contribution to the very large volume of literature on the history of *zamīndārī* as a key institution, social formation and reformatory project of British colonial rule, which has been discussed in Chapter 2. At the very least, it will propose amendments to the Bengal-centred story of little kings turned into absentee landlords and eventually, a proto-colonial intelligentsia, by returning attention to the significantly different trajectories of *zamīndārs* located within a barely known princely state.

[3] M. N. Pearson, 'Shivaji and the Decline of the Mughal Empire', *Journal of Asian Studies*, 35: 2 (1976), 221–35.

[4] On the Maratha empire, see Stewart Gordon, *The Marathas, 1600–1818* (Cambridge: Cambridge University Press. 1993); James Laine, *Hindu King in Islamic India* (Oxford: Oxford University Press, 2003).

[5] Gommans, *Mughal Warfare*, pp. 63–88.

[6] Frank Perlin, 'State Formation Reconsidered', *Modern Asian Studies*, Part I, Part II, 19: 3 (1985), 415–80.

It can also offer some glimpses of the changes that ensued in the process of recording, asserting and disputing entitlements as successive regimes overran the area. The section of the archive that allows us to reconstruct that story is more complex – in terms of language, script and genre – than the rest. New elements – such as new languages, scripts and terms – appear, but the overall picture is that of the reorganisation of existing elements, which begs the question about the continuity or novelty of concepts. Did new concepts of rights, justice and law appear as first the Marathas and then the British acquired control over the area? It is impossible not to speculate, but the fragmentary nature of the surviving record means that any answers can only be provisional.

In terms of language and forms, what strikes us most forcefully is continuity: in the eighteenth and even the nineteenth century, people continued to use Persian. They used it to record transactions, such as sales of houses, as well as to write personal letters to each other. They used the language and its well-established forms even when reporting on political revolutions – for example, in Persian-language *maḥẕar-nāma*s recording the negotiations undertaken by local notables with the incoming Maratha *sardārs* in the 1730s. Once these *sardārs* established their own kingdoms, we find news-writers reporting on each other in Persian-language *akhbarāts*. But there are also changes: we find Marathi-language, Modi-script revenue accounts, which are frustratingly undated, but which we can perhaps place in the middle of the eighteenth century. We also find orders written in Hindi/Rangri, the Central Indian variant of Rajasthani described earlier, and in a version of the Nagri script which, until the end of the seventeenth century, had only appeared in the margins of documents, or the lower half of bi-lingual tax contracts (*qaul qarār*, discussed in chapter 3). These orders refer to the authority of the Puwars – the earliest of the Maratha *sardārs* to invade Malwa, who eventually set up two small states, at Dhar and at Dewas.

Most excitingly, perhaps, as we come close to the present, we find material that offers a fuller view of the principal protagonists. Such material includes a family history, also in Rangri, in two manuscript versions, in which the antecedents of the family are narrated, seemingly without reference to an immediate functional objective. Then, as the nineteenth century arrives, turning Dhar into a 'princely state' under indirect control of the British Indian government, we find family trees in the Persian script, bilingual and bi-scribal Hindi–Urdu documents, English-language petitions, magazine entries and finally, photographs. Such expanded focus, despite the impression of transparency it produces, is of course the product of yet more representational conventions, through which we must hear the story that the protagonists are trying to tell, but also think why they are doing so. That reflection is an opportunity to comment on law and/in empire, especially with reference to British 'indirect rule' in

India.[7] Study of the princely states has the potential for 'provincialising' developments that are taken to be the general course of political, social and cultural change in colonial India. With the notable exception of Hyderabad,[8] that potential remains unrealised, because the implicit assumption appears to be that hybrid political practices were symptomatic of a period of transition,[9] and thereafter limited to theatricality within a broadly shared modernising trend, led by the directly governed British Indian provinces.

Finally, it is worth admitting here that it is impossible for me to fully decipher everything that the authors of these documents are trying to say. Allusions to officers and events are rendered obscure by time, connections between people smudged by badly placed seals, and the sheer linguistic and paleographic challenges of this section of the archive are simply too enormous to be fully tackled within the scope of this book. However, the heterogeneity of this portion of material is an invitation making it too hard to resist expanding upon some of themes that this book has been discussing with reference to the (predominantly) Persian-language sources – such as language and its use in self-representation, especially in the context of assertion of rights.

## The Maratha Empire in Malwa

Sociologically, the Maratha empire was an empire by *zamīndārs*. The classic Maratha claim, that of *sardēśmukhī*, connected landed power to kingship organically. This claim to one-tenth of land revenue was a multi-pronged claim thrust into a mesh of overlapping rights in the countryside. When Shivaji began asserting this claim from the 1660s, and he worked systematically to vanquish and/or recruit other significant *dēśmukh* families into his kingdom. He also began working towards acquiring legitimacy for such moves through concessions from Bijapuri and Mughal overlords. The claim of *sardēśmukhī*, substantively one-tenth of the tax collections of an area, was an innovation based on a much-older Marathi- and Konkani-region title, for which there are grant records from as far back as the twelfth century.[10] Etymologically, the title implied that the holder was the 'head' of *dēśmukh*,

[7] Ramusack, *The Indian Princes*; for studies of specific regimes, see Pamela Price, *Kingship and Political Practice in Colonial India* (Cambridge: Cambridge University Press, 1996); Dirks, *The Hollow Crown*.

[8] Kavita S. Datla, *The Language of Secular Islam: Urdu Nationalism and Colonial India* (Honolulu: University of Hawaii Press, 2013); Eric Beverley, *Hyderabad, British India and the World: Muslim Networks and Minor Sovereignty, 1850–1950* (Cambridge: Cambridge University Press, 2015).

[9] Michael Fisher, *Indirect Rule in India: Residents and the Residency System, 1764–1858* (Delhi: Oxford University Press, 1991).

[10] Principal Balkrishna, 'Nature of Sardeshmukhi during Shivaji's Time', *Proceedings of the Indian History Congress*, 3 (1939), 1189–93.

or a kind of 'first among equals', but it was to Shivaji's credit that he turned this term of landed entitlement into one of sovereign legitimacy.

Following Shivaji's death in 1680 and the succession battles that followed, *dēśmukh* recruited into the Maratha empire project turned into marauding *sardārs*; some of them began spilling into Malwa from the end of the century.[11] In 1713, the Maratha polity began to acquire some structure, mainly because of the new office of Peshwa, a Brahman minister who ruled in the king's name, and led the federation of Maratha *sardārs*. In 1719, Balaji Vishwanath, the first Peshwa, stormed to faction-ridden Delhi and secured three separate orders from the recently and partially enthroned Mughal emperor Muhammad Shah, granting the Marathas the right to *sardēśmukhī* and *chauth* in all six Deccan provinces, and *svarājya* or sovereignty in sixteen districts that constituted the Maratha homelands.[12] It is short-sighted to see *sardēśmukhī* simply as a revenue-sharing arrangement; it was integral to a concession of sovereignty.[13] Although Malwa was not part of these arrangements, from around this time, Maratha bands began to call their demands in Malwa by these names.

Older scholarship had already provided us with the framework of declining Mughal political structure – cornered governors, rival state-builders and so on. Due to the meticulous work by Gordon and Wink, using principally Marathi records, we also have a very detailed picture available about the rise and fall of particular Maratha *dēśmukh* families, the rise of some of these to kingly status, and of administrative consolidation as this formidable new imperial federation expanded into non-Maratha areas, most importantly Malwa, in the eighteenth century.[14] But we know very little about the fortunes of the *zamīndārs* and other middle-ranking powerholders already ensconced in Malwa, about the manner in which they dealt with the incoming overlords and negotiated to retain their existing entitlements.

The Puwars, who would eventually establish two linked kingdoms in Dhar and Dewas, were among the *sardārs* who led the Maratha raids into Malwa, perhaps from as early as the 1690s, and certainly in the 1720s.[15] Two brothers,

[11] Irvine puts the date at 1705; *Later Mughals*, p. 164. But Malcolm was of the opinion that the raids had begun earlier.

[12] James Grant Duff, *The History of the Mahrattas*, 4th ed. (Calcutta: R. Cambray, 1912), Vol. I, pp. 368–9.

[13] Shivaji's grandson, Shahu, who had been captured, brought in the Mughal camp and released to assume the Maratha throne in 1707, was said to refer to himself in 'transaction with the Moghuls' 'merely as a Zumeendar, or head of the Deshmookh of the empire'. Grant Duff, *History of the Mahrattas*, Vol. I, p. 360.

[14] Gordon, 'The Slow Conquest'; Wink, *Land and Sovereignty*, pp. 66–155, but the rest of the book elaborates on the processes involved.

[15] The reason for this long unclear period is the patchiness of Marathi records for the period, and an attitude of denial on the part of Persian-language chroniclers. Malcolm, *Memoir of Central India*, Vol. I, p. 64.

Udaji and Anand Rao, undertook daring raids, and captured the fortress of Dhar for significant lengths of time, punctuated by periods of dislodging, sometimes due to siding with the wrong side in Maratha politics, and at others by energetic Mughal governors, especially Girdhar Bahadur, appointed to Malwa in 1725. Udaji Puwar was also involved in the battle in which Girdhar Bahadur was killed, in 1729.[16]

Given the nature of the early Maratha polity, these commanders were also tax-collectors. In 1724, Bajirao I, the most ambitious of all Peshwas, gave a *sanad* (document) of grant to Udaji Puwar. Malcolm reports having seen this document in the 'old papers of the Puars of Dhar'. The document granted Udaji the obligation-cum-right to collect the *chauth* of Malwa and Gujarat, and keep three-quarters of the proceeds as his *saraṇjām* (expenses for his troops, hence the equivalent of *jāgīr*), while sending the rest to Pune. Substantively, this would have been one of those pre-emptive grants that formed the stuff of the Maratha empire in its predatory, expansive stage – grants to revenue from unconquered lands were made to warlords who had to then win battles in order to actually collect them. Idiomatically, Malcolm's translation, included in *A Memoir of Central India*, appears to have followed the text of an original fairly closely, with its invocations, injunctions and formulaic conclusions. If that is indeed so, then the Maratha empire was bringing new conventions into Malwa: the document began with an invocation to goddess Lakshmi, and used the terms *mōkāsa* and *saraṇjām*, which were new to Malwa, if not the Deccan.[17] There were still the familiar Islamic months (Rabīʿ al-awwal, in this case), combined with the Mughal Faslī year (1123), which Malcolm incorrectly took to be a 'Hindu' calendar. There terse sign offs: 'there is no occasion to write more' was one that Mughal Persian documents shared with their Maratha–Marathi counterparts, across the language divide.[18]

Eventually, Puwar prowess would have made the initial grant worth following up: Malcolm says that he found approximately 150 supplementary orders,

[16] Wink, *Land and Sovereignty*, pp. 135–6; Malcolm, *Memoir of Central India*, Vol. I, p. 78; Sinh, *Malwa in Transition*, pp. 153–66.

[17] Gordon, *The Marathas*, p. 24, note 22, citing the seventeenth-century *Ajnāpatra*, Ramchandra Nilkanth's answer to Abul Fazl's *Āʾīn-i Akbarī*, states that this political treatise-cum-administrative manual proposed a fourfold division of land tenures – *waṭan*, *inām*, *mokāsa* or *saraṇjām* and *vṛttī*. This appears to be a misreading; the translation of the *Ajnāpatra* that Gordon cites does not propose such a division. Instead, it states the importance of *waṭandārs*, and then moves on to lands held as *vṛttī* and as *inām*. The word *mokāsa* or *saraṇjām* are simply not used. 'The Ajnapatra or Royal Edict,' *The Journal of Indian History*, 8: 1 (1929), 81–105, 207–33. Also, for a facsimile of the Modi-script manuscript and Nagri transliteration, see Anuradha Kulkarni, *Ajnāpatra* (Pune: Diamond Books, 2007), pp.165–75. It appears the term *mokāsa* was Persianate; specifically, Bijapuri administrative parlance carried over to the Maratha empire, despite the Sanskritising efforts of Shivaji's Brahmin courtiers.

[18] Malcolm, *Memoir of Central India*, I, pp. 73–4, long note. Malcolm also converted the Faslī year incorrectly to 1724.

dated around 1729, addressed to 'managers of towns of districts, from Bundelcund East to near Ahmedabad West and as far north as Marwar' to pay the said taxes to Udaji Puwar. Here the picture becomes rather murky, because Stewart Gordon found five substantial documents, all dated 1728–9, in the Peshwa *daftar*, which inventorised the revenue received from Malwa, and the military leaders who had collected it; this named Udaji Pawar, but alongside several other military leaders – the Mores, the Shelkes, the Sindhias. Gordon took these documents as evidence of the as-yet-unsettled and military nature of extraction in this early period of Maratha conquest of Malwa;[19] for us, it complicates the story of straightforward usurpation of Malwa by three Maratha generals which was favoured by those that won in the end. In any case, the Puwars continued to collect various grants from the Peshwas, none of which settled their position for very long. In 1725, further *mōkāsa* grants, this time over Dhar and Jhabua, were made to Udaji Puwar[20]; in 1726, he was given some kind of compensation for rights over Malwa and Gujarat,[21] from where he was expelled by the Gaekwad *sardārs*. Anand Rao Puwar once again received a grant to collect the Maratha share of taxes from Malwa and Gujarat in 1734, but it was revoked the following year when the Peshwa himself took over the governorship of Gujarat.[22] Anand Rao's son, Jaswant Rao, who fought and was killed in the third battle of Panipat, fought against the Afghans in 1761. His son, Khande Rao, endangered the family's holdings by siding with the wrong side in the dynastic struggle of the Peshwas, and only when he recanted did he receive a *saraṇjām* grant giving rights to collect taxes from certain districts in Malwa for maintenance of troops.[23] Thereafter, following a period of turmoil due to the minority of heirs, attacks by Holkars, Sindhias and their Pindari agents, a *diwān* who could not agree with his masters and a plucky but inevitably besieged female regent, the state of Dhar was taken under the protection of the British, and treaty being concluded with this 'princely state' in 1818.[24]

Peshwa-era (i.e., eighteenth-century) Marathi documents could have highlighted new forms and formulae of rights creation in Dhar, but they were not available to me until the work on this book was nearly complete. For now, it has to suffice to note that in the early nineteenth century, Malcolm saw many such grant documents, and offered summaries of these in his account of a region that was being 'settled' (i.e., brought under colonial control). The picture that emerges from his account is that of an area with numerous petty principalities left behind in a shatter zone after the demise of the Maratha empire. His

[19] Gordon, 'The Slow Conquest' pp. 8–9, note 14. [20] Sinh, *Malwa in Transition*, p. 156.
[21] Ibid., p. 159. [22] Malcom, *Memoir of Central India,* Vol. I, pp. 98–100.
[23] Malcolm reported having seen the document recording the *saraṇjām* grant to Khande Rao in the hands of the 'pandit of Dhar,' who was rather alarmed at his inspection of it. Ibid. p. 103.
[24] Malcolm, *Memoir of Central India*, pp. 104–15.

informants were naturally eager to assert their historical and hence legal precedence and his narrative is transparently the product of his co-option into that process. Nevertheless, his *A Memoir of Central India* has become a standard reference for historians working on the area. Because of its detailed descriptions and summaries of the documents he saw, in conjunction with reports of his discussions with key political protagonists in the region, it is indeed difficult to resist the ring of authenticity offered by Malcolm's book. Unfortunately, since Malcolm's focus was on the petty princely houses themselves, our family of *zamīndārs* in Dhar does not make an appearance in this work of reference.

There may indeed be archival materials available to trace the evolution of the relationship between the incoming Puwars and Mohan Das's descendants, the *zamīndārs* of Dhar. With the generous help of Amit Choudhary and Dominic Vendell, I discovered a large volume of Marathi records issued by the Dhar state that have been preserved at the Shri Natnagar Shodh Samsthan in Sitamau, the creation of Raghubir Sinh, the 'princely historian'. Raghubir Sinh's efforts mirror those of the famously activist Marathi-reading and -writing historians whose efforts led to the creation of significant archives of material pertaining to the core Marathi- and Kannada-speaking regions. The Bharat Itihasa Samsodhak Mandal of Pune was at the forefront of this activism, which involved searching for, collecting and archiving documentary material held by various land- and office-holders in the region. Many such collections were also published as *daftars* of the respective families, complementing the Peshwa archive, which was taken over by the British and remained difficult to access for Indian researchers. This process of creation, retrieval and recreation of archives, and the linguistic-cum-research activism of the Marathi area is one that has only been partially told,[25] and begs comparison with similar efforts in other linguistic areas, for example, Bengal.[26]

Research in such records, and the regional nationalisms that created such archives, has to take place within another project. Some of the Dhar state's records were collated and published as part of this same historical process.[27] Thus far, I have not been able to identify documents related to Mohan Das's

[25] Dipesh Chakarbarty, *The Calling of History: Sir Jadunath Sarkar and His Empire of Truth* (Chicago: Chicago University Press, 2015), especially chapter 3.

[26] Here I am thinking of activists such as Abdul Karim Sahitya Bisharad, rather than English-writing government-allied historians such as Jadunath Sarkar.

[27] I could not find the book cited in Gordon, 'The Slow Conquest' pp. 7, 13–14, notes 10, 11, 21, 22, K. K. Lele and S. K. Oka, *History of Dhar State: Marathi Saramjyant pawarache dharachya pawarache* [*sic*] *mahaty v daji* (Importance and rank of the Pawars, especially of Dhar, in the Maratha Empire), II (Poona, 1934); the title is somewhat faulty. Instead, I found A. W. Wakankar (ed.) *Dhar State Historical Record Series: Dharkar Pawarancya Itihasaci Sadhane*, Vol. III, Part 1, The Maratha Period (Dhar: The History Department, 1949).This book offers transcriptions in Nagri of Marathi documents, and short English summaries of each document. The book was introduced by the historian G. S. Sardesai, pp. 5–8.

family in those published records, but that may well be because in collating and selecting records for publication, the editors of the Dhar Historical Series predictably looked upwards (towards the Peshwa) rather than downwards, towards pre-existing *zamīndārs* over whom the Puwars had acquired overlordship.

Thus, the story of state-formation that is revealed through the Marathi documents (and documents collected and generated in the British era) is told from the point of view of the conquerors. As for the Malwa *zamīndārs* who faced the Maratha onslaught, we know relatively little except that they ultimately decided or were compelled to acquiesce to the Maratha demands. There are self-congratulatory snippets in the Puwar dynasty's annals which assert respect and good treatment of the *zamīndārs*: contrast this with the otherwise rough handling suffered at the hands of other Maratha imperialists.[28] All of this amounts to little more than royal eulogy. But in that part of the family archive which I discovered in the family mansion in Dhar in December 2016, there are two documents, both classical Mughal *maḥẕar-nāmas*, which offer a more complex and dramatic picture of that transition, one that indicates extensive negotiation, with reference to a range of obligations and rights. Mughal law clearly died a very protracted death.

## Negotiating with the Marathas

In the first *maḥẕar-nāma*, a minor local Mughal official called Shaikh Alimullah outlined his woes. Alimullah said that he was *sharīk* (sharer, co-parcener) in the *taujīh-i jāgīr* of a certain Badakhshi Khan and others, *mansabdārs* of the *khāṣ chaukī*, and also *mutaṣuddī* (official) of the *maḥāl jāgīr* of Safiuddin Muhammad Khan and others. In the beginning of the Faslī year 1142 (1733 CE), said Alimullah, news kept arriving that the imperial (i.e., Mughal) army was about to reach Malwa, which emboldened the *jāgīrdārs* and peasants. But hardly had the imperial army left Shahjahanabad (Delhi), when four '*nā-sardārān-i ghanīm*' (non-leaders of the plunderers/enemy; i.e., Marathas)[29] – Malhar [Rao Holkar], Ranoji Shinde, Anand Rao Puwar and another who is not named – crossed the Narmada and entered Malwa. Straight away, they took over the *bādshāhī* (i.e., Mughal) *jāgīrs*, appointed *mōkāsadārs* (their own version of *jāgīrdār*), and seized the entirety

[28] Malcolm, *Memoir of Central India*, p. 101, in which he repeats a legend popular in the district of Bersiah.

[29] Prachi Deshpande has pointed out that word *ghanīm* was embraced by the Marathas, in a movement of appropriation of a Persian pejorative. By doing so, the Marathas acknowledged their guerrilla military strategy and subversive position, but also expressed pride in being recognised as the archenemy of the Mughals. Personal communication and seminar at Exeter, February 2018.

of the revenues. The *mōkāsadārs* took charge; the *mōkāsadār* Sadashiv Pandit sent his men, including *ghulladārs* (grain-collectors) into the villages, and dismissed the arrangements of the *jāgīrdārs*. At this, the *ʿāmils*, *zamīndārs* and peasants sent a joint message to the Maratha '*nā-sardārs*', saying, 'Since 1141 Faslī (1732), thirty-five percent had been decided as *khandnī* (tribute). Now too, take according to the *dastūr-i sābiq* (old custom) and give over the rest to the *jāgīrdārs*'. After these *jawāb-sawāl* (exchanges), the *nā-sardārs* said, 'Now that the *jāgīrdārs* have brought the *bādshāhī* (Mughal) armies to kill us, what *sulūk* (dealing) and *sulḥ* (treaty) does there remain between us and yourselves, that you want an arrangement?' Some time elapsed in *rad-badal* (negotiation, in Perso-Marathi usage)[30], and then the *sardārs* issued a *parwāngī* (order), that with a view to the *taraddud* (organisation, settling) of the *gumashta-hā* (agents) of the *jāgīrdārs*, half the taxes collected should be given over to them, and the rest taken as *khandnī*. [But] the *mōkāsadārs* took everything from the peasants as *khandnī*, forcing the peasants of many villages to sell up all they had to the *sāhukār* (merchant, moneylender). Many peasants, unable to pay the *saraṇjām*, decided to abscond. Many merchants and *muqaddams* (village headmen) were in the custody of the *mōkāsadārs*, for failing to pay up the arrears. In spite of all this, there remained 3,000 rupees in arrears for the *khandnī*, and for this 1,000 rupees was taken from the *gumashtas* of the *jāgīrdārs*, from the collection of their *ʿamils*, and a *tamassuk* (debt-acknowledgement) was taken for the rest. For this reason, the entire land revenue dues of the *jāgīrdārs* of the district was in arrears. If anyone had information about this matter, Shaikh Alimullah appealed to them to attest to this.

Three *qāẓīs*, with large circular seals and the '*khādim-i shariʿa*' legend, attested that the account was true. There were fifteen other seals in the right-hand margin, all attesting to the veracity of the account. Most of the witnesses were Muslims, including a certain Jamilullah Suhrawardi, two minor Mughal government servants (indicated by the legend on their seals, '*fidwī-yi* (loyal to) *Bādshāh ghāzī*' called Muhammad Baqir and Amir Muhammad. But there were also Jaswant Rao, probably the Rajput chief of Amjhera, and Hamir Chand, the scion of our illustrious family and son of Purshottam Das. The last two names were written in Nagri.

We have, in the family's collection, a second *maḥẓar-nāma* from around the same time,[31] this document also following the Mughal-era format and formulae bearing multiple seals, one possibly of the *qāẓī*, and one of a Mughal government officer called Alimullah, and four more of witnesses. This document is

[30] I thank the first anonymous reader of this manuscript for pointing this out to me.

[31] 1736 BRD 20, Choudhary Family Collection, *Baḍā Rāolā* Dhar. The document dates itself to 5 Ramẓān, RY 17. Since Muhammad Shah was the only Mughal emperor in the eighteenth century with a reign long enough, we can date this document to 1148 AH, that is, 1736 CE.

less well-scribed and on poorer quality paper than the other, but it still has *chaudhrī* Hamir Chand named as one of the witnesses. The main complainant is an individual called Sarup Ram, who is somehow involved with the *jāgīr* of a Sayyid Ali Khan; he complains that on 29 Sha'bān in that year, that is, just a month ago, *bhīlān-i zalīl* (the contemptible *bhīls*) had attacked the village of Akbarnagar in the said *jāgīr*, set it on fire and stolen the crops and animals. Thus, the peasants were not able to pay their taxes.

It is not clear whom Alimullah and Sarup Ram (possibly the agent of a *jāgīrdār*) intended to appeal to with their *maḥẓar-nāmas*, and with what aims in view. It is also not clear why original documents, not copies,[32] were preserved in Hamir Chand's family archives, given that he was not a party, merely a witness. Both documents attest to a time of acute disturbance, of change in regimes, the first very explicitly so. In the first *maḥẓar-nāma,* the terminology used for revenue demand – *khandnī* – relates to the second of four stages Gordon identified in his chronology of administrative and fiscal stabilisation in the Maratha empire in Malwa. This indicates that the demand had moved beyond *ad hoc* raiding demands – called *rakhwālī* – but was still a form of tribute. Only after the 1740s, would such *ad hoc* demands be replaced with tax contracts with civilian official-entrepreneurs, very much like the *ijāras* of Mughal times. Thus the documents are windows to that period when the Maratha empire was being formed in Malwa. But they are also evidence that Mughal-endorsed claims were yet to be extinguished entirely, leading to a jostling between Mughal *jāgīrdārs* and Maratha *mōkāsadārs*, in which both contractual agreement and political loyalty were used as bargaining chips. The times were simply too violent and unstable for either to hold steady, and people like Alimullah appeared to be referring to multiple sources of legitimation at the same time: castigating Maratha warlords for failing to honour agreements that created traditions (*dastūr*), but also resorting to a spot of anti-Maratha snobbery by describing them as '*nā-sardārs*' or non-leaders and *ghanīm* (enemies/plunderers). Sarup Ram's complaint against the *bhīls*, on the other had, was in the nature of reporting a *force majeure*; and it seems to indicate that Mughal tax-collectors were still operational in the area, and required documented evidence of inability to pay. In this process, witnessing by the local *qāẓī*, government officials, and local *zamīndārs* all continued to play a role. As the next rung of powerholders, our protagonists remained an inevitable part of such a documentation process. It is difficult to say whether that co-option was necessitated by the respect for existing landed rights asserted by Maratha political theorists,[33] or simply by the fact of social entrenchment, which even systemic disruption could not alter.

[32] For a discussion of originals and copies, see Chapter 4.
[33] Kulkarni, *Ajnāpatra*, pp. 169–71, where these landed rights are referred to as '*vṛttis*'.

In addition to these documents of transition, we have in the family archive three more documents, these written in Hindi in an archaic Nagri script, which derive from the Maratha regime established in Dhar; two of them definitely related to the Puwar dynasty. The first is an order, bearing a Nagri-script seal, directed at Sahi Ram *ji*, *mōkāsadār* of *pargana* Dhar, instructing him to make regular monthly payments to Bijay Singh and other cavalrymen who had been employed as *cākar* (servant/retainer). The nine horsemen, listed below the main text of the document, are admonished to guard the *chaukī* (police station) night and day.[34] The second document, very similar in appearance and format, is also a Hindi-language order, from Pandit Gangandhar *ji*, on behalf of Yashwant Rao Puwar, who is clearly the sovereign, because his name is elevated above the main text as a mark of respect, just as the names of Mughal emperors and nobles used to be. The document makes a grant of three villages to Sadashiva *mōkāsadār* of *pargana* Dhar, and the grant seems to be very similar to the *qaul-qarār* documents we have seen before, because a *qabūliyat* is mentioned, and the grantee is expected to make earnings out of the grant.[35] The third document of similar appearance and temporal provenance bears a date on the beautifully formed Nagri-script seal: Śaka 1705, which converts to 1783 CE. But the sovereign whose name is elevated in this document is Ramchandra Rao Puwar, who as we know, was the child-king during the transition to British rule in 1818. This is also a royal order, but the contents are unclear to me.[36]

My reading of these three documents is still imperfect, because of the highly eclectic vocabulary and the archaic letterforms used, but they still offer some information about the effects of regime change and the workings of the newly formed Maratha Puwar state. What is striking is that administrative record in the Dhar state was at least partly in Hindi (or Rangri) rather than Marathi, no doubt in response to the linguistic terrain the Puwar dynasty found itself in.[37] Moreover, although written in Hindi and in Nagri script, the documents still use Perso-Arabic formulae – referring to excuses as *ʿujar*, admonishing employees to settle their minds (*khātir jamaʿ*) and so on. In terms of content, the second document appears similar to the *qaul* agreements made with *zamīndārs* in the previous century. The alteration of regime and its cultural-ideological identity is signalled, on the other hand, by the language and script of the authoritative seal in the document. What is unclear, once

[34] 1750 Hin NCD, Choudhary Family Collection, *Baḍā Rāolā* Dhar (here, the date is roughly ascribed).

[35] 1751 Hin NCD Choudhary Family Collection, *Baḍā Rāolā* Dhar (here too, the date is roughly ascribed).

[36] 1783 Hin NCD, Choudhary Family Collection, *Baḍā Rāolā* Dhar (the problem with dating the document has been mentioned).

[37] Hindi usage in Maratha regimes was not limited to Dhar. On official usage of Hindi by Maratha regimes in Central India, including the Holkars and Sindhias, see Rambabu Sharma, *Rājbhāsha Hindī ki kahānī* (Dillī: Aknkur Prakshan, 1980), pp. 50–75.

again, is why these documents found a place in our protagonists' family archive; what role did they play in the making and recording of grants, the hiring of armed horsemen and other administrative activities by the new Puwar regime? These questions are easier to answer in the next period for which we have documentary evidence, when Dhar became a princely state under the authority of the British empire in India.

In addition to these Hindi documents, we also have three Persian-language legal documents: a *fārigh-khaṭṭī* and two *iqrārs* recording sales. All of them are perfectly formulated although scribed poorly (but very legibly) and involve disputes/transactions over property between members of the family with Afghan individuals.

The first document, a *fārigh-khaṭṭī*, is dated 1190 Faslī and 1845 Saṃvat, both of which convert to 1787, with some small variation of months. The document is not sealed, but it narrates that Anwar Beg, son of Jahan Beg, and Sayyid Azam had made a claim to the mango trees in the orchard of Sahib Rai, son of Dianat Rai, but the dispute was resolved and Anwar Beg and his companion wrote a *fārigh-khaṭṭī* in the court, in front of the judge, to the effect that the claim they had made was void. They also made a declaration to this effect in front of *zamīndārs* and *qānūngōs*. The witness clauses were in Perso-Arabic script for Anwar Beg and Sayyid Azam, and in Nagri script for *chaudhrī* Pratap Chand and others.[38]

The two sale documents concern the family more directly, and are from the early nineteenth century. One records the sale of a house and adjoining land in the city of Dhar, and the other a plot of fallow land, adjoining the house of '*Thākur Sāḥeb*' Pratap Chand.[39] The sellers describe themselves, in both cases, as Afghans; the first, was a woman called Chand Bibi, wife of Khairulla Khan, and the second, Sultan Khan, son of Jahan Khan. Although the dates of the two documents are proximate (1803 and 1804) and the handwriting very similar, it is not clear whether there was any family connection between the two Afghan sellers. Both seemed to have lived or owned property in a particular part of the city of Dhar, which they refer to as '*dar al-anwar pīr*' or '*qasba pīrān*'. Both documents are sealed, the one from 1802 has three seals, the largest and most legible one reads Baha al-din Muhammad Abdullah, and bears the sub-script '*khādim-i sharī'a muftī muhr namūd* (the servant of law *muftī* sealed [it])'. Both documents also bear witness clauses in the right-hand margin, in which the names of the Afghan parties are accompanied by symbols that are hard to interpret, but one of which looks like a spinning wheel; the families were weavers. The document from 1804 also has witness clauses with names written in Nagri, this includes one of Pratap Chand himself. In both cases, we have

[38] 1787 NC BRD, Choudhary Family Collection, *Baḍā Rāolā* Dhar.
[39] 1803 AC BRD; 1804 AC BRD, both Choudhary Family Collection, *Baḍā Rāolā* Dhar.

a table at the bottom of the document, describing the extent and nature of the properties.

The first of the two documents (1803 CE) also helpfully offers a genealogy of Pratap Chand, whom the Afghan sellers refer to respectfully as '*Thākur Sāheb*' – he is said to be the son of *Thākur* Nihal Chand and the grandson of *Thākur* Hamir Chand. Pratap Chand was co-buyer with Sarupchand, son of Harchand. All the details match the family trees which we shall discuss in the next chapter, except in one detail. There were two Pratap Chands in the family within the nineteenth century. The Pratap Chand I, who was the buyer of these Afghan-owned properties, was indeed the successor to the main line after Nihal Chand, but he was a younger brother, not a son. Perhaps the difference in ages between the two brothers was significant enough for the brothers to be taken as father and son and the error to pass unchecked into legal documents.

Together, the three documents attest to the continued used of Persian language and legal forms until the very end of independent Maratha rule in Dhar. They also demonstrate the continued relevance of institutions such as the *qāẓī's* court, for resolving disputes as well as recording legal transactions, and the continued involvement of landed powerholders and administrative personnel with the working of such institutions. And above all, they demonstrate continued facility in the use of Persian legal forms among members of the family, a feature we shall also see in the following period, when Dhar became subordinate to British supervision and turned into a princely state.

## *Thākurs* in a 'Princely State'

After nearly half a century of economically ruinous warfare, the armies of the East India Company dislodged the Peshwa and defeated the most important Maratha warlords – and moved into Malwa. In keeping with the symbolism of all previous invading regimes, General (later Sir) John Malcolm 'crossed the Narmada' in November 1817, chasing the Pindaris.[40] In December, he defeated the Holkar's army, and imposed a subordinating treaty in early 2018.[41] Treaties followed with the Sindhia, the Nawab of Bhopal and various important states in subsequently formed 'Rajputana'.

Thus began a process of disentangling claims and polities, and retrieving the rightful possessions of weaker (and more compliant) regimes from those of the larger and more threatening (most importantly, the Sindhias). Each sub-region of South Asia has a pioneering British military-civil officer to its name, whose specific brand of Orientalism, entangled with the subjugation of conquered territory, has continued to shape the region until the present day. If Rajasthan was Tod's creation, 'Central India,' including Malwa, was John Malcolm's.

[40] Grant Duff, *History of the Marathas*, Vol. III, p. 457. [41] Ibid., p. 463–4.

This scion of a minor Scottish aristocratic family had fought in battles against Tipu Sultan and served in the Hyderabad court, becoming fluent in Persian and key to 'restoring' the Hindu Wodeyar *rājās* in Mysore after Tipu's demise. He had also served as commercial-diplomatic envoy to Oman and Qajar Iran, followed by a mission to Awadh in India again. From 1803, he had been involved in the Anglo–Maratha wars and in the diplomatic negotiations that followed, developing a reputation for being a negotiator generous to the Maratha *sardārs*. In 1817, he had several books under his belt, including a history of the princes of India, one on the Sikhs and one on Persia; he had acquired an honorary doctorate, suffered several failed missions and received a large pay-out from the Company on pleading poverty. He reprised his military-diplomatic career in December that year by chasing Pindaris across the Narmada, and then fighting against joint Maratha forces, followed by a typically over-generous settlement with the Peshwa.[42] Then came the five years of his 'settlement' of Central India, creating a vast system of graded treaties by which the many competing principalities formed and re-formed during the days of the Maratha empire were shoehorned into a system of British colonialism by indirect rule.[43]

According to Malcolm, the treaty with Dhar in 1818 was concluded at the invitation of the cornered widow-regent, Maina Bai, whom he clearly admired.[44] Malcolm recorded that the Puwars of Dhar were descendants of the Rajputs of Malwa (thus establishing the legend of the dynasty's connection with Raja Bhoj) who had migrated to the Deccan, and returned as conquerors with the Maratha army. Although lauded as among the most distinguished of Maratha families, and among the earliest Maratha conquerors of Malwa, things looked bleak for the family and its small principality by the end of the eighteenth century. Constantly under attack by the larger and more powerful regimes of the Sindhias and the Holkars, and their allies, the Afghan warlords, they lost territory constantly until annihilation looked imminent. In 1797, Dhar was embroiled with a succession conflict in the Holkar state, which also involved Amir Khan, the Afghan soldier and fortune hunter who eventually founded the state of Tonk.[45] The side they backed, however, repaid their assistance by attacking them and seizing territories together with their Afghan allies. In the early nineteenth century, the widow-regent Maina Bai desperately sought allies

42 R. E. Frykenberg, 'Sir John Malcolm (1769–1833), Diplomatist and Administrator in India', *Oxford Dictionary of National Biography*, 29 May 2018.

43 For an excellent conceptualisation of indirect rule see Kavita Saraswathi Datla, 'The Origins of Indirect Rule in India: Hyderabad and the British Imperial Order', *Law and History Review*, 33: 2 (2015), 321–50.

44 Malcolm, *Memoir of Central India*, Vol. I, 110–11.

45 Busawun Lal, *Memoirs of the Puthan Soldier of Fortune, the Nuwab Ameer-ood-doulah Mohummud Ameer Khan*, translated Henry Prinsep (Calcutta: Military Orphan Press, 1832), p. 93–5.

to save the kingdom for her minor son, including from among the archenemies, the Sindhias, the British and the Gaikwards of Baroda. Eventually, the British entered as saviours, forcing the Sindhia and the Pindaris to return key districts – Badnawar and Bersiah (the latter cannot be located on the map) – to Dhar.[46]

Looking back on his work, Malcolm marvelled at the hugely improved situation in Central India – pointing to the increased revenues and decreased military expenditure in all major and minor states, especially Sindhia, Holkar, Kotah, Bhopal, Dhar and Dewas, but also the petty *rājās* of Amjhera, Ratlam, Sitamau, Jhabua and so on. Dhar had acquired a suitably sensible male *diwān*, Bapu Raghunath. However, this story of peaceful content was clearly also one of de-militarisation and de-politicisation: where in 1817, the Dhar state was reported to have a 'predatory army' of eight thousand men, in 1821, it had a well-paid body of three hundred horse and eight hundred irregulars. The *girāsiyas* of the region were said to be in 'repose,' and the expectation was that their habits would change; the Bhils were being similarly pacified.[47]

The treaty with Dhar provided that the kings would have 'no intercourse, public or private, with any other State, but to act in subordinate connection with the British Government'. They were also to furnish troops according to their ability, when called upon to do so, while in return the British government was to protect the state of Dhar and its dependencies. Certain districts were to be made over to the British government as price of such protection.[48] There was also a list of 'petty chiefs' who paid tribute to the states with which the British government had signed treaties, 'mediated' by the British; this showed a tangled map of formal allegiances – still dominated by the Sindhia, but with shares to Dhar and the Afghan states – spread over non-contiguous territories.[49]

By the early twentieth century, Dhar was part of a constellation of petty states that formed Malwa, mostly Rajput except Dhar and Dewas (although, these too, claimed ancient Rajput ancestry). From this long period of Dhar's transition from a Maratha principality to a colonial 'princely state', we have the only Marathi-language records in the collection. These records appear after a gap of about a hundred years after Alimullah's *maḥẓar-nāma*, that is, from the late nineteenth century. They are also fragmentary and unsatisfactory, but they bear clear signs of regime change and consequent cultural transformation. Here, it is worth underlining that the transformation in question did not consist of a straightforward move to English language and English law. In the continued use of Persian, and the innovative use of Urdu as well as Marathi, this section of the family's archive is striking evidence for the rarely noticed phenomenon of

[46] Malcolm, *Memoir of Central India*, Vol. I, 97–112.

[47] Malcolm, *Memoir of Central India*, Vol. II, pp. 223–63.

[48] *Ibid.*, Vol. II, pp. 408–9, Appendix, No. XVI, F

[49] *Ibid.*, Vol. II, pp. 413–15.

the presence of prolific documentation in 'Modi in the [colonial] archives' that Prachi Deshpande has correctly drawn our attention to.[50]

The 'colonial-era' records can be divided into five types, in which we have Persian-language political newsletters or *akhbārāts*; orders of various kinds, including in Hindi; an English-language petition; private letters in Urdu; and Marathi–Modi accounts. Each of these types attest to different aspects of the transition to colonialism, demonstrating continuities as well as transformations; in the remainder of this chapter, we shall discuss the *akbārāts*, the orders and the petition.

*Akhbārāts* have been studied as emblematic of Mughal information systems and political cultures, as well as their transformation during the extended period of cultural and institutional hybridity that marked the first hundred years of British political power in India.[51] Two *Akhbārāt* fragments in our collection, both from the year 1843, relate to events in Kolkata and Gwalior. The first, titled '*Khulāṣa al-akhbār-i dār al-imārat ṣadar Kalkatta*', is dated to 1843 '*māh-i agast* [August]' the calendar defined as *ʿiswī* [Christian]. It reported, in the typical stream-of-events style that characterises *akhbārāts*, that the *Sāḥebs* of the capital city of Calcutta were engaged in the organisation of the taxes and territories/dominions of the '*sarkār-i kampānī Angrez*'. The news was that the Governor General and the *sipah-sālār* (Commander of the Army) would set out for Hindustan (i.e., North India), in the month of October, to inspect the troops of all areas. A *kharīṭa* (official letter) had been received from Dost Muhammad Khan of Afghanistan and an answer sent. But the crucial news, which may have led to this particular newsletter being preserved in Dhar, was that a *kharīṭa* of the Governor General had been sent to the queen of the *riyāsat* (kingdom) of Gwalior, Bai Sahiba, ordering her that Dada Khasgiwala should be extradited from her kingdom, and Mama Sahib invited, in proper form, and appointed the *mukhtār* (agent) of her kingdom. The reporter ended this section in a watchful, if somewhat ungrammatical note – '*dide bāyad ke che mī shawad* (it has to be seen what transpires)'.[52]

A second newsletter also reports on the unsettled situation in Gwalior, and the impending war with the British. Dated 2 Shaʿbān 1259 (8 August 1843) it reported tense discussions from the court of Maharaja Jayaji Rao Sindia.[53]

Gwalior, the capital of the Sindhia kingdom, took shape in the late eighteenth century, under the leadership of Mahadji Sindhia, an indirect successor of one

[50] Prachi Deshpande, 'Scripting the Cultural History of Language: Modi in the Colonial Archive', in Partha Chatterjee, Tapati Guha-Thakurta and Bodhisattva Kar (eds.), *New Cultural Histories of India* (Delhi: Oxford University Press, 2014). 62–86.

[51] H. Beveridge, 'Colonel Tod's Newsletters of the Delhi court', *Journal of the Royal Asiatic Society*, 40: 4 (1908), 1121–4; Margrit Pernau and Yunus Jaffery (eds.) *Information and the Public Sphere: Persian Newsletters from Mughal Delhi* (New Delhi: OUP, 2009).

[52] 1843 BRD 5, Choudhary Family Collection, *Baḍā Rāolā* Dhar.

[53] 1843 BRD 24, Choudhary Family Collection, *Baḍā Rāolā* Dhar.

of the four Maratha generals whom we have encountered invading Malwa. The Bai Sahiba referred to in this newsletter was Tara Bai, the widow of Jankoji, third in line of succession from Mahadji. Jankoji Sindhia was the adopted son of the formidable and anti-British dowager-regent Baiza Bai, who had been chased out of Gwalior in 1833 in a palace coup by her own son, with the British Resident's connivance. Baiza Bai's departure was followed by the political ascent of Gangadhar Ballal, better known as Dada Khasgiwala, whose title indicated his jurisdiction over the household establishment (*khāsgī*) and entrenchment with harem politics. He, and his father before him, had served as Baiza Bai's interpreter in interactions with the British, and as prime minister, he soon turned out to be her successor as leader of the anti-British lobby. Krishna Rao Kadam, or Mama Sahib, the maternal uncle of Jankoji, on the other hand, was the Company's chosen agent at the Sindhia *darbār*. In 1843, matters were precipitated when Jankoji died, and a child adopted by his widow Tara Bai was placed on the throne under the regency of Mama Sahib, with British approval. In the middle of the year, Khasgiwala, together Tara Bai's father, hounded out Mama Sahib and took over the administration of the kingdom, and forced the British Resident, Col. Speirs, out of Sindhia domains. Finally, in December, the Company army attacked Gwalior and defeated it after two hard-fought battles, imposing a subsidiary alliance with a treaty signed in January 1844.[54]

These two newsletters are evidence for the continued resilience of the Maratha polities of central India well into the nineteenth century, as Amar Farooqi has forcefully argued. In our case, they also offer evidence of the close attention paid by smaller neighbouring states, such as Dhar, to political developments in the vicinity, and their use of traditional (i.e., Mughal-style) newsletter systems in order in order to do so. As with the Hindi orders from the eighteenth century which we have seen in the previous section, it is difficult to say why these two newsletters should have found a place in the family's archive. But they certainly suggest that members of the family held key political and administrative positions in the Dhar state, as we know they did in the twentieth century.[55] That position lent itself to the issuing of certain kinds of orders which we shall now consider.

From 1859, we have a bilingual document, its upper part in Urdu and the lower in Hindi, and bearing the multi-lingual and multi-scribal seal of the Superintendent of Dhar. It is a self-described *parvāna*, addressed to all *ʿilāqedārs* of the area, that *Thākur* Motichand's son was to be married in a few days' time; the *bārāt* (wedding procession) would follow a certain

[54] Farooqi, *Sindhias and the Raj*, pp 58–61, 81–106.

[55] *Who's Who in British India and Burma*, entry on Thakur Nihal Chand, Inam Commissioner and Treasurer of the Dhar state from 1935. Clipping, Choudhary Family Collection, *Baḍā Rāolā* Dhar.

route, which was elaborated. The *'ilāqedārs* were instructed to allow the procession to pass through those areas and to take care of the travellers' possessions. The documents listed the soldiers, ponies, mace-bearers, palanquins, elephants and men who would accompany the procession.[56]

As a *parvāna*, the document situates itself in connection with Mughal documents of order that we have been discussing from the beginning of the book. It also bears the abbreviated invocation '*Alif*', which, as we know, is a shortening of Bismillah. Linguistically, however, this is the first and only legal or administrative document in the collection that is wholly or partially in Urdu, by which I mean Hindi written in the modified Perso-Arabic script with a slightly increased proportion of Persian-origin words. The seal that heads the document is similarly multi-lingual and multi-scribal – the outer rim in Nagri script, spelling out the English word 'superintendent' and the centre in Perso-Arabic script.

Competition and conflicts over processional precedence and ritual hierarchy, and their sublimation and reformulation through colonial judicial processes have been studied in connection with temples in early colonial southern India, as well as monastic groups in the north.[57] These legally and administratively mediated conflicts, apparently derived from pre-modern honours systems, shade into more collective tussles for the physical and metaphorical occupation of public space that, as 'communal riots' came to blight nation-formation in South Asia.[58] Our bilingual document about a wedding procession of a *Thākur*'s son in a princely state offers us a different angle for legal management of public space, which evokes both the aura of 'royal' power and its typical accoutrements (elephants, palanquins and so on) and modern governance (stamp-paper).

The final document that we shall mention in this chapter similarly evokes these dual axes of conceptualising power and entitlements. A slightly incomplete copy of an English-language petition, addressed to the Central Indian Agency, is preserved in the family's traditional home, the *Baḍā Rāolā*. Events mentioned within it, taken together with the dates of *Thākur* Pratap Chand II's active life, suggest that it was from around 1910. I have not been able to trace the petition and its outcome in the archives, but there is no reason to doubt that such a conflict did indeed take place. The dispute was with the Superintendent of the Dhar state over the entitlements of the family and the basis of those

56 1859 NCD, Choudhary Family Collection, *Baḍā Rāolā* Dhar.

57 Arjun Appadurai, *Worship and Conflict under Colonial Rule: A South India Case* (Cambridge: Cambridge University Press, 1981); William Pinch, *Warrior Ascetics and Indian Empires* (Cambridge: Cambridge University Press, 2006).

58 The literature on communal riots is immense, but in relation to conflicts over religious processions, see Kathryn Prior, 'Making History: The State's Intervention in Urban Religious Disputes in the North-Western Provinces in the early Nineteenth Century', *Modern Asian Studies*, 27: 1 (1993), 179–203.

rights, which we shall discuss in more detail in the following chapter. Suffice here to note that while the petition was written in English, and followed the format of many such colonial petitions – with a brief history of antecedents, the claim and the appeal, together with a series of exhibits and depositions – the story it told summarised the stories that had been repeatedly told in the many Persian documents in the collection, and the key pieces of evidence presented included both a translation of a Mughal-era *parvāna* and an excerpt from the *Dhar State Gazetteer*, compiled by Captain Luard and published in 1908.[59]

## Conclusion

Dhar's post-Mughal history as a Maratha kingdom, and then a small princely state, offers us an unusual opportunity for using the family's archive in order to study the many-routed and multi-staged process of conversion to modernity in South Asia. It helps us extend the story of Maratha imperialism beyond its ethnic core in predominantly Marathi-speaking areas and see it for what it really was: an empire replacing another, jostling for the allegiance of entrenched landed powerholders. Documents from this family's collection help open up that process of empire-substitution, demonstrating how people mobilised multiple arguments and norms to negotiate with the incoming regime, but also the cultural power and popularity of the Persianate legal forms both in extraordinary and everyday circumstances. They also reveal the complex and, to some extent, unexpected linguistic developments involved in that transition, such that the fully formed Maratha state in Dhar used old Hindi, rather than Marathi in its official orders.

The documents from the colonial period – when Dhar came under British indirect control – demonstrate this mixed story of continuity and innovation even further. Thus we have Persian newsletters of one princely state spying on another; we have *parvānas*, but in Hindi and Urdu, which had never been used before; and we have English-language petitions that reproduce Mughal *parvānas* as well as colonial gazetteers as evidence, but, as we shall see, refuse the fiscal rationality of a modern state and balanced transactions as the basis of property entitlements. This is, indeed, the story of little kings and big empires.

[59] Petition and exhibits, family collection. This specific issue of the *Dhar State Gazetteer*, which I have not been able to find a copy of, did exist, and is referred to in Luard, *Western States (Malwa) Gazetteer*, p. 2.

# 7 Identity: Professionals or Warlords?

Despite the unusual density and continuity of documentation we have in relation to the family of Mohan Das and his descendants, it remains difficult to answer the question, 'How did the protagonists view themselves?' Because of the formality of the documents which record their activities, disputes and claims, it is tricky to access the self-perception of the protagonists of this story. As we come closer to the present in time, increased familiarity with the forms of address and representation ('*Thākur Sāḥeb*', for example) can create a misleading sense of access to reality.

Fortunately for us, we have disjunctures at every turn. We have *qānūngōs* who were also *chaudhrīs*, we have possible *diwāns* of a princely state addressed as *Thākurs*, and, as we shall see, we have a family that is described in twentieth-century documents as '*Kāyasth Nigam*', but which remembers a family history replete with Rajput-like exploits of blood, death and military valour.

In this final chapter of the book, we shall try to use that family history, in conjunction with other narratives of self-representation, in order to understand how a family of *Kāyasth zamindārs*, who negotiated with first the Mughal, then the Maratha and then the British empire, might have conceptualised themselves and the basis of their entitlements.

## The *Munshī*

Even more than the *qāẕī*, who authenticated documents and their copies, attested to tax payments promised and paid, and adjudicated on important inheritance cases, there was another kind of professional whose hand we can literally see in all affairs of the Purshottam Das family. These were the scribes – *kātib* in Arabic-speaking regions and *munshī* in the Persianate world – who, despite their ubiquitous and indispensible role in the running of empires, received patchy attention until the 1990s.[1] Since that time, a flush of literature

[1] A very important early work was that of Karen Leonard, *Social History of an Indian Caste: The Kayasths of Hyderabad* (Berkeley, London: University of California Press, 1994); since then Alam and Subrahmanyam, 'The Making of a Munshi', pp. 61–72; Chatterjee, 'Scribal Elites', pp. 445–72; Kinra, 'Master and *Munshī*', pp. 527–61; O'Hanlon, 'The Social Worth of Scribes',

about Mughal and post-Mughal *munshīs* has created for us an unusually elaborate picture of a social class – predominantly non-Muslim, most commonly of *Kāyasth* or *Khatrī* caste. From full autobiographical accounts, available from the seventeenth century, to multiple fragments, these protagonists have left detailed accounts of their education, curricular content, entry into the job market and social matrices. The picture this produces is that of a specialist service community, trained from childhood in Persian writing skills and steeped in the commonplaces of Perso-Islamic culture, which, at the top end of the spectrum, extended to full literary immersion, compositional ability and courtly deportment. Complementing this picture of participation is also a narrative of resentment and dislike of passive but powerful bureaucrats, armed with jargon and paperwork, a resentment that was sometimes expressed, at least from the eighteenth century, in sectarian terms, by some Muslim elites, especially jurists.

But were our protagonists *munshīs* themselves? They do not state their caste affiliation in any document scribed prior to the nineteenth century. Only one *parvāna* from the seventeenth-century part of this collection, unambiguously referred to caste, and did so using a classically Indo-Persian usage. This was the *parvāna*, dated 1073 AH/1662 CE, of which we have the original in DAI, Kuwait, and the copy in the NAI, New Delhi, in which an official called Muhammad Hussain granted land for creating a garden in the town of Sultanpur. The recipient of the grant is referred to as Kishan Das '*zunnārdār*'. While the Arabic word *zunnār*, adopted in Persian, originally implied a cord worn around the waist by Christians and Jews and also the Persian magi, in the Indian context, it came to also mean the Brahmanical thread, the *janeū*,[2] with which users may also have discovered a phonetic similarity. The protagonist Kishan Das is not identifiable from the otherwise very useful family trees preserved by the descendants; so we have to discard this eccentric piece of information as an outlier. Kishan Das, the Brahmin, may well have been unrelated to the family, who were informed because of their concern with lands and taxes in the area.

Caste references begin to appear in the collection only in documents that are clearly scribed in the nineteenth century (even if, in some cases, they claim to be older). In these documents, which are, typically, lists of landed properties owned, members of the family refer to themselves as *Kāyasth Nigam*, and this

pp. 563–95; Guha, 'Serving the Barbarian to Preserve the *Dharma*', pp. 497–525; Bellenoit, 'Between Qanungos and Clerks', pp. 1–39; Deshpande, 'The Writerly Self', pp. 449–71; also Spooner and Hanaway, *Literacy in the Persianate World*.

2 Thus Amir Khusrau, the fourteenth-century poet's famous couplet: '*Kāfir-i 'ishq am Musalmānī marā darkār nīst/Har rag-i jān tār gasht hājat-i zunnār nīst* (I am a heretic in love, Of Islam I have no need/Every vein in my body has turned into a string, Of *zunnār* I have no need); S. B. P. Nigam et al., *Amir Khusrau Memorial Volume* (New Delhi: Amir Khusrau Memorial Volume, 1975), p. 72.

is also how descendants of the principal line identify themselves today. This, combined with the fact that the family monopolised the classic village-level profession of *Kāyasths* – that of the *qānūngō* – might suggest that here we have a family of not very eminent Mughal *munshīs*. The family's collective career, as we have seen so far, however, suggests a far more martial social role. It is as pioneering landed gentry that Jayanti Das had received his grant in the late sixteenth century; his son or grandson Mohan Das took the family to new heights, securing their status as *zamīndārs* of several villages, through military entrepreneurship sold to agents of the state in search of local talent. This may have been far less unusual than we might think, despite what may have been the 'stabilisation of service communities' in some parts of the subcontinent around the late medieval period.[3] *Kāyasth zamīndārs* abounded in Bengal in pre-Mughal and Mughal times, including 'Raja' Pratapaditya, one of the '*Bārō Bhūīṇyās*' or 'Twelve Gentry' of legend; a family of *qānūngōs* became the Raja of Darbhanga in the seventeenth century; and even in the eighteenth, *Kāyasth* entered the service of the newly formed state of Hyderabad first as military agents.[4] And indeed, there is no reason to find that surprising, given the demonstration by Peshwas in the eighteenth century that Brahmins could be warriors as well as rulers.

We have an opportunity to explore what some of our protagonists thought of their own condition through the medium of a rather special document. This is a long scroll that I discovered in the family's collection in Dhar. This document, which calls itself a '*haq-o-gal nāma*',[5] narrates the history of the family, which overlaps with the story told by the *maḥẓarnāmas*, but also extends much further back and offers justifications for entitlements that are somewhat different. It is also the story of a journey, the crucial journey of migration that brought the family from Udaipur to Dhar.

The scroll, the top section of which is damaged, bears no date, but the script is very similar to what we have in the margins of the Persian-language documents from the late seventeenth and eighteenth centuries. It appears likely that the language of this manuscript, which is very similar to Rajasthani, is Rangri or the written form of Malwi. If this identification is correct, then it would match with the fact that Rangri was reported by Grierson as being used in keeping administrative records in several princely states in Malwa.[6] The scroll, with its unseparated words, eccentric letter forms and hybrid vocabulary, was illegible to me and to family members (who were rather hoping that it would be

3 O'Hanlon, 'The Social Worth of Scribes', p. 576.

4 Leonard, *Social History of an Indian Caste*.

5 I offer a longer discussion of this document in 'Kayasths in Rajput land: Family Lore in a Dynasty of *qānūngō*-zamindars in early modern Malwa', submitted as part of a special issue to the *IESHR*.

6 Grierson, *Linguistic Survey of India*, pp. 52–9.

a *farmān*), until I realised that it was the verbatim reproduction of the text in another document, about twenty pages long, scribed in a modern and legible Nagri script.

I can only speculate on the dates of scribing of these two documents, and the reason for re-scribing. It is possible that the context and imperatives were similar to those that produced the *kaifiyats* and *yādīs* of landed families in the Marathi-writing region or of temples and other propertied institutions in the Telugu-writing region, both at the behest of the newly formed East India Company government in the early nineteenth century.[7] I can clearly see that the manuscripts tell a story of migration; they say that the family was originally from Udaipur. Their ancestor *Thākur* Gunraj, who was the *diwān* of the *Rāṇā* of Udaipur, saved the *Rāṇā* from an attack of *Bādshāh* Humayun, who was probably a generic 'blessed' emperor, rather than the second Mughal emperor; the dates do not match at all. Whoever the invading *Bādshāh* was, Gunraj saved Udaipur by the clever but predictable ruse of tying torches to the horns of thousands of buffaloes, to present the impression of a huge army. Despite this service, gossips poisoned the *Rāṇā*'s mind, alleging that these *Kāyasths* intended to set up their own kingdom. Faced with such allegations, the *diwān* submitted his inkpot and seal to the king, and set out from Udaipur with around 125 bullock carts full of possessions and people. There is then a genealogical recital of the dispersal and the formation of the diaspora, ending with the branch that reached Dhar.

In Dhar, curiously enough, they again met a rampaging Humayun, although in the improbable year of 1487 Saṃvat (1430 CE). Finding the area depopulated, Humayun *Bādshāh* asked, 'Are there no good people here? (*Is bastī mein kōī bhalā ādmī nahī mālūm hōtā*)'. Somebody mentioned the Udaipuris, so the *Bādshāh* summoned them with due respect, and the family offered hospitality (*mezbānī*) to the emperor. The emperor was so pleased that he wanted to take them along, but on their request, left them behind, bestowing them with a host of rights, which are recited in this string of bowdlerised Persian administrative terms: '*jamīdārī chaudharāt kī parganā majkūr kasbā wagerā hak dastūr ināmī gāoṇ dāmī bhaint jīrāyat sāyer va kalālī wa farōī ki chauthāī dhīvar gāoṇ wa pāṭēlī wa paṭwārā kai gāoṇ kā betī kā shādī gamī hak dastūr rasūm wagerā lag saw sudā sanad kar dī*'.

Of these, the *jamīdārī* (*zamīndārī*) *chaudharāt* (*chaudhrāī*) are easily comprehensible as landlord rights, *dāmī* and *bhaint* refer to rights derived from that position; *hak* (*haq*) and *dastūr* are different registers of talking about rights. *Jīrāyat* could be agricultural land (*zirā'at*) or it could have the Marathi usage,

7 G. C. Vad et al. (eds.), *Selections from the Government Records in the Alienation Office: Kaifiyats, Yadis* (Bombay, 1908); P. Sitapati (ed.), *Srisailam Temple Kaifiyat* [this is a translation of a Telugu *kaifiyat* in the Mackenzie collection] (Hyderabad: Government of Andhra Pradesh, 1981).

meaning unirrigated land, as opposed to orchards. *Sayer* are non-land taxes in which the grant-holders clearly had a share. *Kalālī* and *farōī* are incomprehensible to me; *pāṭēlī* and *paṭwārā* offer an apt combination of landlord and record-keeping rights, in which the former predominate, given the claims on less entitled villagers, during life-cycle occasions, such as weddings (*shādī*).

In this case then, our protagonists claim, once again, that their rights in Dhar derive from the emperor (Mughal or otherwise), rather than a *mansabdār*, an obvious effort to elevate half-remembered claims. Their rights were the result of a service, but the service was simply one of hospitality and largesse, of being well-to-do people of consequence, sort of country squires able to make the necessary arrangements for receiving imperial visitations. A *Kāyasth* past was acknowledged, with the position of *diwān*, and full attributes of the clever *wazīr* and so on. However, that was told as a story of failure and betrayal; by kings who should have known better. The family remade itself, and remade itself as little kings who could host the same emperor whom they had helped repulse in Udaipur.

In the rest of the story, the protagonists refer to themselves as *Thākurs*, and they are seen to be defending a very Rajput notion of honour, against treacherous inferior Rajputs, referred to as '*rangḍa*'. So *rangḍa* Kanha Dewda, who had fled when the emperor was in Dhar, returned to create mischief, sending his retainers to treacherously kill the *Thākur* in his own house, while enjoying his hospitality. At this, the widow demanded revenge, which a twelve-year-old brother-in-law, Jayanti Das, resolved to provide. The frightened Dewda fled towards the hills of Jhabua, taking refuge with *banjāra* Nayaks, who proved to be more manly, refusing to give up their protégé on grounds of hospitality. However, the Nayak's resolve was shaken when Jayanti Das, perched on a tree, had his men shoot the earrings off the Nayak's wife's ear. Now captured, the *rangḍa* was brought back to Dhar fort, where the imperial officer, a Nawab with a garbled name in the manuscripts (Adbud Khan), requested everyone to refrain from violence, but Jayanti Das had to have his revenge. And his sister-in-law then proceeded to become *satī*, bearing the *pāgḍī* (turban) of her husband. This part of the story, then, mimics the Rajputs' intensely sanguinary and self-sacrificial ethos of honour,[8] actuated through the virtuous embrace of violent death – by men, as well as women, albeit on sharply divergent social occasions.[9]

The story then twists, and we find Mohan Das, a descendant of Jayanti Das, living in association with Bira *Rāṇā*, and looting a Mughal tax caravan. Emperor Alamgir, wrathful at the news, sends a *mansabdār* to arrest Mohan

[8] Kamphorst, *In Praise of Death*.

[9] Susan Hoeber Rudolph and Lloyd I. Rudolph, *Essays on Rajputana: Essays on History, Culture and Administration* (New Delhi: Naurang Rai, 1984); Malavika Kasturi, *Embattled Identities: Rajput Lineages and the Colonial State in Nineteenth-Century North India* (New Delhi: Oxford University Press, 2002).

Das and imprison him in the fort of Asirgarh. Years later, Mohan Das's brother Chandar Bhan manages to attract the emperor's attention during a hunting trip in the Deccan. In a story very reminiscent of the Anil Rai episode in *Padshāhnāma*, Chandar Bhan takes on a tiger or lion, once the imperial hunting party fails to shoot the animal. Wrapping cloth around one arm, and with a dagger or *katār* in the other, he kills the animal. The emperor naturally summons him for reward, and Chandar Bhan seeks not only the release of his brother, but the reinstatement of all the rights that had been lost in the arrest and sacking. And the emperor obliges, reinstating our protagonists in Dhar.

This story corresponds with many of the factual details in the legal documents. It offers some plausible explanations of incidents and allusions whose meaning or significance is otherwise elusive in our Persian documents. Mohan Das's temporary fall from favour and residence (imprisonment?) in Asirgarh may be explained by his changing sides and joining the highway robbers, albeit explained as a matter of honour in the family history. The *banjāras*, who made only fleeting appearance so far – in a noble's *dastak* offering tax-free transit and in records of credit transactions – reappear as significant protagonists, of ambivalent moral value in that tale of honour. But it would be facile to think of the family history as a source of additional 'facts'. The narrative it offers has the quality of a dream, in which dates swing across centuries, one emperor is mixed up with another and a protagonist could be a robber-catcher or a robber himself. Rather than regressing towards an early-twentieth-century effort to filter out facts from such stories, or indeed, lurching towards conflating all kinds of stories about the past with history, we can recognise the family history for what it is: an exercise in collective self-representation by a lineage. Only then can we see that this story of military conflicts, assassinations, revenge and women gloriously becoming *satīs*, is really the story of becoming Rajput.

## Refusing Professionalism

Let us skip ahead to the early twentieth century and look at the very last document in our multi-lingual collection – this time, in English. We have already mentioned the petition to the Commissioner of the Central Indian Agency in the previous chapter; here, we shall discuss the arguments and evidence it offered, in order to access the modes of self-representation by this landed family. Once again, such self-representation was occasioned by a legal dispute, and one precipitated by the rationalising efforts of a half-heartedly modernising state, which (for the umpteenth time in South Asian history) attempted to assess revenues predictably, and convert the many nested rights in land to property ownership and salaried service. As the petition demonstrates, the values inherent in such a conversion were alien to landlords such as our family, whose self-perception centred around the royal model.

And so a clearly outraged Pratap Chand II, the patriarch of that generation, produced a printed petition in which he listed the many different rights of his family. The nomenclature of these rights are a bewildering array of arcane Indo-Persian revenue vocabulary, but highly familiar to us, who have encountered and understood these terms, and the rights they stood for, from two centuries worth of Persian documents. The family had clearly come a long way since the few *bīghas* of land in a handful of villages granted to Jayanti Das by an unidentified Mughal noble in the 1570s. Now, Pratap Chand, his descendant, claimed eighteen *istimrāri*[10] villages, 3,657 *bighas* of *zirā'at* (agricultural) land in various villages, and the rights to collect money from the inhabitants for a range of reasons: the *kōtwālī chabūtra* of Dhar, which they managed, *dāmī, bhet,* miscellaneous *rusooms* (traditional dues), *lag, sakri* and *ori.*

To explain and justify these rights, Pratap Chand II told the story of three successive imperial regimes in Dhar – the Mughals, the Marathas and the British – and placed his own family within it. While compared to the family history, this historically accurate story, stripped of all dreaminess, was written in the familiar language of English-language petitions, it asserted the same thing – that rights could never be separated from the politics and wars of empires.

As the Mughal empire declined, said the petition, the *zamīndārs* of the area were compelled to make a deal with the Maratha *sardārs*, especially the Puars, the Holkars and the Sindhias. This deal was formalised in 1743 when the Mughal empire signed a treaty with the Peshwa, handing over Malwa, and the Peshwa, in turn, promised not to disturb the pre-existing rights in the region, especially those of the *zamīndārs* and the *qānūngōs*. The terms of this treaty were quoted in the petition, sourced from none other than Malcolm's *Central India*. In turn, the petition continued, the Maratha *sardārs*, among whom the rights of Malwa were divided, promised to uphold the rights of the *zamīndārs*, and, indeed, they had done so, despite efforts to reduce the military capacity of the *zamīndārs*, and to centralise the administration of the state. Indeed, when, after a troublesome period, the Dhar state was 'saved from extinction' by the British, specifically John Malcolm, by taking it over, the Dhar princes submitted a list of the rights of *zamīndārs* under their control, which was incorporated into the treaty between Dhar state and the British in 1818.

Pratap Chand II acknowledged that:

> The past Maharajas [of the Dhar state] have invariably treated the family of the Dhar Zemindars with marked consideration and esteem. Whenever the zeal of the State officers have raised any dispute affecting the peaceful enjoyment of the heritage, they

[10] Wilson, *Revenue and Judicial Terms*, 221. *Istimrari* was title to land whose revenues were permanently settled.

have always by unambiguous orders, restored the enjoyment to its proper groove, and set matters to right. The *question of specific service and its performance* [italics in original] was never raised in past times by the Durbar, as has been done in 1905 by Rai Bahadur Munshi Roshanlall Saheb, then Superintendent of the State.[11]

Who was this clueless Roshanlal who was so impertinent as to enquire what exactly the *zamīndārs* did for a living?

It appears that he was a British Indian official, appointed in connection with the Dhar state being taken under the authority of the Court of Wards for a second time. And this official, unlike the apparently more conciliatory officers appointed in the past (one Muslim and one British), was so insensitive as to interfere in the '*waṭan*' of the *zamīndārs*, and to deny the rights granted by previous sovereigns – Mughal emperors and Maratha Maharajas – on the petty basis that the *zamīndārs* did not perform the duties enjoined upon them by the grant documents – the *sanads*. This was all wrong-spirited, said Pratap Chand II, because these rights, enjoyed over sixteen generations (as reflected by a family tree submitted as exhibit) were largely rewards for loyal, mostly military services, already rendered. Thus, Pratap Chand II proclaimed himself unwillingly taking up the position of complainant against the Dhar *darbār*, and hoped for justice from the paramount power, that is, the British government of India.

And Mughal law made its final appearance in this story, this time in the form of a translated *parvāna*, purportedly issued by Asad Khan, *wazīr* of emperor Aurangzeb to Narsingh Das *chaudhrī* (son of Purshottam Das) in the year 1696. The original document has not been found among the surviving documents, but it is striking that the English translation follows the correct structure of a *parvāna*, and the conjunction of dates and names are fully plausible. Other exhibits enclosed with the petition were a printed English-language family tree and an excerpt from the Dhar state gazetteers. Royal order, family memory and colonial surveys thus together formed the basis of rights claimed by the long-enduring *zamīndār* family, who had gained their position and possessions through battle, tax-farming, state service and sharp dealing, but refused to be professional about it. This was a very clear declaration of the notion that 'land is to rule'.

## The Shape of Memory: Lineal Descent Versus Outward Blossoming

The petition of the outraged *Thākur* Pratap Chand was accompanied by a family tree, which we have seen in the introduction. This document proposed a straightforward patrilineal line of descent, beginning with a key ancestor

[11] 'Petition' in Choudhary Family Collection, *Baḍā Rāolā* Dhar.

(Gunrajdass), and ending with the petitioner himself. There were, however, other designs to plotting the chronological and genealogical progress of the lineage over time, and a strikingly different design is presented in a type of document that is commonly found in landed families across Malwa and in fact, all over South Asia – the *shajara*.

This depiction of the lineage is shaped literally like a meandering plant with twirling branches, *rising* rather than descending from a common ancestor, offering a literal visualisation of the Arabic word *shajara*, which simply means: a tree. The difference between this document and the English-script genealogical table is stark. This difference, especially the trimming of relations, cannot be explained simply by a change over time, for judging by the paper and the poor handwriting, the *shajara* was probably contemporary to or even written later than the English-language petition and its accompanying genealogical table.

The shapes of the two documents mirror, in many ways, the differences in structure and content of the Persian-language legal documents as compared to the Hindi-language family history. English having taken the place of Persian as the language of governance and record, the memory of the lineage that was presented in the English-script genealogy was one that was restricted to lines of inheritance rather than kinship, and presumably lines of inheritance that the petitioner was particularly keen to establish as exclusively valid. It stuck to one story, geared at producing specific legal entitlements, as the Persian-language documents had done in previous centuries.

The *shajara*, on the other hand, meandered and ran into many lines because here the purpose was probably remembering a flourishing ancient lineage, whose prosperity was not limited to the material possessions of one principal line, but also the fecundity and proliferation of its many sons, just as the family history meandered to tell tales not just of gain, but also bravery and loss.

The family's insignia combined the themes of literacy and martial prowess, with an image of Jayanti *mātā*, the family goddess enclosed in a sword crossed over a pen. The love of books and interest in Persianate literary culture led *Thākur* Pratapchand I's grand-nephew and successor, *Thākur* Motichand, to commission a copy of the famous Persian–Hindi bilingual dictionary, *Khāliq bārī*, attributed to Amir Khusrau. In a beautiful tangling of social circles, the manuscript was copied by a certain *Qāẓī* Fateh al-din, a descendant of the great Khwaja Kamaluddin Chisti Mandavi himself. A memorial volume produced by the community associated with the shrine remembers the family as lovers of Urdu and Persian literature, with a library stacked with hundreds of books in those languages.[12]

[12] Mukhtar Ahmad Khan, *Hazrat Maulāna Khwāja Kamaluddin Chistī* (Piran-e Dhar: Urs Committee Hazrat Maulana Khwaja Kamaluddin Chisti, n.d.), p. 326.

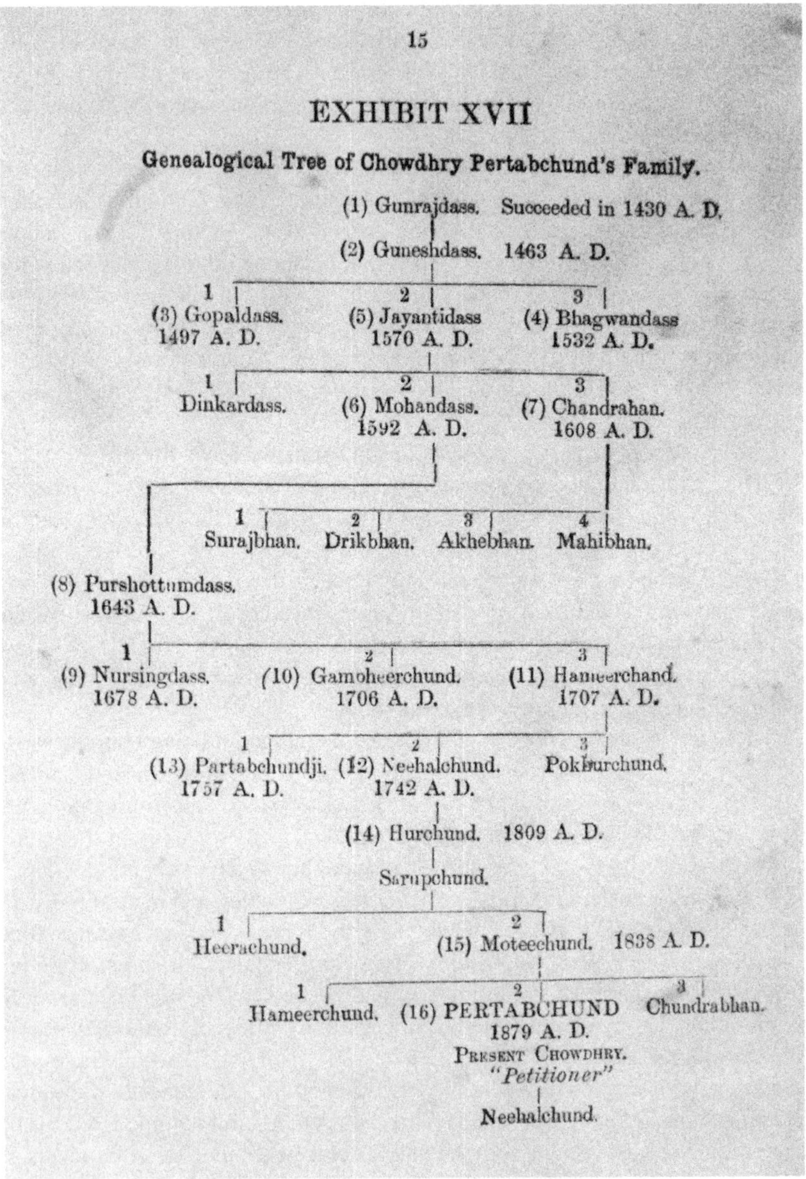

15

EXHIBIT XVII

Genealogical Tree of Chowdhry Pertabchund's Family.

(1) Gunrajdass. Succeeded in 1430 A. D.

(2) Guneshdass. 1463 A. D.

1 (3) Gopaldass. 1497 A. D.
2 (5) Jayantidass 1570 A. D.
3 (4) Bhagwandass 1532 A. D.

1 Dinkardass.
2 (6) Mohandass. 1592 A. D.
3 (7) Chandrahan. 1608 A. D.

1 Surajbhan.
2 Drikbhan.
3 Akhebhan.
4 Mahibhan.

(8) Purshottumdass. 1643 A. D.

1 (9) Nursingdass. 1678 A. D.
2 (10) Gamoheerchund. 1706 A. D.
3 (11) Hameerchand. 1707 A. D.

1 (13) Partabchundji. 1757 A. D.
2 (12) Neehalchund. 1742 A. D.
3 Pokhurchund.

(14) Hurchund. 1809 A. D.

Sarupchund.

1 Heerachund.
2 (15) Moteechund. 1838 A. D.

1 Hameerchund.
2 (16) PERTABCHUND 1879 A. D. PRESENT CHOWDHRY. *"Petitioner"*
3 Chundrabhan.

Neehalchund.

Figure 7.1 Family tree, produced in the early 1900s

Memorabilia preserved in the family include staged formal photographs of Pratap Chand II, which present a combined image of lordliness and erudition.

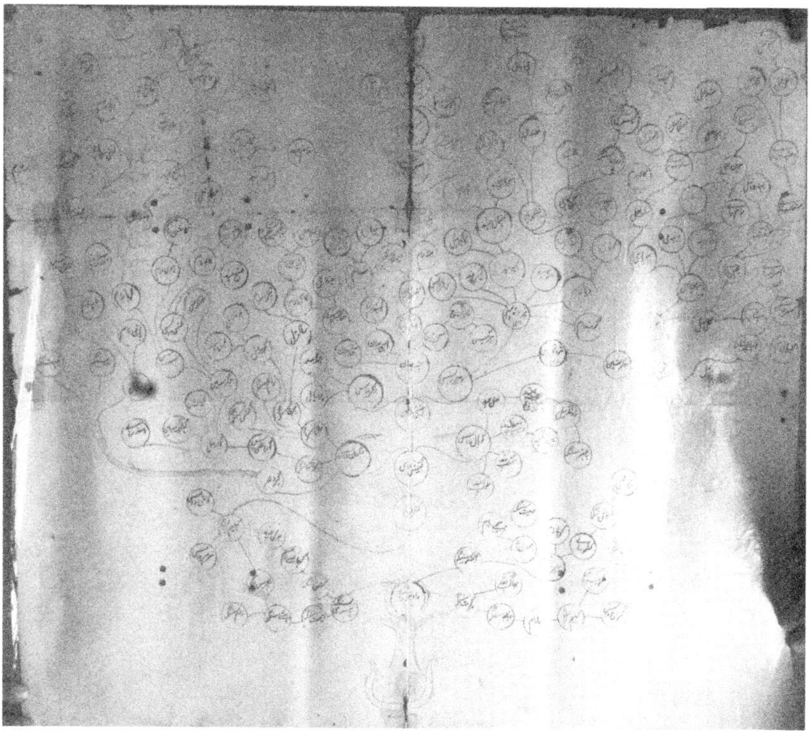

Figure 7.2 *Shajara* (also family tree)

When I discussed the sole photograph of *Thākur* Pratap Chand II with his descendant, Amit Choudhary (presented on the cover of this book) he asked me what I saw as the most striking feature of the photograph. When I couldn't quite identify it myself, he told me: 'Books, it's the books!'

*Thākur* Pratap Chand II's grandson, *Thākur* Nihal Chand is seen in a photograph taken in the courtyard of the *Baḍā Rāolā* mansion, seated on horseback with a young nephew. While this imparts an aura of feudal days, he also featured in the *Who's Who in British India and Burma*, in Indo-Western formal attire – a *sherwānī*, which famously evolved from the English frock-coat. Times were changing, leaving its mark on how rural aristocrats presented themselves. *Thākur* Nihal Chand himself was keen on such change; having studied in the liberal Allahabad University, he found himself better equipped than most landlords to deal with the enormous changes that took place during his lifetime, including the integration of the princely states and, perhaps most momentously, the abolition of *zamīndārī*. He educated his son Hamir Chand in

Figure 7.3 *Thākur* Nihal Chand on horseback in the *Baḍā Rāolā*, Dhar, 1920s. Choudhary Family Collection, *Baḍā Rāolā*, Dhar.

an elite boarding school in Indore, Daly College, and, when the son was grown, actively sought a marital alliance for him with the daughter of a remarkable Gandhian social and political activist. In 1964, when Hamir Chand and Abha were married, the bride and her younger sister still discovered a mansion in Dhar with four wings, hundreds of rooms, huge stores of silverware – a world away from their own.[13] When I met her in Dhar in 2016, *Thākurānī* Abha Choudhary smilingly recalled stepping into that feudal world, where respectable women never went out unveiled. She made her place within that world, combining her mother's social values with the cultural context of her marital home – working quietly for various charitable causes all her life.

## Conclusion

Together, the scroll of family history, the petition, the family trees and the photographs offer us valuable, if belated, access to the self-perception of our principal protagonists. It is also striking that this self-expression took place in languages other than Persian – whether in Hindi or English. In both cases, the protagonists represented themselves in ways that are both in line with the stories told by the Persian legal documents, and divergent from them. Like

[13] Meenal Shrivastava, *Amma's Daughters: A Memoir* (Edmonton: Athabasca University Press, 2018), pp. 189–94.

the Persian documents, the family history and the petition tell stories of war, and of imbrication in empires. They reveal heightened awareness of law, or more accurately, of specific entitlements, and their basis in both their own achievements and in royal grants (or treaties between various sovereigns).

On the other hand, the Hindi family history and the English-language petition assert what the Persian documents do not quite say: that these *zamīndārs* saw themselves as warriors, as little kings in their own right, whose rights arose above all from the virtues of courage, loyalty and attachment to the realm. Both the Mughal-era Persian narrative documents and the Hindi family history emphasised martial ability; the Hindi family history went further, and valorised forms of violence that went far beyond state service, turning towards Rajput-style violent feminine self-immolation, for example. But the Hindi family history also contained in it elements that we would today see as more suitably part of *Kāyasth* self-identity, foregrounding, at crucial moments in the story, symbols such as the inkpot, and traits such as intelligence, diplomacy, hospitality and awareness of legal documentation.

And that is perhaps where we should leave this analysis; reminding ourselves that *Kāyasth*, Rajput and Maratha have not been insular categories from the early modern period until now. The story of this family, and of the many regimes they have inhabited, served and utilised, shows us that claiming entitlement and dominion in this corner of Malwa required travelling boldly between such different identities.

# Fragments to Archives: a Methodological Manifesto

This book is the first micro-history written in the context of studies of the Mughal Empire. Using nearly two hundred Persian-language legal and administrative documents and a significant amount of Hindi-, Marathi- and English-language material, it has told the story of the activities and achievements of one landed family across several generations, from the late sixteenth until the twentieth century. That story traversed several regimes – from remembered connections with pre-Mughal Rajput kingdoms and central Indian sultanates, to the Mughals, then the Marathas, then a minor princely state under the control of the British Empire in India. The central protagonists in the story encountered emperors, princes, nobles, bandits, itinerant merchants, servant-retainers and courtesans. This book has presented the political and social history that emerges from those encounters as a narrative, the story of that family. This is a story that they had themselves worked to produce, through documentation, archiving and excision. The history thus produced and the process of research involved in putting it together forces us, for reasons I shall elaborate, to contend with the relationship of history to memory, especially memories that are significant to individuals and families, and the obligations, both empirical and ethical, that history and the historian owe to such personally significant memories.

In the remaining portion of this book, I will discuss that relationship and my growing understanding of it. I will also offer a description of a process by which the seemingly meaningless fragments of Mughal and Maratha records may be reconstituted as archives that are capable of revealing stories such as this one, about individuals and lineages located in larger political and social structures. And thereby, I argue that, as the best micro-historians have done, we may also achieve better understanding of those broader structures themselves.

Micro-history is in many ways a misnomer. It is not about small events, limited places, fewer people and either insignificant or untenable conclusions. It is instead, as I understand it, a certain attitude towards the subject matter, an attitude that shapes the research process. A great deal of theoretical discussion about micro-history is about the representativeness or typicality of its subject matter, and hence conclusions. If the best micro-histories begin with atypical episodes, data that does not fit, then by exploring it further, can historians really discover anything new about broader ideas, society or politics? Are their efforts merely story-telling indulgences, or alternatively, inventive forays whereby they postulate hidden alternative structures based on their limited evidence?[1] One of the most beautiful answers is offered by Carlo Ginzburg, who suggests that micro-history is a method of following seemingly insignificant clues that in reality offer the truest picture, like an astute detective who refuses to be taken in by overwhelming appearances. Thus whether it be nailing the criminal, the disease or the artist, it is a shared method of attention to 'tiny details [that] provide the key to a deeper reality, inaccessible by other methods. These details may be symptoms, for Freud, or clues, for Holmes, or features of paintings, for Morelli'.[2]

All historians follow clues; following breadcrumb trails is part and parcel of a profession in which most of us write about, and try to understand, people who cannot talk to us and explain why they did what they did. Even in those limited demographic (mostly male, wealthy, literate) and social contexts (that which was worthy of being written about) where they did produce records that have reached us, we do not know what they assume we know already. The ghosts of the past talk to their peers; we are like little children eavesdropping through floorboards trying to make out what the grown-ups are really saying. Meanings are lost in the process of Chinese whispers, in which words pass through multiple layers of articulation and scribing, and it is a struggle to imagine, let alone reconstruct, the many hands that have been at work, across generations, in the producing of a single scrap of paper such as the *nishān* that this book began with.

As a micro-historian, I see it as my duty to pursue what seems unusual or odd about those half-heard whispers, not silence and squeeze them into what we think we already know about the great processes of history. The research necessary to make sense of those shards can be, and has been for me, frighteningly expansive, because these pieces of texts with bizarre word combinations and profusions of symbols can only be decoded if one is prepared to teach oneself a great deal about the usage of such words and symbols – in the immediate context and far beyond. The trouble, as I stated in the beginning, was the situating of my questions and fragments in the appropriate historical field – if I turned to Islamic law, there was a tremendous textual tradition available for referencing, and if I turned to Mughal historiography, there were studies of courtly literature and institutional histories. In the end, I decided to use both – I decided that the Islamic legal vocabulary was not meaningless but

[1] Matti Peltonen, 'Clues, Margins and Monads: The Micro-Macro Link in Historical Research', *History and Theory*, 40: 3 (2002), 347–59.

[2] Carlo Ginzburg and Anna Davin, 'Morelli, Freud and Sherlock Homes: Clues and Scientific Method', *History Workshop*, 9 (1980), 5–36, at 11.

a connection with the practices of the wider Islamic world, and that Mughal institutions and royal traditions produced their own vocabulary, rules and expectations. So a pan-Islamic word like *iqrār* has its many Indian avatars, and they are all part of my story.

But I am not a historian of ideas; my principal tools are not textual analysis and comparison, rather they consist of situating the text in the archive. I prefer instead to try and understand how a certain text, in my case a scrap of a legal deed, may have actually operated (and thus understood) in its own time. For that, I need the archive from which that fragment is derived; but that archive has to be reconstituted.

## Reconstituting the Archive

Intending to write a book on law in the Mughal Empire, I began work in the National Archives of India in the year 2012, and was immediately overwhelmed by two problems, one practical and the other analytical. The practical problem consisted of the sheer bulk of the material available, disrupting the generally held view that Mughal archives have not survived. Archivists in the 'Oriental' section of the National Archives began by telling me about the roughly 130,000 Persian-language documents from the Mughal province of Golconda, which were generally single-page scraps in hideous *shikasta* or 'broken' scribal hand, and, as far as I could see, concerned with routine records related to taxation. When it became clear that I was making no headway at all, the archivists, taking pity on me, introduced me to the 'acquired' Persian documents series, which, as they explained, consisted of collections of documents from various families deposited with the National Archives. This was a much smaller series, but still substantial – around 5,000–6,000 documents – and were thankfully, very well catalogued, with detailed summaries of every document. Even so, how many of these should I read, and to what end? Taking a random and typical page from the catalogues, I struggled to see the connection between a letter about preparing tax records that referred to Bijapur, a copy of a *parvāna* that referred to Malwa, a *baiʿ-nāma* (sale deed) executed in an unknown place and a *rahn-nāma* (mortgage deed) recorded in an unidentified location, all referring to different individuals. What was the connection of any of this with Mughal law? Where were the questions put to the *muftī* and his responses, the judgements of the *qāẓ̤ī* and the *sijillāt* or registers of judgements and deeds – all of which we have been taught to expect in the leading works of Islamic law? As the reader can see, this was the predominant empirical and interpretive structure that I wished to fit my material into, and found myself failing spectacularly in doing so.

I persisted with the catalogues, and plodded through the documents over several months, with the help of the most generous teacher one could ever have – Chander Shekhar, then Head of the Persian department at Delhi University – learning to identify the framing formulae, the logograms that compressed key words and the conventions of transcribing Indic person and place names in the Perso-Arabic script. From him, I learnt to read seals and to reliably identify the position and status of the persons using those seals, especially nobles and *qāẕīs*; I learnt to tell the difference between an original and a copy; I learnt the joys of decrypting dates from calendars that combined a regnal year with an Islamic month. As I did so, certain names and patterns finally began to surface from the dump of scraps; I began to identify some people as they turned up again and again, doing various things in roughly the same cities and villages, and, after a predictable number of years, making way for other individuals who were clearly their descendants.

It is then that I understood how the 'acquired papers' were organised. Clearly, collections of specific families had been acquired by the National Archives, but the integrity of these collections had not been preserved in the catalogues. Instead, the cataloguers took all such documents as a single set of 'acquired documents' and organised them in a chronological order. The only way to re-establish the collections as they had once been would be to read through every single entry in the catalogues, pick out the shelfmarks of the documents pertaining to a single family, and order up and procure copies of those documents. I have told the story of how one individual in particular – Purshottam Das – forced itself on my attention. He was the principal protagonist in the majority of the eighty-four documents related to this family that were held the National Archives, whose dates stretched across the seventeenth century, straddling the reigns of the emperors Shah Jahan and Aurangzeb. The other documents referred to members of the family who inherited his estates after his death; the legacy he had created in the district of Dhar and its environs was clearly persistent. I ended that particular stretch of research with a diverse collection of documents – orders, tax contracts, deeds recording transactions, letters – all united by this individual or his descendants.

But what was the purpose of reconstructing that connection? Could this one obscure individual, not a religious scholar, not even a Muslim, dabbling in taxes and cutting a variety of deals in a corner of the Mughal Empire tell us anything about Islamic law in India? Deciding to suspend that question for a while, I decided instead to study the documents in minute detail, transcribing and translating every one of them in collaboration with my teacher, now research partner, and re-catalogue them. As I did so, I began to see further connections; I began to see the relations between the protagonists, I discovered how fortunes were made and passed on. I learnt about Purshottam Das's father Mohan Das, and his adventures with robber catching,

As I became more familiar with the members of the family across generations, I began to put together a rough genealogy. I then began to see that offices and perquisites did not always pass from one generation to another: Mohan Das passed his title to his brother Chandar Bhan, who passed it to Purshottam Das, his nephew, rather than his own son, Suraj Bhan. Perhaps my most exciting discovery was that a persistently troublesome branch of the family derived from Suraj Bhan's dalliance with a Muslim courtesan, and the son who was born of that relationship. I could see how that son was actively excluded by the patrilineage, but how he, and other such rivals, continued to circle the successful line across generations. There were also important external allies: imperial nobles with whom the family had long-standing connections, and who could sort out not just a mansion or two, but also difficult relatives from time to time. I began to see this as a dramatic narrative that could allow me to use the story of familial/dynastic formation in order to examine how the Mughal state was both substantiated and accessed – for offices, for resources, for selling services and for creating and recording entitlements. This began to accord well with my existing interest in families and in micro-history as a methodology, perhaps with law in practice, although I was still unsure what exactly this 'law' consisted of.

The process of gathering source material continued far longer than I had expected. It was as if every time I thought my story was complete, a completely new store of records would open up, drawing me further and further into a winding cave of wonders, but also despair. Through a process described in the introduction, I managed to find not one but two supplementary archives of material related to the same family, one in the Dar al-Athar al-Islamiyyah Museum in Kuwait and the other in the household of the family, whose descendants I managed to locate, and who chose to be extremely kind to me. Once again, the story of archiving pressed itself forward. Presumably, sometime in the 1950s, one or more members of the family had disposed of some papers from their collection. DAI Kuwait had acquired what appeared, on the face of it, higher-value manuscripts, nicely scribed and sealed, nearly monolingual in Persian. This is a collecting strategy that focusses on the artefact itself rather than the context from which it is derived. The National Archives, on the other, in an immediate post-colonial context, had accepted a more diverse body of material, perhaps in line with the effort to create a people's history and corresponding archive. The residue of the most visually unattractive and linguistically provincial material remained with the family.

In reality, all three collections were part of the same pre-existing archive; together, they told a more complete and comprehensible story, one which not only throws light on how to get ahead in the Mughal empire, but also begins to offer some indication of writing and copying, of recording and archiving practices – all of which point towards the household rather than the state as the location par excellence of Mughal archives. With all the collections of family documents deposited in repositories all over India, Pakistan and

Bangladesh, a small but significant portion of which has been edited and published, we have a tremendous archive of Mughal history. We have just been looking in the wrong place all along.

## Documents as Historical Artefacts

As I began to present some of this work in various articles and conference papers, one question began to force itself upon me; the matter of authenticity. One interlocutor expressed particular concern about the possibility that all these documents may have been forgeries, generated at the cusp of transition to colonialism, when the British urge to stem leakage of revenue and record all entitlements led to the infamous 'Inam commissions' and the rush to produce, if necessary fabricate, records of pre-existing rights.

This pushed me to look wider, and confront the question of Mughal archives – their simultaneous ubiquity as well as absence. There are two tremendous collections of Mughal-era documents, mainly from the seventeenth century, and both related to the newest province, conquered and created in 1685 – Golconda. The first is the Inayat Jung Collection at the National Archives, Delhi, and the other is the series at the Telangana State Archives, Hyderabad. Together, they have around 250,000 individual documents or more, mainly related to taxation and military recruitment and pay. On the other hand, there are smaller collections held in several libraries and archives around the country, which appear to all derive from specific families or religious institutions. Comparable with the latter are sets of documents acquired by European corporations, including the English East India Company, again predictably related to their own rights and privileges. I discovered also that such collections were a combination of sealed originals and copies – the latter designating themselves as such – and learnt that historians of Mughal India have generally paid very little attention to the difference, and, despite periodic concern about forgery, been very trusting of the factual contents of an archive thus presented. My interlocutor's question could potentially undermine the entirety of Mughal historical studies based on documents.

The documents have always been taken to be the same as their content. To take one of the best current exponents, Hasan treats a family collection deposited at the National Archives, New Delhi; 'calendars' or detailed catalogues of documents at the U.P. State Archives, Allahabad; an anonymously composed/ copied collection of documents produced for a French Orientalist; and a *munshāt* all as equivalent sources.[3] Let us a see what difference a more

[3] For a recent example, see Farhat Hasan, 'Property and Social Relations in Mughal India: Litigations and Disputes at the Qazi's Courts in Urban Localities, 17th-18th Centuries', *Journal of the Economic and Social History of the Orient*, 61: 5–6 (2018), 851–77, detailing the sources at 855–7.

careful reading might make. Nile Green's erudite introduction to *The Persianate World*, published in 2019, presents a 'Persian-Marathi *Inam* document of Maloji Bhonsle' as an example of a Mughal secretarial bilingualism.[4] The image of the document shows that it is a *chak-nāma*, which was a document recording the measuring out of lands following a grant. Although *chak-nāmas* are a well-recognised Mughal documentary form, they were also used in the Marathi-writing areas. Maloji, Shivaji's grandfather, had been a high-ranking officer in the Ahmadnagar Sultanate, the archenemy of the Mughals under Malik Ambar, the Abyssinian general-turned-king. If it is indeed an authentic document recording a grant of land being made by Maloji to a Muslim *shaikh* called Muhammad Darvesh Qadri, resident in the town of Chamargonda (Shrigonda, in Ahmadnagar), it would be more correct to call it an Ahmadnagar document rather than Mughal.

However, the authenticity of the document is worth questioning. The document is indeed in Persian and Marathi (in the cursive Modi script) and so presents evidence of (Ahmadnagari) bilingualism; it also bears a superscript saying 'by the *iqrār* of Maloji Bhonsle, a *naql* (copy) according to the original'. The copied document, moreover, does not bear any validating seals, and even so, only a photocopy of this unvalidated copy seems to be held at its current repository. The handwriting suggests that the copy is no older than the nineteenth century, and if so, it may well be the case that the Marathi in Modi summary we have beneath the Persian text is in fact the addition of colonial clerks in western India rather than an instance of Ahmadnagari epistolary tradition.

These thoughts are of course speculative. The aim of this short discussion is pointing out the vast scope and need that remains for the precise reading of these documents, with attention to the entire document as a historical artefact – its formal, material and graphic features – together with constant attention to its archival history. Just as an archaeologist would not be satisfied with receiving a plaster cast of a decorative feature as sole evidence of its historical use, historians of the Mughal and Maratha empires could be both more careful and more exploratory in using such Persian or bilingual documents as historical traces.

## Dealing with Data: a Historian Crunching Numbers

Although one hundred and eighty-eight documents may not seem like big data, when these documents are fiendishly difficult to read, and one is trying to make a story out of a soup of person and place names and seemingly unconnected small events, they do begin to look intimidating. As I moved through this research,

[4] Green, *Persianate World*, p. 31.

I realised that I would have to find a way of searching through my collection, so that I could trace the connections between documents and between people. However, this process of cataloguing and creating a database led me to other difficulties and discoveries, too. The documents sourced from the National Archives had dates assigned to them; I had to establish the dates by reading (and interpreting) the documents from Kuwait and Dhar. This is much more difficult than it sounds, because only a minority of the documents have full Hijri dates, which can be converted will relative ease to dates from the Gregorian calendar (Common Era) using reliable online converters and smartphone apps. The added bonus is that through obvious processes of data mining and tracking of user activity that are ongoing on our phones and computers all the times, I am now regularly sent reminders of the need to pray. There are however more difficult combinations of dates – the Islamic month with the regnal year (*julūs*) – is one that has given me no end of trouble. A date such as 10 Rabi ʿII regnal year 29, for example, requires us to know, first of all which emperor's reign is being referred to. Since none of our documents are imperial orders, we can only know the answer indirectly – by reading the seal of the issuing officer, and hoping that he would declare himself the *banda/murīd* (slave/disciple) of Emperor So-and-So. This of course worked only for high-ranking nobles – *mansabdārs*. For issuing authorities further down the line, for example, from a noble's household, the seal may simply declare allegiance to the noble in question. In such a case, the connection with the emperor and his reign can only be established if the noble can be identified. With some nobles making repeated appearance in our documents, this was relatively easy (over time); it remained difficult for others.

Once at least roughly established, the dates allowed me to organise the documents in a chronological order, which revealed how documents followed each other, as copies, supplementary orders and so on; how events followed each other; and how people related to each other. Tracking Chandar Bhan, Suraj Bhan, Purshottam Das and Muhammad Asad on my spreadsheet, for instance, I could now understand much better why Suraj Bhan, the black sheep and Muhammad Asad's father, was hounded out of his possessions by other members of the family. I could also track the role of certain officials in the activities of the family – *Qāẓī* Muhammad Mustafa, for example, became a familiar name to me, as he must have been for members of the family at the end of the seventeenth century, since he sealed so many of the documents they kept in their collection.

I began disaggregating the data – I separated out information in columns of a table that listed a document by its provenance, date, summary of contents, person and place names, seal, invocation and language. It soon became clear to me that if I wanted to really utilise the data, a table on Microsoft Word was not sufficient; I needed a spreadsheet. And so, to the great joy of my engineer husband, I transferred the data to a Microsoft Excel spreadsheet, discovering immediately that this allowed me to do much more. I could now utilise filters to discern patterns in the documents. For example, I could tell that around 20 per cent of the documents contained some non-Persian elements, and that if we removed the documents from after 1740, the percentage falls slightly lower. However, if we take the 'truly' bilingual documents – that is, with significant sections of non-Persian text in the main body of the document, as opposed to very brief notes in the margins or reverse – the percentage is even lower. The predominant language of giving orders, making contracts and transacting with other subjects of the Mughal empire, even in the villages, was Persian. The other languages played an important and visible, but inevitably limited, role. The language use was also, as I have said in Chapter 4, co-related to the type of document. Tax contracts and *iqrārs* recording sales or other transactions were most likely to have another Indian language, in this case Malwi/Rangri, albeit with a heavily Persianised vocabulary.

Managing and manipulating my spreadsheet also afforded me a highly demonstrable defence of my research method – of re-creating the archive. I could plot the documents in time, and I could add filters to show how the time distribution of documents appeared different at every stage of that archival reconstruction.

Each stage in this chart refers to a stage in the accumulation of these documents. Stage 1 refers to documents collected from the National Archives alone, Stage 2, to the collated documents from National Archives and DAI, Kuwait, and Stage 3, to all documents, from NAI, DAI and Dhar. The NAI documents on their own offer a picture whereby the family's documentation is clustered in the late seventeenth century, with the biggest store of documents being created in the year 1684, the year that Purshottam Das died. Had I stopped my research at this stage, my conclusion would have been that generational boundaries were the causes of most profuse record-making, that is, the imperatives for legal documentation arose from within the family and its structures.

However, as the DAI documents were added, the time distribution shifts to earlier in time, with a peak related, not to Purshottam Das's death, but Dara Shukoh's. As the succession battled raged and then settled, the *zamīndārs* of Dhar, having dealt with Murad Baksh and then Dara Shukoh as *jāgīrdārs*, now had to ensure that their titles remained secure under the new emperor, Aurangzeb.

This peak of documentation, related to imperial politics rather than family dynamics was heightened with the addition of the documents from Dhar. The year 1660 was the one with the most documents now, with significant clusters around that year. The Dhar documents also showed that documentation continued well beyond the Mughal regime, in languages and forms that were familiar as well as novel.

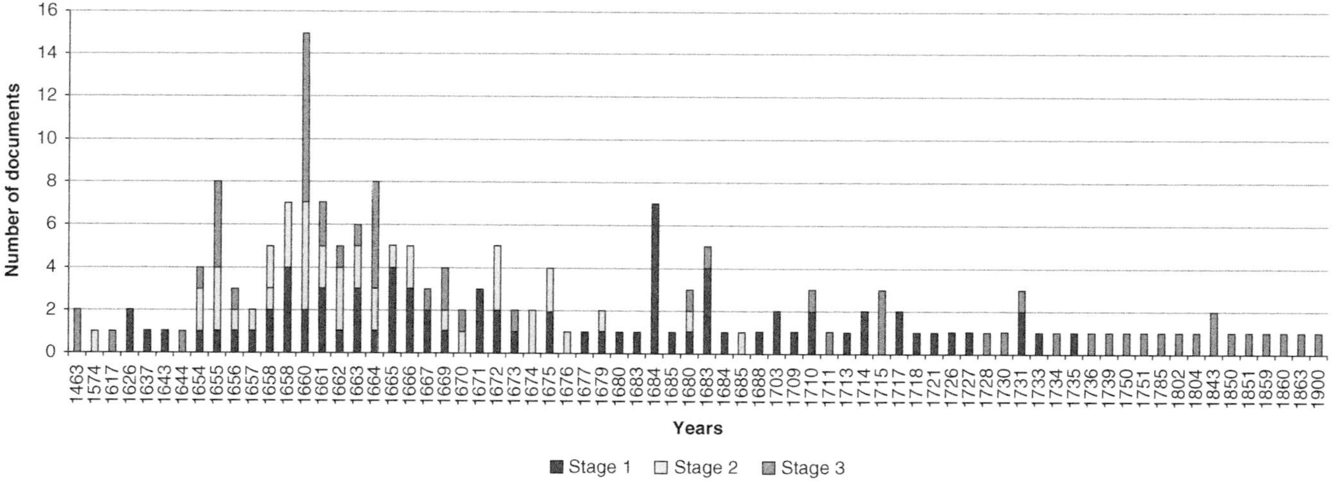


Figure C.1 Time distribution of the number of documents, by stage of research

There is of course no way to assess the completeness of the archive I have recreated. I rest my case, however, on the value of a methodology that is time and labour intensive, but which has the potential to open up archives that are all around us and yet invisible. I propose that we imaginatively restore the fragments to their household archives, and pay attention to the families which acquired and preserved such documents, for the family is the locale for the actuation of the pre-colonial state, activation of law and storing of its records.

### Law and the Uses of Documents

The last scholar to examine such documents on a sufficient scale was Muzaffar Alam. He, however, used such materials to fill out a story about the changing contours of the late Mughal state in two major provinces. More recently, B. L. Bhatia, in writing about Emperor Aurangzeb's relations with Islamic scholars and judges, has made significant use of such documents, especially those from the U.P. State Archives, Allahabad. Farhat Hasan has used catalogue descriptions of the same collection to talk about the meanings of property in South Asia.[5] In other words, the documents are used to tell the stories of greater things, never of the people who are the principal protagonists of the documents themselves.

This book uses the archive to tell the story of the people who populate that archive. This is not a case of reading against the grain; it is in fact reading with the grain, hearing the story that those who created the archive wished to be heard. I reiterate: the purpose of that is not simply to add colour and detail to the bigger picture; it is about answering some of the biggest questions for the field, such as: 'Where are the Mughal archives?' The answer is: 'At home'.

That answer would be less startling if we think of a parallel. There is no central repository of patient records in South Asia, every seeker of medical treatment archiving their own documents, often over years. That makes their grimy, tattered files with fading X-ray plates no less medical, and no less real. It may well be the same with law. If that parallel works, then one has to also keep in mind that what people archive depends on what they believe constitutes medicine, or at least routes to health (similarly, law, or routes to entitlement). Just as medical prescriptions and magical amulets might co-exist in a matriarch's alcove 'medicine-box', *parvānas* and court orders sit comfortably with family history scrolls in a landed family's archive. Reading them together should be the obvious thing to do, especially if we are aiming to find what 'law' really meant to middling people in Mughal India.

Awareness of the range of materials available, and the necessarily incomplete nature of any archive that one might discover or even painstakingly

[5] Farhat Hasan, 'Property and Social Relations in Mughal India'.

reconstitute, also pushes us to think of the archive and library as situated in a spectrum of repositories, language use, genre and even concepts changing dramatically from one end to another. The library-archive concept is Brinkley Messick's update to his powerful schema of 'textual habitus'; both concepts signal a diversity of texts, genres and users, but connected through 'a set of acquired dispositions concerning writing and the spoken word, and the authoritative conveyance of meaning in texts',[6] mainly by the mediation of expert legal mediators (the jurists), who may be a 'local cosmopolitan'.[7] Although many of the documents that this book is based on would be easily recognised by scholars of Islamic law as 'Islamic legal documents', many others, such as the royal and sub-royal orders, the tax contracts and newsletters, would not make it to that trans-regional category. The models that these documents are based on are various too, and if they were indeed united in the Indo-Persian *munshāts*, as I have suggested, then the texts in the higher shelves of this imagined library would contains works of Islamic jurisprudence, stacked next to royal chronicles. In all probability, the mediators would not have been Islamic scholars, not even Muslims, but *munshīs* – Hindu *Kāyasths* like the protagonists of this story. To understand their mindscape, as likewise that of the protagonists, one has to also read family history narratives that emphasise Rajput codes of honour and valour rather than legal doctrine of any kind, and remain aware of a language *and* lexicon very distinct from that of the Persian legal documents. I have been thinking with a notion of circles – *dāi'ra* – to map and interpret the scope and jurisdictions of various levels of knowledge, authority and understanding of law present in the reconstituted archive. By thinking of many circles, not necessarily concentric, I have tried to sidestep a notion of 'Islam-plus' in constituting this version of the Islamicate. The library offers another metaphor, perhaps a more directly realistic one, to refer to a wider, heterogeneous, even discordant field of social life and language use; it also signals the limits of the investigative methodology that this book has proposed.

## The Meaning of Law

Seeing all this material together also helped me resolve, finally, that question of what 'law' is, and what, therefore, are appropriate materials for writing a history of law, especially law in and of the Mughal Empire. As proposed in the Introduction, and as argued throughout the book, I decided that it is unproductive to re-fragment an archive, restored through the process described above, in order to achieve a coherent narrative. The meaning of law derives

[6] Messick, *The Calligraphic State*, p. 251–2.

[7] Brinkley Messick, *Sharī'a Scripts: A Historical Anthology* (New York: Columbia University Press, 2018), pp. 21–8, at 28.

from the integrity of that collection; rather than imposing an external definition and typology, I have observed what functions the documents perform within the collection. Thus observed, a *farmān*, *nishān* or *parvāna*, while an order, can work as a 'charter' creating rights, that are then repeatedly examined and recorded, through the officiation, above all of the local *qāẓī*; but they are also disputed, re-evaluated and re-documented, by the *qāẓī*, but also by other authorities, including the locally resident nobles. And all the time, people transacted – they bought, sold, borrowed, returned, claimed, paid up and gifted; they recorded all this in documentary forms recognisable across the partially overlapping Islamic world and the Persianate world.

The 'law' in such a context derives from a sense of right – both objective (what should be) and subjective (somebody's right) – that is so trenchantly expressed in this totality of documentation. That sense of right/s cannot be attributed to any single learned tradition, whether that be *fiqh* or *dharmaśāstra*, nor to an India-centric notion of Mughal rules, nor simply a purely plastic set of local custom which was a thin veil for social and political power. All these elements may be referenced, especially through a repertoire of terms recognisable trans-locally, but the meaning and content of 'law' has to be derived from what was clearly significant to the protagonists themselves. From this point of view, the family history document is as important a source for accessing that broader understanding as the Persian-language documents recording specific rights and obligations.

The word that is used most frequently in these documents in order to signal a concept of entitlement is *dastūr*. Read in connection with the *dastūr al-ʿamal* manuals we saw in Chapter 3, there emerges a sense of how things ought to be done, which, when done right, renders everyone their due. Twinned with *sharīʿa*, this was the other most common abstract term used to signal 'law'. I propose that *dastūr* may be the window to understanding law in practice in the Mughal empire; the Mughal name for Islamicate law.

## Micro-history and Family History: a Conversation

The family history document also forces us to contend with the implications of memory, especially memories in families about ancestors. This is where I realised that, despite my belief that by using the methodology of micro-history, I had demonstrated my interest in actual human protagonists, this interest was still objective; it was, in the final reckoning, concerned with understanding how social actors operated and a system functioned. I was interested in the abilities, motivations, interests and world-views of my protagonists, but what I discovered had no implication for my own sense of self, or so I thought, until I decided to have an extended conversation with Amit Choudhary, Mohan Das's descendant and my constant interlocutor over the past three years, and his elder sister, Meenal Shrivastava, Professor of Political Economy and Global Studies at Athabasca University, Canada.

In this conversation, which we conducted over Skype, we discussed not just this book but also another 'family history', but of a very different type. That book is *Amma's Daughters*, an imaginative, novelistic, and meticulously researched book based on the diary of an extraordinary woman who defied social conventions, joined Gandhi's *ashram* in Sabarmati, entered an unusual marriage and raised two daughters alongside a punishing regime of work as a social-political activist in post-colonial India.[8] This woman was Meenal's grandmother, *Amma*. Meenal's mother and Amit's were sisters. Two completely different families had been joined by a marriage in the mid-twentieth century and two historians had written stories of those two families.

In recalling the reasons that had brought her to write *Amma's Daughters*, Meenal spoke of the pain and loneliness of being orphaned and simultaneously feeling herself in exile in Canada. She remembered having seized the writings of her grandmother as her one connection to her past, and having embarked upon her project in an effort to revive that connection. As the project entered the stage of archival research, however, the enormous significance of the material to hand dawned on her, and the book became an effort to tell the story of women in the Indian nationalist movement. For Amit, on the other hand, the desire to seek the past of the *thākur* family into which his mother married was more intuitive. Given the family's long pedigree and obvious local significance, how could he not want to know? My arrival in Dhar was, he said, an opportunity too good to miss, to find out about his own family in ways that he could not do himself.

We thus had a subtle binary developing as the rationale for interest in a family's past – emotional connection versus intellectual curiosity. And yet, as Meenal offered to Amit, his curiosity was also born on an emotional connection. Amit agreed, and reconfirmed what he had told me in the past, that his favourite character in the story I had uncovered was the shadowy Jayanti Das, present in one very early document as a grantee but a key protagonist in the Malwi/Rangri family history as the child-warrior who had taken on a rogue Rajput and a Mughal commander in a quixotic mission to revenge the murder of his elder brother. As for me, while I had no connection with the family, my determination to find out about its past had at some point transformed from intellectual curiosity into an emotional investment, in a past that was so very different from our present that it was hard to imagine today.

Were we all interested then, in outliers, misfits? Meenal was very strongly in favour of this explanation; she offered a poetic-ethical exposition of the essential outsiderhood of every person, and thus the need to celebrate outliers

[8] Shrivastava, *Amma's Daughters*.

wherever one finds them. In doing so, said Meenal, we should learn from the techniques of storytelling that had been used by indigenous communities in North America as political protest as well as cultural activism. Both Meenal and Amit expressed their approval for my method of research, including potentially 'embarrassing' discoveries such as the episode with Muhammad Asad. They were looking, they said, for history, not eulogy. Besides this common affiliation to social realism, we found that all three of us had a shared cause in our joy in discovering the people who made up the past, people whom we may like and admire, or not, but people who give us access to other worlds, that were, that may have been. A shared 'interest in the eclectic', as Amit Choudhary put it, had brought us together, and for my commitment to the project of discovering the family's history, Amit offered me the status of an honorary Choudhary. Gratefully receiving that emotional compensation, and on this conversational note, I end this story.

# Appendix: A Catalogue of the P Das Archive[1]

Accession numbers and repositories:

BRD and NCD = Choudhary Family collection, *Baḍā Rāolā*, Dhar (photographed by author or family members)
DAI = Al-Sabah Collection, Dar al-Athar al-Islamiyyah, Kuwait, documents with common shelfmark prefix LNS MS 235
NAI = National Archives of India, New Delhi, Acquired Persian documents, NAI's shelfmarks

1 Twenty-four of these documents, exclusively from the Kuwait DAI collection, were summarised by Syed Bashir Hasan in 'Administration of *Jagirs* in Malwa in the Mid-Seventeenth Century: The Dhar Documents,' in Shahabuddin Iraqi (ed.) *Medieval India 2: Essays in Medieval Indian History and Culture* (Manohar: Centre for Advanced Study, AMU, 2008), pp. 217–30. These are marked with *. Also, images, full transcriptions and translations of several of these documents will be presented on the website lawforms.exeter.ac.uk which is currently under construction.

| Sl. no. | Year CE | Accession no. | Document type | Subject | Seal |
|---|---|---|---|---|---|
| 1 | 1463 | BRD 29 1+2 (R + V) | *Iqrār*; Sale deed | Sale of several villages in *pargana* Dhar by Munji and Mana *mandlōī* to Bhagwan Das, Gopal Das, Jayanti Das, sons of Ganesh Das, son of Gunraj chadhuri for 18,505 golden *Muzaffarīs* (which seems like an enormous amount of money). Long list follows, then Hindi equivalents, which continue on the reverse. | 6 seals, including one *qāẓī*'s |
| 2 | 1463 | BRD 30 1 + 2 (R + V) | *Iqrār*; *Girwī-nāma* | Very similar to BRD 29, exactly same seals and handwriting and similar but not all same parties. Munji *mandlōī* of *tappa qasba* Sadalpur and *mauza*ʿ Kesur of *pargana* Dhar mortgages several villages that belong to him, ancestrally, for 18,505 golden *Muzaffarī* rupees, to *chaudhrī* Bhagwandas, Gopal Das and Jayanti Das, sons of Ganesh Das, son of Gunraj, of *pargana* Dhar. | 6 seals, including one *qāẓī*'s |
| 3 | 1574 | DAI LNS MS 235 (a) R +V * | *Parvāna* | 200 *bīghas* fallow land granted to Jayanti Das, Narhar Das and others for their loyalty and efforts for cultivating and settling *pargan*a Dhar. | 2 seals, to be deciphered |
| 4 | 1617 | BRD 4 R | Copy of *Nishān* | *ʿInām* grant of several villages to Mohan Das, *qānūngō* of *pargana* Dhar | None |
| 5 | 1626 | NAI 2703/2 | *Qaul qarār* | Purshottam Das given the *patta* of *ijāra* of Mohanpur for Rs. 1100 per year. | Sundar Das |
| 6 | 1626 | NAI 2703/31 | Copy of *Nishān* | Mohan Das reappointed *qānūngō* of pargana Dhar and given *ʿinām*; process of issuing a *nishān* discussed. | *Qāẓī* Muhammad Mustafa; 1102/1690 |
| 7 | 1637 | NAI 2733/60 | Copy of *Taṣdīq* | Verification order under the seal of Mirza Khan. Old *ʿinām* grants in favour of Mohan Das, Chandar Bhan and Purshottam Das for several listed villages including Ahu, based on Akbar's and Jahangir's *farmāns* and other *asnād of* past rulers verified and a *taṣdīq* is issued. | Qāẓī Muhammad Mustafa |

| | | | | | |
|---|---|---|---|---|---|
| 8 | 1643 | NAI 2668/2 | *Qaul qarār* | Purshottam Das takes the *patta* of *ijāra* of Nalawada village in the *jāgīr* of a certain Nawab Sahib for Rs. 415 per year; instructions for good treatment of peasants. | To be deciphered |
| 9 | 1644 | BRD 16 (R + V); P Das 1644 NCD | *Parvāna* | Purshottam Das and Paras Ram are instructed to send lists of daily happenings because the writers does not have any such records with him. They are also asked to send any person who comes with news from Gujarat. | Abd al-Islam . . . ? *banda-yi* Sultan Murad Baksh . . . |
| 10 | 1654 | NAI 2703/3 | *Qaul qarār* | Purshottam Das takes the *patta* of *ijāra* of village Mohanpur for Rs 35; this is granted in view of his wish to populate the area and the agreement of peasantry. | To be deciphered |
| 11 | 1654 | DAI LNS MS 235 (c) R+V * | *Parvāna* | Declaration to *chaudhrī* of pargana Dhar regarding their duties of revenue collection and apprehension of thieves. | Diyanat Khan *murīd-i* Hazrat Shah Jahan |
| 12 | 1654 | DAI LNS MS 235 (j) R+V * | *Parvāna* | Dispute over rights to use water from a tank in *pargana* Dhar; peasants v. *zamīndārs*. *Siwāī jama* ʿ taxes mentioned. | . . . [servant of] Sultan Murad Baksh |
| 13 | 1654 | BRD 17 (R + V); Purshottam Das 1654 iii NCD R + V | *Parvāna* | Purshottam Das *chaudhrī* and Paras Ram *qānūngō* of pargana Dhar are informed that their *ʿarẓdāsht* (petition) has arrived. They had written about the war with Audi Singh. [details unclear]. Since they had lots of issues/explanations, their petition, together with the petition of *Sa ʿādat Panāh* (title of the *jāgīrdār*?) has been forwarded to *Ḥuẓūr Nawāb Madār al-Mahām* (a high title, could be *wazīr*). The recipients of the order are admonished to concentrate on the populating of the area and the collection of taxes. | |
| 14 | 1655 | NAI 2703/4 | *Qaul qarār* | Collective *patta* of *ijāra* for *pargana* Dhar, for Rs. 89501; mentions discount for locust attacks on margin. | To be deciphered |
| 15 | 1655 | DAI LNS MS 235 (d) R+V * | *Parvāna* | Order to the effect that since this year is a *sāl kamāl* (perfect year) because of good rains, no excuses will be accepted for not paying full taxes. | . . . Khan *murīd* . . . Shah Jahan |

(*cont.*)

| Sl. no. | Year CE | Accession no. | Document type | Subject | Seal |
|---|---|---|---|---|---|
| 16 | 1655 | BRD 3 (R + V) | *Parvāna* | That peasants have fled due to a natural calamity. Instructions to bring them back and repopulate the villages. | 1 seal, to be deciphered |
| 17 | 1655 | Purshottam Das 1655 NCD R + V | *Parvāna* | *Chaudhrīs* and *qānūngōs* of pargana Dhar told to repopulate the deserted villages, bringing back the villagers. | Illegible |
| 18 | 1655 | DAI LNS MS 235 (b) R+V * | *Parvāna* | In response to an *ʿarẕdāsht* that Chandar Bhan has died and his survivors are struggling to secure livelihood due to high taxes. Some taxes forgiven, also some amount of 4,000 rupees. | Diyanat Khan *murid-yi* Hazrat Shah Jahan |
| 19 | 1655 | BRD 1 (R + V); Purshottam Das 1655 i NCD R + V (same document photographed twice) | *Parvāna* | That Purshottam Das, of the children (i.e., successors) of Chandar Bhan, had appealed to Diyanat Khan (Prince Murad Baksh's *diwān*) about the matter of paying Rs 4,000 as *pishkash* for (becoming, or being confirmed as) *marzbān* (*zamīndār*; governor of hostile borderlands); that he would be pushed to exile if he had to pay so much. So the amount is forgiven. | 1 seal, to be deciphered |
| 20 | 1655 | BRD 7 (R + V); Purshottam Das 1654 ii NCD R (same document photographed twice) | *Parvāna* | Notes that the *ʿarẕdāsht* Purshottam Das and Parasram had sent has arrived. Notes that harmful ideas have been harboured by the *ijāradārs* and *muqaddam*s (headmen). That whatever needs to be done in order to settle the minds of the *riʿaya* (subjects) should be done. Same thing repeated on margin. | 1 seal Abd al-Islam ibn Muhammad . . . Khan *ghulām-i* Sultan Murad Baksh . . . 1053 |
| 21 | 1655 | DAI LNS MS 235 (i) R +V * | *Parvāna* | Order to Purshottam Das and Paras Ram in relation to *girāsiyas* and disturbance caused by them; also about taxes paid in a good year – which, at Rs 9,000, is too low compared to the last year of calamity. | [. . .] Shah Buland Iqbal |

| | | | | | |
|---|---|---|---|---|---|
| 22 | 1656 | DAI LNS MS 235 (k) R+V * | *Parvāna* | The *chaudhrāī* of *pargana* Dhar is confirmed for Purshottam Das, given the exalted *nishān* and *parvāna* of the *diwān*. Assurance that the *peshkash muqarrarī* of the *dihāt ʿināmī* will not be more than Rs. 300. | Ibrahim (?) . . . to be deciphered |
| 23 | 1656 | NAI 2703/5 | *Parvāna* | According to catalogue – an order from Bijay Singh to officers (*kārguzārs*) not to interfere in the villages of pargana Hindola, which have been given to Purshottam Das as *ʿinām*. Is said to bear the seal of Bijay Singh. I have not been able to procure this document. | Bijay Singh |
| 24 | 1656 | 1656 AC-BRD | *Parvāna* | Because of the *nishān* dated 4 Rajab RY 30, which is 1066 (AH), and the *iltimās* (petition) of Mir Ibrahim, an order is issued confirming the service of *chaudhrāī* and certain villages to Purshottam Das. | Persian – illegible |
| 25 | 1657 | NAI 2703/6 | Copy of *Nishān* | Copy of a *nishān* addressed to Rao Amar Singh, that because of the transfer of Prince Murad Baksh, certain *parganas* in *suba* Malwa have been given in the *jāgīr* of the *vukāla-yi sarkār*. Amar Singh is instructed to go to the *maḥāls* (fiscal divisions) with twenty soldiers so that nobody creates a disturbance there. | Śrī Ram *upāsak* Chandrawat Rao Amar Singh Ji . . . [Hindi] |
| 26 | 1657 | DAI LNS MS 235 (l) R * | *Parvāna* | General information and admonishment to local officials to behave well, on change of areas from *jagīr* of Prince Murad Baksh to new appointee [possibly Prince Dara Shukoh] ; this document is connected with document: NAI 2703/6. | Śrī Ram *upāsak* Chand Rawat Rao Amar Singh . . . [Hindi] |
| 27 | 1658 | DAI LNS MS 235 (h) R + V * | *Parvāna* | In response to an *ʿarẕdāsht*; admonition to be loyal and collect taxes, with indication that rewards will be given accordingly on arrival in the area. | Hakim Muzaffar *banda-yi* Shah Buland Iqbal Shah Dara |
| 28 | 1658 | NAI 2668/3 | *Maḥẕar-nāma* | Boundary dispute between two villages; Purshottam Das and others act as arbitrators. | To be deciphered |
| 29 | 1658 | BRD 18 (R+V) | *Parvāna* | In response to the note (*nawishta*) sent by Purshottam Das *chaudhrī*, about the disturbances created on the road near Ahu by Sanuji and Nathu and the efforts he | Very faint. Abd al-Islam, ibn . . . *banda-yi* . . . |

(*cont.*)

| Sl. no. | Year CE | Accession no. | Document type | Subject | Seal |
|---|---|---|---|---|---|
| | | | | (Purshottam Das) had made with his own horsemen to enforce the collection of taxes. He is told to work together with Paras Ram to get rid of the problem. | |
| 30 | 1658 | NAI 2703/28 | Letter | Admonishment to Purshottam Das from a superior for not letting peasants cultivate. | To be deciphered |
| 31 | 1658 | P Das 1658 NCD R+V | Copy of *Parvāna* | FIve villages in *pargana* Hindola, including Ajnai given to Chandar Bhan as *dastūr dāmī*, also other agricultural lands given to him as *ʿinām*. Also that wherever there are *chaukīs* (stations) 1/4 of the *rusūm* of *chaudhrāt* and *qānūngōī* is given over. | Hand-drawn : . . . Khan *murīd-i* Alamgir Bādshāh |
| 32 | 1659 | NAI 2703/8 | *Parvāna* (?) | Response to *ʿarẕdāsht* about their *nānkār* (payment to *chaudhrīs* as tax collectors) villages; a *qāẕī* will reach to settle matters. Related to DAI (e). | No seal, a cypher (hand-drawn decorative monogram) |
| 33 | 1659 | DAI LNS MS 235 (e) R + V * | *Parvāna* | Response to *ʿarẕdāsht* about their *nānkār* villages; *qāẕī* '*jīū*' had already spoken about it, and whatever he decides will be settled. Related to 2703/8. | Nawazish Khan *murīd-i Haẕrat* Shah Jahan |
| 34 | 1659 | DAI LNS MS 235 (f) R + V * | *Parvāna* | Response to *ʿarẕdāsht* about the arrears of 1065 and the arrival of a representative of *wizārat panāh* Kifayat Khan. That they should pay up the arrears, and write whatever they have to say to *wizārat panāh* and do as he says. A *qāẕī* is also mentioned. | Nawazish Khan *murīd-i Haẕrat* Shah Jahan |
| 35 | 1659 | DAI LNS MS 235 (g) R+V * | *Parvāna* | Purshottam Das and Paras Ram told to ensure population and farming. | Nawazish Khan *murid-i Haẕrat* Shah Jahan |
| 36 | 1659 | NAI 2703/7 | *Qaul qarār* | Collective *qaul* for Rs 109,571 | Nawazish Khan |
| 37 | 1659 | NAI 2703/9 | *Qaul qarār* | Purshottam Das takes *ijāra* for *pargana* Jamli for Rs 901. | Nawazish Khan *khānazād-i* Aurangzeb Bahadur Alamgir Bādshāh *Ghazī* |

| | | | | | |
|---|---|---|---|---|---|
| 38 | 1659 | NAI 2733/4 | Letter (giving order) | New *jāgīrdār* of pargana Dhar orders Hamir Das to come to court; the worth of the *jāgīr* is said to be Rs 474, 900 *dāms* (copper coins). | None |
| 39 | 1660 | DAI LNS MS 235 (o1) R+ V | *Parvāna* | Acknowledges letter (*khaṭ*) the Purshottam Das and P Ram had written about [?] and says that the *wakālat panāh* has written 'two words' about it in response, ordered to act accordingly. | . . . .Nawazish Khani |
| 40 | 1660 | DAI LNS MS 235 (y) R + V * | *Parvāna* | In response to an *'arẓdāsht*. That a *parvāna* has already been issued, and admonishment issued on some matter in relation to Narsingh Das. Nothing much on the reverse. | Nawazish Khan *murīd-i Haẓrat* . . . Aurangzeb Alamgir *Bādshāh Ghāzī* |
| 41 | 1660 | DAI LNS MS 235 (p1) R + V * | *Parvāna* | Shaikh Abdul Rasul has reported that the *muqaddam* of the *mauza'* Thanpur/Nihanpur has gone to *pargana* Jamli and is living there. His *mata'* (possessions) and cattle are not being given, orders that they be handed over. | To be deciphered |
| 42 | 1660 | P Das 1660 i NCD R + V | *Parvāna* | House of Bulaqi Chand given to Purshottam Das; house to be repaired and the wood to be sent to his Lord (the issuer of the order). | . . . Khan *murid* Aurangzeb Alamgir *Bādshāhi* |
| 43 | 1660 | P Das 1660 iii NCD R + V | *Parvāna* | House of Suraj Bhan, which is attached to that of Purshottam Das, is given to the latter; wood and 200 rupees for the costs of the land to be sent to the *sarkār* (i.e., the noble ordering). | Nawazish Khan *murīd-i Haẓrat* Muhammad Aurangzeb Alamgir *Bādshāh Ghāzī* |
| 44 | 1660 | P Das 1660 BRD 22 | *Parvāna* | In response to an *'arẓdāsht* sent by Purshottam Das and P Ram, which has sent detailed information about the building of a lake (?) Sang/Nak/Tank in the village Niwasa. The architect has been sent (?) As per what they had said, 200 bullock-carters have been collected and it is necessary that they be put to work and not kept on the road. The putting of lime (*chūna-puran*) should be completed; *chūna* is to be supplied. About what you had said about the inspector (*mushrif*), it is Muhammad Hashim Shiqdar for 3 years. Same thing on marginal note. | . . . *murīd-i Hazrat* Muhammad Aurangzeb Alamgir *Bādshāh Ghāzī* |

(*cont.*)

| Sl. no. | Year CE | Accession no. | Document type | Subject | Seal |
|---|---|---|---|---|---|
| 45 | 1660 | P Das BRD 21 (R + V) | *Parvāna* | In response to an *ʿarẕdāsht* sent by Purshottam Das chaudhrī and Paras Ram qānūngō of pargana Dhar. They had written that they are making no mistakes in keeping the peasants content. But the peasants were not relying on their words and aims, they did not know why. The order admonishes them to do all that is needed to improve the administration and cultivation of the pargana, leaving no suitable land fallow. And if any doubts remain, they can be cleared when the *Wakālat Panāh* (title = a noble, possibly Nawazish Khan) and when the writer himself comes to Mandu, they could send their *vakīl*. | . . . Nawazish Khanī (servant of Nawazish Khan) 1067 (old seal) |
| 46 | 1660 | P Das1660 AC-BRD | *Parvāna* | Hamid has repaired a house, which is attached to that of Bulaqi Chand, which is now given to Purshottam Das, for a *pishkash* of 150 rupees. | Illegible, damaged |
| 47 | 1660 | P Das BRD 8 (R + V) | *Parvāna* | Notes, in response to an *ʿarẕdāsht* to the effect that the house of Bulaqi Chand belongs to him (Purshottam Das), and out of kindness it is given to him. The house must be destroyed (*mismār*) and the wood sent to His Lord (the noble who issued the *parvāna*). According to old tradition, take possession of it, and be engaged in the work of the government. | 1 seal . . . Khan *murīd-i* Aurangzeb Alamgir *Bādshāh Ghāzī* |
| 48 | 1660 | P Das 1660 AC-BRD-ii | *Parvāna* | This is an order addressed to *qāẓī ʻjīū'*, informing him that he (Nawazish Khan) has given the house that used to belong to Muhammad Hashim Siqdar, to Purshottam Das, wood and tiles should be dispatched to his Lord and make the land over to the said *chaudhrī*, on payment of 150 rupees as *pishkash*. | Nawazish Khan, *murīd-i Hazrat* Muhammad Aurangzeb Alamgir *Bādshāh Ghāzī* |
| 49 | 1660 | P Das BRD 2 (R + V) | *Parvāna* | In response to an *ʿarzdāsht:* that the house of Suraj Bhan, attached to house of Purshottam Das and his children, | Nawazish Khan, *murīd-i Hazrat* Muhammad |

| | | | | | |
|---|---|---|---|---|---|
| | | | | has been forfeited and is given over to Purshottam Das, subject to the payment of Rs 200 for the land and walls of the house. He should repair it for staying in it, and nobody should cause trouble. | Aurangzeb Alamgir *Bādshāh Ghāzī* |
| 50 | 1660 | DAI LNS MS 235 (l1) * | *Parvāna* | Purshottam Das and Paras Ram are told that they must investigate the theft of a camel and find it, not consider themselves excused. | Muhammad . . . servant of Nawazish Khan |
| 51 | 1660 | DAI LNS MS 235 (z) R + V | *Parvāna* | In response to a letter. Told to come to court to sort out some dispute? | To be deciphered |
| 52 | 1660 | NAI 2668/4 | *Farigh Khaṭṭī* | Purshottam Das repays loan taken by Mohan Das, Chandar Bhan and Dinkar Das from *banjāra* (itinerant) traders. | *Qāẓī* (?) Fath Ilyas (?) bin Fazl Allah |
| 53 | 1660 | NAI 2733/3 | *Parvāna* | Purshottam Das asks for copy of *tūmā*r (rent rolls) Rao Narsingh Das asks him to send a Persian scribe to get copies. | |
| 54 | 1661 | DAI LNS MS 235 (m1) * | *Parvāna* | Purshottam Das and Paras Ram told to deposit the fee for the measurement of *tafrīq* (measurement, separation) of 18 *parganas* to *Khwāja* J. Narayan. | Nawazish Khan . . . |
| 55 | 1661 | 1661_AC_BRD | *Bai ʿ-nāma* | Nathu son of Maqbul sells house in Burhanpur, which he had built on Purshottam Das's land, to Purshottam Das, for 13 rupees. | |
| 56 | 1661 | BRD P23 | *Parvāna* | In response to *ʿarẓdāsht* sent by Purshottam Das, that some time ago, Kanwal Das and Tilok Chand had petitioned that the *qānūngōī* (and? missing) of the *chabūtra-yi kōtwālī* (police station) of *qasba* Dhar was theirs through generations (lit. from father and grandfather) and Chandar Bhan had forcibly taken possession of the *qānūngōī* and they have the purchase deed (called *maḥẓar-i kharīd*) with the seal of the *qāẓī*. On the basis of this maḥẓar, the exalted *parvāna* is issued in their name, that rights be given to right-holders in this way: You did not agree to understand that in no way can heirs be destroyed. You are, from an | . . . *khās* Nawazish Khanī (special servant of Nawazish Khan) |

*(cont.)*

| Sl. no. | Year CE | Accession no. | Document type | Subject | Seal |
|---|---|---|---|---|---|
| | | | | old greed, and from short-sightedness, fighting with brothers and the sons of brothers. Behave well with your brothers and brothers' sons and keep that old greed under control. There is no need to write about this. Engage yourself in your work. | |
| 57 | 1661 | NAI 2668/6 | *Maḥẕar-nāma* | An account of how Mohan Das defeated Bira the highwayman of Hindola, employing Bharmal Rajput, getting the latter a *mansab* and *jāgīr*, and himself *qānūngōī*, how later Bharmal's son Paras Ram became a highwayman, his grandson hiding in hills near Jhabua and aspiring for *zamīndārī*, List of Purshottam Das's rights. | *Qāẕī* (?)Fath Ilyas (?) bin Fazl Allah |
| 58 | 1661 | NAI 2703/10 | Copy of a *Qabẕ* | Receipt given to Purshottam Das and Paras Ram for Rs 8850, as payment of surety for Hari Ram *chaudhrī* of Amjhera, who is absconding. The servant of Wazir Khan who has taken the money declares that he has deposited it in with the *fōtedār* (treasurer) of the *pargana*. | Fath Ilyas (?) bin Fazl Allah |
| 59 | 1661 | NAI 2733/23 | Copy of *Tamassuk* | Related to 2703/10 = *ẕāminī* (surety) of Hari Ram *chaudhrī* | None |
| 60 | 1661 | DAI LNS MS 235 (e1) R + V | *Parvāna* | *Chaudhrīs* and *qānūngōs* of *pargana* Hindola are told that the *muchalka* of *raẕamandī* about the taking of *ijāra* by the old *ijāradār*, which they had sent, has been received. Asks for various tax record documents – *muwāzana dah-sāla*, *dastūr al-ʿamal* and copy of *tūmar* to be sent – not clear where to. | . . . *banda-yi Bādshāh* Alamgir |
| 61 | 1662 | DAI LNS MS 235 (s) R + V * | *Parvāna* | Since Nathmal has asked for 15 *bīghas* of land for creating garden in *mauza*ʿ Sindhauri/ Sindhuri and it will be good for travellers, it is granted. | . . . Nawazish *Khānī* (servant of Nawazish Khan) |

| | | | | | |
|---|---|---|---|---|---|
| 62 | 1662 | DAI LNS MS 235 (a1) | *Parvāna* | Original of NAI 1665 2703/11. | Muhammad Hussein |
| 63 | 1662 | DAI LNS MS 235 (c1) * | *Parvāna* | Instruction to Mutammad Lal Muhammad, in response to *ʿarẓdāsht* of Purshottam Das; that M. Lal M has threatened the peasants of *pargana* Jamli; he should not do it again and write a petition when needed. | Nawazish Khan *murīd-i Hazrat* Muhammad Aurangzeb *Bādshāh Ghazī* |
| 64 | 1662 | NAI 2703/13 | *Qabẓ* | Purshottam Das and Paras Ram pay Rs 1,600 to a servant of Nawab Wazir Khan, due to surety for Hari Ram *chaudhrī*; related to 2703/10 | To be deciphered |
| 65 | 1662 | BRD 28 1 + 2 + 3 (R + V) | *Qaul qarār* | *Qaul qarār* (tax contract) for village (Ekalduna?) and others in *pargana* Dhar in the *jāgīr* of the Nawab (i.e., Nawazish Khan) by the acceptance of *chaudhrī* Purshottam Das, from the beginning of season of Kharif and Rabi 1072 *ʿAmlī*. Details beneath. Hindi/Nagri equivalent beneath the Persian. | 2 seals, very light. Seal 2, . . . Nawazish *Khānī* (servant of Nawazish Khan) |
| 66 | 1663 | DAI LNS MS 235 (n1) R + V * | *Dastak* | *Banjāras* Nayak Singha, etc., are assured that no one will trouble them for taxes; that they should come to Dhar to buy grains. | Asadullah Nawazish *Khānī* (servant of Nawazish Khan) |
| 67 | 1663 | DAI LNS MS 235 (k1) R + V * | *Parvāna* | In answer to an *ʿarzdāsht*; that whatever amount was promised in the *qabuliyat* (agreement/contract for tax payable) should be collected without excuses. | Asadullah Nawazish *Khānī* (servant of Nawazish Khan) |
| 68 | 1663 | NAI 2703/12 | *Parvāna* | *Nigāhbāns* of highway Katha that a man Purshottam Das has been appointed there; should be given a fourth of collections. | Chandar Bhan, *banda-yi Shāh* Alamgir |
| 69 | 1663 | NAI 2703/11 | Copy of *Parvāncha* | 20 *bīghas* of *banjar pokhta* (fallow) land given to Kishan Das to make a garden in *qasba* Sultanpur, which would help travellers. | To be deciphered |
| 70 | 1663 | NAI 2668/5 | *Qaul qarār* | *Qaul of patta-yi chauth* and *gautha* (?) of the villages of Kacchadhiya in *pargana* Hindola, etc., by the *qabuliyat* of Lonkaran/Naukaran (name unclear) for Rs. 23. | Chandar Bhan, *banda-yi Shāh* Alamgir |

(*cont.*)

| Sl. no. | Year CE | Accession no. | Document type | Subject | Seal |
|---|---|---|---|---|---|
| 71 | 1663 | NAI 2733/7 and /7a & 8 | Copy of *Parvāna* | Copy of a *parvāna* from Nawab Najabat Khan, confirming possession of *ʿinām* villages for Darka Das and his descendants; list on reverse. | 0 |
| 72 | 1664 | DAI LNS MS 235 (d1) R +V * | *Parvāna* | Purshottam Das told to set his son to collecting taxes and come with his horsemen and infantry as soon as possible. | Nawazish Khan . . . Aurangzeb *Bādshāh Ghāzī* |
| 73 | 1664 | NAI 2703/15 | *Qaul qarār* | Contract for Rs 894 for the taxes of village Nalawada. | . . . Nawazish Khan [?] to be deciphered |
| 74 | 1664 | BRD 11 (R + V) | *Parvāna* | Routine administration – in response to an ʿarẕdāsht written by Purshottam Das and Paras Ram, with regards to taxes (?) on the purchase of cows by the subjects (peasants) of the area. An order is made, to not trouble the peasants (?) | Asad . . . Nawazish *Khānī* (servant of Nawazish Khan) |
| 75 | 1664 | P Das 1664 I NCD R | *Parvāna* | In response to the petition Purshottam Das and P Ram had sent about the *maḥṣūl* (impost) on the purchase of cows by the peasantry (?) which is cancelled? | . . . Nawazish *Khānī* (servant of Nawazish Khan) |
| 76 | 1664 | Purshottam Das1664 ii NCD R + V; same as P Das BRD P 28 | *Qaul qarār* | *Qaul qarār* of the *patta* of *ijāra* for the *mauza* ʿ (village) of Ekalduna (?), etc., in *pargana* Dhar in the jagīr of the Nawab, by the *qabūliyat* of Purshottam Das, for 1072 (?) for Rs. 2,119, to be deposited in the treasury. Details given below – village by village. This includes Mohanpur. Full Hindi section below. | 2 seals (. . . Nawazish *Khānī* (servant of Nawazish Khan |
| 77 | 1664 | NAI 2703/14 | *Qabẕ al-waṣūl* | Rai Singh *muqaddam*, Godar, Manji, etc., agriculturists of village Jiwara in pargana Dhar in the *jāgīr* of Mir Syed Inayat Ali declare that, following a petition by officers of the *jāgīrdār*, they have received armed assistance from the *faujdār* against an attacker called Indar Singh; they acknowledge the return of the animals that they had been robbed of. | 0 |

| | | | | | |
|---|---|---|---|---|---|
| 78 | 1664 | DAI LNS MS 235 (m) R + V | *Parvāna* | Note from [Najabat Khan?] that Suraj Bhan has complained against Purshottam Das, that the latter is not giving his share of villages, and also that he is depopulating Bhan's villages. Both warned severely not to quarrel and create such disturbances. Related to NAI 2703/17. | . . . Khan *murīd-i Bādshāh* Alamgir |
| 79 | 1664 | NAI 2733/10 | Copy of *Parvāna* | Copy of *parvāna* giving Narsingh Das, son of Purshottam Das, son of Mohan Das the rights of *khidmat* (service) of *muqadammī* of villages Naogaon Buzurg, etc., and relevant *haq-dastūrs* (customary rights) on the basis of old orders. | 0 |
| 80 | 1665 | NAI 2668/8 | Letter | Their petition, together with copy of letter of Muhammad Hussain, has arrived. The contents of this to be clarified, but they are urged to increase cultivation and be loyal. | Illegible |
| 81 | 1665 | DAI LNS MS 235 (g1) R+ V | *Parvāna* | About sending *shīsham* wood to Baroda | Muhammad . . . |
| 82 | 1665 | NAI 2703/17 | Copy of *maḥẕar-nāma* | Maḥẕar of a decision given by *qāẕī* Abul Fath, about dispute between Suraj Bhan and Purshottam Das about certain *nānkār* villages. | *Qāẕī* Muhammad Mustafa |
| 83 | 1665 | NAI 2703/18 | *Qabẕ al-wasūl* | Daya Ram *fotedār* (treasurer) acknowledges receiving money; will transfer to Amjhera in 7 days. | |
| 84 | 1665 | NAI 2733/11 | | Since villages in *pargana* Jamli were in the *ijāra* of Purshottam Das, a *sanad* (document) given in writing that all dues have been received. | 0 |
| 85 | 1666 | NAI 2733/14 | Copy of *Parvāncha* | Purshottam Das alerted by Nawab Wazir Khan that there is Rs 9,000 outstanding as *ẕāminī* of Amjhera which is due from *chaudhrī* Kanpil. Related to DAI (v). | |
| 86 | 1666 | DAI LNS MS 235 (v) R + V | *Parvāna* | About the *ẕāminī* of *chaudhrī* Kanpil of Amjhera, for which Purshottam Das of Dhar and *chaudhrī* of Nalcha had stood surety. | Wazir Khan *murīd-i* Bādshāh Alamgir |
| 87 | 1666 | NAI 2733/15 | Copy of *Yāddāsht* | Hari Ram *chaudhrī's dastūr* (rights, title) confiscated in favour of Purshottam Das. | |

(*cont.*)

| Sl. no. | Year CE | Accession no. | Document type | Subject | Seal |
|---|---|---|---|---|---|
| 88 | 1666 | DAI LNS MS 235 (f1) R+V | *Parvāna* | Because Hariram *chaudhrī* failed to fulfil his obligations and appear and pay his dues; his perquisites are transferred to those that stand surety for him according to *sharī' a* (Islamic law) and *'urf* (customary law, according to Islamic jurisprudence). | Wazir Khan *murid-i Bādshāh* Alamgir |
| 89 | 1666 | NAI 2733/13 | *Sanad* | Purshottam Das and Paras Ram take a loan of Rs 2,000 from Nawab. | |
| 90 | 1667 | NAI 2703/20 | Copy of *Parvāna* | Shyam Das's *qānūngōī* of Amjhera has been transferred to Purshottam Das, who was the *māl-ẕāmin* (guarantor for payment of land taxes). | To be deciphered |
| 91 | 1667 | NAI 2733/16 | Copy of *Parvāna* | Nawab Ahmad Beg Khan instructs *Qāẕī* Abdul Ghani that the *qānūngōī* of Amjhera has been transferred to Purshottam Das; told to hand over *dastūr dāmī*, etc. | 0 |
| 92 | 1667 | P Das 1667 Hin NCD R | *Parwana* (in Rajasthani/ Malwi) | Maharaja Amar Singh *ji* gives an order entirely in Rajasthani – acknowledging the news about Hari Ram, asking Nathmal to remain in touch and expressing his satisfaction with him. | None |
| 93 | 1669 | NAI 2703/21 | Statement – genre not sure | Conflict with *amīn*, *karōrī* and *faujdār*; visit to imperial court; new officials appointed but large amount forcibly demanded in revenue (Rs 1 lakh?). | No seal |
| 94 | 1669 | DAI LNS MS 235 (w) R + V | *Parvāna* | Five *bīghas* land in *mauza'* Maliwada given to Nathmal, son of *chaudhrī* Purshottam Das for creating a garden. Notes on reverse to same effect. Maybe connected with NAI 2703/21. | Muhibb Ali *murīd-i Shāh* Alamgir |
| 95 | 1669 | BRD 13 (R + V) | *Parvāna* | Purshottam Das, *chaudhrī* of *pargana* Jamli and Hindola is told that his *'arẕdāsht* has arrived. He had written that the good people of the area had been displaced and the well-being of *qasba* Sultanpur disturbed by the behaviour of | 1 seal, to be deciphered |

| | | | | | |
|---|---|---|---|---|---|
| | | | | the *karōrī* (imperial or *jagīrdār*'s tax-collector). A note has been sent to the *karōrī* about this, it (the note) should be reached to him and mutual satisfaction should be established so that you (the addressee) can engage yourself in the real aim – populating the area and increasing the earnings from agriculture. Marginal note probably repeats this – to be read. | |
| 96 | 1669 | P Das 1669 NCD R + V | *Parvāna* | Purshottam Das chaudhrī of *pargana* Jamli and Hindola told, in response to his petition about the dislodging of the *mahājans* and well-to-do people of Sultanpur, due to the bad behaviour of the *karōrī*, that the *karōrī* has been written to about this business, which should have reached him, and the peasants should be settled. (Possibly the same document as above) | 1 seal – to read |
| 97 | 1670 | DAI LNS MS 235 (n) R + V | *Parvāna* | Appears to be a matter of division of inheritance between Purshottam Das and his brother. Odd document, different handwriting, and very repetitive. Not clear if related to a dispute or not. Very detailed *zimn* – appeared to be a list of shares. The word *yād-dāsht* is used. There is a very clear '*baiza'* or terminal symbol. | Asad Khan *murīd-i* Alamgir *Bādshāh* |
| 98 | 1670 | P Das 1670 NCD R + V | *Parvāna* | That villages Ajnai, etc., in the parganas of Hindola and Jamli were given as *'inām* to Chandar Bhan, and now too, based on the old documents, these are upheld. This document seems genuine, but a later extension is added on different paper and handwriting with many more villages. | Asad Khan *murīd-i* Alamgir *Bādshāh* |
| 99 | 1671 | NAI 2733/17 | Copy of *Parvāna* | The copy of a *parvāna* apparently issued in Hindi originally, Sale of part of *qānūngōī* of Amjhera by Shyam Das to Purshottam Das and his son. | No seal |
| 100 | 1671 | NAI 2733/18 | Copy of a Hindi *Parvāna* | The copy of a *parvāna* apparently issued in Hindi originally, by which 101 *bīghas* of land are given to Nathmal, son of Purshottam Das, for creating a garden. | No seal |

(*cont.*)

| Sl. no. | Year CE | Accession no. | Document type | Subject | Seal |
|---|---|---|---|---|---|
| 101 | 1671 | NAI 2703/24 | *Parvāna* | Confirmation, according to old documents about the right to certain garden lands in village Gondhra, pargana Dhar; *parvāna* of a certain Sheikh Ibrahim, according to the marginal notes. | To be deciphered |
| 102 | 1672 | DAI LNS MS 235 (r) R + V | *Parvāna* | Matter of payment related to a tax called '*nalī*'. | Rafi' Muhammad *khānazād-i Bādshāh* Alamgir |
| 103 | 1672 | DAI LNS MS 235 (p) R + V | *Parvāna* | Confirmation of *inam* of Purshottam Das, because of *nishān* of Prince Murad Baksh and the orders of previous *jāgīrdārs*, and because Purshottam Das is loyal and hardworking. The *'inām* consists of Ahu and other villages, 500 *bīghas* of lands and trees. The writer also confirms on own authority. Detailed notes on reverse. Note: Nawab . . . Khan. | . . . *shāh* Alamgir |
| 104 | 1672 | NAI 2733/20 | *Parvāna* | Grant of land in certain villages to Hamir Chand. | No seal |
| 105 | 1672 | DAI LNS MS 235 (x) R + V | *Parvāna* | That since nineteen villages including Ahu, three thousand . . . hundred and fifty *bīghas* of land and mango trees have been granted to Purshottam Das and his sons by the exalted *nishān* and *asnad* of *jagīrdārs*, hence '*ba-dastūr-i sābiq* (in line with ancient custom)' these titles are confirmed. | Islam Khan bin Hussein Ali *murīd-i* Alamgir *Bādshāh*. 2 seals on reverse: Muhammad Amin . . . Islam Khan; . . . |
| 106 | 1672 | NAI 2733/19 | Copy of *Parvāna* | That since the loyalty and good works of Purshottam Das are well known, Nawab Maham (?) Khan orders that ten villages, including Ahu, are confirmed to him as *'inām*, as per the *sanad* secured from Nawab Nawazish Khan. | None |
| 107 | 1673 | NAI 2668/25 | | That Suraj Bhan *baqqāl*, resident of village Kharpura came to Ghulam Muhammad, *kōtwāl* saying that he had nowhere to live, and begged for a house. The | *Qāẓī* Muhammad Mustafa 1123 |

| | | | | | |
|---|---|---|---|---|---|
| | | | | *kōtwāl* asked Bhagwati Das and Bardman of *ahl-i hirfa* for it. Since the house of Santokni who was dead, and which belonged to Sundar Das, resident of Sultanpur, was empty, it was given to him, along with its contents | |
| 108 | 1673 | BRD 6 (R + V) | Copy of *Farmān* | Sultanpur, etc., five *mauza*ʿs (villages) within *pargana* Hindola, *sarkār* Mandu were given to Purshottam Das and Narsingh Das as ʿ*inām* by the orders of previous rulers/governors. Now, Hamirchand and Nihalchand, the grandsons of Purshottam Das and Narsingh Das, have the said villages allocated to them by the order that the whole world obeys (i.e., this *nishān*), on condition of the services detailed on the reverse. The officials of the said villages should make these over to them, and not demand fresh documentation every year. | 1 elaborate *qāẓī*'s seal on reverse. Saad al-din. *qāẓī-yi Sharīʿa* . . . |
| 109 | 1674 | DAI LNS MS 235 (i1) R + V | *Parvāna* | Ten villages including Ahu, 3,300 *bīgha* of lands and mango trees confirmed due to *nishān* of Prince Murad Baksh and other *asnad*. Very detailed notes on reverse. Contains a very clear '*baiẓa*' or terminal symbol. | *Az jān wa dīn gardida murīd-i . . . Ali . . . Alamgir* [RY]13. Absolutely same seal and note as on DAI (u) |
| 110 | 1674 | DAI LNS MS 235 (u) R + V | *Parvāna* | *Mauza*ʿ Koswada given as ʿ*inām* and *nānkār* to Purshottam Das and his children for his service. Detailed note on *zimn* (verso) to same effect, and two more seals. One note says Parvāna -yi Ali Beg Khan. Contains a very clear '*baiẓa*' or terminal symbol. | . . . Ali . . . *murīd-i* Alamgir . . .[RY] 13 |
| 111 | 1675 | DAI LNS MS 235 (h1) R+V | *Parvāna* | *Mauza*ʿ given as *nānkār* to Purshottam Das for service. | Islam Khan, son of Hussein Ali, servant of Alamgir *Bādshāh* |
| 112 | 1675 | DAI LNS MS 235 (q1) R + V * | *Parvāna* | In response to an ʿ*arzdāsht*; which was about certain villages being put aside by a certain '*shahangiya*' (official?) Abd al-Hamid; who (and Khuda Dost) are instructed to withdraw their forces. Purshottam Das, etc., are given a discount of Rs 3,000. | Asadullah *murīd-i khāṣ* Nawazish *Khanī* (special disciple of Nawazish Khan) |

(*cont.*)

| Sl. no. | Year CE | Accession no. | Document type | Subject | Seal |
|---|---|---|---|---|---|
| 113 | 1675 | NAI 2668/10 | *Āwarja* (accounts) | Statement of Rs 43 which are arrears on the *ijāra* of *sayer* (custom duties) of *pargana* Dhar, which has been given as salary to Muhammad Baqir, son of Muhammad Aqil, holding a rank of 50 *sawārs*. | Islam Khan bin Hussein *murīd-i* Alamgir *Bādshāh* |
| 114 | 1675 | NAI 2733/21 | Copy of *Parvāna* | Because of his loyalty, *mauza*ʿ (Kasawadha?) given to Purshottam Das. | None |
| 115 | 1676 | DAI LNS MS 235 (o) R + V | *Parvāna* | That 10 *dar-o-bist* (entire villages) and 550 *bīghas* of land and 43 mango trees and a garden are confirmed to Purshottam Das as ʿ*inām* because of old *asnad* and because he is loyal. Detailed notes on reverse. | Munir or Mir Khan, . . . Auragzeb Alamgir |
| 116 | 1677 | NAI 2733/22 | *Parvāna* | 150 *bīghas* of land, tax-free is confirmed to Chandar Bhan‘s son (name unclear). | |
| 117 | 1679 | DAI LNS MS 235 (b1) R+V | *Parvāna* | That since 1/3 of the *qānūngōī* of *pargana* Amjhera belonged to Purshottam Das *chaudhrī* of *pargana* Dhar, according to the old *asnad* and old orders and since he is loyal, the villages detailed in the reverse are allocated as *dāmī*, etc. Very detailed notes on reverse. | Muhammad Ismail Ibn . . . Khan *Khānazād-i* Alamgir *Bādshāh* |
| 118 | 1679 | NAI 2703/26 | Copy of a *Parvāna* | Purported copy of an order by Asad Khan to the officials of pargana Dhar saying that Purshottam Das, Lok Chand and Amar Chand came to court to say that the *chaudhrāī* of the *pargana* belonged to them hereditarily because of old *asnad*. Thus, these titles are confirmed to them. List follows. This is an obvious forgery, written so late that the scribes have forgotten the format of a *parvāna* and included a Mughal imperial genealogical seal for good measure. | |
| 119 | 1680 | NAI 2703/25 | Copy of a *Parvāna* | Same as NAI 2703/26. | |

| | | | | | |
|---|---|---|---|---|---|
| 120 | 1683 | NAI 2703/27 | Court order | Dispute before a *qāẕī* about lands left behind by Purshottam Das. Decision given. | No seal |
| 121 | 1684 | NAI 2703/61 | *Maḥẕar-nāma* | Narrates the antecedents of Narsingh Das, starting from the story of Mohan Das and his receipt of grants, followed by the loss of some villages and resources by Purshottam Das because of the interference of *ʿāmils*. Because of the loss of such resources, Purshottam Das had not been able to maintain the necessary troops, leading to the Bhils and *girāsiyas* creating trouble and even blocking the royal mail from going to Gujarat. The eminent people declared that Narsingh Das was as competent as his father, and that his *nānkār sanads* should be renewed to help him protect their life and property. | No seal |
| 122 | 1684 | NAI 2703/62 | Copy of *Maḥẕar-nāma* | Family history and rights of Purshottam Das (very similar to NAI 2703/61). | No seal |
| 123 | 1684 | NAI 2733/26 | Letter | Responding to an application (*darkhwast*) about villages in Mandu, in response to which a sanad has been prepared and sent. | None |
| 124 | 1684 | NAI 2733/61 | Letter | Responding to letter about Purshottam Das (written by?) has arrived and the *parvāna* about the *chaudhrāīs* of Jamli and Hindola have been sent. | None |
| 125 | 1684 | NAI 2733/62 | Letter | To '*Khwāja*' Purshottam Das. | None |
| 126 | 1684 | NAI 2733/75 | Letter | Letter to '*Khwāja*' Purshottam Das. | |
| 127 | 1684 | NAI 2733/108 | Copy of a *Parvana* | Narsingh Das given 500 *bīghas* of fallow untaxed land for his loyalty, etc., in Navgaon. | None |
| 128 | 1685 | NAI 2703/29 | *Sanad* – court order | Purshottam Das died, conflict between Hamir Chand and other sons, and a division of property by the *maḥkama aqẕia*. | None |
| 129 | 1690 | BRD 19 | *Parvāna* | 25 *bīghas* (amount unclear) land are allocated as (share) of *chaudhurāī* in the name of Tilok Chand, etc., descendants (?) of Gopal Das, *chaudhrī* of Dhar, because of *sanad* (order) of Ḥuẕur Madār al-Mahām | Illegible, damaged. |

(*cont.*)

| Sl. no. | Year CE | Accession no. | Document type | Subject | Seal |
|---|---|---|---|---|---|
| | | | | (Wazir?), on the basis of a deed of division/separation (*taqsīmnāma*). On this basis, 100 *bīghas* of land are allocated as *ʿinām* on the basis of asnad of past gvoernors. Since their good service is apparent, according to the *sanad* of the *Ḥuẕūr*, the said lands, etc. are confirmed. They are admonished to do all that is necessary for the comfort of the subjects/peasant (*riaʿya*). | |
| 130 | 1690 | NAI 2733/29 | Copy of *Hiba-nāma* (gift deed) | Nine villages including Chikliya, some *dāmī* and some *muqadammī*, one garden and two houses gifted to Narsingh Das and Gambhir Chand by their female relative Puran (wife of Dinkar Das), who also appends a curse. | *Qāẕī* Muhammad Muhsin |
| 131 | 1690 | DAI LNS MS 235 (q) R+V | *Parvāna* | Fifteen bīghas of *banjar pokhta* (fallow) land, *khārij jamaʿ* (untaxed) from village Nauganda Buzurg, is given to Gambhir Chand, son of Purshottam Das *chaudhrī*, to create a garden and pray for the permanent glory of the regime/donor. This is summarised on the reverse. | . . . Alamgir |
| 132 | 1693 | NAI 2668/12 | Letter | Letter of Ashraf, officer of Azam Shah. | |
| 133 | 1693 | NAI 2668/2 | *Qaul qarār* | *Qaul qarār* of *mauzaʿ* Nalawada for Rs. 450, for. the year 1051 Faslī although the document is written in 1053. | Illegible |
| 134 | 1693 | NAI 2703/32 | Copy of Nishān | That eleven villages including Ahu, 3,607 *bīghas* of land and eighteen *istimrārī* villages, etc., given to Prusrhottam Das on the basis of *farmāns* of past emperors. | Azam Shah bin Alamgir Bādshāh Ghazi 1096, hand-drawn |
| 135 | 1693 | NAI 2703/33 | Qaul qarār | Agreement for Rs 159 as tax for village Nekpur, in the *jāgīr* of Nawab Abid Khan, with *chaudhrī* Narsingh Das. | Keshav Rai; Mania Ram or Mansa Ram *kārkun* |

| | | | | | |
|---|---|---|---|---|---|
| 136 | 1693 | NAI 2668/15 | *Taqsīmnāma* | Division of lands with seals of *qāẕī* as well as noble – Asad Khan. Mentions shares of Tilokchand and Lalchand son of Gopalchand; and in another section, Hari Ram, Narsingh, Kodarmal, etc. Lots of seals and witness statements, in Persian and Hindi. | |
| 137 | 1694 | NAI 2733/31 | Copy of *Parvāna* | Order from Asad Khan confirming the grant of ten villages including Ahu to Narsingh Das as *wajh-i nānkār*. | |
| 138 | 1695 | DAI LNS MS 235 (t) R+V | Parvāna | *Mauza'* Gondra given to Narsingh Das as *'inām*, on condition of loyalty. | Rahmat Allah *khānazāda-yi Bādshāh* Alamgir |
| 139 | 1698 | NAI 2668/17 | Unclear | Order to officials of *pargana* Dhar to confirm certain villages as *muqaddamī* to Purshottam Das, on the basis of the petition he had sent to the emperor claiming that the *chaudhrāī* of pargana Dhar belonged to him as ancestral right, along with all associated perks. | None |
| 140 | 1703 | NAI 2703/36 | Copy of *Parvāna* | Instruction to Muhammad Hussain that a third of the *qānūngōī* of *pargana* Amjhera, given to chaudhrī Purshottam Das because of death of Shyam Das *qānūngō*. *Dastūr* to be given him. | To read |
| 141 | 1703 | NAI 2703/35 | *Qabuliyat* | *Qabuliyat* of Rupa and Badan Chand that the year 1111 Faslī Syed Ghulam Muhammad officer of *jazya* has assessed Rs 2,200 on the houses, and they have accepted. | [. . .] *Khadim-i Sharī 'a* |
| 142 | 1709 | NAI 2703/42 | *Lā dawa sulḥ-nāma* | That Bardman, son of Rupa chaudhrī of Dhar had sent Daulat Khan to find news about his servant from *jagīrdār* Jadrup in Amjhera, but Jadrup killed him. Daulat Khan's female heirs seek diyat and invoke *qāẕī* as well as *muftī*. Given Rs 55. | *Qāẕī* Muhammad Mustafa |
| 143 | 1710 | NAI 2668/22 | *Fārigh Khaṭṭī* | Hamir Das and Nihal Chand return the money borrowed by Narsingh Das and Gambhir Chand from Kale Afghan and Ganesh Sahu to the respective sons. | *Qāẕī* Muhammad Mustafa |

*(cont.)*

| Sl. no. | Year CE | Accession no. | Document type | Subject | Seal |
|---|---|---|---|---|---|
| 144 | 1710 | NAI 2703/38 | Copy of a Tawārīkh | That following the resolution of a boundary dispute between two villages – Bijur in pargana Dhar and Sakrod in pargana Dipalpur – a mosque was constructed on the boundary to prevent further encroachments. | |
| 145 | 1710 | P Das 1710 NCD R + V | Copy of *Farmān* | That *mauza'* Sultanpur, etc., five villages in *pargana* Hindola are confirmed as *'inām* for Hamir Chand and Nihal Chand, grandsons of *chaudhrī* Purshottam Das, because of the *farmān*. | On reverse, Saad al-din, *qāẕī-yi Sharī 'a* |
| 146 | 1711 | P Das 1711 NCD R + V | *Parvāna* | The *vakīl* of Hamir Chand and Nihal Chand have complained to the court that Muhammad Asad is calling himself *chaudhrī*, order issued, agreement signed. | None |
| 147 | 1713 | NAI 2733/34 | *Iltimās* | Hamir Chand and Gambhir Chand ask for confirmation of their title after the end of the Muhammad Asad dispute. | No seal |
| 148 | 1714 | NAI 2668/21 | Copy of *Maḥẕar-nāma* | *Maḥẕar* describing the long dispute over Muhammad Asad's claim that Suraj Bhan had converted to Islam and married his mother – Parwar – who was a courtesan. Describes several episodes in the protracted conflict; ultimately a huge assembly decides that Muhammad Asad's claims are invalid. | *Qāẕī* Muhammad Mustafa |
| 149 | 1714 | NAI 2703/46 | Copy of *Maḥẕar-nāma* | Muhammad Asad's claim. | *Qāẕī* Muhammad Mustafa |
| 150 | 1715 | BRD 25 1+ 2 (R + V) | Copy of *Maḥẕar-nāma* | This is a copy of an earlier *maḥẕar*, sealed by *qāẕī* Abdul Wahid. This current copy is also sealed, by *qāẕī* Mustafa. Rupa *chaudhrī* of *pargana* Dhar asks for evidence that on (date?) Rajab RY 7, which is 1125 | *Qāẕī* Muhammad Mustafa *Khādim-i Sharī 'a* |

| | | | | | |
|---|---|---|---|---|---|
| | | | | AH (certain events which are not very clear, happened). Amjhera and Jasrup Singh, *mansabdār* with *jāgīrs* in Amjjera, are involved, and there is some monetary transaction at the end. There appears to be a list of gold and silver items involved in the transaction at the end. | |
| 151 | 1715 | BRD 26 1+ 2 (R + V) | Copy of *Maḥẓar-nāma* | Same as above, but without seals. | |
| 152 | 1715 | BRD 27 1 + 2 (R + V) | *Maḥẓar-nāma* | Appears to be nearly same as above. | |
| 153 | 1717 | NAI 2703/40 | *Qaul qarār* | *Ijāra* for *mauza'* Antarah in pargana Dhar for Rs. 475 in the name of Hamir Chand and Kesho, based on assessment of Ab al-Qadir Amin. Discount will be given if natural calamity or Deccani enemies (Marathas) attack. | Abd al-Qadir Khan . . . |
| 154 | 1717 | NAI 2703/41 | *Parvāna* | Jaswant Singh and other *chaukīdārs* of Bilwara told to take 505 *bīghas* land for upkeep of eight horsemen and fifteen infantry soldiers. | Nand Lal |
| 155 | 1718 | NAI 2668/23 | *La dawa sulḥ-nāma* | About the murder of Hira, who was killed on a mission to Amjhera. Rs 32 (8 months * 4 pm) given in compensation to his family. | *Qāẓī* Muhammad Mustafa; Muhammad Hussein. |
| 156 | 1721 | NAI 2668/20 | *Tamassuk* | Hamir Chand borrows Rs 2240 from Mir Muhib Allah in lieu of his *'inām* village. | *Qāẓī* Muhammad Mustafa |
| 157 | 1726 | NAI 2703/43 | *Qaul qarār* | Mentions discount if Marathas attack. | |
| 158 | 1727 | NAI 2703/19 | Copy of *Parvāna* | That one *chaudhrī* has paid another's surety. | |
| 159 | 1728 | BRD | | Not supplied – but appears to be about lands; date probably wrong. | 0 |
| 160 | 1730 | P Das 1730 Trans NCD | Hindi translation of a *Farmān* | Sultanpur, etc., five villages were given to Purshottam Das and Narsingh Das as *'inām* on the basis of old documents, these are kindly reissued to Hamir Chand and Nihal Chand. | Hand-drawn |

(*cont.*)

| Sl. no. | Year CE | Accession no. | Document type | Subject | Seal |
|---|---|---|---|---|---|
| 161 | 1731 | P Das 1731 NCD R+V | *Parvāna* | Sultanpur, etc., five villages were given as *ʿinām* to Hamir Chand and Nihal Chand, grandsons of Purshottam Das and Narsingh Das because of copy of a *farmān* sealed by *qāẕī* so these may be given over to them. | Saad Khan fidwī (loyal to) Muhammad *Shāh Bādshāh Ghāzī*,1144 |
| 162 | 1731 | NAI 2703/44 | Copy of *Parvāna* | Confirms hereditary *chaudhrāī* of Hamir Chand based on old *sanads*, a *nishān* of Prince Murad Baksh, and *mawāzana* and *taqsīm* papers of the *pargana*. | |
| 163 | 1731 | NAI 2668/24 | Copy of *Farmān* | Confirming hereditary lands in *ʿinām* to Purshottam Das, according to *farmān* of Aurangzeb and nishān of Prince Murad Baksh. | Hand-drawn imperial seal |
| 164 | 1733 | NAI 2703/45 | *Chak-nāma* | *Chak-nāma* of lands in Dhar for Daya Ram Bhat astrologer; according to Qamar al-din Khan's *parvāna*, lands released by officials of Umar Khan and the agents of Hamir Chand and Nihal Chand. | Hand-drawn seal of Umar Khan Bahadur. Muhammad Shah |
| 165 | 1734 | P Das 1734 NCD R | *Maḥẕar-nāma* | Sheikh Alimullah and other *mansabdārs* of *pargana* Dhar complain that they had made a deal with the Maratha '*na-sardārs*' that the latter would respect their dues, but this has not happened because the Marathas have taken all that the peasants had. Very important document – showing regime change. | 18 seals including three seals of *qāẕīs* |
| 166 | 1735 | NAI 2668/27 | *Fārigh Khaṭṭī* | Jagannath demands his money and *patta* of *naukrī* (employment) from Hamir Chand and his son; arbitrators appointed, he gets what he wants. | 4 seals; 1 Hindi |
| 167 | 1736 | BRD 20 | *Maḥẕar-nāma* | Sarup Ram (name unclear, crucial part torn) asks for evidence from Saiyid Ali Khan, from the kind aristocrats, from the people of court and many others that on 29 Shaban RY seventeen Bhils robbed the harvest of Kharif of *mauzaʿ* Akbarnagar (?) (which is the writer's *maḥāl-* | 6 seals. Seal 1= Largest, likely to be of the *qāẕī*, top left, part legible – 'Inayat . . . Shaikh Azim . . . Muhammad' above note |

| | | | | | |
|---|---|---|---|---|---|
| | | | | *jāgīr*) and burnt the village. They carried off all the cattle/ livestock and the harvested but unthreshed corn. The peasants cannot pay the taxes of the *jawārī* (harvest of *jawār*?) so the *dāmī* (*zamindār's* share) in the taxes on *jawārī* have not been collected. Several attestations on the right-hand margin, apart from the *qāẓī*'s note an seal. Five notes of '*Gawāh shud* (witnessed)' one of which is by Abd Al-Karim *Khātib-i Jamīa* and two attestations in Nagri. One is of Hamir Chand, the other (illegible to me) of *pargana* Dhar. | 'Witness statement sealed'. Seal 2 = Alimullah, *Fidwī* Muhammad *Shāh Ghāzī*. Seal 3 = |
| 168 | 1739 | P Das 1739 NCD R+V | *Parvāna* | *ʿInāms* of Lala Parmanand, etc., confirmed on the basis of old documents. | 1 seal Muhib Allah . . . . |
| 169 | 1750 | P Das 1750 HIN NCD R+V | *Parvāna* Hindi | Ram *Ji mōkāsadār* hires Vijay Singh to supply soldiers for a fixed payment. They must guard the *chaukī*, names of soldiers listed. | Shri Pandurang *charanat sar Sadashiv Ram nirantar* |
| 170 | 1751 | P Das 1751 Hin NCD R | *Parvāna* Hindi | An order from Gangadhar and Sadasiva *mōkāsadār* . . . . refers to a *qabūliyat* and the seasons *Kharif* and *Rabi* . . . . seems to be a tax agreement . . . . 3 *mauza*ʿs seem to be listed. | 2 Hindi seals |
| 171 | 1783 | P Das 1783 Hin NCD R+V | *Parvāna* Hindi | Order issued under a beautiful Hindi seal, which bears the date1705 *Śaka*, and the elevated name (i.e., the authority is Shrimant Rajeshri Ramchandra Rao Puwar). Illegible so far, but the last line, in Modi, is 'Such are the facts. In the month of *Ẕu al-qaʿda* it was registered, *murattab shud'*. | Hindi seal to be read |
| 172 | 1787 | P Das 1787 NCD R | *Fārigh Khaṭṭī* | That Anwar Beg and Syed Azam had made a claim on the mango tress in the garden of Sahib Rai, son of Dianat Rai; after they failed to produce documents in a court, claims are relinquished. | |
| 173 | 1803 | 1803_AC_BRD | *Iqrār; Baiʿ-nāma* | A certain Chand Bibi of qaum Afghan makes an *iqrār* that a mansion and some lands are sold to Thakur Pratap Chand; interesting symbols. | . . . Allah *fidwī* Bādshāh Ghazi Muhammad Shah |

(*cont.*)

| Sl. no. | Year CE | Accession no. | Document type | Subject | Seal |
|---|---|---|---|---|---|
| 174 | 1804 | 1804_AC_BRD | *Iqrār; Bai ‘ -nāma* | A certain Afghan person sells land to *Thākur Sāḥib*. | Persian to read |
| 175 | 1843 | BRD 5 R; 1843 NCD | *Khulāṣa* (extract) of *Akhbarāt* (newsletter) | News of developments in Calcutta – including impending military expedition to Afghanistan; instructions given to the *riāsat* of Gwalior, etc. | None |
| 176 | 1843 | BRD 24 1 (R+V) | *Kaifiyat* | *Kaifiyat* (account) of the news of the court of Maha Rao Jayaji Sindhia Bahadur, Gwalior from 22 Rajab-2 Shaaban 1259. | None |
| 177 | 1850 | P Das 1850 NCD R + V | Private letter | Letter to Thakur Saheb; ends by urging him to say ‘Ram Ram’ to whoever asks after them and to write every week. | 0 |
| 178 | 1851 | P Das 1851 NCD R | *Girwī-nāma* (pawn deed) Hindi | A certain tailor called Kalu makes a transaction for an Rs 20 and refers to Rajeshri Thakur Pratap Chand and Chiranjivi Kunwarji. A house/land and its limits are described and there are witnesses at the bottom. Very hard to read. | 0 |
| 179 | 1859 | P Das 1859 NCD R + V | *Parvāna* | Order to all *ilaqedārs* to let the wedding party of Thakur Motichand’s son pass through. | Trilingual Company seal |
| 180 | 1860 | P Das 1890 NCD | *Ishtehār-i Maḥkama* | Order to *jagīrdāran*, *taluqdārān*, *zamindārān*, conveying an order of the sardar of the Angrez, the Governor General, from London (*sic.*) with regards to the *uhdedārs* of Dhar, whose situation declined since the rebellion. | 0 |
| 181 | 1900 | P Das Mar NCD 1–10 | Accounts? | Accounts in Modi script, several pages in a *bahī*-type book. Lists various crops. | 0 |
| 182 | 19th or 20th century | BRD 12 (R + V) | Letter | Addressed to ‘*Thākur Sāheb*’. Laments not having received a letter for a long time. Personal tone. From . . . Singh. No date, seems nineteenth century or later. | None |

| | | | | | |
|---|---|---|---|---|---|
| | | | | Also notes that for the letter of a Jhashu ? *Thākur*, which has been forwarded to the addressee, a tax/fee of 3 annas has been paid. | |
| 183 | Pre-1707 (original). Copy after 1830. | BRD 10 (R + V) | Copy of *Parvāna* | Order to the effect: the officials of *pargana* Hindola should know that the *dāmī* (revenue collecting rights for being chaudhrī) of five villages including Ajnai, were given to Chandar Bhan, *chaudhrī* of that district, as *ʿinām* by *asnad* (legal deeds) of the governors of the past. Now too, I confirm this *ʿinām*. These must be made over to them so that they may concentrate on being loyal to the government. It is also decreed that they get shares 1/3 for chaudhurai and 1/4 for *qānūngōī* for villages with *chaukīs* (police stations). | Hand-drawn copy of seal of a noble: Karim Khan (?) murid-i Alamgir |
| 184 | | BRD 14 (R + V) | Copy of *Parvāna* | In response to an *ʿarẓdāsht* about the doubts regarding the *chaudhurāī* of Purshottam Das, that he owns twenty villages in Sitapuri in pargana Hindola and a certain Mirza Muhammad Mashhadi had created disputing claims during the tenure of *jagīrdār* (name?) and for this reasons the *gumashtas* (agents) of Mirza Rafi ud-daula are taking possession of those villages. An order given to refrain from doing so. | None |
| 185 | | DAI LNS MS 235 (j1) R + V | | Not received, in error. | |
| 186 | | BRD 9 (R + V) | Not clear | Now/recently, the *vakīl* of Hamir Chand and Nihal Chand, the hereditary *chaudhrīs* of pargana Dhar have appealed to court that a person called Muhammad Asad has declared himself *chaudhrī*. The order that the world obeys was issued that . . . (some proceedings should take place) . . . (after consideration of . . . ?) the events and happenings of this matter . . . a *raẓī-nāma* was sent to *Ḥuẓūr*. | None |

*(cont.)*

| Sl. no. | Year CE | Accession no. | Document type | Subject | Seal |
|---|---|---|---|---|---|
| 187 | | BRD 15 (R + V) | *Parvāna* | The officials present and future of *pargana* Dhar are told that Lala Parmanand and his brothers Rai Bhan and Kripa Ram '*sarkārī naukar*' and of *qaum* 'Kayashtha Nigam' petitioned through the officials of the *'Adālat-i Aliya* and it was ordered to the chaudhrīs, *qānūngōs* and *muqaddams* (headmen) of the said pargana that 15 bīghas of land suitable for a garden with mango trees, etc., is appointed to them (the petitioners) due to *asnad* of previous governors, so give it over to them. | 1 seal, to be deciphered |
| 188 | | BRD 24 2 (R + V) | | Similar or continuation, to check. | None |

# Glossary

| | |
|---|---|
| *bai‘-nāma* | Sale deed |
| *banda* | Slave, self-deprecating usage for an imperial official or servant of a noble |
| *dastak* | A low-level order |
| *dastūr* | Custom or customary dues |
| *farmān* | An imperial order |
| *fidwī* | A liegeman, an imperial official or servant of a noble |
| *fiqh* | Islamic jurisprudence |
| *‘inām* | Literally: reward; a tax-free grant of land |
| *iqrār* | A legally binding declaration in Islamic law |
| *jāgīr* | Temporary assignment of revenue proceeds of a certain area as salary and expenses for holding a state office, *mansab*, and for maintaining troops |
| *jāgīrdār* | Holder of a *jāgīr*, usually also a *mansabdār* |
| *maḥz̤ar-nāma* | Document of testimony |
| *mansabdār* | A rank-holding noble/official in the Mughal Empire |
| *mauza‘* | Smallest unit of Mughal tax administration, usually a village |
| *maẕhab* | Islamic school of law |
| *mōkāsa* | A revenue assignment as payment for military duties, similar to *jagīr* |
| *muftī* | Islamic juriconsult |
| *muhr* | Seal |
| *muḥtasib* | Islamic censor |
| *nikāḥ-nāma* | An Islamic marriage contract |
| *nishān* | An order by a prince of the imperial dynasty |
| *pargana* | District |
| *parvāna* | An order issued by a Mughal noble |
| *qānūngō* | Keeper of village tax records |
| *qasba* | Town |
| *qāz̤ī* | Islamic judge |
| *rahn-nāma* | A pawn/mortgage deed |
| *saraṇjām* | Temporary assignment of revenues proceeds for maintaining troops in the Maratha Empire; similar to *jāgīr* |

| | |
|---|---|
| *sarkār* | Territorial division in the Mughal Empire, smaller than a province |
| *sharīʿa* | Islamic law |
| *suba* | Province in the Mughal Empire |
| *tughra* | Cipher or calligraphically stylised name, usually of the emperor |
| *zamīndār* | Landlord |
| *ʿurf* | Custom in Islamic law |

# Bibliography

## Primary Sources

### *Manuscripts*

#### *British Library*


Anon., *Dastūr al-ʿamal-i ʿAlamgīrī*, Add. 6598
Anon., *Dastūr al-ʿamal-i Shāhjahānī*, Add. 6588
Anon., *Khulāṣat al-siyāq*, Add. 6588
Khawaja Yasin's dictionary, Add. 6603
*Munshī* Thakur Lal, *Dastūr al-ʿamal-i Shāhenshāhī*, Add. 22831


### *Archives*

#### *National Archives of India, New Delhi*


Acquired Persian Documents


#### *Dar al-Athar al-Islamiyyah, Kuwait*


LNS MS 235


#### *Baḍā Rāolā Dhar, India*


Choudhary Family Collection


#### *Shri Natnagar Shodh Samsthan, Sitamau, India*


Letterbook of Nawazish Khan – No. 14 under 'Aurangzib Histories' in handlist of Natnagar Shod Samsthan, Sitamau


## Published Primary Sources


Abul Fazl. *Ā'īn-i Akbarī* (Persian) (ed.) H. Blochmann, 2 vols. (Calcutta: Printed for the Asiatic Society of Bengal by the Baptist Mission Press, 1872)

Abul Fazl, *Ain-i Akbari* (English) translated H. Blochmann and H. Jarrett, 3 vols. (Calcutta, 1873–94)

Abul Fazl, *Akbar Nāma*, translated H. Beveridge, 3 vols. (Calcutta: Asiatic Society, 1907–39)

Ahmed, Mohammed Ziauddin. *Mughal Archives: a Descriptive Catalogue of the Documents Pertaining to the Reign of Shah Jahan, 1628–1658* (Hyderabad: State Archives, 1977)

Amedroz, H. F. 'The Mazalim Jurisdiction in the Ahkam Sultaniyya of Mawardi', *Journal of the Royal Asiatic Society*, 2 (1911), 635–74

Badauni, Abdul Qadir. *Muntakhabu-t-Tawarikh*, translated George Ranking and W. H. Lowe, 2 vols. (Calcutta: Asiatic Society, 1864)

Baillie, Neil. *The Land Tax of India, According to the Moohummudan Law, Translated from the Futuwa Alumgeeree*, 2nd ed. (London: Smith, Elder & Co., 1873)

Barani, Zia. *Tarīkh-i Firūz Shāhī*, (ed.) Saiyid Ahmad Khan (Calcutta: Bibliotheca Indica, 1862)

*Dastūr al-ʿamal mutaẕammin bar navad va panj āʾīn barā-yi intiẓām-i umūr-i ʿadālathā-yi dīvānī-i ṣadr va mufaṣṣal* (A Persian Translation of the Regulations for the Administration of Justice in the Courts of Suddur and Mofussil Dewannee Adauluts) (Calcutta: Charles Wilkins, 1782)

Elliot, Henry M. *Memoirs on the History, Folklore and Distribution of the Races of the Northwestern Provinces of India* (ed.) J. Beames (London: Hertford 1869)

Elliot, Henry, and Dawson, John. *History of India as Told by Its Own Historians*, 8 vols. (London, Trübner and Co., 1871), Vol. III

Elliott, Charles Alfred. *The Chronicles of Oonao, A District in Oudh* (Allahabad: Allahabad Mission Press, 1862)

Erskine, William. *A History of India under the Two First Sovereigns of the House of Timur*, 2 vols. (London: Longmans, 1854)

Ferishta, *History of the Rise of Mahomedan Power in India till the year A.D. 1612*, translated John Briggs (first published 1829, reprint New Delhi: Oriental Books, 1981)

Firminger, W. K. (ed.). *Fifth Report from the Select Committee of the House of Commons on the Affairs of the East India Company* (Calcutta: R. Cambray & Co., 1918)

*The Formularies of Angers and Marculf: Two Merovingian Legal Handbooks*, translated Alice Rio (Liverpool: Liverpool University Press, 2008)

Forster, William (ed.). *The Embassy of Sir Thomas Roe to India, 1618–1619* (London: Hakluyt Society, 1899)

Goswamy, B. N., and Grewal, J. S. (eds.). *The Mughals and the Jogis of Jakhbar: Some Madad-i Ma'ash and Other Documents* (Simla: Indian Institute of Advanced Study, 1967)

Grant, James. An *Inquiry into the Nature of Zemindary Tenures in the Landed Property of Bengal* (London: J. Debrett, 1790)

Grant Duff, Cunningham James. *A History of the Mahrattas*, 4th ed., 3 vols. (Calcutta: R. Cambray, 1912)

Greville, Charles Frances. *British India Analyzed: the Provincial and Revenue Establishment of Tippoo Sultan and of Mahomedan and British Conquerors of Hindostan*, 3 vols. (London: R. Faulder, 1795)

Grewal, J. S. *In the By-Lanes of History: Some Persian Documents from a Punjab Town* (Simla: Institute of Advanced Study, 1975)

Grierson, George Abraham. *Linguistic Survey of India* (Calcutta: Office of the Superintendent of Government Printing, 1903–1928), Vol. IX, Part 2 (1908)

Gune, V. T. *The Judicial System of the Marathas* (Pune: Deccan College Postgraduate and Research Institute, 1953)

*Imperial Gazetteer of India*, new ed., 26 vols. (Oxford: Clarendon Press, 1908), Vols. XIX, XVII

Khan, Ali Muhammad. *Mirat-i Ahmadi*, translated M. F. Lokhandwala, 2 vols. (Baroda: Oriental Institute, 1965)

Khan, Ali Muhammad. *Mirat-i Ahmadi Supplement*, translated Syed Nawab Ali (Baroda: Oriental Institute, 1928)

Khan, Geoffrey. *Arabic Legal and Administrative Documents in the Cairo Genizah Collections* (Cambridge: Cambridge University Press, 1993)

Khan, Mukhtar Ahmad. *Hazrat Maulāna Khwāja Kamaluddin Chistī* (Piran-e Dhar: Urs Committee Hazrat Maulana Khwaja Kamaluddin Chisti, n.d.)

Khan, Saqi Mustad. *Maāsir-i-'Ālamgiri*, translated Jadunath Sarkar (Calcutta: Asiatic Society, 1947, reprint 2008)

Khan, Shahnawaz, and Hayy, Abdul. *Maasir al-Umara*, 2 vols., translated Henry Beveridge and Baini Prashad (Patna: Janaki Prakashan, 1979)

Khan Naqshbandi, Shujauddin (ed. and translator). *Fārsi Farmānon je Prakāsh mein Mughalkālin Bhārat ewaṃ Rājput Shāsak*, 4 vols. (Bikaner: Rajasthan State Archives, n.d.)

Khobrekar, V. G. (ed.). *Records of Shivaji Period* (Bombay: Government of Maharashtra, 1974)

Kulkarni, Anuradha (ed.). *Ajnāpatra* (Pune: Diamond Books, 2007)

Lal, Busawun. *Memoirs of the Puthan Soldier of Fortune, the Nuwab Ameer-ood-doulah Mohummud Ameer Khan*, translated Henry Prinsep (Calcutta: Military Orphan Press, 1832)

Lele, K. K. *Parmar Inscriptions in Dhar State, 875–1310* (Dhar: Dhar State Historical Records Series, 1944)

Luard, C. E. *The Central India State Gazetteer Series: Western States (Malwa) Gazetteer*, Vol. V, Part A (Bombay: British India Press, 1908)

Lyall, Alfred. 'The Rajput States of India', in *Asiatic Studies: Religious and Social* (London: J. Murray, 1882)

Malcolm, John. *A Memoir of Central India*, 3rd ed., 2 vols. (Calcutta: Thacker & Spink, 1880)

Mandavi, Muhammad Ghawsi. *Azkār-i Abrār*, Urdu translation of *Gulzar-i Abrar* translated Fazl Ahmad Jewari (Agra, 1908, reprint Lahore, 1975)

Merutunga, *The Prabandhacintamani or the Wishing Stone of Narratives*, translated C. L. Tawney (Calcutta: Asiatic Society, 1899)

Mundy, Peter. *The Travels of Peter Mundy, in Europe and Asia, 1608–1667*, (ed.) Richard Temple, Vol II: *Travels in Asia, 1618–1624* (London: Hakluyt Society, 1914)

Prasad, Pushpa (ed.). *Lekhapaddhati: Documents of State and Everyday Life from Ancient and Early Medieval Gujarat, 9th to 15th Centuries* (New Delhi: Oxford University Press, 2007)

Ramsbotham, R. B. *Studies in the Land Revenue History of Bengal, 1769–1787* (Bombay: Humphrey Milford, 1926)

*Rathōḍān ri Khyāt*, (ed.) Hukm Singh Bhatti, 3 vols. (Jodhpur: Itihas Anusandhan Sansthan, 2007)

*The Rehla of Ibn Batuta*, translated Mahdi Husain (Baroda: Oriental Institute, 1976)

*Report on the Administration of the Dhar State, 1920–21 to 1925–26* (Dhar, n.d.)

Russell, R.V., and Lal, Hira. *Tribes and Castes of the Central Provinces*, 4 vols (London: Macmillan, 1916)

Shafi, Muhammad. 'Ahd-i Sher Shah ke do farmānein', *Lahore Oriental College Magazine* IX (1933), 115–28

Shakespear, John. *A Dictionary of Hindustani and English* (1834)

Sheikh Nizam and others, *Fatāwáyi 'Alamgīrī*, translated to Urdu by Maulana Saiyid Amir Ali, 10 vols. (Lahore: Maktaba Rahmaniya, n.d.), Vols. VIII, X

Shekhar, Chander (ed.). *Waqāi' Asad Beg* (Delhi: National Mission for Manuscripts and Dilli Kitab Ghar, 2017)

Sitapati, P. (ed.). *Srisailam Temple Kaifiyat* (Hyderabad: Government of Andhra Pradesh, 1981)

Smyth, D. Carmichael. *Original Bengalese Zumeendaree Accounts, accompanied with a translation* (Calcutta: Baptist Mission Press, 1829)

Stewart, Charles. *Original Persian Letters and Other Documents* (London: William Nicol, 1825)

Tavernier, Jean-Baptiste. *Travels in India*, translated V. Ball (London: Macmillan, 1889)

Tilley, Norah M. (ed.). *The Ni'mat Nāma Manuscript of the Sultans of Mandu: the Sultan's Book of Delights* (London: Routledge, 2005)

Tod, James. *Annals and Antiquities of Rajasthan, or the Central and Western Rajpoot States of India*, William Crooke (ed.), 2nd ed., 3 vols. (London: Humphrey Milford, 1920)

*The Travels of Ibn Batuta, 1304–1377*, translated Samuel Lee (London: J. Murray, 1829)

Vad, G. C., Mawjee, P. V., and Parasnis, D. B. (eds.). *Selections from the Government Records in the Alienation Office: Kaifiyats, Yadis & c.* (Bombay: P. V. Mawjee, 1908)

Venkasawmy Row, T. A. (ed.). *Indian Decisions: Old Series*, 17 vols. (Madras: Law Print, 1911–16), Vols. 6–17

Wakin, Jeanette (ed. and translator). *The Function of Documents in Islamic Law: the Chapters on Sales from Ṭaḥāwī's Kitāb al-shurūṭ al-kabīr* (Albany:State University of New York Press, 1972)

Wakankar, A. W. (ed.). *Dhar State Historical Record Series: Dharkar Pawarancya Itihasaci Sadhane* (Dhar: History Department, 1949), Vol. III, Part 1

Wilson, H. H. *A Glossary of Revenue and Judicial Terms* (London: W.H. Allen and Co., 1855)

## Secondary Sources

Ahmad, Muhammad Bashir. *The Administration of Justice in Medieval India* (Aligarh: Aligarh Muslim University, 1941)

Ahmad, Qeyan Uddin. 'Origin and Growth of Darbhanga Raj (1574–1666), Based on Some Contemporary and Unpublished Documents', *Indian Historical Records Commission*, 36: 2 (1961), 89–98

Ahmed, Shahab. *What Is Islam?: the Importance of Being Islamic* (Princeton: Princeton University Press, 2016)

Alam, Muzaffar. 'The Mughals, the Sufi Shaikhs and the Formation of the Akbari Dispensation', in Richard Eaton, David Gilmartin, Munis Faruqui and Sunil Kumar (eds.) *Expanding Frontiers in South Asian and World History: Essays in Honour of John F. Richards* (Cambridge: Cambridge University Press, 2013), pp. 124–63

Alam, Muzaffar. *Languages of Political Islam: India 1200–1800* (London: Hurst, 2004)

Alam, Muzaffar. 'The Pursuit of Persian: Language in Mughal Politics', *Modern Asian Studies*, 32: 2 (1998), 317–34

Alam, Muzaffar, and Subrahmanyam, Sanjay. *Writing the Mughal World: Studies on Culture and Politics* (New York: Columbia University Press, 2012)

Alam, Muzaffar, and Subrahmanyam, Sanjay. 'The Deccan Frontier and Mughal Expansion, ca. 1600: Contemporary Perspectives', *Journal of the Economic and Social History of the Orient*, 47: 3 (2004a), 357–89

Alam, Muzaffar, and Subrahmanyam, Sanjay. 'The Making of a Munshi', *Comparative Studies of South Asia, Africa and the Middle East*, 24: 2 (2004b), 61–72

Alam, Muzaffar, and Subrahmanyam, Sanjay. *The Mughal State, 1526–1750* (Oxford: Oxford University Press, 1998)

Alavi, Seema. *Islam and Healing: Loss and Recovery of an Indo-Muslim Medical Tradition, 1600–1900* (Basingstoke: Palgrave, 2008)

Ali, M. Athar. *Mughal India: Studies in Polity, Ideas, Society and Culture* (New Delhi: Oxford University Press, 2006)

Ali, M. Athar. *The Apparatus of Empire: Awards of Ranks, Offices and Titles to the Mughal Nobility, 1574–1658* (Delhi: Oxford University Press, 1985)

Ali, Athar. *The Mughal Nobility under Aurangzeb* (Bombay: Aligarh Muslim University, 1966)

Al-Qattan, Najwa. 'Dhimmis in the Muslim Court: Legal Autonomy and Religious Discrimination', *International Journal of Middle Eastern Studies*, 31: 3 (August, 1999), 429–44

Altekar, V. *A History of Village Communities in Western India* (Bombay: Humphrey Milford, Oxford University Press, 1927)

Amanat, Abbas, and Ashraf, Assef (eds.). *The Persianate World: Rethinking a Shared Sphere* (Leiden: Brill, 2019)

Amin, Shahid. *Conquest and Community: the After-Life of Warrior Saint Ghazi Miyan* (Chicago: Chicago University Press, 2017)

Amin, Sonia Nishat. The *World of Muslim Women in Colonial Bengal, 1896–1939* (Leiden: Brill, 1996)

Anderson, Michael. 'Islamic Law and the Colonial Encounter', in Peter Robb and David Arnold (eds.) *Institutions and Ideologies: a SOAS South Asia Reader* (Richmond: Curzon Press, 1993), pp. 165–85

Appadurai, Arjun. *Worship and Conflict under Colonial Rule: a South India Case* (Cambridge: Cambridge University Press, 1981)

Appellaniz, Francisco. 'Judging the Franks: Proof, Justice and Diversity in Late Medieval Alexandria and Damascus', *Comparative Studies in Society and History*, 58: 2 (2016), 350–78

Asher, Catherine. 'Kacchavaha Pride and Prestige: the Temple Patronage of Raja Mana Simha', in Margaret H. Case (ed.) *Govindadeva: a Dialogue in Stone* (New Delhi: IGNCA, 1996), pp. 215–40

Asif, Manan Ahmed. *A Book of Conquest: the Chachnāma and Muslim Origins in South Asia* (Cambridge, MA: Harvard University Press, 2017)

Aspinall, A. S. *Cornwallis in Bengal* (Manchester: Manchester University Press, 1931)

Baevskiĭ, Solomon. 'Farhang-e Anandraj' in *Encyclopedia Iranica*, online edition, 1999, www.iranicaonline.org/articles/farhang-e-anandraj, accessed 11 December 2019

Balabanlilar, Lila. *Imperial Identity in the Mughal Empire: Memory and Dynastic Politics in Early Modern South and Central Asia* (London: I.B. Tauris, 2011)

Baldwin, James. *Islamic Law and Empire in Ottoman Cairo* (Edinburgh: Edinburgh University Press, 2017)

Baldwin, James. 'Petitioning the Sultan in Ottoman Egypt', *Bulletin of the School of Oriental and African Studies*, 75: 3 (2012), 499–524

Balkrishna, Principal. 'Nature of Sardeshmukhi during Shivaji's Time', *Proceedings of the Indian History Congress*, 3 (1939), 1189–1193

Banga, Indu. *Agrarian System of the Sikhs: Late Eighteenth and Early Nineteenth Centuries* (Delhi: Manohar, 1978)

Barak, Guy. *The Second Formation of Islamic Law: the Hanafi School in the Early Modern Ottoman Empire* (Cambridge: Cambridge University Press, 2015)

Bellenoit, Hayden. *Formation of the Colonial State: Scribes, Paper and Taxes* (London: Routledge, 2017)

Bellenoit, Hayden. 'Between Qānūngōs and Clerks: the Cultural and Service Worlds of Hindustan's Pensmen, c. 1750–1850', *Modern Asian Studies*, 48: 4 (2014), 1–39

Benton, Lauren. *A Search for Sovereignty: Law and Geography in European Empires, 1400–1900* (Cambridge: Cambridge University Press, 2009)

Benton, Lauren. *Law and Colonial Cultures: Legal Regimes in World History, 1400–1900* (Cambridge: Cambridge University Press, 2002)

Benton, Lauren. 'Introduction', *The American Historical Review*, 117: 4 (2012), 1092–100, at 1093

Beveridge, H. 'Colonel Tod's Newsletters of the Delhi Court', *Journal of the Royal Asiatic Society*, 40: 4 (1908), 1121–4

Beverley, Eric. *Hyderabad, British India and the World: Muslim Networks and Minor Sovereignty, 1850–1950* (Cambridge: Cambridge University Press, 2015)

Bhatia, M. P. *The Ulama, Islamic Ethics and Courts under the Mughals* (New Delhi: Manak, 2006)

Bhatt, S. K. 'Five Persian Documents of Aurangzeb's Reign from Malwa', *Proceedings of the Indian History Congress*, 39: 1 (1978), 398–401

Bishara, Fahad Ahmad. 'No Country but the Ocean': Reading International Law from the Deck of an Indian Ocean Dhow, ca. 1900', *Comparative Studies in Society and History*, 60: 2 (2018), 338–66

Bishara, Fahad Ahmad. *A Sea of Debt: Law and Economic Life in the Western Indian Ocean, 1780–1950* (Cambridge: Cambridge University Press, 2017)

Blake, Stephen P. 'The Patrimonial-Bureaucratic Empire of the Mughals', *Journal of Asian Studies*, 39: 1 (1979)

Bochor, Guy. *God in the Courtroom: the Transformation of Courtroom Oath and Perjury between Islamic and Franco-Egyptian Law* (Leiden: Brill, 2012),

Bose, Mellia Belli. *Royal Umbrellas of Stone: Memory, Politics and Royal Identity in Rajput Funerary Art* (Leiden: Brill, 2015)

Busch, Alison. 'The Classical Past in the Mughal Present: the Braj Bhasha Riti Tradition', in Yigal Bronner, David Shulman and Gary Tubb (eds.) *Innovations and Turning Points: Towards a History of Kavya Literature* (New Delhi: Oxford University Press. 2014), pp. 648–690

Busch, Allison. *Poetry of Kings: the Classical Hindi Literature of Mughal India* (New York: Oxford University Press, 2011)

Brooks, Christopher, and Lobban, Michael (eds.) *Communities and Courts in Britain, 1150–1900* (London: Hambledon, 1997)

Burke, Peter (ed.). *New Perspectives on Historical Writing* (Cambridge: Polity, 1991)

Burke, Peter, and Porter, Roy (eds.) *Languages and Jargons: Contributions to a Social History of Language* (Cambridge:Polity Press, 1995)

Burns, Kathryn. *Into the Archive: Writing and Power in Colonial Peru* (Durham, NC: Duke University Press, 2010)

Burns, 'Notaries, Truth, and Consequences', *American Historical Review*, 110 (2005), 350–79

Case, Margaret H. (ed.). *Govindadeva: a Dialogue in Stone* (New Delhi: Indira Gandhi National Centre for the Arts, 1996)

Chakarbarty, Dipesh. *The Calling of History: Sir Jadunath Sarkar and His Empire of Truth* (Chicago: Chicago University Press, 2015)

Chandra, Jnan. 'Alamgir's grants to Hindu Pujaris', *Journal of the Pakistan Historical Society*, 6: 1 (1958), 54–65

Chatterjee, Kumkum. 'Scribal Elites in Sultanate and Mughal Bengal', *Indian Economic and Social History Review*, 47 (2010), 445–72

Chatterjee, Nandini. '*Mahzar-namas* in the Mughal and British Empires: the Uses of an Indo-Islamic Legal Form', *Comparative Studies in Society and History*, 58: 2 (2016), 379–406

Chatterjee, Nandini. 'Hindu City and Just Empire: Banaras and India in Ali Ibrahim Khan's legal imagination', *Journal of Colonialism and Colonial History*, 15: 1 (2014a), online only

Chatterjee, N. 'Law, Culture and History: Amir Ali's Interpretation of Islamic Tradition', in Shaunnagh Dorsett and John McLaren (eds.) *Legal Histories of the British Empire: Laws, Engagements and Legacies* (London: Routledge, 2014b), pp. 46–48

Chatterjee, Nandini. 'Reflections on Religious Difference and Permissive Inclusion in Mughal Law', *Journal of Law and Religion*, 29: 3 (2014c), 393–415

Chatterjee, Nandini. 'Muslim or Christian? Family Quarrels and Religious Diagnosis in a Colonial Court', *American Historical Review*, 117: 4 (2012), 1101–22

Chatterjee, Partha. *A Princely Impostor? The Strange and Universal History of the Kumar of Bhawal* (Princeton: Princeton University Press, 2002)

Chatterjee, Partha. *The Nation and Its Fragments: Colonial and Postcolonial Histories* (Princeton: Princeton University Press, 1993)

Chattopadhyaya, B. D. 'Origin of the Rajputs: the Political, Economic and Social Processes in Early Medieval India', in Chattopadhyaya, *The Making of Early Medieval India*, 2nd ed. (Delhi: Oxford University Press, 2012), pp. 59–92

Chattopadhyaya, B. D. 'The Emergence of the Rajputs as Historical Process in Early Medieval Rajasthan', in Karine Schomer et al., *the Idea of Rajasthan: Explorations in Regional Identity* (Delhi: Manohar, American Institute of Indian Studies, 2001) Vol. II, pp. 161–91

Chaudhri, K. N. *The Trading World of Asia and the English East India Company, 1660–1760* (Cambridge: Cambridge University Press, 1978)

Claessen, H. J. M., and Skalnik P. (eds.). *The Study of the State* (The Hague: Mouton, 1981)

Cohen, Mark R. 'A Partnership Gone Bad: Business Relationships and the Evolving Law of the Cairo Geniza Period', *Journal of the Economic and Social History of the Orient*, 56 (2013), 218–63

Cohn, Bernard S. *Colonialism and Its Forms of Knowledge* (Princeton: Princeton University Press, 1996)

Cohn, Bernard. 'Structural Change in Indian Rural Society, 1596–1885', in Robert E. Fryckenberg (ed.) *Land Control and Social Structure in Indian History* (Madison: Wisconsin University Press, 1969), pp. 53–122

Coulson, N. J. *Conflicts and Tensions in Islamic Jurisprudence* (Chicago: University of Chicago Press, 1969)

Coulson, N. J. 'Doctrine and Practice in Islamic Law: One Aspect of the Problem', *Bulletin of the School of Oriental and African Studies*, 18: 2 (1956), 211–26

Dale, Stephen. *The Garden of the Eight Paradises: Bābur and the Culture of Empire in Central Asia, Afghanistan and India (1483–1530)* (Leiden, Boston:Brill, 2004)

Dale, Stephen. 'The Legacy of the Timurids', *Journal of the Royal Asiatic Society*, 3: 8 (1998), 43–58

Darnton, Richard. *The Great Cat Massacre: and Other Episodes in French Cultural History* (London: Allen Lane, 1994)

Datla, Kavita Saraswathi. 'The Origins of Indirect Rule in India: Hyderabad and the British Imperial Order', *Law and History Review*, 33: 2 (2015), 321–50

Datla, Kavita S. *The Language of Secular Islam: Urdu Nationalism and Colonial India* (Honolulu: University of Hawaii Press, 2013)

Davidoff, Leonore, Doolittle, Megan, Fink, Janet, and Holden, Katherine. *The Family Story: Blood, Contract and Intimacy 1830–1960* (London: Longman, 1999)

Davis, Donald. 'Recovering the Indigenous Legal Traditions of India: Classical Hindu Law in Practice in Late Medieval Kerala', *Journal of Indian Philosophy*, 27 (1999), 159–213

Day, Upendranath. *Medieval Malwa: A Political and Cultural History, 1401–1562* (Delhi, 1965)

Derrett, J. D. M. *Religion, Law and the State in India*, 2nd edition (New Delhi: Oxford University Press, 1999)

Derrett, J. D. M. 'The Administration of Hindu Law by the British', *Comparative Studies in Society and History*, 4: 1 (1961), 10–52

Deshpande, Prachi. 'The Writerly Self: Literacy, Discipline and Codes of Conduct in Early Modern Western India', *Indian Economic and Social History Review*, 53: 4 (2016), 449–71

Deshpande, Prachi. 'Scripting the Cultural History of Language: Modi in the Colonial Archive', in Partha Chatterjee, Tapati Guha-Thakurta and Bodhisattva Kar (eds.) *New Cultural Histories of India* (Delhi: Oxford University Press, 2014), pp. 62–86.

Deshpande, Prachi. *Creative Pasts: Historical Memory and Identity in Western India, 1700–1960* (New York: Columbia University Press, 2007)
Deshpande, Prachi. 'Property, Sovereignty and Documentation: Marathi *Kaulnāmas* from Persianate to Colonial Eras', unpublished MSS in the author's possession
Digby, Simon. 'Before Timur Came: Provincialization of the Delhi Sultanate through the Fourteenth Century', *Journal of the Economic and Social History of the Orient*, 47: 3 (2004), 298–356
Dirks, Nicholas. *The Hollow Crown: Ethnohistory of an Indian Kingdom* (Cambridge: Cambridge University Press, 1987)
Eaton, Richard. *India in the Persianate Age, 1000–1765* (London: Penguin Books, 2019)
Eaton, Richard. 'The Persian Cosmopolis (900–1900) and the Sanskrit Cosmopolis (400–1400)', in Abbas Amanat and Assef Ashraf (eds.) *The Persianate World: Rethinking a Shared Sphere* (Leiden: Brill, 2018), pp. 63–83
Eaton, Richard M. *A Social History of the Deccan, 1300–1761: Eight Indian Lives* (Cambridge: Cambridge University Press, 2005)
Eaton, Richard. *The Rise of Islam and the Bengal Frontier, 1204–1760* (Berkeley: University of California Press, 1993)
Eaton, Richard. *Sufis of Bijapur, 1300–1700: Social Role of Sufis in Medieval India* (Princeton: Princeton University Press, 1978)
Eaton, Richard, and Wagoner, Philip (eds.). *Power, Memory, Architecture: Contested Sites on India's Deccan Plateau, 1300–1600* (Oxford: Oxford University Press, 2014)
Emon, Anver M. *Religious Pluralism and Islamic Law: 'Dhimmīs' and Others in the Empire of Law* (Oxford: Oxford University Press, 2012)
Ergene, Boğaç A. 'Why Did Ümmü Gülsüm Go to Court? Ottoman Legal Practice between History and Anthropology', *Islamic Law and Society*, 17: 2 (2010), 210–44
Ernst, Carl. *Eternal Garden: Mysticism, History and Politics at a South Asian Sufi Center* (New York: State University of New York Press, 1992)
Ewing, Katherine (ed.). *Sharī'a t and Ambiguity in South Asian Islam* (Berkeley: University of California Press, 1988)
Farooqui, Amar. *Sindhias and the Raj: Princely Gwalior c. 1800–1850* (Delhi: Primus Books, 2011)
Farooqui, Amar. *Smuggling as Subversion: Colonialism, Indian Merchants and the Politics of Opium, 1790–1843* (Lanham: Lexington, 2005)
Farooqui, Amar. 'Opium Enterprise and Colonial Intervention in Malwa and Western India, 1800–1824', *Indian Economic and Social History Review*, 32: 4 (1995), 447–74
Faruqui, Munis. *The Princes of the Mughal Empire, 1504–1719* (Cambridge: Cambridge University Press, 2012)
Febvre, Lucien. 'La Sensibilité et l'Histoire: Comment Reconstituer La Vie Affective d'Autrefois?', *Annales d'Histoire Sociale*, 3: 1/2 (1941), 5–20
Fernandez, Alex Hertel. *State Capture: How Conservative Activists, Big Businesses and Wealthy Donors and Reshaped the American States – and the Nation* (New York: Oxford University Press, 2019)
Finn, Margot. 'Family Formations: Anglo India and the Familial Proto-State', in David Feldman and Jon Lawrence (eds.) *Structures and Transformations in Modern British History* (Cambridge: Cambridge University Press, 2011), pp. 100–17

Fisher, Michael. *Indirect Rule in India: Residents and the Residency System, 1764–1858* (Delhi: Oxford University Press, 1991)

Flatt, Emma J. 'Practicing Friendship: Epistolary Constructions of Social Intimacy in the Bahmani Sultanate', *Studies in History*, 33: 1 (2017), 61–81

Flood, Finbarr B. *Objects of Translation: Material Culture and Medieval 'Hindu-Muslim' Encounter* (Princeton: Princeton University Press, 2009)

Flood, Finbarr B. 'Architecture of Malwa Sultanate', in Abha Narain Lambah and Alka Patel (eds.) The Architecture of the Indian Sultanates (Mumbai: Marg on behalf of IGNCA, 2006), pp. 81–91

Foltz, Richard C. (ed.). *Mughal India and Central Asia* (Karachi, Oxford: Oxford University Press, 1998)

French, Henry. 'The Common Fields of Urban England: Communal Agriculture and the Politics of Entitlement, 1500–1750', in R. W. Hoyle (ed.) *Custom, Improvement and the Landscape in Early Modern Britain* (Farnham: Ashgate, 2011), pp. 149–74

French, Henry, and Doyle, R. 'English Individualism Refuted and Reasserted: the Land Market of Earls Colne (Essex), 1550–1750', *Economic History Review*, 56: 4 (2003), 595–622

Friedmann, Yohanan. *Shaykh Ahmad Sirhindi: an Outline of His Thought and a Study of His Image in the Eyes of Posterity* (New Delhi: Oxford University Press, 2000)

Friedmann, Yohanan. 'The Naqshbandis and Awrangzeb', in Marc Gaborieu, Alexandre Popopvic and Thierry Zarcone (eds.) *Naqshbandis: Cheminements et Situations Actuelle d'un Ordre Mystique Musulman* (Istanbul, Paris: Institute Français d'etudes Anatoliennes d'Istanbul, 1990), pp. 209–20

Frykenberg, R. E. 'Sir John Malcolm (1769–1833), diplomatist and administrator in India', *Oxford Dictionary of National Biography*, 2009, https://doi.org/10.1093/ref:odnb/17864, accessed 11 December 2018

Fuess, Albrecht. 'Zulm by Mazālim? The Political Implications of the Use of Mazālim Jurisdiction by the Mamluk Sultans', *Mamluk Studies Review*, 13 (2009), 121–47

Furber, Holden. *Rival Empires of Trade in the Orient, 1600–1800* (Oxford: Oxford University Press, 1990)

Gerber, Haim. *Crossing Border: Jews and Muslims in Ottoman Law, Economy and Society* (Istanbul: The ISIS Press, 2008)

Gerber, Haim. *State, Society and Law in Islam: Ottoman Law in Comparative Perspective* (Albany: State University of New York Press, 1994)

Ginzburg, Carlo. *The Cheese and the Worms: the Cosmos of a Sixteenth-Century Miller*, translated by John and Anne Tedeschi (London: Routledge, 1980 [1981])

Glushkova, Irina, and Vora, Rajendra (ed.). *Home, Family and Kinship in Maharashtra* (Delhi: Oxford University Press, 1989)

Gommans, Jos. 'Afghans in India', in *Encyclopaedia of Islam*, 3rd ed., 2007

Gommans, Jos. *Mughal Warfare: Indian Frontiers and Highroads to Empire, 1500–1700* (London: Routledge, 2002)

Gommans, Jos. *The Rise of the Indo-Afghan Empire, c. 1710–1780* (Leiden: Brill, 1995)

Gordon, Stewart. *The Marathas: 1600–1818* (Cambridge: Cambridge University Press, 1993)

Gordon, Stewart. 'The Slow Conquest: Administrative Integration of Malwa into the Maratha Empire, 1720–1760', *Indian Economic and Social History Review*, 11: 1 (1977), 1–40

Gordon, Stewart. 'Scarf and Sword: Thugs, Marauders and State Formation in 18th Century Malwa', *Indian Economic and Social History Review*, 6: 4 (1969), 403–29

Gould, Eliga. 'Entangled Histories, Entangled Worlds: the English-Speaking Atlantic as a Spanish Periphery', *American Historical Review*, 112: 3 (2007), 764–86

Gould, William, Fuller, C.J., and Bénéï, Véronique (eds.). *The Everyday State and Society in Modern India* (Delhi: Social Science Press, 2009)

Green, Nile (ed.). *The Persianate World: the Frontiers of a Eurasian Lingua Franca* (Oakland: University of California Press, 2019)

Guha, Ranajit. *Elementary Aspects of Peasant Insurgency in Colonial India* (Delhi: Oxford University Press, 1983)

Guha, Ranajit. *A Rule of Property for Bengal: an Essay on the Idea of Permanent Settlement* (Paris: Mouton, 1967)

Guha, Sumit. 'Rethinking the Mughal Economy: Lateral Perspectives', *Journal of the Economic and Social History of the Orient*, 58 (2015), 532–75

Guha, Sumit. 'Property Rights, Social Structure and Rural Society in Comparative Perspective: Evidence from Historic South Asia', *International Journal of South Asian Studies*, 5 (2013), 13–22

Guha, Sumit. 'Serving the Barbarian to Preserve the *Dharma*: the Ideology and Training of a Clerical Elite in Peninsular India, c. 1300–1800', *Indian Economic and Social History Review*, 47: 4 (2010), 497–525

Guha, Sumit. 'Margi, Desi and Yavani: High Language and Ethnic Speech in Maharashtra', in H. Kotani (ed.) *Marga: Ways to Liberation, Empowerment and Social Change in Maharashtra* (Delhi: Manohar, 2008), pp. 129–46

Guha, Sumit. 'The Family Feud as Political Resource in Eighteenth Century India', in Indrani Chatterjee (ed.) *Unfamiliar Relations: Family and History in South Asia* (New Brunswick: Rutgers University Press, 2004a), pp. 73–94

Guha, Sumit. 'Speaking Historically: the Changing Voices of Historical Narration in Western India, 1400–1900', *The American Historical Review*, 109: 4 (2004b), 1084–103

Guha, Sumit, *Environment and Ethnicity in India, 1200–1991* (Cambridge: Cambridge University Press, 1999)

Gupta, Akhil. 'Blurred Boundaries: the Discourse of Corruption, the Culture of Politics and the Imagined State', *American Ehtnologist*, 22: 2 (1995), 375–402

Gupta, Satya Prakash, and Khan, Sumbul Halim. *Mughal Documents: Taqsim (c. 1649-c. 1800)* (Jaipur: Publication Scheme, 1993)

Habib, Irfan. *The Agrarian System of Mughal India 1556–1707*, 3rd ed. (New Delhi: Oxford University Press, 2014)

Habib, Irfan. 'From Arith to Rādhākund: the History of a Braj Village in Mughal Times', *Indian Historical Review*, 38: 2 (2011), 211–224

Habib, Irfan. 'Mercant Communities in Precolonial India', in James D. Tracy (ed.) *The Rise of Merchant Empires: Long-Distance Trade in the Early Modern World, 1350–1750* (Cambridge: Cambridge University Press, 1990), pp. 371–99

Habib, Irfan. *An Atlas of the Mughal Empire* (Delhi: Oxford University Press, 1982)

Habib, Irfan. 'Aspects of Agrarian Relations and Economy in a Region of Uttar Pradesh in the 16th Century', *Indian Economic and Social History Review*, 4: 3 (1967a), 205–32

Habib, Irfan. 'The Mansab System, 1595–1637', *Proceedings of the Indian History Congress*, 29: 1 (1967b), 221–42

Habib, Irfan, and Raychaudhri, Tapan (eds.). *Cambridge Economic History of India*, Vol. I, 79–80

Habib, Mohammad, and Afsar Umar Salim Khan, *Political Theory of the Delhi Sultanate: Including a Translation of Ziauddin Barani's Fatawa-i Jahandari, Circa, 1358–9 AD*. (Delhi: Kitab Ghar, 1961)

Hadi, Nabi. *Dictionary of Indo-Persian Literature* (New Delhi: Indira Gandhi National Centre for Arts, 1995)

Haidar, Najaf. 'Language, caste and the secretarial class in Mughal India', unpublished paper, on author's academia.edu pages

Haidar, Najaf. 'Norms of Professional Excellence and Good Conduct in Accountancy Manuals of the Mughal Empire', *International Review of Social History*, 56 (2011), 263–74.

Haim, Ofir. 'An Early Judeo-Persian Letter Sent from Ghazna to Bāmiyān (Ms. Heb. 4° 8333.29)', *Bulletin of the Asia Institute*, 26 (2012), 103–19

Hakala, Walter. *Negotiating Languages: Urdu, Hindi and the Definition of Modern South Asia* (New York: Columbia University Press, 2016)

Hallaq, Wael. *Shari'a: Theory, Practice, Transformations* (Cambridge: Cambridge University Press, 2009)

Hallaq, Wael. 'Model *Shurūṭ* Works and the Dialectic of Doctrine and Practice', *Islamic Law and Society*, 2: 2 (1995), 109–34

Hallaq, Wael. 'From *Fatwā*s to *Furū'*: Growth and Change in Islamic Substantive Law', *Islamic Law and Society*, 1: 1 (1994), 17–56

Hallaq, Wael. 'Was the Gate of Ijtihad Closed?' *International Journal of Middle East Studies*, 16: 1 (1984), 3–4

Hasan, Farhat. 'Property and Social Relations in Mughal India: Litigations and Disputes at the Qazi's Courts in Urban Localities, 17th–18th centuries', *Journal of the Economic and Social History of the Orient*, 61: 5–6 (2018), 851–77

Hasan, Farhat. *State and Locality in Mughal India: Power Relations in Western India, c. 1572–1730* (Cambridge: Cambridge University Press, 2006)

Hasan, Farhat. 'The Mughal Fiscal System in Surat and the English East India Company', *Modern Asian Studies*, 27: 4 (1993), 711–18

Hasan, Farhat. 'Indigenous Cooperation and the Birth of a Colonial City, Calcutta c. 1698–1750', *Modern Asian Studies*, 26: 1 (1992), 65–82

Hasan, Nurul. 'Zamīndārs under the Mughals', in Muzaffar Alam and Sanjay Subrahmanyam (eds.) *The Mughal State* (Oxford: Oxford University Press, 1998) pp. 284–98

Hasan, Syed Bashir. 'Chisti and Shattari Saints of Malwa: Relations with the State', *Journal of Business Management and Social Science Research*, 3: 3 (2014), 51–54

Hasan, Syed Bashir. 'Administration of *Jagirs* in Malwa in the Mid-Seventeenth Century: the Dhar Documents, ' in Shahabuddin Iraqi (ed.) *Medieval India 2: Essays in Medieval Indian History and Culture* (Manohar: Centre for Advanced Study, Aligarh Muslim University, 2008), pp.217–30

Hodgson, Marshall. *The Venture of Islam: Conscience and History in a World Civilization*, Vol. I (Chicago: University of Chicago Press, 1974)

Horstmann, Monika (ed.). *In Favour of Govinddevji: Historical Documents Relating to a Deity of Vrindavan and Eastern Rajasthan* (Manohar: Indira Gandhi National Centre for the Arts, 1999)

Hussain, S. M. Azizuddin. '*Kalimat-i-Aurangzeb*: a Source of Aurangzeb's Reign', *Proceedings of the Indian History Congress*, 40 (1979), 314–18

Hussain, Zakir. 'A "Zamindar" Family of "Sarkar" Mandu "Suba" Malwa during the 17th Century (Archival Evidence)', *Proceedings of the Indian History Congress*, 53: 9 (1992), 311–20

Ikram, S. M. *Muslim Civilization in India*, (ed.) Ainslee T. Embree (New York: Columbia University Press, 1964)

Iraqi, Shahabuddin (ed.). *Medieval India 2: Essays in Medieval Indian History and Culture* (Manohar: Centre for Advanced Study, AMU, 2008)

Irvine, William. *The Army of the Indian Moghuls: Its Organization and Administration* (London: Luzac & Co., 1983)

Irvine, William. *Later Mughals*, (ed.) Jadunath Sarkar, Reprint (New Delhi: Oriental Books Reprint Corporation, 1971)

Irwin, R. 'The Privatization of 'Justice' under the Circassian Mamluks', *Mamluk Studies Review*, 5 (2002): 63–70

Jackson, Peter. *The Delhi Sultanate: a Political and Military History* (Cambridge: Cambridge University Press, 1999)

Jafri, Saiyid Zaheer Hussain. 'The Sarkar Qānūngō 16th–17th century documents' *Proceedings of the Indian History Congress*, 46th session (Delhi: Indian History Congress, 1986), 253–64

Jain, M. P. *Outlines of Indian Legal History* (Bombay: N. M. Tripathi, 1966)

Jain, Ravindra K. *Between History and Legend: Status and Power in Bundelkhand* (Delhi: Orient Longman, 2002)

Jalal, Ayesha. *Self and Sovereignty: Individual and Community in South Asian Islam since 1850* (London: Routledge, 2001)

Jha, Pankaj. 'Beyond the Local and the Universal: Exclusionary Strategies of Expansive Literary Cultures in Fifteenth Century Mithila', *Indian Economic and Social History Review*, 51: 1 (2014), 1–40

Jones, Justin. '"Signs of Churning": Muslim Personal Law and Public Contestation in Twenty-First Century India', *Modern Asian Studies*, 44: 1 (2010), pp. 175–200

Kaderi, A. A. 'A Mahdar from Hukeri in Karnataka', in *Epigraphica Indica: Arabic and Persian Supplement* (Delhi: Archaeological Survey, 1972), pp. 51–77

Kamphorst, Janet. *In Praise of Death: History and Poetry in Medieval Marwar* (Leiden: Leiden University Press, 2008)

Kane, P. V. *History of the Dharmaśāstra (Ancient and Mediaeval Religious and Civil Law in India)*, 2nd ed., 5 vols. (Poona: Bhandarkar Oriental Research Institute, 1968–77)

Kasturi, Malavika. *Embattled Identities: Rajput Lineages and the Colonial State in Nineteenth-Century North India* (New Delhi: Oxford University Press, 2002)

Khadgawat, Mahendra (ed.). *Phārsī farmāṇo ke Prakāsh mein Mughalkālīn Bhārat evaṃ Rājput Shāshak*, Vol. IV (Bikaner: Rajasthan State Archives, 2018)

Khalfaoui, Mouez. 'Mughal Empire and *Law'*, in *The [Oxford] Encyclopedia of Islam and Law*. Oxford Islamic Studies Online, accessed 04 August 2016

Khalfaoui, Mouez. 'Al-Fatawa Al-ʿAlamgiriyya (al-Hindiyya)', in *The Encyclopedia of Islam*, 3rd ed., Part 3, Kate Fleet, Gudrun Krämer, Denis Matringe, John Nawas, Everett Rowson (eds.). http://dx.doi.org.uoelibrary.idm.oclc.org/10.1163/1573-3912_ei3_COM_27028 First published online: 2012, accessed 11 December 2019

Khalfaoui, Mouez. 'Together but Separate: How Muslim Scholars Conceived of Religious Plurality in South Asia in the Seventeenth century', *Bulletin of the School of Oriental and African Studies*, 74 (2011a), 87–96

Khalfaoui, Mouez. 'From Religious to Social Conversion: How Muslim Scholars conceived of the *Rites de Passage* from Hinduism to Islam in Seventeenth-Century South Asia', *Journal of Beliefs and Values*, 32: 1 (2011b), 85–93

Khan, Jasim. *Being Salman* (Gurgaon: Penguin, 2015)

Kia, Mana. Early Modern Persianate Identity between Iran and India (Unpublished Ph.D. Thesis, Harvard University, 2011)

Kinra, Rajeev. 'Master and *Munshī*: a Brahman Secretary's Guide to Mughal Governance', *IESHR*, 47: 4 (2010), 527–61

Knost, Stefan (ed.). *Lire et Écrire l'Histoire Ottoman* (Beirut: Orient-Institut Beirut, 2015)

Kolff, Dirk H. A. *Naukar, Rajput, Sepoy: the Evolution of the Military Labour Market in Hindustan, 1450–1850* (Cambridge: Cambridge University Press, 1990)

Kolff, Dirk H. A. 'The Rajput in Ancient and Medieval India: a Warrior-Ascetic', in N. K. Singhi and R. Joshi (eds.) *Folk, Faith and Feudalism* (Jaipur, New Delhi: Rawat Publications, 1995), pp. 257–934

Kothiyal, Tanuja. *Nomadic Narratives: a History of Mobility and Identity in the Great Indian Desert* (New Delhi: Cambridge University Press, 2016)

Kozlowski, Gregory. *Muslim Endowments and Society in British India* (Cambridge: Cambridge University Press, 1985)

Kugle, Scott Alan. 'Framed, Blamed and Renamed: the Recasting of Islamic Jurisprudence in Colonial South Asia', *Modern Asian Studies*, 35: 2 (2001), 257–313

Kumar, Sunil. '*Bandagī* and *Naukarī*: Studying Transitions in Political Culture and Service under the North Indian Sultanates, Thirteenth-Sixteenth Centuries', in Francesca Orsini and Samira Sheikh (eds.) *After Timur Left: Culture and Circulation in Fifteenth-Century North India* (New Delhi: Oxford University Press, 2014), pp. 60–108

Kumar, Sunil. *The Emergence of the Delhi Sultanate, 1192–1286* (New Delhi: Permanent Black, 2007)

Lahori, Abdul Hamid. *King of the World: the Padshahnāma*. Milo Cleveland Beach and Ebba Koch (eds.), translated by Wheeler Thackston (London: Azimuth, 1997)

Laine, James. *Hindu King in Islamic India* (Oxford: Oxford University Press, 2003)

Lambton, Ann. 'Pīs̲h̲kas̲h̲': Present or Tribute?' *Bulletin of the School of Oriental and African Studies*, 57: 1 (1994), 145–58

Lambton, Ann K. S. *State and Government in Medieval Islam: an Introduction to the Study of Islamic Political Theory: the Jurists* (New York: Routledge/Curzon, 1981), pp. 138–52

Lefèvre, Corinne. 'Beyond Diversity: Mughal Legal Ideology and Politics', in Gijs Kruitjtzer and Thomas Ertl (eds.) *Law Addressing Diversity: Premodern Europe and India in Comparison (13th–18th centuries)* (Berlin: De Gruyter, 2017)

Lelyveld, David. *Aligarh's First Generation: Muslim Solidarity in British India* (Princeton: Princeton University Press, 1978)

Leonard, Karen. *Social History of an Indian Caste: the Kayasths of Hyderabad* (Berkeley, London: University of California Press, 1994)

Leonard, Karen. 'The Hyderabad Political System and Its Participants', *Journal of Asian Studies*, 20: 3 (1971), 569–82

Levi, Giovanni. 'On Microhistory', in Peter Burke (ed.) *New Perspectives on Historical Writing* (Cambridge: Polity, 1991), pp.93–113

Levi, Scott. *The Indian Diaspora in Central Asia and Its Trade, 1550–1900* (Leiden: Brill, 2002)

Lewis, Bernard 'Siyasa', in A. H. Green (ed.) *In Quest of an Islamic Humanism: Arabic and Islamic Studies in Memory of Mohamed al-Nowaihi* (Cairo: American University in Cairo Press, 1984), pp. 3–14

Loualich, Fatiha. 'In the Regency of Algiers: the Human Side of the Algerian Corso', in Maria Fusaro, Colin Heywood and Mohamed-Salah Omri (eds.) *Trade and Cultural Exchange in the Early Modern Mediterranean: Braudel's Maritime Legacy* (London: I.B. Tauris, 2010), pp. 69–96

Lutfi, Huda. 'A Study of Six Fourteenth Century Iqrārs from Al-Quds Relating to Muslim Women', *Journal of the Economic and Social History of the Orient*, 26: 3 (1983), 246–94

Majeed, Javed. 'The Jargon of Indostan': an Exploration of Jargon in Urdu and East India Company English', in Peter Burke and Roy Porter (eds.) *Languages and Jargons: Contributions to a Social History of Language* (Cambridge: Polity, 1995), pp. 182–205

Makdisi, George. The *Rise of Colleges: Institutions of Learning in Islam and the West* (Edinburgh: Edinburgh University Press, 1981)

Makdisi, J. 'Legal Logic and Equity in Islamic Law', *The American Journal of Comparative Law*, 33: 1 (1985), 63–92

Malgonkar, Manohar. *The Puars of Dewas Senior* (Bombay: Orient Longmans, 1963)

Mallat, Chibli. 'From Islamic to Middle Eastern Law: a Restatement of the Field (Part 2)', *The American Journal of Comparative Law*, 52: 1 (2004), 209–86

Manucci, Niccolao. *Storia do Mogor*, translated William Irvine (London: John Murrary, 1907), Vol. I, pp. 67–8

Marglin, Jessica 'Cooperation and Competition among Jewish and Islamic Courts: Double Notarization in Nineteenth-Century Morocco', in *Studies in the History and Culture of North African Jewry*, Volume III, Moshe Bar-Asher and Steven Fraade, eds. (New Haven and Jerusalem: Yale Program in Judaic Studies and the Hebrew University Center for Jewish Languages and Literatures), pp. 111–29

Markovits, Claude. *The Global World of Indian Merchants, 1750–1947: Traders of Sind from Bukhara to Panāma* (Cambridge: Cambridge University Press, 2000)

Marglin, Jessica. *Across the Lines: Jews and Muslims in Modern Morocco* (New Haven: Yale University Press, 2016)

Marshall, P. J. 'Indian Officials under the East India Company in Eighteenth-Century Bengal', *Bengal Past and Present*, 84, Part 2, Serial no. 158 (1965), 95–120

Masud, Muhammad Khalid, Messick, Brinkley and Powers, David S. (eds.). *Islamic Legal Interpretation: Muftis and Their Fatwas* (Cambridge, MA: Harvard University Press, 1996)

Meharda, B. I. *History and Culture of the Girasias* (Jaipur: Jawahar Nagar, 1985)

Melchert, Christopher. *The Formation of the Sunni Schools of Law, 9th–10th Centuries C.E.* (Leiden: Brill, 1997)

Messick, Brinkley. *Sharīʿa Scripts: a Historical Anthology* (New York: Columbia University Press, 2018)

Messick, Brinkley. *The Calligraphic State: Textual Domination and History in a Muslim Society* (Berkeley: University of California Press, 1993)

Metcalf, Barbara. *Islamic Revival in British India, Deoband, 1860–1900* (Princeton: Princeton University Press, 1982)

Metcalf, Thomas. *Land, Landlords, and the British Raj: Northern India in the Nineteenth Century* (Berkeley and Los Angeles: University of California Press, 1979)

Mitchell, Colin. 'Safavid Imperial *Tarassul* and the Persian *Inshā* Tradition', *Studia Iranica*, 27 (1997), 173–209

Mohiuddin, Momin. *The Chancellery and Persian Epistolography under the Mughals, from Babur to Shah Jahan, 1526–1658* (Calcutta: Iran Society, 1971)

Monckton-Jones, M. E. *Warren Hastings in Bengal, 1773–74* (Oxford: Clarendon Press, 1918)

Moreland, W. H. 'The Pargana Headman (Chaudhrī) in the Mogul Empire', *The Journal of the Royal Asiatic Society of Great Britain and Ireland*, 4 (1938), 511–21

Moreland, W. H. 'Ranks (mansab) in the Mughal service', *Journal of the Royal Asiatic Society* (1936)

Morgenstein Fuerst, Ilyse R. 'A Muslim Bhagavad Gita: 'Abd al-Rahman Chisti's Interpretative Translation and Its Implications', *Journal of South Asian Religious History*, 1 (2015), 1–29

Morley, W. H. *Administration of Justice in British India* (London: Williams and Norage, 1858)

Moosvi, Shireen. *The Economy of the Mughal Empire c. 1595*, 2nd ed. (New Delhi: Oxford University Press, 2015)

Moosvi, Shireen. *People, Taxation and Trade in Mughal India* (New Delhi: Oxford University Press, 2008)

Moosvi, Shireen. 'Evolution of the Mansab System under Akbar', *Journal of the Royal Asiatic Society*, 2 (1981)

Mukherjee, Mithi. *India in the Shadows of Empire: a Legal and Political History, 1774–1950* (New Delhi: Oxford University Press, 1950)

Mukhia, Harbans. The *Mughals of India* (Oxford: Blackwell, 2004)

Müller, Christian H. O. 'Acknowledgement', in *Encyclopedia of Islam*, 3rd edition (eds.) Kate Fleet, Gudrun Krämer, Denis Matringe, John Nawas and Everett Rowson. Brill Online, 2015, http://0-www.brillonline.nl.lib.exeter.ac.uk/entries/encyclopaedia-of-islam-3/acknowledgement-COM_0166, accessed 11 July 2015

Nayeem, M. A. 'Mughal Documents Relating to the Pīshkash of Zamīndārs of South India, 1694–1752 A.D.' *Indian Economic and Social History Review*, 12: 4 (1975), 425–32

Neale, Walter C. 'Land is to Rule', in Robert E. Fryckenberg (ed.) *Land Control and Social Structure in Indian History* (Madison: Wisconsin University Press, 1969), pp. 3–15

Nielsen, Jørgen S. 'Mazalim', in P. Bearman, Th. Bianquis, C. E. Bosworth, E. van Donzel and W. P. Heinrichs (eds.) *Encyclopaedia of Islam*, 2nd ed. (Published Online, 2012)

Nielsen, Jørgen S. *Secular Justice in an Islamic State: Maẓālim under the Baḥrī Mamlūks, 662/1264–789/1387* (Leiden: Nederlands Historisch-Archaeologisch Instituut te Istanbul, 1985)

Nigam, S. B. P. et al. *Amir Khusrau Memorial Volume* (New Delhi: Publications Division, Ministry of Information and Broadcasting, Government of India, 1975)

Nobuaki, Kondo (ed.). *Persian Documents: Social History of Iran and Turn in the 15th-19th Centuries* (London: Routledge, 2017)

Nora, Pierre. 'Between Memory and History: Les Lieux de Memoire', *Representations*, 26 (1989)

Nussdorfer, Laurie. *Brokers of Public Trust: Notaries in Early Modern Rome* (Baltimore, MD: Johns Hopkins University Press, 2009)

O'Hanlon, Rosalind. 'Speaking from Siva's temple: Banaras Scholar Households and the Brahman 'ecumene' of Mughal India', *South Asian History and Culture*, 2: 2 (2011), 253–77

O'Hanlon, Rosalind. 'The Social Worth of Scribes: Brahmins, Kayasthas and the Social Order in Early Modern India', *Indian Economic and Social History Review*, 47: 4 (2010), 563–595

O'Hanlon, Rosalind. 'Letters Home: Banaras Pandits and the Maratha Regions in Early Modern India', *Modern Asian Studies* 44: 2 (2010), 201–40

O'Hanlon, Rosalind, and Minkowski, Christopher. 'What Makes People Who They Are? Pandit Networks and the Problem of Livelihood in Early Modern Western India', *Indian Economic and Social History Review*, 45: 3 (2008), 381–416

O'Hanlon, Rosalind, and Washbrook, David (eds.). Special issue on Munshis, Pandits and Record-Keepers: Scribal Communities and Historical Change in India, *IESHR*, 47: 4 (2010): 441–615

Okawara, Tomoko. 'Reconsidering Ottoman Qadi Court Records: What Are They? Who Produced, Issued and Recorded Them?' in Vanessa Gueno and Stefan Knost (eds.) *Lire et écrire l'histoire ottoman* (Beirut: Orient-Institut Beirut, 2015), pp. 15–37.

Othman, Aida. '"And Amicable Settlement Is Best": Sulh and Dispute Resolution in Islamic Law', *Arab Law Quarterly*, 21 (2007), 64–90

Paul, Jürgen. '*Inshā'* Collections as a Source of Iranian History', in Bert Fragner et al. (eds.) *Proceedings of the Second European Conference of Iranian Studies (Bamberg, 1991)* (Rome: IsMEO, 1995), pp. 535–40

Peabody, Norbert. *Hindu Kingship and Polity in Precolonial India* (Cambridge: Cambridge University Press, 2003)

Peabody, Norbert. 'Tod's Rajasthan and the Boundaries of Imperial Rule in Nineteenth-Century India', *Modern Asian Studies*, 30: 1 (1996), 185–220

Pearce-Moses, Richard. *A Glossary of Archival and Records Terminology* (Chicago: Society of American Archivists, 2005)

Pearson, M. N. 'Shivaji and the Decline of the Mughal Empire', *Journal of Asian Studies*, 35: 2 (1976), 221–35

Peel, H. G. L. *The Vengeance of God* (Leiden: Brill, 1995), pp.236–38

Peirce, Leslie. *Morality Tales: Law and Gender in the Ottoman Court of Aintab* (Berkeley: University of California Press, 2003)

Perlin, Frank. 'State Formation Reconsidered', *Modern Asian Studies*, Part 1, Part 2, 19: 3 (1985), 415–80

Perlin, Frank. 'The Precolonial Indian State as History and Epistemology: a Reconstruction of Societal Formation from the Western Deccan from the Fifteenth to the Nineteenth Century', in H. J. M. Claessen and P. Skalnik (eds.) *The Study of the State* (The Hague: Mouton, 1981), pp. 272–302

Pernau, Margrit, and Jaffery, Yunus (eds.). *Information and the Public Sphere: Persian Newsletters from Mughal Delhi* (New Delhi: Oxford University Press, 2009)

Peters, Rudolph. *Crime and Punishment in Islamic law: Theory and Practice from the Sixteenth to the Twenty-First Century* (Cambridge: Cambridge University Press, 2005)

Pickett, James. 'The Persianate Sphere during the Age of Empires: Islamic Scholars and Networks of Exchange in Central Asia, 1747–1917', Unpublished Ph.D. dissertation, Princeton University, 2015

Pinch, William. *Warrior Ascetics and Indian Empires* (Cambridge: Cambridge University Press, 2006)

Pollock, Sheldon. 'Cosmopolitan and Vernacular in History', *Public Culture*, 12: 3 (2000), 591–62

Pollock, Sheldon. 'India in the Vernacular Millennium: Literary Culture and Polity 1000– 1500', *Daedalus* 127: 3 (1998): 41–74

Powell, Avril. *Muslims and Missionaries in Pre-Mutiny India* (London: Routledge, 1993)

Powers, David. *The Development of Islamic Law and Society in the Maghrib: Qadis, Muftis and Family Law* (Burlington: Ashgate, 2011)

Powers, David. *Law, Society and Culture in Maghrib, 1300–1500* (Cambridge: Cambridge University Press, 2002)

Powers, David S. '*Kadijustiz* or *Qāḍī*-Justice? A Paternity Dispute from Fourteenth-Century Morocco', *Islamic Law and Society*, 1: 3 (1994), 332–66

Prakash, Om. *European Commercial Enterprise in Pre-Colonial India* (Cambridge: Cambridge University Press, 1998)

Preston, Laurence W. *The Devs of Cincvad: a Lineage and the State in Maharashtra* (Cambridge: Cambridge University Press, 1989)

Prior, Kathryn. 'Making History: the State's Intervention in Urban Religious Disputes in the North-Western Provinces in the early Nineteenth Century', *Modern Asian Studies*, 27: 1 (1993), 179–203

Qureshi, I. H. 'The Army of the Great Mughals', *Pakistan Historical Society*, 6: 1 (1958), 34–54

Qureshi, I. H. *The Administration of the Delhi Sultanate*, 4th ed. (Karachi: Pakistan Historical Society, 1958)

Raman, Bhavani. *Document Raj: Writing and Scribes in Early Colonial India* (Chicago: University of Chicago Press, 2012)

Ramsbotham, R. B. *Studies in the Land Revenue History of Bengal, 1769–1787* (Bombay: Humphrey Milford, 1926, pp. 99–134

Ramusack, *The Indian Princes*; for studies of specific regimes, see Pamela Price, *Kingship and Political Practice in Colonial India* (Cambridge: Cambridge University Press, 1996)

Ranawat, Manohar Singh. *Mālwa Itihās ke Phārsī Kāgaz-Patroṇ kā Vivaranātmak Sūchī-Patra* (Sitamau: Shri Natnagar Shodh-Samsthan, 2000)

Rapoport, Yossef. 'Royal Justice and Religious Law: Siyāsah and Shariʿah under the Mamluks', *Mamluk Studies Review*, 15 (2012): 71–102

Ray, Ratnalekha. *Change in Bengal Agrarian Society 1760–1850* (Delhi: Manohar, 1979)

Ray, Rajat, and Ray, Ratnalekha. 'Zamīndārs and Jotedars: a Study of the Rural Politics in Bengal', *Modern Asian Studies, Modern Asian Studies*, 9: 1 (1975), 81–102

Rezai, Omid. 'Dilbastagī mazhabī angize-yi dīgar barā-yi muhājirāt az shabe qare be falāt Iran', in Iraj Afshar and Karim Isfahani (eds.) *Pazūhesh-hā-yi Irānshanashī*, [Iranian Studies] (Tehran: Chapkhane-yi Tarana, 2014), pp. 198–213

Richards, John F. *The Mughal Empire* (Cambridge: Cambridge University Press, 1993)

Richards, John F. (ed. and translator). *Document Forms for Official Orders of Appointment in the Mughal Empire* (Cambridge: E.J.W. Gibb, 1986)

Richards, J. F. 'Norms of Comportment among Mughal Imperial Officers', in Barbara Metcalf (ed.) *Moral Conduct and Authority: the Place of Adab in South Asian Islam* (Berkeley: University of California Press, 1984), pp. 255–89

Richards, J. F. *Mughal Administration in Golconda* (Oxford: Clarendon Press, 1975)

Ritchie, Robert C. *Captain Kidd and the War against the Pirates* (Cambridge, MA: Harvard University Press, 1986)

Ricci, Ronit. *Islam Translated: Literature, Conversion and the Arabic Cosmopolis of South and Southeast Asia* (Chicago and London: University of Chicago Press, 2011)

Risso, Patricia. *Merchants and Faith: Muslim Commerce and Culture in the Indian Ocean* (Boulder, CO: Westview Press, 1995), pp. 104–106

Robinson, Francis. *The 'ulama of Farangi Mahal and Islamic Culture in South Asia* (London: Hurst, 2001)

Rudolph, Susan Hoeber, and Rudolph, Lloyd I. *Essays on Rajputana: Essays on History, Culture and Administration* (New Delhi: Naurang Rai, 1984)

Rustow, Marina. 'The Legal Status of Dhimmis in the Fatimid East: a View from the Palace in Cairo', in Maribel Fierro and John Victor Tolan (eds.) *The Legal Status of Dhimmis in the Islamic West* (Turnhout, Belgium: Brepols, 2013), pp.307–32

Saksena, Rai Chatarman. *Chahar Gulshan* (ed.) Chander Shekhar (Delhi: Dilli Kitab Ghar for National Mission for Manuscripts, 2011)

Sandla, Thakur Raghunath Rathor. *Amjhera Rājya ka Itihās* (Jodhpur: Maharaja Mansingh Pustak Prakash Kendra, 2007)

Sangar, S. P. *The Nature of the Law in Mughal India and the Administration of Criminal Justice* (New Delhi: Sangar, 1998)

Saran, P. *The Provincial Government of the Mughals, 1526*–1658, 2nd ed. (Bombay: Asia Publishing House, 1973)

Sarat, Austin and Kearns, Thomas R. (eds.). *History, Memory and the Law* (Ann Arbor: University of Michigan Press, 2002)

Sarkar, Jadunath. *History of Jaipur* (New Delhi: Orient Longman, 1984)

Sarkar, Jadunath. *Mughal Administration* (Patna: Patna University, 1920a)

Sarkar, Jadunath. *Shivaji and His Times*, 2nd ed. (London: Longmans, Green and Co., 1920b)

Sarkar, Jadunath. 'The Revenue Regulations of Aurangzeb', *Journal and Proceedings of the Asiatic Society of Bengal*, New Series (1906), 225

Sarkar, Jadunath, and Sinh, Raghubir. *A History of Jaipur, 1503–1938* (Hyderabad: Orient Longman, 1968)

Sartori, Paolo. *Visions of Justice: Shari'a and Cultural Change in Russian Central Asia* (Leiden: Brill, 2017)

Sartori, Paolo. 'Constructing Colonial Legality in Russian Central Asia: On Guardianship', *Comparative Studies in Society and History*, 56: 2 (2014), 419–47

Sartori, Paolo. 'Introduction: On the Social in Central Asian History: Notes in the Margins of Legal Records', in P. Sartori (ed.) *Explorations in the Social History of Modern Central Asia (19th–Early 20th Century)* (Leiden: Brill, 2013), 1–22

Sartori, Paolo. 'The Evolution of Third-Party Mediation in Sharī'a Courts in 19th- and Early 20th-Century Central Asia', *Journal of the Economic and Social History of the Orient*, 54: 3 (2011), 311–52

Sartori, Paolo. 'Colonial Legislation Meets Sharī'a: Muslims' Land Rights in Russian Turkestan.' *Central Asian Survey*, 29: 1 (2010), 43–60

Schacht, Joseph. *An Introduction to Islamic Law* (Oxford: Clarendon, 1964)

Schneider, Irene. *The Petitioning System in Iran: State, Society and Power Relations in the Late 19th Century* (Wiesbaden: Harrassowitz, 2006)

Sen, S. N. *Administrative System of the Marathas* (Calcutta: University of Calcutta, 1976)

Seyller, John. *The Hamza Nāma: Painting and Storytelling in Mughal India* (London: Azimuth, 1997)

Shaked, Shaul. 'Early Persian Documents from Khorasan', *Journal of Persianate Studies*, 6 (2013), 153–162

Sharma, G. N. *Rajasthan through the Ages, Vol. II from 1300 to 1761 A.D.* (Bikaner: Rajasthan State Archives, 2014)

Sharma, Rambabu, *Rājbhāsha Hindī ki kahānī* (Dillī: Aknkur Prakshan, 1980)

Sharma, Vishwanath. *Glimpses of Mandu* (Mandu, 1943)

Sheikh, Samira. *Forging a Region: Sultans, Traders and Pilgrims in Gujarat, 1200–1500* (New Delhi: Oxford University Press, 2010)

Sherman, Taylor C., Gould, William, and Ansari, Sarah (eds.) *From Subjects to Citizens: Society and the Everyday State in India and Pakistan, 1947–70* (Cambridge: Cambridge University Press, 2014)

Shrivastava, Meenal. *Amma's Daughters: a Memoir* (Edmonton: Athabasca University Press, 2018)

Siddiqi, Noman Ahmad. *Land Revenue Administration under the Mughals* (London: Asia Publishing House for Aligarh Muslim University, 1970)

Singh, Chetan. *Region and Empire: Panjab in the Seventeenth Century* (Delhi: Oxford University Press, 1991)

Singh, Chetan. 'Centre and Periphery in the Mughal State: the Case of Seventeenth-Century Panjab', *Modern Asian Studies*, 22: 2 (1988), 299–318

Singh, M. P. *Town, Market, Mint and Port in the Mughal Empire (1556–1707)* (New Delhi:Adam Publishers, 2015), p. 213

Singha, Radhika. *A Despotism of Law: Crime and Justice in Early Colonial India* (Delhi:Oxford University Press, 1998)

Singha, Radhika. ''Providential' Circumstances: the Thuggee Campaign of the 1830s and Legal Innovation', *Modern Asian* Studies, 27: 1 (1993), 83–146

Sinh, Raghubir. *Malwa in Transition, First Phase 1698–1765* (Bombay: D.B. Taraporevala, 1936)

Siebenhüner, Kim. 'Approaching Diplomatic and Courtly Gift-Giving in Europe and Mughal India: Shared Practices and Cultural Diversity', *Medieval History Journal*, 16: 2 (2013), 525–46

Speciale, Fabrizio. *Hospitals in India and Iran, 1500–1950* (Leiden: Brill, 2010)

Spooner, Brian, and Hanaway, William L. (eds.). *Literacy in the Persianate World: Writing and the Social Order* (Philadelphia: University of Pennsylvania Press, 2012)

Sreenivasan, Ramya. *The Many Lives of a Rajput Queen: Heroic Pasts in India, c. 1500–1900* (Seattle: University of Washington Press, 2007)

Stern, Philip. *The Company-State: Corporate Sovereignty and the Early Modern Foundations of the British Empire in India* (Oxford: Oxford University Press, 2011)

Subramanian, Lakshmi. *The Sovereign and the Pirate: Ordering Maritime Subjects in India's Western Littoral* (New Delhi: Oxford University Press, 2016)

Subrahmanyam, Sanjay. *Europe's India: Words, People, Empires, 1500–1800* (Harvard: Harvard University Press, 2017)

Subrahmanyam, Sanjay. 'The Mughal State: Structure or Process? Reflections on Recent Western historiography', *IESHR*, 29: 3 (1992), 291–321

Sutton, Deborah. 'Devotion, Antiquity and Colonial Custody of the Hindu Temple in British India', *Modern Asian Studies*, 47: 1 (2013), 135–66

Szyszko, Aleksandra. *The Three Jewels of the Desert: the Dhola-Maru Story: a Living Narrative Tradition of Northern India* (Warsaw: Elipsa, 2012)

Talbot, Cynthia. *The Last Hindu Emperor: Prithviraj Chauhan and the Indian Past, 1200–2000* (New York: Cambridge University Press, 2016)

Talbot, Cynthia. 'Becoming Turk the Rajput Way: Conversion and Identity in an Indian Warrior Narrative', *Modern Asian Studies*, 43: 1 (2009), 211–243

Thompson, E. P. *Whigs and Hunters: the Origin of the Black Act* (London: Allen Lane, 1975)

Thompson, E. P. 'The Moral Economy of the English Crowd in the Eighteenth Century', *Past and Present*, 50 (1971), 76–136

Thompson, E. P. 'The Peculiarities of the English', *The Socialist Register*, 2 (1965): 311-62

Toorn, K. van der. *Sin and Sanction in Israel and Mesopotamia: a Comparative Study* (Assen/Maastricht: Van Gorcum, 1985)

Travers, Robert. *Ideology and Empire in Eighteenth Century India: the British in Bengal* (Cambridge: Cambridge University Press, 2011)

Tucker, Judith. *In the House of the Law: Gender and Islamic Law in Ottoman Syria and Palestine* (Berkeley: University of California Press, 1998)

Tuck, Richard. *Natural Rights Theories* (Cambridge: Cambridge University Press, 1979)

Van Berkel, Maiike, Buskens, Leon, and Sijpesteijn, Pertra M. (eds.). *Legal Documents as Sources for the History of Muslim Societies* (Leiden: Brill, 2017)

Vassie, Roderic. *Persian Interpretations of the Bhagavadgīta in the Mughal Period: With Special Reference to the Sufi Version of Abd al-Rahman Chisti* (Unpublished PhD Thesis, SOAS, London, 1988)

Vaudeville, Charlotte. 'Leaves from the Desert: the Dhola-Maru-ra-Duha – An Ancient Ballad of Rajasthan', in Charlotte Vaudeville (ed.) *Myths, Saints and Legends in Medieval India* (Calcutta: Oxford University Press, 1996), pp. 273–334

Vogel, F. E. 'Siyāsah', in C. E. Bosworth et al. (eds.). *The Encyclopaedia of Islam*, 2nd ed. (Leiden: Brill, 1997), Vol. IX, 693–96

Werner, Christoph. *Vaqf en Iran: Aspects Culturels, Religieux et Sociaux* (Paris: Association pour l'Avancement des Études Iraniennes, 2015)

Werner, Christoph, 'Formal Aspects of Qajar Deeds of Sale', in Kondo Nobuaki (ed.) *Persian Documents: Social History of Iran and Turan in the Fifteenth to Nineteenth Centuries* (London: Curzon, 2003), pp. 13–50

Werner, Christoph. *An Iranian Town in Transition: a Social and Economic History of the Elites of Tabriz, 1747–1848* (Wiesbaden: Harrasowitz, 2000)

Willis, Michael. 'Dhār, Bhoja and Sarasvatī: from Indology to Political Mythology and back', *Journal of the Royal Asiatic Society*, 22: 1 (2012), 129–53

Wilson, Jon E. *The Domination of Strangers: Modern Governance in Eastern India, 1780–1835* (Basingstoke: Palgrave, 2009)

Wink, André. *Land and Sovereignty in India: Agrarian Society and Politics under the Eighteenth Century Maratha Swarajya* (Cambridge: Cambridge University Press, 1986)

Zaman, Muhammad Qasim. *The Ulama in Contemporary Islam: Custodians of Change* (Princeton: Princeton University Press, 2002)

Zemon Davis, Natalie. *The Return of Martin Guerre* (Cambridge, MA: Harvard University Press, 1983)

Ziegler, Norman P. 'Marvari Historical Chronicles: Sources for the Social and Cultural History of Rajasthan', *Indian Social and Economic History Review*, 13: 2 (1976), 219–50

Ziegler, Norman P. 'Some Notes on Rajput Loyalties in the Mughal Period', in John F. Richards (ed.) *Kingship and Authority in South Asia* (Madison: University of Wisconsin South Asia Publication Series, no. 3, 1978), pp. 215–52.

Ziegler, Norman. 'Evolution of the Rathor State of Marwar: Horses, Structural Change and Warfare', in Karine Schomer et al., *The Idea of Rajasthan: Explorations in Regional Identity* (Delhi: Manohar, American Institute of Indian Studies, 2001) Vol. II, 193–201

Zilli, I. A. 'Development of Inshā Literature to the End of Akbar's Reign', in Muzaffar Alam, Francoise 'Nalini' Delvoye, and Marc Gaborieau (eds.) *The Making of Indo-Persian Culture: Indian and French Studies* (New Delhi: Manohar, 2000), pp.309–49

Zutshi, Chitralekha. *Kashmir's Contested Pasts: Narratives, Sacred Geographies, and the Historical Imagination* (New Delhi: Oxford University Press, 2015)

# Index

Note: Locators in *italics* denote figures. Locators followed by a 't' and a number refer to a footnote, e.g. 51n135 refers to footnote 135 on page 51.

Printed in Great Britain
by Amazon

55324177R00175